Cambridge IGCSE®
Economics

Susan Grant

CAMBRIDGE
UNIVERSITY PRESS

CAMBRIDGE
UNIVERSITY PRESS

University Printing House, Cambridge CB2 8BS, United Kingdom

One Liberty Plaza, 20th Floor, New York, NY 10006, USA

477 Williamstown Road, Port Melbourne, VIC 3207, Australia

4843/24, 2nd Floor, Ansari Road, Daryaganj, Delhi – 110002, India

79 Anson Road, #06–04/06, Singapore 079906

Cambridge University Press is part of the University of Cambridge.

It furthers the University's mission by disseminating knowledge in the pursuit of education, learning and research at the highest international levels of excellence.

www.cambridge.org
Information on this title: www.cambridge.org/9781107612334

© Cambridge University Press 2014

First published 2014
20 19 18 17 16 15 14 13 12 11 10 9

Printed in Italy by Rotolito Lombarda S.p.A.

A catalogue record for this publication is available from the British Library

ISBN 978-1-107-61233-4 Paperback

....

....

....

Every effort has been made to trace the owners of copyright material included in this book. The publishers would be grateful for any omissions brought to their notice for acknowledgement in future editions of the book.

....

® IGCSE is the registered trademark of Cambridge International Examinations.

To the memory of my mother, Pat Grant,
who was a woman of great cheerfulness and courage.

CONTENTS

INTRODUCTION

This book is designed to introduce you to the study of economics and to help you progress through your IGCSE Level course. The book follows the structure of the IGCSE courses closely.

It covers all the topics of the course. In places, the book goes beyond the syllabus to include concepts which will stretch your understanding and which will provide you with additional possible ways to approach particular topics and strengthen the depth of your answers. These are:

Allocative, productive and dynamic efficiency (pages 87–89)

Cost-benefit analysis (page 114)

Aggregate demand and aggregate supply analysis (page 312)

Velocity of circulation (page 367)

Flexible employment (page 376)

Purchasing power parity (page 399)

Lorenz curve (page 427)

The capital and financial accounts of the balance of payments (pages 463–464)

Absolute and comparative advantage (pages 476–478)

The terms of trade (page 479).

The Book is divided into 52 units. Each of these units explores a key economic topic and provides activities and multiple choice questions to assess your understanding of the same. At the end of each unit a teacher's tip is given. This may remind you of a key point, warn you about a common confusion, give you advice on how to approach a question or recommend an activity which will enhance your understanding. There is also a summary of the main points covered in the unit.

The units have been arranged into eight sections. At the end of each section, there are answers to the activities and multiple choice questions. Do not look at them until you have worked through the questions. Besides 'Answer Key', a section on 'Examination Practice' also contains ten multiple choice questions covering the whole section and some structured questions from past examination papers. Answers to these multiple choice questions and structured questions can be found at the end of the book. You must remember that the answers, included for structured questions, are only suggested answers. There can be different approaches, particularly in the case of the higher marked questions, which are equally valid.

Economics

Economics is an important, well-respected and exciting subject. Economists play a key role in the world. They give advice to firms and governments to improve their performance and also comment on their success or failure. The work of economists can make a significant difference to people's lives. For instance, the policies they recommend to governments may reduce poverty and improve the quality of the environment.

Whilst some of the people, who study economics, go on to become economists, others enter a range of professions including accountancy, banking, education, journalism and the law. Economists enjoy a lot of respect in universities and professional organisations. They regard it as a rigorous subject, that develops logical thinking and analytical and mathematical ability.

There are certain concepts – such as opportunity cost and price elasticity of demand, and certain topics – including price determination, unemployment and inflation, that are central to economics. The subject, however, is ever changing as new theories develop, new institutions are created and new problems are encountered. This makes it an interesting and challenging subject.

The Skills of an Economist

To be a good economist, you need to be informed of the developments in your economy and other economies. You need to be able to think and write clearly and apply relevant economic terms and concepts. You need to be confident in handling figures. This involves being able to add, divide, subtract, multiply, calculate percentage changes and understand index numbers. You also need to be able to draw relevant, well-labelled and accurate diagrams. This book is designed to help you develop these skills.

PREPARING FOR EXAMINATION

Revision is a continuous process. After every lesson, check your work and if necessary, add extra notes. As an examination approaches, you will need to do intensive revision. Try to engage in active revision. This involves, not just reading notes, but also using the information. There are a number of ways through which this can be done. These include testing other members of the class and getting them to test you, drawing spider diagrams and producing tables and revision cards.

Examination Technique

It is not sufficient to have a sound knowledge and good skills in the subject. You also have to demonstrate these under examination conditions. So, it is essential to develop examination techniques.

Before an examination, check out the duration of the examination and the number of questions you have to answer. Read the instructions on the examination paper carefully. Do not rush into writing your answers.

In answering multiple choice papers, consider every option in a question carefully. If you are uncertain of an answer to a particular question, proceed further and return to it when you have answered the other questions. At the end, check that you have answered all the questions. Never leave a question unanswered, even if you have to guess.

In answering structured questions read the questions very carefully, paying particular attention to the directive (instruction) words. A questions which asks you to identify or state something will only require a brief answer, consisting of a few words. In contrast, a question which asks you to explain, assess or discuss something will require a longer answer, written in sentences and paragraphs. Unless specifically asked for, do not produce a list. Such an approach is likely to gain you a few marks.

The marks allocated to a question or part of a question should give you a clear indication of the extent of detail required. It is often useful to include a diagram (or diagrams) in your answers. These should be clear, accurate, well-labelled and backed up by an explanation in the text.

ACKNOWLEDGEMENT

Photo credits : Shutterstock
Section I: 24164749, 61753705, 117364918, 71048386, 59788057, 430205, 60779491, 54791671 **Section II**: 84084331, 77951401, 3844432, 109624334, 1380985, 50418028, 102745670, 101904619, 95330008, 54151870, 111999368, 86325814, 89663761, 61547215, 1748151, 65030281, 72653824, 29434846, 8864401, 4646644, 114104152, 33111940, 79657726, 115490365, 56239708, 89343070 **Section III**: 76590274, 91539893, 65714203, 12196441, 88516873, 109392416, 83133064, 80324677, 111946214, 101827642, 95521039, 115151443, 80227009, 116667094, 9203965, 114541927, 77192542 **Section IV**: 77042365, 64124296, 100158233, 107447666, 109515845, 88781662, 79172839, 111328973, 103588754, 110533598, 81974545, 56131003, 38412814, 56239708 **Section V**: 63608758, 85259425, 72852049, 114871843, 66673771, 114440692, 99014546 **Section VI**: 94986733, 106095458, 81155452, 86416297, 93928222, 32739469, 54279004, 68716657, 57367663, 80334658 **Section VII**: 80548063, 98264402, 77179411, 59788057, 86843710, 68148946 **Section VIII**: 48918724, 104212088, 38104051, 11430322

The questions taken from past examination papers are reproduced by permission of Cambridge International Examinations.

Syllabus Name & Code	Paper & Question Number	Month/Year	Section/Page in book
Cambridge IGCSE Economics 0455	Paper 2 Q5	Nov 1997	Section I Page 26
Cambridge IGCSE Economics 0455	Paper 4 Q3a	May/June 2006	Section I Page 26
Cambridge IGCSE Economics 0455	Paper 2 Q2a and b	May/June 2002	Section II Page 136
Cambridge IGCSE Economics 0455	Paper 2 Q2	Oct/Nov 2007	Section II Page 136
Cambridge IGCSE Economics 0455	Paper 2 Q3	Oct/Nov 2003	Section II Page 136
Cambridge IGCSE Economics 0455	Paper 2 Q4	May/June 2005	Section III Page 222
Cambridge IGCSE Economics 0455	Paper 4 Q7	Oct/Nov 2005	Section III Page 222
Cambridge IGCSE Economics 0455	Paper 4 Q6	May/June 2004	Section III Page 223
Cambridge IGCSE Economics 0455	Paper 4 Q2	May/June 2006	Section IV Page 301
Cambridge IGCSE Economics 0455	Paper 6 Q1	May/June 2006	Section IV Page 302
Cambridge IGCSE Economics 0455	Paper 4 Q3	May/June 2005	Section IV Page 302
Cambridge IGCSE Economics 0455	Paper 4 Q4	Oct/Nov 2002	Section V Page 355
Cambridge IGCSE Economics 0455	Paper 6 Q2	May/June 2002	Section V Page 355
Cambridge IGCSE Economics 0455	Paper 2 Q6	Oct/Nov 2006	Section V Page 355
Cambridge IGCSE Economics 0455	Paper 6 Q2	May/June 2003	Section VI Page 413
Cambridge IGCSE Economics 0455	Paper 4 Q4	May/June 2006	Section VI Page 413
Cambridge IGCSE Economics 0455	Paper 6 Q2	May/June 2004	Section VI Page 414
Cambridge IGCSE Economics 0455	Paper 4 Q7	May/June 2006	Section VII Page 457
Cambridge IGCSE Economics 0455	Paper 4 Q7	May/June 2005	Section VII Page 458
Cambridge IGCSE Economics 0455	Paper 4 Q7	May/June 2004	Section VII Page 458
Cambridge IGCSE Economics 0455	Paper 4 Q5	May/June 2005	Section VIII Page 507
Cambridge IGCSE Economics 0455	Paper 4 Q5	Oct/Nov 2005	Section VIII Page 507
Cambridge IGCSE Economics 0455	Paper Q6	Oct/Nov 2004	Section VIII Page 508
Cambridge IGCSE Economics 0455	Paper 2 Q2	May/June 2004	Section I Page 551
Cambridge IGCSE Economics 0455	Paper 22 Q2	Oct/Nov 2011	Section I Page 551
Cambridge IGCSE Economics 0455	Paper 2 Q2	May/June 2004	Section II Page 551
Cambridge IGCSE Economics 0455	Paper 4 Q7	May/June 2002	Section II Page 552
Cambridge IGCSE Economics 0455	Paper 2 Q3	Oct/Nov 2006	Section III Page 552
Cambridge IGCSE Economics 0455	Paper 4 Q2	May/June 2002	Section III Page 552
Cambridge IGCSE Economics 0455	Paper 2 Q7	Oct/Nov 2006	Section IV Page 553
Cambridge IGCSE Economics 0455	Paper 4 Q7	Oct/Nov 2003	Section IV Page 553
Cambridge IGCSE Economics 0455	Paper 4 Q6	May/June 2005	Section V Page 553
Cambridge IGCSE Economics 0455	Paper 4 Q3	Oct/Nov 2004	Section V Page 553
Cambridge IGCSE Economics 0455	Paper 2 Q4	Oct/Nov 2006	Section VI Page 554
Cambridge IGCSE Economics 0455	Paper 4 Q7	Oct/Nov 2002	Section VI Page 554
Cambridge IGCSE Economics 0455	Paper 4 Q6	Oct/Nov 2005	Section VII Page 554
Cambridge IGCSE Economics 0455	Paper 4 Q5	Oct/Nov 2002	Section VII Page 555
Cambridge IGCSE Economics 0455	Paper 4 Q6	May/June 2006	Section VIII Page 555
Cambridge IGCSE Economics 0455	Paper 4 Q5	May/June 2004	Section VIII Page 555

The Basic Economic Problem

Scarcity

In this first unit you will be introduced to the basic problem facing all economies. This is the problem of scarcity.

The Nature of Scarcity

In all the countries throughout the world, people would like to have more goods and services. It was estimated that in India, in 2006, at least 6 million people were living in slums. These people would clearly like to have better quality housing. Even many of those living in the rich suburbs would like to improve the quality of their living accommodation by, for instance, adding a swimming pool. What stops people enjoying all the products they would like to have? It is a lack of resources to produce them. Resources, including workers and machinery, are scarce.

Key Point

Scarcity: a situation where there is not enough to satisfy everyone's wants.

The Continuing Nature of Scarcity

Scarcity continues to exist. More goods and services are being produced today than ever before but the growth in wants is exceeding the growth of economic resources. People still want more products than the resources available can produce. Over a period of time, wants continue to grow and change.

 # The Economic Problem

The economic problem arises because of scarcity. There is no limit to people's wants – they are infinite. For instance, people want more and better clothing and health care and improved transport infrastructure. The number of workers, machines, offices, factories, raw materials and land used to produce these products, however, is limited. At any given time, for example, there are only a limited number of workers and they can produce only a specified amount. This mismatch, between what people want and the maximum that can be produced, gives rise to the economic problem.

Key Point

The economic problem: unlimited wants exceed scarce resources.

 # Evidence of the Existence of Scarcity

The fact that people have to choose which products to buy, which subjects to study, what jobs to do and which products to produce shows that there are insufficient resources, As consumers, we cannot have everything we want. We have limited incomes. Students have to select which courses to study. It is not possible to study economics and chemistry at the same time. Some teachers may carry out other work in the evening but when they are teaching, they are not working as writers! Time is in limited supply. Farmers cannot grow rice and wheat on the same land. They have to select one crop as land is scarce.

Activity 1

Decide which of the following are scarce:

a. vacancies for university degree courses
b. foreign holidays
c. health care.

Summary

- People's wants continue to grow.

- Resources such as workers, machines and land are limited in supply.

- The economic problem of scarcity arises because wants exceed resources.

Teacher's Tip

It is very important to learn definitions. The more you apply a term such as scarcity in your work, the more you will become familiar with it. You may also want to compile your own economics dictionary by writing down terms in alphabetical order, as you come across them.

Multiple Choice Questions

1. Why does scarcity exist?
   a. Each year workers tend to produce less than previously.
   b. Machines wear out with time.
   c. There are not sufficient resources to produce all the products people want.
   d. There is a limit to people's wants.

2. Why will scarcity continue to be a problem in the future?
   a. Prices will rise.
   b. The quantity of resources will decline.
   c. Wants will continue to increase.
   d. World population will fall.

Factors of Production

This unit explores the key characteristics of the factors of production, the influences on their supply and also discusses the mobility of these factors. It also mentions the payments to factors of production. Factors of production is another term for economic resources. Unit 1 explained that economic resources are used to produce goods and services and are in limited supply.

 ## What are the Factors of Production?

Most economists identify four factors of production. These are land, capital, labour and enterprise. Some economists, however, claim that there is really only three factors of production and that enterprise is a special form of labour.

 Key Point

Factors of production: the economic resources of capital, enterprise, labour and land.

Land

Land in general terms includes the earth in which crops are grown and on which offices and factories are built, but in economics it has a wider meaning. It covers any natural resource which is used in production. So besides the land itself, it also includes what is beneath the land, such as coal, what occurs naturally on the land e.g. rainforests and the sea, oceans and rivers and what is found in them, for instance fish.

To attract foreign tourists, for instance, a travel company will make use of water in its swimming pools, good climate and beaches in the holidays it provides. Equivalently, the land used by a safari park includes not only the grass on which some of the animals graze but also the animals themselves.

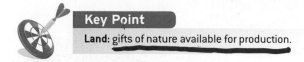

The Supply of Land

The amount of physical land in existence does not change much with time. There is a certain degree of soil erosion which reduces the supply of arable land but also a certain amount of land reclamation which increases its supply.

Other natural resources, however, can change quite significantly. Rainforests are currently declining at a rapid rate.

Some natural resources are renewable whilst others are non-renewable. Renewable resources, for instance wind power, are replaced by nature and hence can be used again and again. In contrast, non-renewable resources, e.g. gold and oil, are reduced by use. There is a risk that renewable resources can be turned into non-renewable resources if they are over-exploited, that is used at a faster rate than they are replenished. Over-fishing and the hunting of wildlife can diminish numbers to a point where they cannot be restored.

The Mobility of Land

Most land is occupationally mobile. This means that it can be used for a number of purposes. Land which is currently being used for farming may instead be used to build houses. Trees can be used to make tables or sleepers for railway lines.

Land, in its traditional sense, is however geographically immobile. It is not possible to move a section of land from Sri Lanka to India, for instance. Some forms of land, in its wider meaning, can be moved to a certain extent. For example, the course of rivers can be diverted and wildlife can be moved.

Activity 1

Identify two forms of land that are used by a paper mill.

Capital

Capital would have to be used in the diversion of the course of a river. Capital is any human-made (manufactured) good used to produce other goods and services. It includes, for example, offices, factories, machinery, railways and tools.

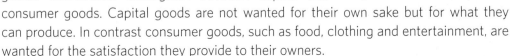

Capital is also referred to as capital goods and producer goods. Economists distinguish between capital and consumer goods. Capital goods are not wanted for their own sake but for what they can produce. In contrast consumer goods, such as food, clothing and entertainment, are wanted for the satisfaction they provide to their owners.

In deciding whether a good is a capital or a consumer good, it is necessary to consider who the user is and the purpose of its use. A computer, for example, will be a capital good if it is used by an insurance company to process insurance claims – it is producing a service. If, however, it is used by a person to play games, it is a consumer good.

Key Point

Capital: human-made goods used in production.

Activity 2

Decide which of the following are capital goods and which are consumer goods:

a. a chocolate bar
b. a car
c. a child's toy
d. a farm tractor
e. a dentist's drill
f. a courtroom.

The Supply of Capital

The supply of capital tends to increase with time. Every year some capital goods physically wear out and some become outdated. A farm barn may fall down, for instance, and some machinery may be replaced by newer, more efficient machinery.

New capital goods, however, usually take the place of those goods, which firms are unable (or choose not) to use any more. The total value of the output of capital goods produced is referred to as **gross investment** or sometimes just investment. Some of the capital goods being produced will be replacing those which have worn out or become obsolete. The value of replacement capital is called **depreciation** or capital consumption.

Net investment is the value of the extra capital goods made. It is equal to gross investment minus depreciation. For instance, if a country produces $200m capital goods one year and there is depreciation of $70m, net investment is $130m. The country will have more capital goods. These additional capital goods will allow it to produce more goods and services.

Occasionally gross investment may be lower than depreciation. This means that some of the capital goods taken out of use, are not replaced. This is said to be *negative net investment*.

Key Point

Investment: spending on capital goods.

 **Activity 3**

A firm is currently using 12 machines. Each machine is capable of producing 100 units of output. It anticipates that by the end of the year, 3 of its machines will wear out. If it expects to sell 1 600 units next year:

a. How many machines will it buy?
b. Why in the future may fewer machines be needed to produce the same output?

The Mobility of Capital

The geographical and occupational mobility of capital varies according to the type of capital goods. Some types of capital goods can be transferred from one part of the country to the other. A photocopier used by a bank in one area of a country can be sold to and then used by a bank in another area. A coal mine and a dock, however, are fixed in position and so are geographically immobile. They are also occupationally immobile since their use cannot be changed, as they have been made for a specific purpose. In contrast, a delivery van, used originally by a book publisher may be bought and employed by a toy manufacturer to distribute its products. Similarly, an office block may be used for a variety of purposes. It may house a call centre or an accountancy firm.

Labour

Labour covers all human effort – both mental and physical, involved in producing goods and services. A road sweeper, a steel worker and a bank manager all contribute their labour.

Some what confusingly, reference is sometimes made to human capital. This means the education, training and experience that workers have gained. The more human capital workers have, the more they should be capable of producing.

The Supply of Labour

The supply of labour is influenced by two key factors. One is the number of workers available and the second is the number of hours for which they work.

The number of available workers is determined by:

- **The size of the population.** The larger the population, the more workers there are likely to be.

- **The age structure of the population.** A country with a high proportion of people of working age will have more workers than a country with the same population size but a higher proportion of younger or older people.

- **The retirement age.** The higher the retirement age, the more potential workers there will be.

- **The school leaving age.** Raising the school leaving age would reduce the number of workers.

- **Attitude to working women.** Countries, where it is acceptable for women to work, have more workers to draw on.

Those people who are working or are seeking work form, what is known as, the **labour force**. This is also known as the workforce or working population. Those of working age are people between the school leaving age and the retirement age. In the UK, this covers people aged between 17 and 65. Not all of these people, however, are in the labour force. Some may be in full time education, some may have retired and some may be sick or disabled.

The number of hours, for which people work, is influenced by (among other factors):

- the length of the average working day. For instance, full time workers in USA tend to work for longer hours than those in the European Union.

- whether they work full or part time. For example, more people in the UK work part time than those in France.

- the duration of over-time.

- the length of holidays availed by workers.

- the amount of time lost through sickness and illness.

As with all the factors of production, it is not just the quantity of labour which is important but also the quality. More can be produced with the same number of workers if the workers become more skilled. Increase in productivity is a major cause of an increase in a country's output.

Key Point

Productivity: output per worker hour.

 Activity 4

Decide which of the following would raise labour productivity:
a. improved education and training
b. better equipment
c. worse working conditions.

The Mobility of Labour

The mobility of labour varies. Some workers may find it difficult to move from one area of the country to another or from one country to another (geographical immobility) and some may find it difficult to switch from one type of job to another type (occupational immobilty).

The causes of geographical immobility include:

- **differences in the price and availability of housing in different areas and countries.** Workers who lose their jobs in poor areas may not be able to take up jobs in rich areas because they cannot afford or find housing there.

- **family ties.** People may be reluctant to leave the country they are currently living in because they do not want to live away from friends and relatives.

- **differences in educational systems in different areas and countries.** People may not be willing to move to a job elsewhere if it disrupts their children's education.

- **lack of information.** People without jobs or those in poorly paid jobs may stay where they are because they are unaware of job opportunities elsewhere.

- **restrictions on the movement of workers.** It is often necessary to obtain a work visa to work in another country and these can be limited in supply.

There are also a number of causes of occupational immobility. Again there may be a lack of information about vacancies in other types of jobs. The main cause, however, is a lack of appropriate skills and qualifications. A shortage of doctors cannot be solved by hiring street hawkers!

Enterprise

Enterprise is the willingness and ability to bear uncertain risks and to make decisions in a business. Entrepreneurs are the people who organise the other factors of production and who crucially bear the risk of losing their money, if their business fails. Entrepreneurs decide what to produce – taking into account consumer demand, and how to produce it. Some of the risks faced by any business can be insured against. These include fire, flood and theft. Other risks, however, have to be borne by entrepreneurs. This is because some events are not anticipated, based on past events and so cannot be insured against. These include the uninsurable risks of other firms bringing out rival products and rising costs of production.

The two key tasks of an entrepreneur can be carried out by different people. In large companies, it is the shareholders who run the risk of losing their money if the companies go out of business whilst the managing directors take production decisions and organise the factors of production.

Key Point

Enterprise: risk bearing and decision making in business.

The Supply of Entrepreneurs

A good education system, including university degree courses in economics and business studies, may help to develop entrepreneurs in an economy. Lower taxes on firms' profits (corporate taxes) and a reduction in government regulations may encourage more people to set up their own businesses. Sometimes, a disproportionate number of immigrants become entrepreneurs. These are people who have had the drive to leave home in search of a better life and this drive often leads them to become entrepreneurs in the new country.

The Mobility of Enterprise

Enterprise is the most mobile factor of production. The skill involved can be applied in every industry. Someone who has borne uncertain risks and organised factors of production in the car industry should be able to do this in, for instance, the textile industry too. Apart from being occupationally mobile, enterprise is also geographically mobile. Someone who has been successful in starting up and running a business in one country is likely to be successful in another country also.

 Activity 5

The following is a list of economic resources. In each case, decide whether the resource is an example of capital, enterprise, labour or land:

a. chemical fertiliser
b. a school
c. a lake
d. the work of a nurse
e. the initiative needed to set up and run a bicycle repair shop.

 # Payments to Factors of Production

Payments are made for the use of factors of production. Firms pay wages for the services of the workers. For bearing uncertain risks and organising the other factors of production, entrepreneurs earn profit. Land receives rent and interest is a payment for capital.

 **Summary**

- The four factors of production are capital, enterprise, labour and land.

- Whilst most land is occupationally mobile, land in its traditional meaning is geographically immobile.

- Net investment increases a country's stock of capital goods.

- The supply of labour is influenced by the number of workers and the number of hours for which they work.

- Entrepreneurs bear uninsurable risks and make production decisions.

 Teacher's Tip

Remember when economists refer to capital, they mean human-made goods, such as machinery and office buildings, that are used to produce other products.

Multiple Choice Questions

1. Which factor of production's function is to make decisions and take risks?
   a. Capital
   b. Enterprise
   c. Labour
   d. Land

2. Which type of factor of production is a road?
   a. Capital
   b. Enterprise
   c. Labour
   d. Land

3. A country produces 3 000 new capital goods in a week. 500 of these replace worn out capital goods. What is the net investment made?
   a. 500
   b. 2 500
   c. 3 000
   d. 3 500

4. Which factor of production is the most mobile?
   a. Capital
   b. Enterprise
   c. Labour
   d. Land

Opportunity Cost

There are not enough economic resources to produce all the goods and services we would desire, as was noted in Unit 1. Capital, enterprise, land and labour are scarce and so decisions have to be made about the method and purpose of their use. A classroom can be used to teach English or economics in the some room but not at the same time. In deciding what to use the classroom for, and in making other decisions, the concept of opportunity cost is important as this unit will seek to explain.

Opportunity Cost

When we decide to do one thing, we are deciding not to do something else. To ensure that we make the right decisions, it is important that we consider the alternatives, particularly the best alternative. Opportunity Cost is the cost of a decision in terms of the best alternative given up to achieve it. For instance, there are a variety of things you could do tomorrow between 5pm and 6pm. These may be to go shopping, to read a chapter of an economics book, to do some paid work or to visit a friend. You may narrow those choices down to reading the chapter or visiting a friend. You will have to consider very carefully which one will give you the best return. If you choose to read the chapter, you will not be able to visit your friend and vice versa.

Key Point

Opportunity cost: the best alternative forgone.

Opportunity Cost and Consumers

Consumers are buyers and users of goods and services. We all are consumers. The vast majority of us cannot buy everything we like. I may, for example, have to choose which economics dictionary to buy. I will probably consider a number of different ones, taking into account their prices. The choice will then tend to settle on two of them. I will select the one with the widest and the most accurate informative coverage. The closer the two dictionaries are in quality and price, the harder the choice will be.

Opportunity Cost and Workers

Undertaking one job involves an opportunity cost. People employed as teachers might also be able to work as civil servants. They need to carefully consider their preference for the jobs available. This would be influenced by a number of factors, including the wage paid, chances of promotion and the job satisfaction to be gained from each job. If the pay of civil servants or their working conditions improve, the opportunity cost of being a teacher will increase. It may even increase to the point where some teachers resign and become civil servants instead.

Opportunity Cost and Producers

Producers have to decide what to make. If a farmer uses a field to grow sugar beet, he cannot keep cattle on that field. If a car producer uses some of his factory space and workers to produce one model of a car, he cannot use the same space and workers to make another model of the car at the same time.

In deciding what to produce, private sector firms will tend to choose the option which will give them the maximum profit. They will also take into account, the demand for different products and the cost of producing those products.

Opportunity Cost and the Government

Government has to carefully consider, its expenditure of tax revenue on various things. If it decides to spend more on education, the opportunity cost involved may be a reduced expenditure on health care. It could, of course, raise tax revenue in order to spend more on education. In this case, the opportunity cost would be put on the taxpayers. To pay higher taxes, people may have to give up the opportunity to buy certain products or to save.

![Activity 1]

In each of the following cases, consider what might be the opportunity cost.
a.   A person wanting to buy fruit, decides to buy apples.
b.   A person decides to study economics at a university.
c.   A factory is built on farm land.
d.   A woman has a television set which cost her $800 two years ago. A new set would cost her $1 000 and she could sell her television set for $450. What is the opportunity cost of keeping the old television?

Economic Goods and Free Goods

A vast majority of goods are economic goods. This means that it takes resources to produce them and hence, their production involves an opportunity cost. Also, they are limited in supply. For example, a carpet is an economic good. The material and labour used to produce it, could have been used to make another good (or goods). It is easy to find examples of economic goods. Almost every good and service you can think of is an economic good. Your education is an economic good, since your teachers and the other resources used to provide it could have been employed for making other products.

Free goods are much rarer. When most people talk about free goods, they mean products they do not have to pay for. These are not usually free goods in the economic sense since

resources have been used to produce them. Economists define a free good as one, which takes no resources to make it and thus does not involve an opportunity cost. It is hard to think of examples of free goods. Sunshine is one such example, so is water in a river. However, as soon as this water is processed for drinking or used for irrigation of fields, it becomes an economic good.

 ## Key Points

Economic good: a product which requires resources to produce it and therefore has an opportunity cost.

Free good: a product which does not require any resources to make it and so does not have an opportunity cost.

Activity 2

Decide whether each of the following is an economic or a free good:

a. air
b. education
c. newspapers
d. public libraries
e. state education.

Production Possibility Curves

A good way to illustrate opportunity cost is to use a production possibility curve (PPC). In fact, a PPC can also be called an *opportunity cost curve*. Its other names are a production possibility boundary (PPB) and a production possibility frontier (PPF).

A PPC shows the maximum output of two products and combinations of these products that can be produced with existing resources and technology. Figure 1 shows, that a country can produce either 100 units of manufactured goods or 150 units of agricultural goods or a range of combinations of these two goods.

A country may decide to produce 80 units of manufactured goods and 75 units of agricultural goods. If it then decides to produce 100 units of agricultural goods, it will have to switch resources away from producing manufactured goods. The diagram shows the reduction of output of manufactured goods to 60 units. In this case, the opportunity cost of producing 25 extra units of agricultural goods is 20 units of manufactured goods.

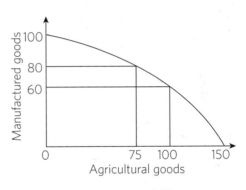

Fig. 1 A production possibility curve

 **Key Point**

Production possibility curve: a curve that shows the maximum output of two types of products and combination of those products that can be produced with existing resources and technology.

 Activity 3

Using Figure 2:

a. state the maximum number of capital goods the country can produce if it devotes all of its resources for making capital goods.

b. calculate the opportunity cost of increasing the output of consumer goods from 80 to 90 units.

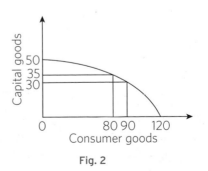

Fig. 2

Summary

- Opportunity cost is an important concept as it emphasises that people have to consider what they are sacrificing when they decide what to buy, what job to do and what to produce and when governments are deciding what to spend their tax revenue on.

- Economic goods have an opportunity cost as the resources used to produce them could have been used to make something else.

- Free goods exist without the use of resources and hence do not have an opportunity cost.

- PPC curves can be used to illustrate opportunity cost. They show what can be produced with the given economic resources.

Teacher's Tip

In explaining opportunity cost, it is always useful to give an example.

Multiple Choice Questions

1. What is meant by 'opportunity cost'?
    a. The best alternative forgone.
    b. The cost of the item selected.
    c. The cost of exploring business opportunities.
    d. The labour used in producing the product.

2. A person decides to go to the university for three years, to study economics. If he had not gone, he could have taken up a job which would have paid him $15 000 a year. After he graduates he expects to find a job paying him $40 000 a year. What is the opportunity cost of going to the university for him?
    a. $15 000   b. $40 000
    c. $45 000   d. $120 000

3. Which of the following is a free good?
    a. Inoculation provided without charge by the state.
    b. Prizes of food items given away by a supermarket.
    c. Recycled paper.
    d. Wind coming in from the sea.

4. Using Figure 3, determine the opportunity cost of increasing the output of luxury goods from 25 to 35.

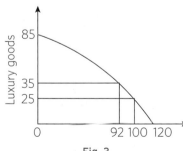

Fig. 3

    a. 8 basic goods
    b. 10 luxury goods
    c. 25 luxury goods
    d. 92 basic goods

Answer Key

Unit 1

Activity 1

All three items are scarce. In each case, people want more than what is currently being produced. More people want to study at university than there are places available. Most of us would like to holiday abroad and those of us fortunate enough to do so, would like to undertake more trips. Also there are not enough resources to provide good quality health care quickly, to every one who requires it.

Multiple Choice Questions

1. c

   Scarcity arises because wants are greater than the resources that can be used to produce them. Workers tend to produce more each year, as they become more experienced and work with better machinery. Machines wear out with time but they are usually replaced by more efficient ones and are often added to. There is no limit to people's wants.

2. c

   Both wants and resources will continue to increase with time. World population is likely to rise. Prices are also likely to increase in the future but such a change will reflect changes in demand and supply and will not be a cause of scarcity.

Unit 2

Activity 1

Among the forms of land used by a paper mill, are the land on which the mill is built and the water and wood used in the process of making paper.

Activity 2

a. a consumer good
b. a consumer or capital good depending on who uses it
c. a consumer good
d. a capital good
e. a capital good
f. a capital good

Activity 3
a. It will need 16 machines in total. It starts with 9 machines (12 – 3) so it needs to buy 7 machines – 3 for replacement and 4 to expand capacity.

b. There may be advances in the technology.

Activity 4
a. and b. would raise labour productivity. Improved education and training would make workers more skilful and hence capable of producing a higher output. Better equipment should also enable each worker to produce more. On the other hand, c. would probably cause a fall in output per worker. Worse working conditions would reduce workers' motivation and may make it more difficult for them, to carry out their tasks.

Activity 5
a. capital
b. capital
c. land – if a naturally formed lake but capital, if man made
d. labour
e. enterprise

Multiple Choice Questions
1. a
    Enterprise is the ability and willingness to bear uncertain risks and make production decisions.

2. a
    Capital is a human made good used to produce other goods and services. A road enables passengers to travel and freight to be transported.

3. b
    Net investment is gross investment minus depreciation. In this case, it is 3 000 – 500.

4. b
    Enterprise and the entrepreneurs that provide it, find it relatively easy to switch from one industry to another and from one location to another.

Unit 3

Activity 1

a.   Other types of fruits e.g. bananas, mangoes or pears.

b.   Another degree course e.g. mathematics or a job.

c.   Other uses of the land including housing, an office or a park.

d. $450 – by keeping the TV, she is forgoing $450.

Activity 2

a.   free good   b.   economic good
c.   economic good   d.   economic good
e.   economic good

Economic resources are used to produce b – e.

Activity 3

a.   50 capital goods
b.   5 capital goods are given up. To increase the output of consumer goods from 80 to 90, the output of capital goods has to fall from 35 to 30.

Multiple Choice Questions

1.   a
     A straightforward question.

2.   c
     By going to the university, the student is giving up the opportunity to earn $15 000 a year for three years – a total of $45 000.

3.   d
     Wind coming in from the sea does not take resources to produce it. All the other items mentioned have to be produced and, in each case, the production involves an opportunity cost.

4.   a
     To produce 10 more luxury goods, the output of basic goods has to fall from 100 to 92. The opportunity to make 8 basic goods has been given up.

Examination Practice

Multiple Choice Questions

1. What gives rise to the problem of scarcity?
   a. A lack of money.
   b. An uneven distribution of income.
   c. Capital equipment being greater than labour.
   d. Wants exceeding resources.

2. As an economy becomes richer, what happens to resources and wants?

	Resources	Wants
a.	decrease	decrease
b.	decrease	increase
c.	increase	decrease
d.	increase	increase

3. Which of the following is an example of the factor of production 'capital'?
   a. The money a farmer has borrowed to buy livestock.
   b. The money a farmer has saved in the bank.
   c. A farm worker.
   d. A tractor.

4. Which type of factor of production can be described as a 'natural resource'?
   a. Capital
   b. Entrepreneur
   c. Labour
   d. Land

5. A woman owns a TV which she bought for $300. She is considering buying a better model for $450. Her neighbour offers her $200 for her TV. What is the opportunity cost of her rejecting this offer?
   a. $100
   b. $200
   c. $300
   d. $450

6. A man presently works as a builder. His previous jobs included working as a farm labourer and a street trader. His next best-paid job is that of a carpenter but he would rather choose to work as a gardener, if not a builder. What will be the opportunity cost of him working as a builder? Working as:
    a.   a carpenter
    b.   a farm labourer
    c.   a gardener
    d.   a street trader

Structured Questions

1. After studying for this examination you decide to continue your studies and take further examinations.
    a.   How does this decision involve an opportunity cost? Explain your answer. (4)
    b.   What are the economic factors you might consider while making such a decision? (6)

    (Cambridge 0455 Paper 2 Q5 Nov 1997)

2. Explain the terms scarcity and opportunity cost. (4)

    (Cambridge 0455 Paper 4 Q3a May/June 2006)

Market and Mixed Economies

The previous section explored the nature of resources and explained that wants exceed resources. Hence, decisions have to be made as to how the resources need to be used. This unit examines how these choices are made in different economic systems.

 ## The Three Main Economic Systems

All economies have to answer three fundamental economic questions.

These are:

*   what to produce

*   how to produce it and

*   who is to receive the products produced.

These questions arise because of the basic economic problem of *unlimited wants exceeding finite resources*. A decision has to made as to how the economy's resources are to be allocated. For example, how many resources should be devoted to health care, how many to leisure goods and services and how many to defence.

Once this decision has been taken, an economy has to decide on how the products are to be manufactured. For example, whether a large number of workers should be used in agriculture or more reliance be placed on capital equipment? Finally, because as many goods and services cannot be produced, as required to satisfy the needs of everyone, a decision has to be reached as to how the products should be distributed. Should products be distributed to people according to their needs or their ability to earn a high income?

The answers to the above questions differ in different economic systems. An economic system covers the institutions, organisations and mechanisms in a country that influence economic behaviour.

Different Economic Systems

There are three main economic systems. One is a *planned economy*, which can also be called a centrally planned, command or collectivist economy. It is one in which the state (government) makes the decisions about what to produce, how to produce it and who receives it. The state owns all or at least most of the land and capital and employs workers. It gives instructions, sometimes called **directives**, to state-owned enterprises (SOEs) on what to produce and how to produce it. It determines who gets the products made, both by deciding on the remuneration paid to the workers and by controlling prices. It will usually provide basic necessities and important products such as housing, transport and education free of cost or at a low price.

The other two type of economic systems are a *market economy* and a *mixed economy*. Given the decline in the number of countries operating planned economies, this unit will focus largely on these two types.

> **Key Point**
>
> **A planned economy:** an economy where the government makes the crucial decisions, land and capital are state-owned and resources are allocated by directives.

A Market Economy

A market economy, also known as a *free enterprise economy*, is one in which consumers determine what is produced. They signal their preferences through the price mechanism. If they want more of a product, they will be willing to pay more for it. The higher price offered will encourage firms to produce the good in more amounts as then the firms make more profit.

In a market economy, resources switch from products that are becoming less popular to those which are becoming more popular. Fig. 1 shows the effect of demand for bananas increasing whilst demand for apples decreases.

In a market economy, government intervention is minimum. Land and capital are privately owned. Private sector firms decide how to produce the products consumers want to buy. Some firms, for instance steel firms, may employ large amounts of capital relative to labour. They are said to be **capital intensive**. Others, for example, hotels may use a relatively high numbers of workers in comparison with the amount of capital used. They

Bananas	Apples
Increase in demand	Decrease in demand
↓	↓
Rise in price	Fall in price
↓	↓
Rise in profit	Fall in profit
↓	↓
Firms produce more	Firms produce less
↓	↓
Hire more workers, use more capital and land	Reduce number of workers, capital and land employed

Fig. 1 Changes in resource allocation in a market economy.

are **labour intensive**. In making their decision on which factors of production to employ, firms will seek to achieve the **least cost method of production**. This may also involve use of new, more productive capital equipment, to replace older equipment.

In a market economy, those who earn the highest incomes exercise the maximum influence on what is produced. Those workers whose skills are in highest demand and the most successful entrepreneurs will be able to buy more products than those whose skills are in low demand and unsuccessful entrepreneurs.

Key Point

A **market economy**: an economy where consumers determine what is produced, resources are allocated by the price mechanism and land and capital are privately owned.

The Advantages of a Market Economy

A market economy should be very responsive to changes in consumer demand. In fact, in this economic system, consumers are said to be *sovereign*.

There is also *choice* in a market economy. Consumers can choose which firms to buy from, firms can decide what they want to produce and workers can choose who to work for.

The profit motive and competition promote *efficiency* also. Those firms, which produce what consumers want at the lowest possible prices, are rewarded with high profits. But those which do not change their output quickly to reflect what is in demand and have high costs (and consequently high prices) are likely to go out of business.

High incomes provide an *incentive* for people to work hard and for entrepreneurs to set up and expand firms. (See unit 10 for a more detailed discussion of the merits of the market system.)

Disadvantages of a Market Economy

There is a risk that the market forces of demand and supply may not work well. In fact, there may occur, what is called *market failure* with market forces failing to ensure the maximum benefit for society. There are a number of reasons for this.

a. One is that consumers and private sector firms only take into account the costs and benefits to themselves and not the costs and benefits of their decisions on others. For example, some people may smoke even if it annoys and endangers the health of those around them. To keep their costs and prices down, firms may dump waste material in local rivers rather than process it.

b. Competition between firms should ensure efficiency but, in practice, there may be little competition. A market may become dominated by one or a few firms. These firms have considerable market power leading to limited or no choice for consumers. They can raise the prices of their products and produce poor quality products, as people have no choice but to buy from them.

c. Even when there is competition and firms want to respond to desires of consumers, they may not be able to do this. This may be because they cannot attract more workers as workers lack the right skills or are geographically immobile.

d. Firms will not make products unless they think they can charge for them. There are some products, such as defence, which most people may want but know that if they are provided for some, they will have to be provided for all. In such cases people can act as *free riders*. They can enjoy the product even if they do not pay for it. When it is not possible to exclude non-payers, private sector firms do not have the financial incentive to produce the product.

e. Advertising can distort consumer choice. It can persuade people to buy products they would not otherwise have wanted or encourage them to buy larger quantities. Consumers and producers may also lack information and hence may make inefficient choices.

f.   In a market economy, some consumers will also have a lack of income. There can be a very uneven distribution of income, with some people being very rich while some others being very poor. The sick and disabled may find it difficult to earn incomes. The old may not have made adequate financial provision for their retirement. Some workers may become unemployed and may find it difficult to find new jobs.

Differences in income will increase over time. Those earning high incomes can afford to save and buy shares. Their savings and shares will earn them interest and dividends (a share of profits). In contrast, the poor cannot afford to save. The children of the rich will be more likely, than the children of the poor, to earn high incomes. This is because their parents are able to spend more on their education, provide better equipment such as computers at home for them and thus they have high hopes of what they can achieve. (See unit 11 for a more detailed exploration of market failure.)

Activity 1

In USA, there is a considerable gap between the rich and the poor. Explain, how in a market economy, some people can be:

a.   rich

b.   poor.

Activity 2

Decide which of the following may be found in a market economy:

a.   most people working for SOEs

b.   controls on the prices of most products

c.   entrepreneurs earning high profits

d.   most land being privately owned.

A Mixed Economy

A mixed economy has a combination of the features of a planned and a market economy. Some firms are privately owned (in the private sector) and some are government owned (in the public sector). Some prices are determined by the market forces of demand and supply and some are set by the government. In this type of economic system, both consumers and the government influence what is produced.

A mixed economy seeks to gain the advantages of both a market and a planned economy whilst avoiding their disadvantages. Having some products produced by the private sector may generate choice, increase efficiency and create incentives. Benefits may also be gained as a result of state intervention. These are listed below.

- The government should take into account all the costs and benefits that will arise from their decisions. This should mean, for example, that even if a railway line and station would not make a profit in the private sector, they would be maintained by the state if the benefit to society is greater than the cost.

- Government can also encourage the consumption of products that are more beneficial for consumers and others than they realise by granting subsidies, providing information or passing legislation.

- Government can discourage the consumption of products that are more harmful for consumers and others than they appreciate by imposing taxes on such products, providing information or passing legislation.

- Government can finance the production of products that cannot be charged for directly, for example, defence.

- Government can seek to prevent private sector firms from exploiting consumers by charging high prices.

- Government is likely to seek to make maximum use of resources, including labour, and hence try to ensure that those people willing and able to work can find jobs.

- There is a possibility that the government will plan ahead to a greater extent than private sector firms and hence may devote more of its resources to capital goods.

- Government can help vulnerable groups, ensuring that they have access to basic necessities. It can also create a more even distribution of income, by taxing the rich at a high rate.

There are, nevertheless, risks attached even to a mixed economy and there is no guarantee that it will perform better than the other two types of economies. Market failure can occur and government intervention may make the situation worse.

Examples of the Different Economic Systems

To a certain extent, all economies are mixed economies. This is because there is some government intervention in all economies and some private sector production. The term – a mixed economy, however, is largely used to describe an economy which has market and government sectors of reasonably similar sizes. An example of such an economy is Sweden.

Whilst there is no economy without a government sector, USA is often described as a market economy. The US government does carry out some functions, for instance, providing defence. The economy is, nevertheless, considered to be a market economy as most capital and land is owned by individuals and groups of individuals and market forces play the key role in deciding the fundamental economic questions.

In Cuba, there is a limited degree of small scale private sector agricultural production but the economy is largely a planned economy. Most land and capital is owned by the government and it makes most of the decisions as to what to produce, how to produce it and who receives the output.

 ## Changes in Economic Systems

In the 1980s and 1990s a number of economies, including the UK and New Zealand, moved from being largely mixed economies to being mainly market economies. The role of the government was reduced by removing a number of government regulations, selling off SOEs and parts of SOEs (privatisation) and lowering taxation.

There was an even more dramatic change in the economies of Eastern Europe, including Poland and Russia, in the 1990s. They moved from being planned economies to market economies. These economies have experienced a significant increase in consumer choice and a rise in the quality of products produced. They have also, however, seen a rise in income inequality and poverty.

Recent years have witnessed an increasing role of market forces in a number of economies in Asia, including China and India, and in Africa, including South Africa. In contrast, there has been a rise in government intervention in a number of Latin American economies, including Bolivia and Venezuela.

Activity 3

India has a long tradition of government planning but the degree of government intervention in the economy has been reduced in the last two decades. Privatisation started in 1991, with the creation and sale of a small number of shares in some SOEs. This process speeded up in the first decade of the 2000s. In 2004, for instance, the Indian government sold off some of its shares in the Oil and National Gas Corporation and some shares in the airports of Delhi and Mumbai, hoping that this would stimulate more investment and greater efficiency. This privatisation has been opposed by the communist parties of India which argue that firms perform better in the public sector.

a.　What is meant by privatisation?
b.　Explain one reason for better performance of a firm when:
　　(i)　it is in the private sector
　　(ii)　it is in the public sector.

Summary

- The main factors that determine the type of economic system are – who decides what is produced, how resources are allocated and who owns the capital and land.

- The three main economic systems are (i) planned economy, (ii) market economy and (iii) a mixed economy. Over the last three decades there has been a decline in the number of planned economies.

- The main advantage claimed for a market economy are that output reflects consumer tastes, consumers have greater choice, competition promotes efficiency and financial incentives encourage hard work and enterprise.

continued····>

- Among the disadvantages that may arise from operating a market economy are that output may not reflect the full costs and benefits, private sector firms may abuse their market power, resources may be immobile, products that consumers want but cannot be charged for directly cannot be produced and there may be poverty.

- In a mixed economy, resources are allocated by means both of the price mechanism and government decision.

- Recent decades have seen a number of countries in Eastern Europe, Asia and Africa move towards a market economy.

Teacher's Tip

Be careful not to confuse a market and a mixed economy. In a market economy, it is the price mechanism which allocates resources. In a mixed economy, it is both the price mechanism and the government which decide the use of resources.

Multiple Choice Questions

1. What are the three questions faced by all economies?
    a.   What to produce, when to produce it and who receives it
    b.   What to produce, how to produce it and who receives it
    c.   Where to produce, how to produce and when to produce
    d.   Where to produce, when to produce and how to produce

2. How are resources allocated in a market economy?
    a.   By directives
    b.   By the price mechanism
    c.   By directives or the price mechanism
    d.   By directives and the price mechanism

3. What is an advantage of a market economy?
    a.   An absence of poverty
    b.   Consumer sovereignty
    c.   Firms having considerable market power
    d.   Full employment

4. What is an argument for state intervention in an economy?
    a.   To encourage the consumption of harmful products
    b.   To increase the role of the price mechanism in allocating resources
    c.   To make the distribution of income more uneven
    d.   To prevent private sector firms from overcharging consumers

Equilibrium Price

The prices of goods and services are determined by the amount consumers wanting to buy them are prepared to pay for them and the amount the producers wishing to sell them are prepared to accept. In this unit, demand, supply and price determination are explored in more depth.

 Demand

When economists discuss demand, they are discussing effective demand. They define this as the *willingness* and *ability* to buy a product. I may want a product but if I cannot afford it, my demand is not effective as a firm will not be prepared to sell it to me. Demand and price are inversely related. This means demand will rise as price falls and fall as price rises. A higher price will mean that fewer people will be able to afford the product. They will also be less willing to buy it and will be more likely to switch to rival products. So as price rises, the willingness and ability to buy a product falls.

Key Point
Demand: the willingness and ability to buy a product.

Individual and Market Demand

Economists study individual and, more commonly, market demand. As its name suggests individual demand is the amount of a product an individual would be willing and able to buy, at different prices. Market demand is the total demand for a product at different prices. It is found by adding up each individual's demand at different prices.

Key Point
Market demand: total demand for a product.

A Demand Schedule

A demand schedule lists the different quantities demanded of a product, at different prices over a particular time period. Table 1 shows a demand schedule for tickets on trains from Oxford to London.

Table 1 Daily demand for train tickets from Oxford to London in the winter months.

Price (£)	Quantity demanded
50	2 200
45	2 500
40	3 000
35	3 800
30	5 000
25	7 000

A Demand Curve

The information from a demand curve can be plotted on a diagram. Price is measured on the vertical axis (the line going up) and quantity demanded on the horizontal axis (the line going across). Fig. 1 shows the above information on a diagram.

This demand curve and the demand schedule on which it is based do not show the demand over the full range of prices. It is possible to do this. Fig. 2 illustrates such a curve.

The curve shows the price, £90, at which people would stop buying tickets – the service is priced out of the market. It also shows how many tickets people would want, if they were provided free of cost. As it is unusual for firms to charge either such a high price that demand is zero or a zero price, demand curves are often not taken to the axes.

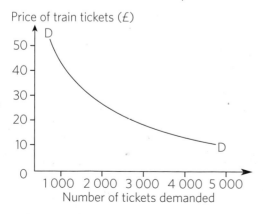

Fig. 1 Daily demand for train tickets from Oxford to London

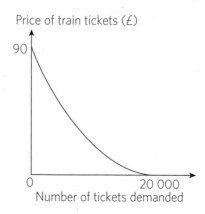

Fig. 2 A demand curve over the full range of prices

To save time and for the sake of clarity, economists also often draw demand curves as straight lines as shown in Fig. 3. (It is interesting to note that they are still referred to as curves).

Such lines do not usually show exact quantities and prices but can be used to illustrate the relationship between demand and price and the effect of price changes on demand.

Fig. 3 A straight line demand curve

 **Activity 1**

Using the following demand schedule, plot the demand curve for rooms in a hotel in Delhi.

Price (rupees)	Number of rooms
800	10
700	20
600	35
500	55
400	80
300	110

The Effect of a Change in Price on Demand

As noted earlier, a fall in the price of a product is likely to lead to a rise in demand for it. Economists refer to this as extension in demand, expansion in demand or an increase in the quantity demanded. Seeing the words 'an extension in demand', 'expansion in demand' or 'an increase in the quantity demanded' will tell an economist that the cause of the change in demand is a change in the price of the product itself.

Such a change can be illustrated on a demand curve (Fig. 4).

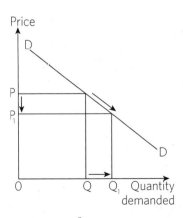

Fig. 4 An extension in demand

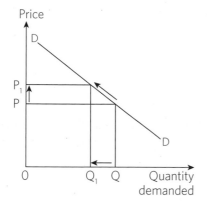

Price

D

P₁

P

D

0   Q₁   Q   Quantity demanded

Fig. 5 A contraction in demand

The diagram shows that a fall in price from P to P_1 has caused the demand to extend from Q to Q_1. In contrast, a rise in price will cause a contraction in demand which can also be referred to as a decrease in quantity demanded.

Fig. 5 shows the impact of a rise in price.

Demand contracts from Q to Q_1 as a result of a rise in price from P to P_1.

Key Points

An extension in demand: a rise in the quantity demanded caused by a fall in the price of the product itself.

A contraction in demand: a fall in the quantity demanded caused by a rise in the price of the product itself.

Activity 2

A shop changes the price of a can of soft drink from $3 to $2 and as a result, demand changes from 40 cans a day to 50 cans.
a. Illustrate this change on a demand curve.
b. Identify whether demand has extended or contracted.

Supply

Supply is the willingness and ability to sell a product. It is important not to confuse supply with production. Supply is influenced by the amount produced but is not the same as production. This is because some of the amount produced today may be stored, in order to be sold at a later date. Conversely, it is possible that some of the output offered for sale today may have come from stocks.

In contrast to demand, supply is directly related to price. A rise in price will lead to a rise in supply. Firms will be more willing to supply the product, as they are likely to earn higher profits. They will also be able to supply more as the higher price will make it easier for them to cover the costs of production.

Individual and Market Supply

Individual supply is the supply of one plant/firm whereas market supply is the total supply of a product produced by all the firms in the industry. Market supply is calculated in a similar way to market demand. The quantities that would be supplied at each price are added up.

A Supply Schedule

A supply schedule records the different quantities supplied at different prices. Table 2 shows a supply schedule for train tickets from Oxford to London.

Table 2 Daily supply of train tickets from Oxford to London in winter months

Price (£)	Quantity Supplied
50	6 000
45	5 000
40	4 300
35	3 800
30	3 600
25	3 500

From this information, a supply curve can be plotted as shown in Fig. 6.

As with demand curves, supply curves can be drawn as straight lines.

The Effect of a Change in Price on Supply

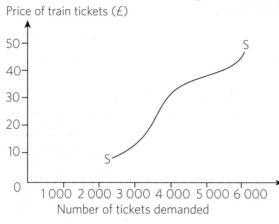

Fig. 6 Daily supply of train tickets from Oxford to London

Again as with demand, a change in price of the product will cause an extension in supply (expansion or an increase in the quantity supplied) or a contraction in supply (a decrease in the quantity supplied).

This time, however, it is a rise in price which will cause an extension in supply and a fall in price which will cause a contraction in supply. Fig. 7 illustrates both these changes.

Key Points

An extension in supply: a rise in the quantity supplied caused by a rise in the price of the product itself.

A contraction in supply: a fall in the quantity supplied caused by a fall in the price of the product itself.

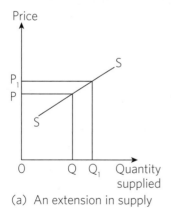

(a) An extension in supply

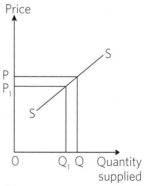

(b) A contraction in supply

Fig. 7

Price Determination

Consumers want low prices whilst sellers want high prices. So how is the price of a product determined? In some cases, there is direct bargaining between buyers and sellers.

Buyers often haggle with market traders, seeking to drive the price down and the traders aim to keep the price relatively high. In other cases, the bargaining is more indirect. Firms estimate and then charge what they think is the equilibrium price, that is the price where demand and supply are equal. If they find that they cannot sell all of their output at this price, they will lower it. If, on the other hand, they find that consumers want to buy more than what they are offering for sale at this price, they will raise the price.

Key Point

Equilibrium price: the price where demand and supply are equal.

Equilibrium Price

Equilibrium price is also sometimes referred to as the *market clearing price*. This is because it is the price, where demand and supply are equal and so there are no shortages or surpluses of the product. The equilibrium price of a product can be found by comparing the demand and supply schedules of that product and seeing where demand and supply are equal. Table 3 uses the information previously given on train tickets.

Table 3 The daily demand for and supply of train tickets from Oxford to London in winter months.

Price (£)	Quantity demanded	Quantity supplied
50	2 200	6 000
45	2 500	5 000
40	3 000	4 300
35	3 800	3 800
30	5 000	3 600
25	7 000	3 500

In this case the equilibrium price is £35, since at this point demand and supply are equal.

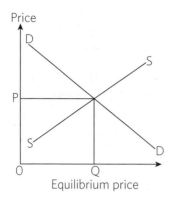

Price

Fig. 8

Equilibrium price

Equilibrium price can also be found by examining a demand and supply diagram. It occurs where the demand and supply curves intersect.

Fig. 8 shows that equilibrium price is P and the equilibrium quantity is Q.

Price will stay at P until demand and supply conditions change.

How is equilibrium price achieved?

Market forces move price towards the equilibrium. If a firm sets the price above the equilibrium level, it will not sell all of the products it offers for sale – there will be a **surplus**. To ensure it sells all of the products it wants to, it will lower price until the market clears, with the quantity demanded equalling the quantity supplied. Fig. 9 shows a market, initially being in a state of disequilibrium with supply exceeding demand.

At \$6, the firm is willing and able to sell 10 000 products but consumers buy only 4 000. This leaves 6 000 unsold products. As a result price will fall, causing demand to extend and supply to contract until price reaches the equilibrium level. Fig. 10 shows this adjustment.

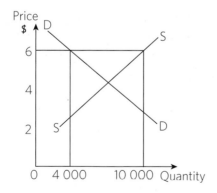

Fig. 9 Supply exceeding demand

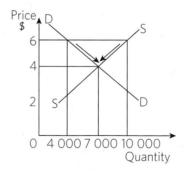

Fig. 10 Return to equilibrium

Key Point

Disequilibrium: a situation where demand and supply are not equal.

Market forces will also move the price, if it is initially set below the equilibrium level. In this case, there will initially be a shortage of the product with demand exceeding supply as shown in Fig. 11.

Some consumers anxious to buy the product will be willing to pay a higher price and suppliers recognising this demand, will raise the price. Fig. 12 shows the price being pushed up to the equilibrium level of $5.

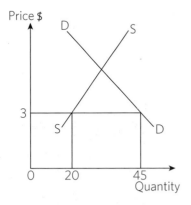

Fig. 11 Demand exceeding supply

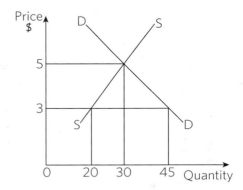

Fig. 12 Return to equilibrium

 **Activity 3**

As the 2006 World Cup approached, sales of Brazilian football shirts increased not only in Brazil but also in a number of other countries. Two weeks before the competition started, shops in London and Sao Paulo reported that demand for shirts was outstripping supply.

a.   On a demand and supply diagram, illustrate the market for Brazilian football shirts in Sao Paulo two weeks before the 2006 World Cup.

b.   What would you have expected to happen to the price of Brazilian football shirts in Sao Paulo in this situation? Explain your answer.

 **Summary**

- A fall in the price of a product will make the people more willing and able to buy it.

- A demand schedule lists, and a demand curve shows, the different quantities of a product that would be demanded at different prices.

- An extension in demand is caused by a fall in the price of the product whereas a contraction is caused by a rise in price.

- A fall in the price of a product will make suppliers less willing and able to sell it.

- Supply schedules and supply curves show the relationship between the price and the quantity supplied.

- A fall in price causes a contraction in supply whereas a rise in price causes an extension in supply.

- Price is determined by the interaction of demand and supply.

- At the equilibrium price, demand is equal to supply.

- If price is not at the equilibrium level initially, market forces will move it towards equilibrium.

 Teacher's Tip

In answering questions on demand and supply, it is useful to draw diagrams. A diagram must be accurately and fully labelled. It should also be large enough and clear. It is advisable to use at least one third of an A4 size page for drawing a diagram. Also, explain the diagram in your text.

Multiple Choice Questions

1. What is the relationship between demand and price and the relationship between supply and price?

	demand and price	supply and price
a.	directly related	directly related
b.	directly related	inversely related
c.	inversely related	directly related
d.	inversely related	inversely related

2. What happens to people's willingness and ability to buy a product when its price falls?

	willingness	ability
a.	increases	increases
b.	increases	decreases
c.	decreases	decreases
d.	decreases	increases

3. What does a market supply curve show?
   a. The proportion of total output produced by different firms in the industry
   b. Proportion of total output sold
   c. The relationship between the total quantity supplied and demand for the product
   d. The relationship between the total quantity supplied and the price of the product

4. Equilibrium price is the price at which:
   a. everything that is produced is sold
   b. the amount consumers demand is equal to the amount sellers supply
   c. the number of buyers equals the number of sellers
   d. supply exceeds demand.

Changes in Demand

In this unit you will learn about the main causes of changes in demand and the effects, that such changes have, on a market.

 ## A Change in Demand

In the previous unit you learned that a change in the price of a product will result in a new quantity demanded. Price, however, is not the only influence on demand. There are a range of causes for more or less being demanded even if price is unchanged. For example, in a period of hot weather there is likely to be an increase in demand for ice cream. The quantities demanded will rise at each and every price. A new demand schedule can be drawn up to show the higher level of demand.

Table 1 Demand for ice cream

Price per ice cream	Quantities demanded per day	
$	Original demand	New demand
5	2 000	4 000
4	3 000	5 000
3	4 000	6 000
2	5 000	7 000
1	6 000	8 000

On a diagram, an increase in demand is shown by a shift to the right of the demand curve. Fig. 1 shows that at any given price, a larger quantity is demanded. At a price of $2, for instance, initially 5 000 ice creams would be demanded a day. The hot weather would encourage people to buy more ice creams. Demand would increase to 7 000.

Besides increasing, demand for ice cream may decrease too due to extraneous factors.

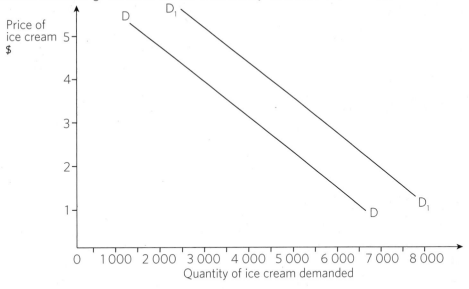

Fig. 1 An increase in demand

During periods of cold weather, consumers tend to demand less ice cream.
Such a decrease in demand is illustrated by a shift to the left of the demand curve.

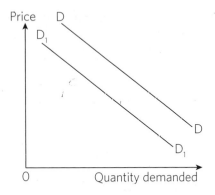

Fig. 2 A decrease in demand

Key Points

Changes in demand: shifts in the demand curve.

An increase in demand: a rise in demand at any given price, causing the demand curve to shift to the right.

A decrease in demand: a fall in demand at any given price, causing the demand curve to shift to the left.

Causes of Changes in Demand

Among the factors that can cause consumers to demand different quantities of a product, even if the price has not changed, are changes in disposable income, changes in the price of related products, advertising campaigns, changes in population and changes in taste and fashion.

Key Point

Disposable income: income after income tax and national insurance contributions have been deducted.

Changes in Disposable Income

An increase in disposable income raises consumers' purchasing power. For most of the products, this results in an increase in demand. In fact, so common is this positive relationship between income and demand, that such products are referred to as normal goods.

A few products have a negative relationship with income. These products are called inferior goods. When income rises, demand falls as consumers switch to better quality products.

Key Points

Normal good: a product whose demand increases when income increases and decreases when income falls.

Inferior good: a product whose demand decreases when income increases and increases when income falls.

Activity 1

In China, urban incomes rose by more than 11% in 2011. This contributed to a rise in demand for mobile phones, making China the world's largest mobile phone market, with approximately 350 million handsets.

a.   Illustrate the change in demand for mobile phones in China on a diagram.

b.   Is a mobile phone, a normal or an inferior good? Explain your answer.

Changes in the Price of Related Products

An increase in demand can be caused by a rise in the price of a substitute product. If the price of holidays to Egypt rises, demand for holidays to Mauritius may increase. Demand will also increase if the price of a complement falls. If travel insurance becomes cheaper, demand for holidays to most of the destinations will increase.

Activity 2

Decide whether each of the following is a substitute or a complement to a Volkswagen car:

a.   public transport.

b.   petrol

c.   a Ford car.

Advertising

A successful advertising campaign will increase demand for a product. It may bring the product to the notice of some new consumers and may encourage some existing consumers to purchase more quantities of the product.

Changes in Population

The population of a country can change in terms of both size and age composition. If there is an increase in the number of people in the country, demand for most products will increase. If there is an ageing population, with people living longer, and a fall in the birth rate, demand for wheelchairs is likely to increase while demand for toys is likely to decrease.

Changes in Taste and Fashion

Certain products are particularly influenced by changes in taste and fashion. These include food, clothes and entertainment. A rise in vegetarianism in a number of countries has caused the demand for meat to decrease. Health reports can have a significant influence on demand for particular foods. Designer trainers have become more popular in many countries and the rise in the popularity of football in the Far East has increased demand for football shirts and football merchandise.

Other Factors

A range of other factors can influence demand for a product. It was mentioned earlier that a change in weather conditions will affect the demand for ice cream. Such a change would also shift the demand curve for umbrellas, soft drinks and clothing.

Expectations about future price rises can influence current demand. Demand for oil increased during the revolution in Libya. This was because it was widely anticipated that a conflict was imminent and that such event would disrupt supplies of oil and raise price. Special events can have an impact on demand for a particular product. For instance, the Olympic Games held in London in July 2012 increased the demand for holidays in the UK.

Activity 3

Youngsters throughout the world are turning away from buying newspapers to new forms of media for their information and entertainment. For instance, in the UK, in 1973, 80% of 15–24 year olds read a (paid for) national newspaper. By 2005, this percentage had fallen to 46%. A study carried out by *News International* in 2004 found a number of reasons for this trend. These include young people having less time, less need, less interest and less opportunity to buy newspapers and declining importance of newspapers for youngsters. There are now many rivals to newspapers including television, radio and the internet. The youngsters who do buy newspapers tell the researchers that they read them more for entertainment than news.

a. What percentage of 15-24 year olds did not read a 'paid for' national newspaper in 2005?

b. Explain two reasons why young people throughout the world are demanding fewer newspapers.

c. Does the extract suggest that internet is a substitute for or a complement to newspapers? Explain your answer.

d. Discuss two ways through which newspaper publishers could raise demand for their newspapers.

The Effect of Changes in Demand

Changes in demand will cause a change in price and a movement along the supply curve. Fig. 3 shows the effect of an increase in demand. Initially there is a shortage of xy. This shortage forces the price to move up.

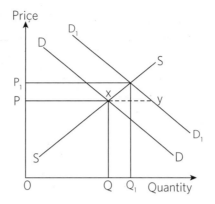

Fig. 3 The effect of an increase in demand

The higher price encourages an extension in supply until a new equilibrium price of P_1 is reached. At this price, demand and supply are again equal. In contrast, a decrease in demand will cause a fall in price and a contraction in supply. Fig. 4 shows demand decreasing from DD to D_1D_1. With lower demand, there will be a surplus of unsold products at the initial price of P. This surplus pushes down the price. As a result supply contracts until the new equilibrium price of P_1 and a new quantity of Q_1 are reached.

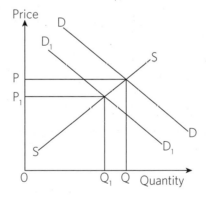

Fig. 4 The effect of a decrease in demand

 **Activity 4**

Use a demand and supply diagram to illustrate the effect of the following events on the market for economics books in India:

a. a successful advertising campaign run in the country by publishers of economics books,

b. a decrease in the number of students studying economics.

 **Activity 5**

Decide in each case, whether the following would cause an extension in demand, a contraction in demand, an increase in demand or a decrease in demand for fish in a country:

a. a rise in the price of fish

b. a report that eating fish reduces heart diseases

c. net emigration

d. a fall in the price of chicken.

Summary

- Causes of a change in demand include changes in disposable income, changes in the price of substitutes and complements, advertising campaigns, changes in the size and age composition of the population and changes in taste and fashion.

- An increase in demand shifts the demand curve to the right.

- A decrease in demand shifts the demand curve to the left.

- An increase in demand will raise price and cause an extension in supply.

- A decrease in demand will lower price and cause a contraction in supply.

 Teacher's Tip

Be careful to distinguish between a movement along a demand curve and a shift in demand. The only thing that can cause a movement *along* a demand curve is a change in the price of the product itself. Anything else that causes demand to change would be shown by a *shift* in the demand curve.

Multiple Choice Questions

1. The diagram shows a change in the market for coffee.

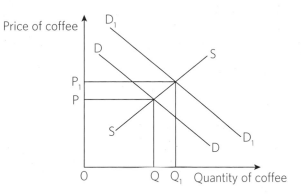

   What could explain this change?
   a. A rise in the price of coffee
   b. A rise in the price of tea
   c. A successful advertising campaign for tea
   d. A health report indicating that drinking coffee can cause headaches

2. An increase in demand is represented by:
   a. a movement down the demand curve
   b. a movement up the demand curve
   c. a shift to the left of the demand curve
   d. a shift to the right of the demand curve.

3. Which of the following diagrams illustrates the effect of an increase in income on the market for an inferior good?

a. Price

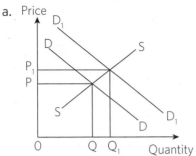

b. Price

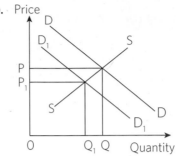

c. Price

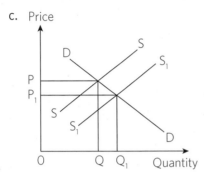

d. Price

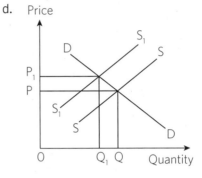

4. The price of a product rises. What will happen to the demand for its complement?

a. It will contract.

b. It will extend.

c. It will decrease.

d. It will increase.

Changes in Supply

The last unit examined the causes and consequences of changes in demand. In this unit, the focus switches to changes in supply. Also, more examples of market changes are discussed.

 Changes in Supply

A change in supply occurs when the conditions facing suppliers alter. In such a situation, a different quantity will be offered for sale at each price. For instance, a good period of weather may increase the rice crop in a country. This will make it possible for rice farmers to supply more. Table 1 shows the original supply schedule in the previous season and the supply schedule in the current season.

Table 1 Rice production

Price per ton (rupee)	Supply in previous season (millions of tonnes)	Supply in current season (millions of tonnes)
1 000	110	130
900	100	120
800	90	100
700	80	90
600	70	80
500	60	70

Shifts in the Supply Curve

While a change in the price of the product itself causes a movement along the supply curve, a change in supply conditions causes the supply curve to shift. An increase in supply is illustrated by a shift to the right as shown in Fig. 1. At each and every price, more is supplied.

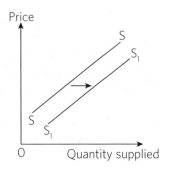

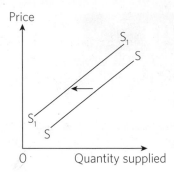

Fig. 1 An increase in supply

Fig. 2 Decrease in supply

In contrast, a decrease in supply results in a movement of the supply curve to the life, as shown in Fig. 2. Now whatever the price, less will be supplied.

Key Points

An increase in supply: a rise in supply at any given price, causing the supply curve to shift to the right.

A decrease in supply: a fall in supply at any given price, causing the supply curve to shift to the left.

Causes of Changes in Supply

Among the factors that can cause a change in supply are changes in the costs of production, improvements in technology, taxes, subsidies, weather conditions, health of livestock and crops. It is also affected by the price of other products. Disasters, wars, discoveries of new sources and depletion also contribute to this change of commodities.

Key Point

Changes in supply: changes in supply conditions causing shifts in the supply curve.

Activity 1

In the last fifty five years, the world production of rice has increased considerably from 215m tonnes in 1961 to more than 600m tonnes in 2006. This has largely been the result of breakthroughs in seed generation and cultivation techniques.

a. Draw a diagram showing the change in supply of rice, since 1961.

b. Identify two factors that can cause the supply curve for rice to move in the opposite direction.

Changes in the costs of production

If it costs more to produce a product, suppliers will want a higher price for it. For example, if it costs $200 to produce four units, firms would supply four units at a price of $50 per unit. If costs rise to $280, they would be prepared to sell only four units, at a price of $70 each.

The two basic reasons for a change in costs of production are

- a change in the price of any of the factors of production

- a change in their productivity.

If, for example, the price of raw materials used increases, it will be more expensive to produce a product. One cost which changes frequently is the cost of transporting goods. This is because the price of oil used in petrol, is itself very volatile.

A rise in the productivity of a factor of production will reduce unit cost. For example, if a worker who is paid $200 a week produces 100 units, the labour cost per unit is $2. If her or his productivity rises to 200, the labour cost per unit would fall to $1.

An increase in the wages paid to workers by itself would raise the costs of production and therefore cause a decrease in supply. It is interesting to note, however, that if it is accompanied by an equal rise in productivity, then unit costs and supply will remain unchanged.

Key Point

Unit cost: the average cost of production. It is found by dividing total cost by output.

Activity 2

A firm employs ten workers and pays $50 a day to each of them. The total output of ten workers is 100 units initially. The firm then raises the wage rate to $60 a day and the output per worker rises to 20.

a. Showing your workings, calculate:
  (i) the initial unit cost
  (ii) the new unit cost.

b. Will supply decrease, stay the same or increase? Explain your answer.

Improvements in Technology

This influence is closely related to the previous one, since improvements in technology raise the productivity of capital, reduce costs of production and result in an increase in supply. It has become much cheaper to produce a range of products due to the availability of more efficient capital goods and methods of production.

For instance, whilst world demand for personal computers has increased in recent years, the supply has increased even more as it has become easier and cheaper to produce them. Fig. 3 shows these changes and the resulting fall in price.

Fig. 3 Changes in the market for PCs

Key Point

Improvements in technology: advances in the quality of capital goods and methods of production.

Taxes

Taxes on firms, including corporation tax and indirect taxes such as VAT and excise duty, are effectively a cost that firms have to pay. They are likely to try to recover at least some of this extra cost by raising the price paid by the consumers. Nevertheless, the firms themselves are largely responsible for passing on the tax revenue to the government.

A rise in the rate of an existing tax or the imposition of a new tax will make it more expensive to supply a product and hence will reduce supply. In contrast, a cut in a tax or its removal will increase supply.

Key Points

A tax: a payment to the government.

Indirect taxes: taxes on goods and services.

Subsidies

A subsidy given to the producers provides a financial incentive for them to supply more. Besides being paid by the consumer, they are now being paid by the government also.

As a result, the granting of a subsidy will cause an increase in supply whilst the removal of a subsidy will cause a decrease in supply.

Most countries, throughout the world, subsidise some agricultural products. A number of them also give subsidies to new and important industries.

Less frequently, a government may also give a subsidy to consumers, to encourage them to buy a particular product. For example, grants may be given to households to enable them to buy houses. In this case, of course, it is demand and not supply conditions which change.

Key Point

A subsidy: a payment by a government to encourage the production or consumption of a product.

Weather Conditions and Health of Livestock and Crops

Changes in weather conditions affect particular agricultural products. A period of good weather around harvest time is likely to increase the supply of a number of crops. Very dry, very wet or very windy weather, however, is likely to damage a range of crops and thereby reduce their supply. The amount of agricultural products produced and available for supply is also influenced by the health of livestock and crops. The outbreak of a disease, such as foot and mouth in cattle or blight in crops, will reduce supply.

Prices of other Products

Firms often produce a range of products. If one product becomes more popular, its price will rise and supply will extend. In order to produce more of this product, the firm may divert the resources from the production of other products. The prices of these other products have not changed but the firm will now supply less at each and every price. For example, if a farmer keeps cattle and sheep, a rise in the price and profitability of lamb is likely to result in the farmer keeping fewer cows and a corresponding decrease in the supply of beef.

Besides the products being supplied in a competitive environment, they can also be jointly supplied. This means that one product is automatically made when another product is produced i.e. one product is a by-product of the other one. For example, when more beef is produced, more hides will be available to be turned into leather.

In the case of products which are jointly supplied, a rise in the price of one product will cause an extension in supply of the other product. Firms make more of one product because its price has risen. The supply of the other product will increase outomatically. More is produced, not because it has risen in price but because the price of a related product has risen.

Disasters and Wars

Natural disasters, such as hurricanes, floods and wars, can result in a significant decrease in supply. The earthquake and resulting tsunami that hit Japan in March 2011 caused extensive damage to infrastructure and killed workers. These effects reduced the supply of a range of products.

Discoveries and Depletions of Commodities

The supply of some commodities, such as coal, gold and oil, is affected by discoveries of new sources. For instance, the discovery of new oilfields will increase the supply of oil. In contrast, if coal mines are expended, the supply of coal will be reduced in the future.

The Effect of Changes in Supply

Changes in supply cause a change in price and a movement along the demand curve. Initially, an increase in supply will cause a surplus. This surplus will drive down the price and result in an extension in demand, as shown in Fig. 4.

A decrease in supply will have the opposite effect. It will cause a rise in price, which in turn causes a contraction in demand, as shown in Fig. 5.

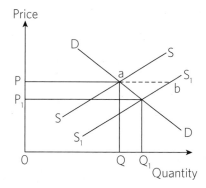

Fig. 4 The effect of an increase in supply

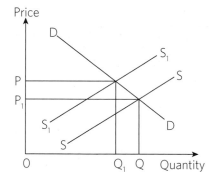

Fig. 5 The effect of a decrease in supply

In each case, using a demand and supply diagram, analyse the effect on the market for Ghanaian football shirts:

a. a fall in incomes in Ghana and neighbouring countries

b. a rise in the productivity of workers making Ghanaian football shirts

c. Ghana winning the world cup

d. a tax being placed on Ghanaian football shirts

e. new, cheaper but more efficient machinery being introduced to make Ghanaian football shirts.

 # Changes in Demand and Supply

It is, of course, possible for both the conditions of demand and the conditions of supply to change at the same time. In this case, the impact on the market will depend not only on the direction of the changes but also on the size of the changes. For example, a report may come out stating that eating apples is good for people's complexion and at the same time, that good weather contributes to a record harvest. In this case, both demand and supply will increase. This will result in an increase in the quantity being bought and sold. The effect on price, however, will depend on relative strengths of shifts in demand and supply. Fig. 6 shows the increase in demand being greater than the increase in supply. As a result, price rises.

In contrast, Fig. 7 shows the increase in supply exceeding the increase in demand, causing price to fall.

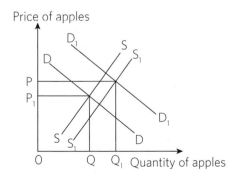

Fig. 6 The effect of demand increasing more than supply

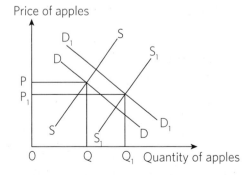

Fig. 7 The effect of supply increasing more than demand

 **Activity 4**

In September 2005, Vietnam suffered an outbreak of avian (bird) flu. Thousands of chicken, suspected of having the disease, were slaughtered and millions of healthy chicken were vaccinated. This action was taken to prevent the spread of the disease not only among the chicken population but also to the human population.

Use a demand and supply diagram to analyse the effect, this is likely to have on the market for chicken in Vietnam.

 Summary

- Causes of a change in supply include changes in the costs of production, improvements in technology, taxes, subsidies, weather conditions, health of livestock and crops, changes in the price of related products, disasters, wars and discoveries of new sources of commodities.

- An increase in supply shifts the supply curve to the right.

- A decrease in supply moves the supply curve to the left.

- An increase in supply will lower the price and cause an extension in demand.

- A decrease in supply will raise the price and cause a contraction in demand.

 Teacher's Tip

Do not mix up supply and demand curves. Remember supply curves slope up from left to right whilst demand curves slope down from left to right.

Multiple Choice Questions

1. How would an increase in supply be illustrated?
   a. A movement up the supply curve
   b. A movement down the supply curve
   c. A shift to the left of the supply curve
   d. A shift to the right of the supply curve

2. What would cause an increase in the supply of milk?
   a. An increase in the price of cattle feed
   b. An increase in wages paid to farm workers
   c. The introduction of a subsidy to cattle farmers
   d. The outbreak of a disease affecting cows

3. The diagram shows the demand for and supply of a product. The initial equilibrium is at point X. The cost of raw materials used to produce the product falls. Which point represents the new equilibrium?

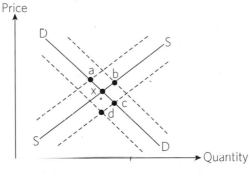

Fig. 8

4. What effect would a decrease in supply of a product have on its price and demand?

	Price	Demand
a.	decreases	contracts
b.	decreases	extends
c.	increases	contracts
d.	increases	extends

Price Elasticity of Demand

Unit 6 discussed the causes and effects of changes in demand for products. This unit examines the extent of such changes and the factors affecting the same.

 Importance of Changes in Price

A change in a product's price is often the main influence on its demand. This is one of the reasons why economists study the effect of a price change in some depth.

It is widely recognised that a fall in price will result in an extension in demand. An entrepreneur, however, in considering whether to cut the price of a product will need to know the extent of any rise in demand. If demand is going to rise by only a relatively small amount, it may not pay to reduce the price. For instance, the entrepreneur's firm may be currently selling 100 units a day at $4 each and hence earning a total revenue of $400. If it is expected that lowering its price to $3, demand will only rise to 120, the firm would experience a fall in revenue of $40.

While taking a decision on its subsidy and taxation policies, a government also needs to know the responsiveness of demand to a change in price. It may, for instance, be seeking to discourage consumption of a certain product. If, however, demand for a product does not alter much with a change in price, placing a tax on such a product will not be a very effective way of achieving this aim.

 Definition of Price Elasticity of Demand

Price elasticity of demand (PED) measures the extent to which the quantity demanded changes when the price of the product changes. The formula used to calculate it is:

$$PED = \frac{\text{Percentage change in quantity demanded}}{\text{Percentage change in price}}$$

This is often abbreviated to:

$$PED = \frac{\% \, \Delta \, QD}{\% \, \Delta \, P}$$

Key Point

Price elasticity of demand: a measure of the responsiveness of demand to a change in price.

Calculating PED

To work out elasticity of demand, it is necessary to first calculate the percentage change in quantity demanded and a percentage change in price. To do this, the change in demand is divided by the original demand and multiplied by 100. The same process is used to work out the percentage change in price. For instance, demand may rise from 200 to 240 as a result of price falling from $10 to $9. In this case, the percentage change in quantity demanded is:

$$\frac{\text{Change in demand}}{\text{Original quantity demanded}} \times 100 \text{ i.e. } \frac{40}{200} \times 100 = 20\%$$

The percentage change in price is:

$$\frac{\text{Change in price}}{\text{Original price}} \times 100 \text{ i.e. } \frac{-\$1}{\$10} \times 100 = -10\%$$

When these changes have been calculated, the percentage change in quantity demanded is divided by the percentage in price to give the PED. In this case, this is 20%/–10%. Remember that a division involving different signs gives a minus figure. Hence the PED is –2.

Activity 1

In each case, calculate the PED:
a. A fall in price from $4 to $3 causes the demand to extend from 60 to 105.
b. Demand falls from 200 to 180 when price rises from $10 to $12.
c. A reduction in price from $12 to $6 results in an extension in demand from 100 to 140.

Interpretation of PED

The PED figure provides two pieces of information. One is given by the **sign**. In the vast majority of cases, it is a minus. This tell us that there is an *inverse relationship* between demand and price – a rise in price will cause a contraction in demand and a fall in price will cause an extension in demand.

The other piece of information is provided by the **size** of the figure. This indicates the extent by which demand will extend or contract when price changes. A figure of – 2, for instance, indicates that a 1% change in price will cause a 2% change in quantity demanded.

  **Activity 2**

Demand for a luxury product falls from 500 to 200 when price rises from $2 000 to $2 200.

a.   Calculate the PED.

b.   In this case, by what percentage would demand contract, if price rose by 1%?

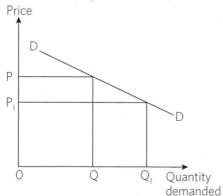

Elastic and Inelastic Demand

Most products have either elastic or inelastic demand. **Elastic demand** occurs when a change in price results in a greater percentage change in demand, giving a PED figure (ignoring the sign) of more than 1 but less than infinity.

When demand is elastic, price and total revenue move in opposite directions. For instance, initially ten products may be demanded at a price of $5 each, giving a total revenue of $50. If price falls to $4 each and demand rises to 20 (giving a PED of –5 i.e. 100%/–20%), then total revenue would increase to $80. In the case of elastic demand, a firm can raise total revenue by lowering the price but it must be aware that if it raises the price, its total revenue will fall. Elastic demand is usually illustrated by a shallow demand curve. Fig. 1 shows that the percentage change in quantity demanded is greater than the percentage change in price.

Fig. 1 Elastic demand

Inelastic demand is when demand changes by a smaller change than the price and the PED is less than 1 but greater than zero. In this case, price and total revenue move in the same direction. If price is raised, demand will fall but by a smaller percentage than the change in price and hence more revenue will be earned. If price is lowered, more products will be demanded but not enough, to prevent the total revenue from falling. In this case, if a firm wants to raise revenue, it should raise its price.

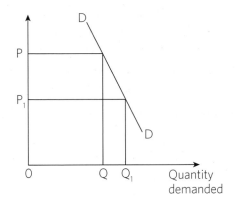

Fig. 2 Inelastic demand

Inelastic demand is usually represented by a relatively steep demand curve, as shown in Fig. 2.

Key Points

Elastic demand: when demand changes by a greater percentage than the change in price.

Inelastic demand: when demand changes by a smaller percentage than the change in price.

Factors Determining the Degree of Elasticity

The main factor that determines whether demand is elastic or inelastic is the *availability of substitutes* of a similar quality and price. If a product does have a close substitute, it is likely to have elastic demand. In this case, a rise in price will be likely to cause a significant fall in demand as consumers will switch to the substitute. However, if there is no close substitute available, demand will probably be inelastic. Demand will not fall much in response to a rise in price because there is no suitable alternative to switch over to.

The other influencing factors are all linked to the availability of substitutes. These factors include the proportion of income spent on the product, whether the product is a necessity or a luxury, whether the product is addictive or not, whether its purchase can be postponed, how the market is defined and the time period under consideration.

If purchase of a product takes up a small proportion of people's income, demand is likely to be inelastic. For example, if the price of salt rose by 20%, demand is likely to alter by a much smaller percentage. This is because a 20% rise in price is likely to involve consumers paying only a little more. In fact, some may not even notice the rise in price. In contrast, products which take up a large proportion of people's income to be bought, tend to have elastic demand. In this case, a 20% rise in price would involve consumers paying significantly more. Such a rise in the price of a new car would be likely to cause a greater percentage contraction in demand.

Besides taking up a large percentage of income, a new car may also be regarded as a luxury. Luxury products usually have elastic demand. They do not have to be purchased, so a rise in price may result in a greater percentage fall in demand. If their prices fall, however, demand is likely to rise by a greater percentage as more of the population can afford to buy them now.

In contrast to luxuries, necessities such as soaps tend to have inelastic demand. People cannot cut back significantly on their use, even if their prices rise.

People also find it difficult to cut back on their purchases of products which are addictive, such as cigarettes and coffee. This means that such products have inelastic demand.

If the purchase of a product can be delayed, demand tends to be elastic. A rise in price will result in a greater percentage fall in demand as people will postpone the purchase of the product, hoping that its price will drop back in the future. If it does, demand will rise by a greater percentage, with the build up of sales.

The more narrowly defined a product is, the more elastic its demand is. Demand for one brand of tea is more elastic than demand for tea in general and even more elastic than demand for hot drinks in general. This is because the narrower the definition, the more substitutes a product is likely to have. Demand also becomes more elastic, if the time period under consideration is long. This is because it gives consumers more time to switch their purchases. In the short term – if the price of a product rises, customers may not have enough time to find alternatives and if it falls, new customers will not have sufficient time to notice the change in price and switch away from rival products.

Decide in each case, whether demand is likely to be elastic or inelastic:

a. cut flowers
b. gold jewellery
c. coffee
d. train travel by commuters
e. food.

Differences in PED

PED for the same products can differ with time. What were once seen as luxuries can turn into necessities as people become richer. This changes their demand from elastic to inelastic. In Europe and the US, almost every teenager now has a mobile phone and a rise in price would not discourage many from buying the latest model. A wide range of other products, including TVs and cars, are seen as being essential requirements to sustain a modern lifestyle.

Due to different tastes, different income levels and different cultures, PED can also be found to vary between countries. Demand for rice is more inelastic in Bangladesh than it is in US, where it competes with a greater range of food products. In India, where cricket has a devoted following, demand for tickets to international cricket matches is more inelastic than it is in the Netherlands where it is a relatively new sport.

 # Other Degrees of Elasticity

The most common degrees of elasticity are elastic and inelastic. Very occasionally other types are found. These are perfectly elastic demand, perfectly inelastic demand and unit elasticity of demand.

(i) **Perfectly elastic demand** occurs when a change in price causes a complete change in demand. For instance, if one of the many wheat farmers raises his price, he may lose all of his sales with buyers switching to rival farmers. In this case, PED is infinity.

(ii) **Perfectly inelastic demand** is when demand does not change when price changes. Consumers buy the same quantity despite the alteration in price and PED is zero.

(iii) **Unit elasticity of demand** is found when a percentage change in price results in an equal percentage change in demand, giving a PED of one.

 ## Changes in PED

PED becomes more elastic as the price of a product rises. Consumers become more sensitive to price changes, the higher the price of the product. This is because, for instance, a 10% rise in price when price was initially $10 000 would involve consumers having to spend considerably more (i.e. $1 000) to buy the product. If a supplier was foolish enough to keep raising the price, a point would come when the product would be priced out of the market. At this point, demand would be perfectly elastic.

As the price falls, demand becomes more inelastic. For e.g. a 10% fall in price when the price was initially $1 is not very significant and is unlikely to result in much extra demand. If price falls to zero, there will be a limit to the amount people want to consume. At this point, demand is perfectly inelastic. Fig. 3 shows how PED varies over a straight line demand curve. At the mid-point there is unit PED, with the percentage change in quantity demanded matching the percentage change in price.

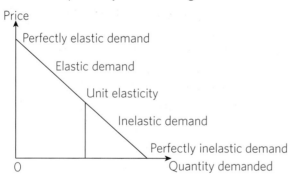

Fig. 3 **Variation of PED over a demand curve**

PED also changes when there is a shift in the demand curve. The more consumers want and are able to buy a product, the less sensitive they are to price changes. So a shift in the demand curve to the right reduces PED at any given price. In Fig. 4, PED is initially –5 (50%/–10%) when price falls from $10 to $9. Then when demand increases to D_1D_1, PED falls to –2.5 (25%/–10%).

When demand decreases, consumers become more sensitive to price changes and demand becomes more elastic. Fig. 5 shows PED rising from –5 to –10 (100%/–10%).

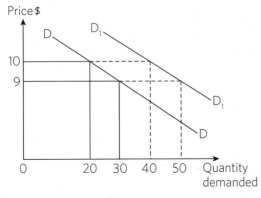

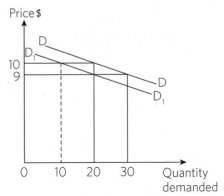

Fig. 4 The effect of an increase in demand on PED

Fig. 5 The effect of a decrease in demand on PED

 **Activity 4**

In each of the following examples, first calculate the PED and then decide if the PED is elastic, inelastic, perfectly elastic, perfectly inelastic or unity.

a. The price of a product falls from $8 to $6, causing demand to extend from 10 000 to 12 500.

b. Demand contracts from 500 to 400 when price rises from $40 to $42.

c. Demand extends from 2 000 to 2 800 when price falls from $20 to $18.

d. Price rises from $15 to $30 but demand stays unchanged at 5 000.

e. An increase in price from $80 to $90 and as a consequence, a decrease in quantity demanded from 400 to 300.

 Summary

- It is important for economists, firms and the government to know the extent to which demand changes as a result of a change in price.

- Price elasticity of demand is a measure of the extent to which demand changes as a result of a change in price.

- The most common types of PED are elastic and inelastic. Elastic demand is when demand changes by a greater percentage than price whereas inelastic demand is when demand changes by a smaller percentage than price.

continued····>

- The main factor that determines whether demand is elastic or inelastic is the availability of close substitutes of the product.

- Demand for a product is likely to be inelastic if it has no close substitutes, takes up a small proportion of income to be bought, is a necessity, addictive or its purchase cannot be postponed.

- PED can vary with time and between countries.

- The categories of PED are elastic, inelastic, perfectly elastic, perfectly inelastic and unity.

- As price rises, demand becomes more elastic.

- An increase in demand will make the demand more inelastic.

Teacher's Tip

Remember that inelastic demand does not mean that demand does not change with price changes. It does alter, but by a smaller percentage than price. It is only when demand is perfectly inelastic that demand does not change with price.

Multiple Choice Questions

1. What is price elasticity of demand?
    a. A measure of the extent to which price changes when the quantity demanded changes
    b. A measure of the extent to which the quantity demanded changes when price changes
    c. A measure of the extent to which total revenue changes when price changes
    d. A measure of the extent to which price changes when total revenue changes

2. Demand for a product is inelastic. What effect will a fall in price have?
    a. Demand will not change.
    b. Demand will change by a greater percentage.
    c. Total revenue will fall.
    d. Total revenue will rise.

3. What characteristic is likely to make the demand for a product elastic?
    a. It is a necessity.
    b. It is habit-forming.
    c. It is relatively cheap.
    d. It has close substitutes.

4. The price of a product rises from £60 to £90. This causes demand to contract from 800 to 600. What type of price elasticity of demand does this product have over this price range?
    a. Perfectly inelastic
    b. Inelastic
    c. Unity
    d. Elastic

Price Elasticity of Supply

Just as economists study the extent to which demand reacts to a change in price, similarly they also study how responsive supply is to a change in price.

 Definition of Price Elasticity of Supply

Price elasticity of supply (PES) measures the extent to which the quantity supplied changes when the price of a product changes. The formula is:

$$PES = \frac{\text{Percentage change in quantity supplied}}{\text{Percentage change in price}}$$

The abbreviated form of this is:

$$PES = \frac{\% \Delta QS}{\% \Delta P}$$

 Key Point

Price elasticity of supply: a measure of the responsiveness of supply to a change in price.

Calculating PES

PES is calculated in the same way as PED. This time, however, it is the percentage change in supply which has to be calculated. Again it is found by dividing the change in supply by the original supply and multiplying by 100. Similarly, the percentage change in price is calculated by dividing the change in price by the original price and multiplying by 100.

For example, supply may rise from 100 to 130 as a result of price increasing from $10 to $12. In this instance, the percentage change in quantity supplied is:

$$\frac{\text{Change in quantity supplied}}{\text{Original quantity supplied}} \times 100 \text{ i.e. } 30 \times 100 = 30\%$$

And the percentage change in price is:

$$\frac{\text{Change in price}}{\text{Original price}} \times 100 \text{ i.e. } \frac{\$2}{\$10} \times 100 = 20\%$$

This means that the PES is:

$$\frac{30\%}{20\%} = 1.5$$

Activity 1

In each case, calculate the PES:

a. A fall in price from $5 to $4 causes supply to contract from 10 000 to 4 000.

b. Supply extends from 200 to 210 when price rises from $10 to $14.

c. An increase in price from $4 000 to $4 400 results in an extension of supply from 80 to 90.

Interpretation of PES

As supply and price are directly related, PES is a positive figure. The figure indicates the degree of responsiveness of supply to a change in price. The higher the figure, the more responsive supply is. A PES of 2.6, for example, means that a 1% rise in price will cause a 2.6% extension in supply.

Activity 2

Supply of a product rises from 5 000 to 7 000 due to a rise in price from $4 to $5.

a. Calculate the PES.

b. In this case, by what percentage would supply extend if price rose by 1%?

 # **Elastic and Inelastic Supply**

Supply is usually found to be elastic or inelastic. Elastic supply is when the percentage change in quantity supplied is greater than the percentage change in price. In this case, PES is greater than 1 but less than infinity. The higher the figure, the more elastic supply is. Elastic supply is usually illustrated by a shallow curve, as shown in Fig. 1.

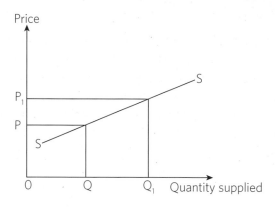

Fig. 1 Elastic supply

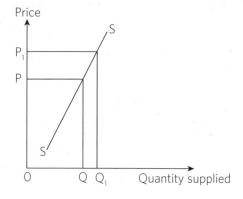

Fig. 2 Inelastic supply

In contrast, inelastic supply is when the percentage change in quantity supplied is less than the percentage change in price and so PES is less than 1 but greater than zero. A PES of 0.2 would mean that supply is more inelastic than that for a PES of 0.7. Fig. 2 illustrates inelastic supply. The supply curve is steep, showing that supply changes by less than the price in percentage terms.

Key Points

Elastic supply: when supply changes by a greater percentage than the change in price.

Inelastic supply: when supply changes by a smaller percentage than the change in price.

Factors Influencing PES

The three main factors which determine the PES of a product are:

  (i) the time taken to produce it

  (ii) the cost of altering its supply and

  (iii) feasibility of storing it.

If the product can be made quickly, the cost of altering its supply is low. Also, if it can be stored, supply can be adjusted relatively easily in the event of a price change. In such a case, a rise in price will result in a greater percentage change in supply. This is because firms can alter the amount they offer for sale by making more, using up spare capacity and shifting resources, and by drawing on stocks. If price falls, firms will cut back on production, remove some products from the market and place them in storage.

In contrast, if it takes a long time to make a product, it is expensive to change production (perhaps because firms are working at full capacity). Again, if product cannot be stored, it will be more difficult to adjust its supply in response to a change in price. As a result, supply will be inelastic. Supply of many agricultural products is inelastic. This is because it takes time for crops to grow and animals to mature and many agricultural products cannot be stored. If the price of apples falls, for instance, it is unlikely that the quantity offered for sale will decline significantly. This is because once picked, apples have a relatively short shelf-life. If the price of apples rises, again farmers cannot alter the quantity supplied substantially. It can take years before new apple trees start producing a significant crop. The supply of apples in one area or one country, however, may be relatively elastic if apples can be moved from one place to another in response to difference in demand, and hence price.

 **Activity 3**

Decide, in each case, whether supply is likely to be elastic or inelastic:
a. elastic bands
b. tee-shirts
c. aircraft
d. pencils
e. lamb.

Other Degrees of PES

In addition to elastic and inelastic supply, three other degrees of elasticity may be found, although not nearly as frequently as elastic and inelastic supply.

(i) **Perfectly inelastic supply** is when the quantity supplied does not alter with price changes and PES is zero. If, for instance, more people are demanding to see a film at a particular cinema, ticket prices may rise. However, it is unlikely to increase the seating capacity in the short run. In the longer run, if demand remains high, the owners of the cinema are likely to increase its size.

(ii) **Perfectly elastic supply.** This is when a change in price will cause an infinite change in supply, giving a PES of infinity.

(iii) **Unity PES** occurs when a given percentage change in price causes an equal percentage change in supply.

Changes in PES

As already hinted at, PES can vary with time. The supply for most of the products becomes more elastic as the time period increases. This is because producers have more time to adjust their supply. This may involve, switching production from/to other products and building new factories and offices or selling off existing plants.

Advances in technology, by reducing the production period and lowering costs of production, make the supply more elastic. In recent years, it has become much easier and cheaper to produce magazines. As a result, not only has the number of magazines on offer increased but also the speed with which new titles appear and titles, which are declining in popularity, disappear.

Producers want their supply to be as elastic as possible. Their profits will be higher, the quicker and more fully they can adjust their supply in response to changes in demand and hence price. Many governments are seeking to promote flexibility in production by making it easier for firms to hire and fire.

 Summary

- PES is a measure of the extent of changes in supply, as a result of a change in price.

- The most common types of PES are elastic and inelastic supply. Elastic supply is when supply changes by a greater percentage than price whereas inelastic supply is when supply changes by a smaller percentage than price.

- The main factors that determine whether supply is elastic or inelastic is whether production can be changed cheaply and quickly and whether the product can be stored.

- Supply of a product is likely to be inelastic if it takes a long time to produce it, if it is expensive to alter production and if it cannot be stored.

- Supply tends to become more elastic with time.

- The categories of PES are elastic, inelastic, perfectly elastic, perfectly inelastic and unity.

 Teacher's Tip

In the case of both PED and PES, do not forget to divide the change by the **original** figure and multiple by 100, while calculating percentages.

Multiple Choice Questions

1. What is the formula for PES?

   a. $$\frac{\text{Change in quantity supplied}}{\text{Change in price}}$$

   b. $$\frac{\text{Percentage change in quantity supplied}}{\text{Percentage change in price}}$$

   c. $$\frac{\text{Change in quantity supplied}}{\text{Change in quantity demanded}}$$

   d. $$\frac{\text{Percentage change in quantity supplied}}{\text{Percentage change in quantity demanded}}$$

2. What does a PES of 0.8 indicate?
   a. Supply is elastic.
   b. Supply is perfectly elastic.
   c. Supply is perfectly inelastic.
   d. Supply is inelastic.

3. In what circumstance would supply of a product be elastic?
   a. It is costly to produce.
   b. It takes time to produce.
   c. It can be stored.
   d. It uses resources which are in short supply.

4. Which figure illustrates elastic supply?

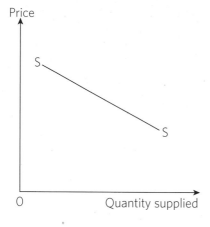

a.

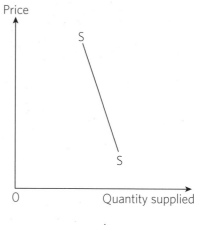

b.

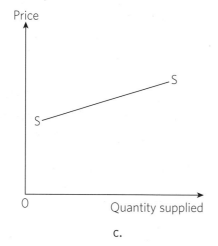

c.

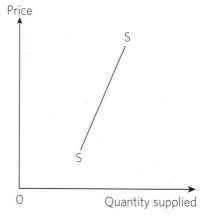

d.

Merits of the Market System

In a market system, resources move automatically as a result of changes in price. In turn, price changes are determined by the interaction of demand and supply. As its name suggests, a market economy relies on the market system. A mixed economy relies, in part, on the market system. This section explores the advantages of a market system mentioned in unit 4, in greater depth.

 ## Reallocation of Resources

The use of resources is changing all the time in response to changes in consumer demand and costs of production. As mentioned in unit 4, resources move towards those products whose demand is rising and away from those which are becoming less popular. Fig. 1 shows an increase in demand for air travel and a decrease in demand for sea travel.

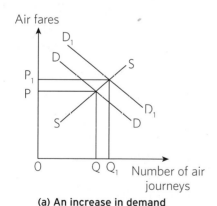

(a) An increase in demand

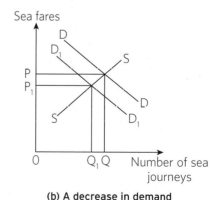

(b) A decrease in demand

Fig. 1

The changes in demand cause prices to change. These alterations in price encourage firms to switch their resources from sea travel to air travel.

Market forces also ration out products when their supply falls short of demand. If, for instance, a disease attacks a potato crop, supply will decrease. Initially this may result in a *shortage* with demand exceeding supply, as shown in Fig. 2a. This shortage, however, will drive up price until the market again clears with demand equalling supply as shown in Fig. 2b. The market sorts out who will receive the products by raising the price. Those who are able to pay the higher price will be able to consume the product.

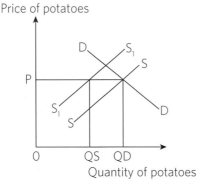

(a) Initial response to a decrease in supply

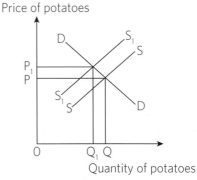

(b) The market clearing

Fig. 2

 Activity 1

The price of onions tripled in India in 2006. Traders blamed the hike in price on a poor crop after unusually light monsoon rains. In the same year in India, the price of tomatoes rose largely due to higher demand caused by an increase in urban incomes.

a. Draw a diagram, in each case, to show why the price of onions and the price of tomatoes rose in India in 2006.

b. Explain how, in each case, the markets responded to changing circumstances.

The Importance of Competition and Incentives

The advantages of a market system, rely in large part, on competitive pressures. One of the benefits claimed for a market system is **choice**. If there is a large number of firms producing a product, consumers will have a choice of producers. This should increase the prospects of consumers deciding what is made, with producers competing with each other to meet their demand. In such a case, consumers are said to be *sovereign*.

Competition, whether actual or potential, should also result in low prices. Actual competition arises when there are rival firms in the industry. Potential competition occurs when it is easy for firms to enter or leave the industry. If it is possible for consumers to switch from high price firms to low price firms or for other firms to start producing the products if prices and profits are high, there will be pressure on firms to keep their prices low in order to stay in business. To do this, they will seek to keep their costs low. The more successful a firm is in keeping its costs low and the more it targets the desires of consumers, the more efficient it is said to be.

The market system encourages efficiency by rewarding those entrepreneurs and workers, who respond to market signals and punishes those who do not. This is sometimes referred to as the market system providing both a *carrot* (a reward) and a *stick* (punishment) to promote efficiency.

Entrepreneurs, who are quick to pick up on changes in consumer demand, are likely to earn high profits. These provide them with the incentive and ability to innovate and expand. In contrast, those entrepreneurs who are unresponsive to changing consumer demand are likely to suffer losses.

In labour markets, workers increase their chance of earning high wages by developing those skills which are in high demand, working hard, accepting more responsibility and by being willing to change their nature and place of work. Those who are not prepared (or able) to work, who lack the appropriate skills and who are geographically or occupationally immobile may receive no or low incomes.

Activity 2

In 2007, shortages of lorry drivers in the US led some US companies to recruit truckers from India. The companies attracted the drivers by offering them higher wages than they could earn at home. In fact the wages were twelve times those paid in India.

a. What market incentive is touched on in the passage?
b. Explain (using a diagram) what is likely to have happened to the wages paid to lorry drivers in India, in 2007.

Allocative Efficiency

Allocative efficiency occurs when resources are allocated in a way that maximises consumers' satisfaction. This means that firms produce the products, that consumers demand, in the right quantities.

Fig. 3a shows allocative efficiency being achieved with supply matching consumers' demand. In contrast, Fig. 3a and 3b depict allocative inefficiency. In the case of **3b**, there are too few resources being devoted to the product, which results in a *shortage*. In **3c**, too many resources are allocated for producing the product and there is a *surplus*.

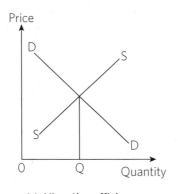

(a) Allocative efficiency

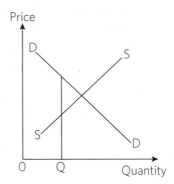

(b) Allocative inefficency: under-production

Fig. 3

Market forces, by changing prices, should eliminate shortages and surpluses and move markets towards allocative efficiency. Competition can play a key role in this process. This is because in a competitive market, a firm has both an incentive in the form of profit and a threat of punishment in the form of a risk of going out of business to be allocatively efficient. If it is more responsive to the needs of consumers as compared to its rivals, it should gain a larger market share and earn high profits at least for a while. In contrast, if it does not produce commodities demanded by consumers, it will lose sales to rivals and may be driven out of the market.

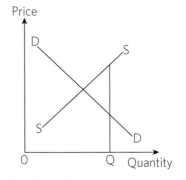

(c) Allocative inefficiency: over-production

Activity 3

In recent years, UK consumers have become more health conscious. This has led to a fall in demand for crisps. A number of crisp producers have gone out of business.

a. What effect is a fall in demand likely to have on price?

b. What evidence is there in the passage, of the UK crisp market working efficiently?

Productive Efficiency

A firm is said to be productively efficient when it produces at the lowest possible cost per unit. Again in a competitive market, a firm has both an incentive and a threat of punishment which should drive it towards being productively efficient. If it can drive its costs down to the lowest possible level, it may capture more sales and gain more profit. If, however, its costs per unit are higher than its rivals, it will lose market share and possibly all of its sales.

If a firm is productively efficient, it means that it is not wasting resources. If all producers in a country are productively efficient, the economy will be able to make full use of its resources and hence will be producing on its production possibility curve.

In Fig. 4, production point A is productively efficient. With its given resources and technology, the economy is making as many products as possible. Point B is productively inefficient as some resources are either not being used or not being put to good use. For instance, some workers may be unemployed, some workers may be lying idle and some factory and office space may be empty. Also, there may be some workers involved in jobs to which they are not best suited and the capabilities of some capital goods may not be fully exploited.

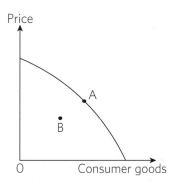

Fig. 4 Productive efficiency (A) and inefficiency (B)

Dynamic Efficiency

Dynamic efficiency arises when resources are used efficiently, over a period of time. The profit incentive and threat of going out of business can encourage firms in a market system to spend money on research and development and to innovate. Those firms, that introduce new methods of production and bring out new, improved products, increase their chance of gaining high profits. Those, that do not seek to keep up with new ideas to produce products and do not develop new products, run the risk of being driven out of the market.

In 2004 *Dyson*, a UK company, introduced a miniature version of its vacuum cleaner in Japan, modified to take into account the smaller size of Japanese homes. A year later, it overtook *Hoover* to become the market leader in vacuum cleaners in the US. In 2006, it announced record profits and its intention to spend more on research and development and to launch new products.

a.   What evidence is there in the passage, that Dyson was responding to consumer demand?

b.   How may consumers benefit from the high profits earned by Dyson?

Advantages of a Market System

A market system has the potential to provide some significant benefits and benefits which can grow over time. These include providing consumers with the power to determine what is produced, choice, low prices and high quality products.

If a market system is working well, it will be automatically allocating resources according to the consumer demand. By rewarding efficiency and punishing inefficiency, it may encourage the manufacture of products that consumers want and are prepared to pay for, in the right quantities and at the lowest possible cost per unit.

Market forces can also promote the improvement of methods of production and a rise in the quality of products made. It does this by putting competitive pressure on entrepreneurs and workers and by providing them with incentives to respond to changes in market conditions. For instance, if demand for books is increasing whilst the demand for cinema tickets is falling, profits and wages will be rising in the publishing industry while they will be falling in the film industry. These changes will encourage some firms to switch production and some workers to change their jobs.

Summary

- In a market system, changes in prices cause the shift in resources, from making products that are becoming less popular to making those that are becoming more popular.

- Competition and incentives, including higher profits and higher wages, play key roles in a market system.

- Allocative efficiency is achieved when the products desired by consumers are made in the right quantities.

- A firm that produces at the lowest possible average cost is productively efficient.

- Innovation can lead to dynamic efficiency.

- A market system rewards efficiency and punishes inefficiency.

Teacher's Tip

Efficiency is a key economic concept. In assessing the performance of an economy or firm, consider whether it is efficient or not.

Multiple Choice Questions

1. What encourages firms to produce what consumers demand?
   a. The chance to earn a high profit
   b. The chance to experience high unit costs of production
   c. The desire to attract new firms into the industry
   d. The desire to keep revenue as low as possible

2. The diagram below shows the current position in a market. How will market forces move the situation towards allocative efficiency?

	Price	Demand	Supply
a.	fall	fall	rise
b.	fall	rise	fall
c.	rise	fall	rise
d.	rise	rise	fall

   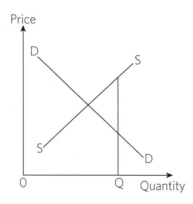

3. In a market system, what encourages firms to keep their costs low?
   a. Competition
   b. Government regulations
   c. Subsidies
   d. Taxation

4. In the diagram below, which movement shows an increase in productive efficiency?

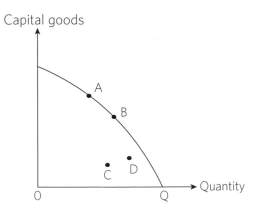

a. A to B
b. B to C
c. C to D
d. A to D

Market Failure

The previous unit described the benefits that arise when markets work well. In practice, however, there are a number of reasons why markets may fail to be efficient. These reasons were introduced in unit 4, but are explained in more depth in this unit. Some of the measures that governments can take, to correct market failure, are also outlined briefly.

The Nature of Market Failure

Market failure occurs when market forces fail to produce the products that consumers demand, in the right quantities and at the lowest possible cost. In other words, *market failure arises when markets are inefficient.* There are a number of indicators of market failure including shortages, surpluses, high prices, poor quality and lack of innovation.

If left to market forces, some products may be under-produced, some over-produced and some may not be produced at all. Prices may be high due to lack of competitive pressure and difficulties in lowering the costs. A lack of investment and reduction in expenditure on research and development can also slowdown the improvement in products.

Failure to Take into Account all Costs and Benefits

The consumption and production of some products may affect people, who are not involved in their consumption or production directly. (Those indirectly affected are often referred to as *third parties*.) In such cases, the total benefits and total costs to society, called **social benefits** and **social costs**, are greater than the benefits and costs to the consumers and producers, known as **private benefits** and **private costs**. For instance, the social costs of a firm producing chemicals will include costs not only to the firm but also to people living nearby. Costs to third parties are called **external costs**. Among the private costs to the firm, will be the cost of

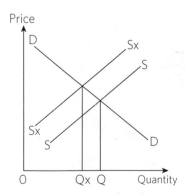

Fig. 1 Over-production

buying raw materials, fuel and wages. The external costs imposed on those living nearby may include noise pollution, air pollution and water pollution. If the decision to produce chemicals is based only on the private costs to the firm, there will be over-production. Fig. 1 shows that if only the private costs to the firm are taken into account, then the supply would be SS whereas the full cost to society is higher at SxSx. The difference between the two is accounted for by the external costs. The allocatively efficient output is Qx but the market output is Q.

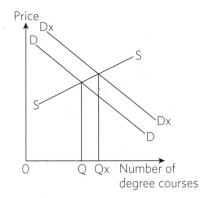

Fig. 2 Under-production

Demand, based just on the private benefits to those consuming the product, will lead to under-consumption and hence under-production if the total benefit to society is greater. For example, among the benefits students may receive by undertaking university degree courses are greater number of career choices, higher future earnings, life long interests and life long friends. The social benefits include not only these private benefits but also the benefits to other people (external benefits) who will be able to enjoy a higher quantity and quality of output as graduates are usually highly productive workers. In Fig. 2 demand for degree courses, based on private benefits, is DD whilst the total benefit to the economy is DxDx. The number of degree courses that would be undertaken, if left to market forces, is Q whereas the number which would cause the maximum benefit to the society is Qx.

Whenever there is a gap between the total effects on society and the effects on those directly consuming and producing the products, markets will fail to allocate resources efficiently. This problem is examined further in the next unit.

Key Points

Private costs: costs borne by those directly consuming or producing a product.

Private benefits: benefits received by those directly consuming or producing a product.

External costs: costs imposed on those who are not involved in the consumption and production activities of others directly.

External benefits: benefits enjoyed by those who are not involved in the consumption and production activities of others directly.

Social costs: the total costs to a society of an economic activity.

Social benefits: the total benefits to a society of an economic activity.

 **Activity 1**

In March 2006, demonstrations by Argentineans held up the construction of two large cellulose factories on the Uruguary-Argentina border. The demonstrators claimed that the factories would pollute the local river – harming local tourism, farming and fishing.

a.   Identify two private costs of building the factories.

b.   Explain why pollution is an external cost.

Information Failure

For consumers to buy the products, that will give them the highest possible satisfaction at the lowest possible prices, they have to be fully informed about the nature of the products on offer, the benefits they can receive from them and their prices. Workers need to know what jobs are on offer, the location of the workplace, the qualifications required and the remuneration they would receive. They should also be aware about the nature of jobs, for which their skills are best suited. Similarly, producers need to know what products are in demand, where good quality raw materials can be purchased at lowest possible prices and what are the most cost-effective methods of production. If they lack this information, they will make decisions that are not in their best interests. Besides consumers paying more than required and buying products of lower quality than available, workers may end up in the wrong jobs and producers costs may be higher and revenues lower than possible due to information failure.

Information failure can occur in a number of ways. There may be a lack of information or inaccurate information. There may also be asymmetric information which occurs when consumers and suppliers do not have equal access to information. For instance, if a car mechanic tells a motorist that her or his car needs an expensive repair, the motorist may lack the technical knowledge to question the advice.

 **Merit Goods**

In the case of some products, there is both a problem of information failure and a problem of social benefits or costs being greater than the private benefits or costs.

Merit goods are products that are more beneficial to the consumers than they themselves realise and that have benefits for those who are not involved in their consumption directly i.e. external benefits. This failure of the consumers to acknowledge the true value to themselves and to others means that these products would be under-consumed and hence underproduced, if left to market forces.

Health care is an example of a merit good. For instance, some people may not recognise the importance of regular medical check-ups and or visiting a doctor. Hence, they are unlikely to take into account the benefits of their fitness to others. The associated external benefits may include higher output as a result of workers having less time off work (hence being more productive) and prevention of spread of diseases.

There are various measures that a government may adopt to overcome the problem of a lack of consumption, in the case of merit goods. One is by providing information on the benefits of consuming the products. If successful, there should be an increase in demand. In the absence of an increase in demand, the government may need to try another approach. Fig. 3a shows the demand, which will exist if left to market forces, DD, and demand based on the full benefits to society, DxDx. To persuade consumers to purchase the allocatively efficient quantity of Qx, the price of the product needs to fall to P1. Fig. 3b shows this being achieved, as a result of a subsidy – shifting the supply curve to the right.

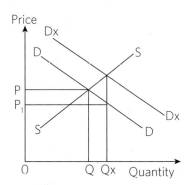

(a) Under-consumption if left to market forces

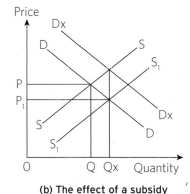

(b) The effect of a subsidy

Fig. 3

If a government thinks that consumers undervalue the product significantly or there are considerable external benefits, it may provide the product free to consumers and/or make its consumption compulsory. For example, inoculation against a range of diseases is provided free and the wearing of seat belts in cars is compulsory in the UK.

 **Activity 2**

Some African countries provide free primary education. In a number of other African countries, state schools charge fees.
a. Identify two arguments for providing free primary education.
b. Explain why, if left to market forces, education is likely to be under-consumed.

 # Demerit Goods

As their name suggests, demerit goods are the opposite of merit goods. Demerit goods are more harmful to consumers than they realise and they generate external costs. For example, cigarettes are a demerit good. Some people do not fully realise the damage, smoking inflicts on their health. Their smoking also imposes costs on people around them by polluting the air, causing a number of them to develop cancer through passive smoking and generating litter.

Demerit goods are over-consumed and hence over-produced. To tackle this problem, a government could raise their price by imposing a tax on them. It could also seek to discourage consumption, by providing information about their harmful effects. Also, if it thinks that the consumption of certain products causes serious problems, it may ban them.

Recently a number of countries, including the countries of the UK and Ireland, have imposed a ban on smoking in public places. This measure is designed not only to discourage smoking but also to protect the health of non-smokers. Other measures, that governments use to reduce smoking, include government sponsored health campaigns, placing health warnings on packets of cigarettes, taxation and banning the advertising of cigarettes. Bhutan has gone further than most countries in banning the purchase of cigarettes in the country.

Activity 3

Between 1977 and 2006, alcohol-related medical emergencies and hospital treatments doubled in the UK. In 2006 the state funded, National Health System (NHS), carried out more than a quarter of a million treatments for medical problems caused by excessive drinking, including liver disease and severe alcohol poisoning.
a. Explain why alcohol is a demerit good.
b. Explain two ways which the UK government could use to reduce the consumption of alcohol.

Public Goods

The degree of market failure is greater in the case of public goods than merit goods and demerit goods. Whilst too few merit goods and too many demerit goods will be produced if left to market forces, no public goods would be made.

As mentioned in unit 4, private sector firms will not have any incentive to make products

they cannot charge for. It is not possible to exclude non-payers from enjoying the benefits of products such as defence. If these public goods are provided for some people, others can consume them without paying for them. Those who do take advantage in this way are called *free riders*. For instance, if a flood defence system is built to protect a coastal town, all homes in the area would be protected whether their owners are prepared to pay for it or not.

Besides **non-excludability**, public goods have another characteristic. This is **non-rivalry**. This means that consumption of the product by one more person does not reduce someone else's ability to consume it. For example, one more person walking down a lit street does not reduce the benefit that other people receive from the street lights.

Most products, including merit and demerit goods, are private goods. These products are both rival and excludable. In these cases, it is possible to stop non-payers from enjoying the products and if one person consumes a unit of the product, someone else cannot. For example, I cannot take a computer out of a shop without paying for it and if I do buy it, no-one else can have that particular computer. Even though primary and secondary education and health care are not directly charged for in some countries, they are nevertheless private goods. This is because they can be charged for, and also because they are rival goods (in some cases). If one child is occupying a place in a class or one patient is occupying a hospital bed, no one else can occupy these places. Of course, education and health care are examples of a special type of private goods i.e. merit goods.

Markets will supply private goods, although not necessarily in the right quantities. They will not, however, supply public goods. This means that public goods have to be financed through taxation. The government can then produce them itself or pay a private sector to produce them.

Abuse of Market Power

Market failure can arise due to producers having more market power than consumers. If one firm dominates a market, it may not be allocatively, productively or dynamically efficient. It will lack competitive pressure to respond to consumer demands, to keep its costs low and to improve its product. If it is the only firm selling the product, consumers will have no choice but to buy from it, even if the price of the product is high, the product is not in accordance to the needs of the consumers and its quality is poor.

Abuse of market failure can also occur, when there is more than one firm producing the product. If there are, for instance, five major producers in a market there is a risk that they may collude to reduce competition. For example, they may all agree to charge the same high price. This is referred to as **price fixing**.

There are various ways, through which governments try to promote competition and prevent firms from abusing their market power. These include removing restrictions on the entry of new firms into a market and making uncompetitive practices such as price fixing illegal. They may also stop some firms from merging, i.e. joining together to form one new firm, if it is thought that the merged firm will act against the interests of consumers by charging high prices and producing poor quality products.

 **Activity 4**

Under an 'open skies' deal reached in March 2007 between the US and European Union, it was agreed to allow more airlines to fly between the two areas, including between Heathrow Airport in London and the US. The deal is due to come into effect in March 2008.

Up to 2008, only four airlines – British Airways (BA), Virgin Atlantic, American Airlines and United Airlines, were permitted to fly between London and New York. It is expected that increased competition will come from airlines such as bmi, Lufthansa and Delta and that prices will fall significantly. BA has announced that it is going to upgrade its business class cabins and lounges to prevent its customers being lured away.

a. What incentive would encourage more airlines to fly on a particular route?

b. Explain two benefits offered by increased competition to consumers.

Immobility of Resources

To achieve allocative efficiency, it is necessary for resources to move from producing products that are decreasing in demand towards those which are experiencing an increase in demand. This requires resources to be both occupationally and geographically mobile. In practice, some resources may be immobile. If, for example, demand for a country's financial services might be increasing whilst demand for its steel may be decreasing, there may be a shortage of financial services, unemployment of workers and under-utilisation of capital equipment if resources cannot easily move between the two.

The main measures, a government can take to promote occupational mobility of labour, are to improve education and to provide training in the new skills needed. Also, government can provide investment grants to make it easier for firms to change the use of land and buildings. Geographical mobility of workers can be encouraged by making it easier for them to buy or rent housing in areas where demand for labour is high. This might be achieved by construction of more houses in such areas or by providing financial help for those workers who move to these locations by the government.

 # Short Termism

There is a risk that market forces may not result in sufficient resources being devoted to capital goods. If a country produces a high quantity of consumer products, people can enjoy a high living standard. For them to enjoy more consumer products in the future, some resources have to be diverted for making capital goods. Private sector firms may be interested in making quick profits and may not plan for times ahead. Such a myopic approach can result in a lack of investment. As a result, a government may have to stimulate private sector investment by, for instance, cutting taxes on firms and undertake some investment itself.

Unfairness

Besides intervening in a market economy to correct market failure, governments also intervene on grounds of equity, i.e. fairness. As mentioned in unit 4, income distribution can become very uneven if it is solely determined by market forces. Some people will be very rich but some will be very poor. Private sector firms will only produce those products that people are willing to buy and able to pay for. This may mean that they will not produce products, needed by the poor.

A government is likely to try and ensure that everyone in the country has access to basic necessities including housing, education and health care. To achieve this, it can give financial assistance to the poor and provide some essential products to them free of cost. In fact in a number of countries, state education and health care is provided free, not only because they are merit goods but also to make them accessible to the poor. Such free state services are financed by taxation. Taxation and benefits may also be used to reduce income and wealth inequality. A big difference in the income and wealth of the rich and poor, besides being unfair, can be socially divisive and

can result in some workers being less productive. Some people in the country, including the elderly and the sick, may be unable to earn incomes. There may be social unrest if there is considerable income inequality. Also, if people are poor they may be less healthy, less well educated and consequently less productive.

Government Failure

Government failure occurs when government intervention worsens the situation instead of improving it. It can arise due to a number of reasons. A government may lack information about, for instance, the extent of externalities. It may overestimate the extent of the private benefits, offered to the people by consuming merit goods and it may find it difficult to calculate the most efficient quantity of public goods to supply.

Governments can take time to make decisions and those decisions may be influenced by political factors. For example, a government may decide not to raise the tax on petrol, despite concerns about the environment, because it may be politically unpopular and may lose it votes.

Government intervention may also reduce economic efficiency by reducing incentives. If taxes on earned income and unemployment benefits are high, some people may be discouraged from working. High taxes on firms' profits can reduce entrepreneurs' willingness and ability to invest.

 **Summary**

- Market failure occurs when markets do not operate efficiently.

- If left to market forces, those products whose social benefits exceed their private benefits will be under-consumed and hence underproduced. There will be over-consumption and over-production of products, if their social costs exceed their private costs.

- Consumers, workers and producers may not make the right choices due to lack of information, inaccurate information or because they have less information than the other party in a transaction (asymmetrical information).

- Merit goods would be under-consumed, if left to market forces, because people do not realise their true value to themselves and because they generate benefits to third parties.

- Demerit goods would be over-consumed in a market system. They are more harmful to the consumers than they realise and involve external costs.

- Public goods are both non-excludable and non-rival. They would not be produced in a market system, as it is not possible to stop free riders from enjoying them.

- Where there is a lack of competition, a firm may not keep its costs down, may charge a high price and may produce a poor quality product.

- The most efficient allocation of resources may not be achieved due to a lack of mobility of resources.

- Private sector firms, keen to earn high profits in short term, may under-invest.

- Besides correcting market failures, governments intervene in economies to protect vulnerable groups and to ensure an evern distribution of income and wealth.

 Teacher's Tip

In discussing whether a market system works well, or any other economic issue, consider arguments for and against and where appropriate come to a conclusion.

Multiple Choice Questions

1. In which case is market failure occurring?
    a. Consumers determining what is produced
    b. Firms producing above the lowest possible cost
    c. Price falling as a result of a decrease in demand
    d. Price rising as a result of an increase in costs of production

2. A merit good is one which:
    a. has an absence of external benefits
    b. has higher private benefits than consumers realise
    c. imposes costs on those who are not involved in its production directly
    d. is both non-excludable and non-rival

3. Which type of goods would be over-produced if left to market forces?
    a. Basic necessities
    b. Capital goods
    c. Demerit goods
    d. Public goods

4. What is a cause of market failure?
    a. Competition between firms
    b. Consumers lacking information about where the lowest prices can be found
    c. Differences in pay between skill and unskilled workers
    d. Resources being both geographically and occupationally mobile

Use of Resources

One area, in which there is a high risk of market failure, is in the use of non-renewable resources and the environment. Private sector firms may be more concerned with making a quick profit than sustainability. Also, there may be information failure regarding the effects of exploiting resources and the external costs and benefits generated by their use. This unit touches on the conflict between the conservation and exploitation of resources. It also examines the nature of social, external and private costs and benefits.

Conflicts in the Use of Resources

Non-renewable resources include coal, gold, iron ore and oil. Other resources, including fish stocks, may be turned from renewable to non-renewable, if they are over-harvested. The quality of resources can also be adversely affected by over use. For example, the beauty of a beach may be reduced, if too many tourists visit it.

Exploiting resources, however, can raise employment, income and improve the trade position of the country and living standards of its people. For example, if Venezuela extracts large amounts of oil in the next five years, the country will probably experience a rise in employment. Selling it abroad will raise export revenue and Venezuelan citizens will enjoy a higher living standard. The government will receive more tax revenue, which will enable it to spend more on education, health care and creating a climate conducive for the growth of other industries. However, if a non-renewable resource is being exploited, it is important that some of the revenue earned is used to ensure that other industries can develop, as future sources of income.

The faster Venezuela exploits its oil reserves, the sooner these supplies will be exhausted. It may be better to conserve most of the reserves. This approach would allow future generations to continue to benefit from the resources. It may also mean that the country becomes a more balanced economy, encourages the development of other industries and does not become too dependent on one export.

The choice, whether to exploit or conserve reserves, is influenced by a number of factors. These include the current living standards of the country, the country's need for income, products where the country's comparative advantage lies, current world demand and future world demand. If a country is very poor, it may have to use resources to raise its people out of poverty. The country may also be in debt to other countries and may need to obtain export revenue in order to service its debt. It may also exploit its resources,

if current world demand is high. However, there are uncertainties about future world demand. If it is found that currently the country does not have a comparative advantage in the product, the country may wait until cost conditions change. In the meanwhile, it may import the product. An efficient use of resources is more likely to occur, if social costs and benefits are taken into account while deciding on the use of resources.

 Activity 1

The Organisation of the Petroleum Exporting Countries (OPEC) often restricts the supply of oil, in order to keep its prices high. There are signs, however, that OPEC is now thinking about increasing the amount of oil it extracts and sells. This is thought to be the result, in part, of fears that high prices may trigger the adoption of alternative fuels such as ethanol.

a.   How may market forces compel OPEC to sell more oil?

b.   Explain one reason (other than to raise price) for OPEC to restrict the supply of oil.

Private Costs and Benefits

The rainforests, in the Amazon region of Brazil, are being cleared at a relatively rapid rate. The firms that are engaged in logging, in the forests, are only taking into account private

costs and benefits. Private costs (as noted in the previous unit) are the costs borne by those who are directly involved in the decision to consume or produce a product. In the case of a logging company, private costs will include, for example, the cost of transporting the wood and the cost of labour. Private benefits are the benefits received by those directly involved in the consumption and production of a product. The private benefit, logging company receives from selling the wood, is the revenue it earns. The company will continue cutting down trees, as long as the revenue received by it exceeds it costs.

 # External Costs and Benefits

When firms produce products and households consume them, they often affect other people. For example, someone smoking in a factory may harm the health of other workers and a clothing firm, that dumps waste into a river, may damage the fishing stocks of a fish farmer and harm the environment.

The effects on *third parties*, due to the consumption and production activities of others, are known as external costs and external benefits. External costs caused by the logging companies may include damage to wildlife habitats, loss of plant species that could be used to develop medicines, global warming and interference with the lifestyle of local tribes. External benefits may include reduced transport costs for tourist firms in the area due to construction of roads by logging companies. While making its decisions on the number of trees to be cut down, a logging company will not take these external costs and benefits into account.

 # Social Costs and Benefits

Social costs are the total costs of an economic activity to society. The social cost of cutting down trees in the Amazon, will consist of both external and private costs. When social costs exceeds private costs, there are external costs involved. Social benefits are the total benefits to the society, arising from an economic activity. They include both private and external benefits. Again, where social benefits are greater than private benefits, external benefits exist.

The level of output which will cause maximum benefit to the society (socially optimum output) will occur when the social benefit of the last unit produced is equal to the social cost of that unit. If the social cost exceeds the social benefit, it implies that too many resources are being devoted to the production of the product. Society would benefit from reducing its output. In contrast, if the benefit society would gain from producing more of the product is greater than the cost to society of producing more output, then more resources should be devoted to its production.

A case, where the social cost (in most countries) exceeds the social benefit, is the use of road space by private cars. When people are thinking of making a trip in their car, they take into account the private costs and benefits, that is the cost and benefits to themselves. If the benefits received by them by undertaking the journey exceed the costs – for example the cost of petrol and wear and tear on the vehicles, they will make the journey. What they do not consider is the external costs caused by them, including air pollution, noise

pollution, congestion and accidents. A number of governments, including Singapore and the UK, have introduced *road pricing schemes*. These seek to charge the full costs of their journeys. Different amounts are charged according to when and where people drive. Someone driving along a deserted country road is likely to cause lower external costs than someone driving into a city centre at peak time.

Activity 2

Emissions of carbon dioxide from the British aviation industry doubled from 1990 to 2006 and are forecasted to double again, by 2030. Britain generates more flights than any other European country and a fifth of all international air passengers worldwide, are on flights that arrive or leave from British airports. The UK government is supporting the idea of taxing airlines for the pollution caused by them.

a.   Identify two external costs caused by air travel.

b.   What impact is a tax on air travel, likely to have on the number of flights?

c.   Explain one external benefit that could arise from the operation of a new airport.

Summary

- There may be a conflict between conserving and exploiting resources. Exploitation of resources gives rise to income and employment but depletes them.

- When households and firms make their consumption and production decisions, they take into account private costs and benefits only. External costs and benefits are the beneficial and harmful effects on third parties respectively, arising from the actions of others.

- Social costs are the total costs to society, arising from the production or consumption of a product.

- Social benefits are the total benefits to society, arising from the production or consumption of a product.

Teacher's Tip

It is a common mistake to confuse social and external costs and benefits. Remember social costs and benefits are the total costs and benefits of an economic activity. They include both the external and private costs and benefits.

Multiple Choice Questions

1. A country, whose main export is fish, decides to place a limit on the quantity of fish fishermen can catch. What is the likely reason for this decision?
    a. To improve the trade in goods position in the next year.
    b. To protect future living standards.
    c. To reduce government intervention.
    d. To raise employment in the fishing industry.

2. What are external costs?
    a. Costs borne by those consuming or producing the product.
    b. Fixed costs plus variable costs.
    c. Social costs minus private costs.
    d. Total costs of all the firms in the industry.

3. A government decides to subsidise rail travel. What will be an external benefit of this move?
    a. A rise in government expenditure
    b. Increased crowding on trains
    c. Lower fares for train passengers
    d. Reduced congestion on roads

4. A firm, concerned about its reputation, decides to install new equipment in order to reduce the pollution created by it. What impact will this have, on private and external costs?

	private costs	external costs
a.	fall	fall
b.	fall	rise
c.	rise	fall
d.	rise	rise

Public Expenditure versus Private Expenditure

This unit examines the nature of public expenditure, its purposes, methods to finance it, government influences on the private sector and comparisons between the effectiveness of public expenditure and private expenditure.

 Public Expenditure

Public expenditure is the expenditure done by the public sector. It includes expenditure by the central government, local authorities or regional bodies and state owned enterprises. There are two broad categories of public expenditure. One is called **exhaustive spending**. This involves the public sector directly buying goods and services, such as buying medical equipment, paying the police and building roads. In this case, the public sector determines the use of resources.

The other category is **transfer payments** – transfers of money to people (for instance, pensioners and the unemployed) and to firms (in the form of subsidies and grants). This is non-exhaustive expenditure. In this case, the government does not decide on the allocation of resources. The people and firms, receiving the financial support, make the decision through their purchases.

The Uses of Public Expenditure
National and regional governments spend money on:
- public goods
- merit goods
- supporting vulnerable groups

- helping private sector industries

- covering any losses incurred by state owned enterprises and

- managing the economy, including promoting employment.

Financing Public Expenditure

Public expenditure can be financed by:

- taxation

- borrowing, from the profits of state owned enterprises

- privatisation.

The amount of tax a government can raise is influenced by the income of the country, the willingness of the citizens to pay taxes, reaction of firms and workers to tax changes and tax rates in other countries. If a country has a high real GDP, it should be able to raise a considerable amount in taxes, even with relatively low tax rates. In a democracy, people may not be prepared to vote for a political party which is planning to raise tax rates. If people resent paying taxes, a rise in tax rates may not be very successful in increasing tax revenue but may instead increase the size of the *informal economy*. A government may also be reluctant to raise taxes, if it thinks that workers will work for fewer hours or emigrate and multinational companies (MNCs) will leave the country. It may be particularly worried about raising tax rates, if other countries have lower rates. In recent years, a number of Eastern European countries have introduced **'flat taxes'**. A flat tax is a tax with only one rate, which is often low. Estonia, for instance, does not even tax firms' profits if they are reinvested.

Ability of a government to borrow will depend on its credit worthiness at home and abroad. If people, firms, foreign governments and international organisations believe that they will be repaid, they will be willing to lend to the government. Amount borrowed by a government will be influenced by the state of the economy, level of economic development and acceptable rate of interest. The more the number of state-owned enterprises in a country and higher the profit made by them – the more revenue a government may raise. If, however, state owned enterprises make losses, they will drain the government revenue and won't be able to act as a source of revenue.

Selling off state owned assets, including state owned enterprises, to the private sector can raise revenue in the short term. If the assets, however, were profitable, the sales may reduce government revenue in the long term.

A government borrows money to build new schools, hire more teachers and buy educational equipment, in order to raise the school leaving age. This action may, in the longer term, increase tax revenue, some of which can be used to repay the loan.

a. Apart from borrowing, identify one other way the government could have been influenced about its expenditure on education

b. Why may a government spend more on education?

c. Why may spending money on education, 'increase the tax revenue'?

Government Influence on Private Sector Expenditure

The government influences private sector expenditure in a number of ways. These include:

- taxing income and expenditure

- providing subsidies

- giving grants

- influencing the level of economic activity.

Private sector investment, for instance, would be increased by the introduction of government investment grants, a cut in corporation tax and a cut in the rate of interest. Investment grants would encourage private sector firms to buy more capital goods. A cut in corporation tax will increase the willingness and ability of firms to invest. A lower interest rate would reduce the cost of borrowing to buy capital goods and would reduce the opportunity cost of using retained profits to buy capital goods.

Comparison of Expenditures by Public and Private Sectors

There is some debate as to whether public or private sector expenditure, leads to a more efficient allocation of resources. Do households and firms make better decisions than the government? In practice, there are advantages and disadvantages of both private and public sector expenditure.

A new airport, for instance, could be built by the private or public sector. There may be a number of advantages in it being built by a private sector firm. The profit incentive and force of competition may imply that it will build a high quality airport at low cost and in less time.

There is a risk, however, that a private sector firm may be a monopoly and hence may not be forced to keep its costs down. Thus, it may charge a high price for building the airport. Also, a private sector firm will also take only private costs and benefits into account.

Using public expenditure to build an airport may also have its own drawbacks. Knowing that the state is paying, a state owned enterprise or private sector firm hired by the government, may not keep its costs down. A state owned enterprise may lack the commercial expertise to complete the project on time. There may also be delays in decision making by the government to go ahead with the project. A major benefit, however, of a major investment project being undertaken by government is that it will base its decision (as to whether to proceed with it) on the consideration of all factors involved, that is social impact, costs and benefits. It is likely to carry out a **cost benefit analysis** (CBA) in the first place. This involves measuring all the private costs and benefits involved. In the case of an airport, the private costs will involve the cost of the land, the cost of the labour employed to build and run the airport and the cost of the building material and maintenance. The major private benefit is the revenue that will be earned.

After measuring the private costs and benefits, the economists carrying out a CBA, then seek to place a value on external costs and benefits. This is not an easy process. The external costs may include – operation of the airport damage to the environment, noise due to risk of accidents and congestion near the airport. The external benefits may include employment in the area due to tourism and making it a more attractive as a site for domestic firms and MNCs.

When all the calculations have been made, the social costs and benefits are compared. If social costs exceed social benefits, the government will not proceed with the project. If social benefits exceed social costs, it will go ahead (if the net social benefit is greater than that on rival projects). There will still be a debate, however, on whether it is the best use of government money. Government expenditure on one item always involves a significant opportunity cost. The money could have been spent on, for instance, education.

Key Point

Cost benefit analysis: a method of assessing investment projects which takes into account, social costs and benefits.

 **Activity 2**

The private sector in China is responsible for a growing amount of output and employment. Some economists argue that private sector firms are more profitable and efficient than the state sector.

a.   How may the government benefit, from private sector firms being more profitable?

b.   Why may private sector firms be more efficient than state owned enterprises?

 Summary

- Public expenditure can be (directly) on goods and services or on transfer payments to people and firms.

- Public expenditure is used to finance public and merit goods, help vulnerable groups, cover losses of state owned enterprises and manage the economy.

- The government influences private sector expenditure by means of taxation, subsidies, grants and macroeconomic policies.

- Expenditure by the private sector on an investment project may ensure efficiency but a private sector firm considers only private costs and benefits.

 Teacher's Tip

Be careful with the word 'public'. Sometimes, it refers to the government as in 'public expenditure' and 'public sector'. It can, however, also refer to people as a whole as in the 'general public' or open to all people, as in a 'public limited company'.

Multiple Choice Questions

1. The production of which of types of goods, given below, has to be financed by the government?
    a. Capital
    b. Consumer
    c. Merit
    d. Public

2. Which of the following is an example of a transfer payment?
    a. Government expenditure on teachers' salaries
    b. Government expenditure on student grants
    c. Government expenditure on the building of schools
    d. Government expenditure on the maintenance of school buildings

3. How may an increase in government expenditure, on the education of the poor, benefit the rich?
    a. In the short term, some government expenditure on higher education may have to be reduced.
    b. In the short term, the rates of progressive taxes may have to rise.
    c. In the longer term, the productivity of workers may rise and if hence the productive capacity of the economy might increase.
    d. In the longer term, more workers may emigrate which may raise the dependency ratio on those remaining.

4. Which of the following is a possible aim of public sector expenditure but not that of private sector?
    a. To ensure that all costs of production are covered
    b. To ensure full employment of resources
    c. To finance the purchase of capital goods
    d. To finance the expenditure on research and development

Answer Key

Unit 4

Activity 1

a. Those people whose labour skills are in high demand are well paid. Entrepreneurs, who produce what consumers want, can make high profits. Those with high incomes can save and earn income from their savings.

b. The sick, disabled and old will find it hard to earn an income.

Activity 2

c. and d. – the profit motive and private ownership of land are key features of a market economy. a and b are found in a planned economy.

Activity 3

a. Privatisation involves the sale of state owned enterprises (SOEs) and parts of SOEs to the private sector.

b. (i) A firm may perform better in the private sector due to the profit incentive and competitive pressure.

   (ii) A firm in the public sector may do better than the one in the private sector, as it may base its production decisions on the full costs and benefits of those decisions.

Multiple Choice Questions

1. b

    A relatively easy question.

2. b

    Resources are allocated by the price mechanism in a market economy. If a product becomes more popular, consumers will be willing to pay more for it and hence more resources will be devoted for its production. Directives allocate resources in a planned economy. Directives and the price mechanism are used in a mixed economy.

3. b

    Consumers determine what is produced in a market economy. Poverty and unemployment can occur in a market economy. Firms having considerable market power may be a disadvantage, as they would be able to charge high prices.

4. d

The government can increase economic efficiency by preventing the private sector from abusing its market power. A government would want to reduce the consumption of harmful products and is likely to desire a more equitable distribution of income. Its intervention would reduce the role of the price mechanism.

Unit 5

Activity 1

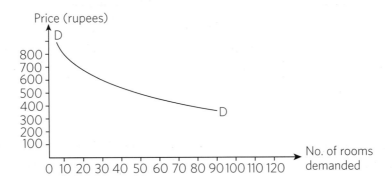

Activity 2

a.

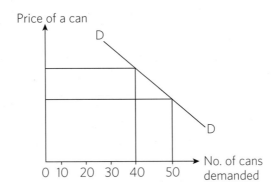

b. Demand has extended – more is being demanded because price has fallen.

Activity 3

a.

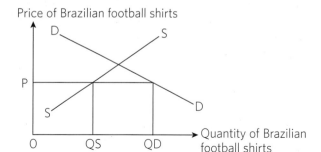

Price of Brazilian football shirts

b. Price would be expected to rise due to surplus demand. Customers, eager to buy the shirts, would be prepared to pay more.

Multiple Choice Questions

1. c

   Demand and price move in the opposite directions and hence are inversely related. In contrast, supply and price move in the same direction, which means that they are directly related.

2. a

   If the price of a product falls, people are not only likely to buy more of it but they will also be able to afford to buy greater quantities of the same product.

3. d

   A market supply curve shows the total amount supplied at different prices.

4. b

   Equilibrium price occurs when the quantity demanded equals the quantity supplied. There is the possibility that everything that is produced may not be offered for sale or what is sold consists of more than that has recently been produced (in such a case stocks may be drawn on). The number of buyers and sellers do not have to be equal – it is the quantity demanded and supplied, which is significant. If supply exceeds demand, the market will be in disequilibrium.

Activity 1

a.

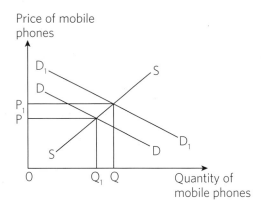

Demand for mobile phones increased in China. This would have caused their price to rise and their supply to extend.

b. A mobile phone is a normal good. This is because demand for mobile phones increases as income rises. Some of those without phones, purchase them and those with phones, upgrade them for better models.

Activity 2

a. Usually a substitute. People may travel to a place by car or by bus or by train. Occasionally, they may drive to a train or bus station and then use public transport – in which case they are a complement.
b. A complement. People buy petrol to use their cars.
c. A substitute. People choose from a range of models of cars.

Activity 3

a. 54% (100% – 46%)
b. One reason is that young people do not have the time to read newspapers and so do not by them. Another reason is that young people have less need to buy newspapers, as they can receive the news from a variety of other sources.

c. It suggests that internet is a substitute to newspapers. It mentions that it is a rival to newspapers – a number of young people get their news from the internet rather than newspapers.

d. Newspaper publishers could raise demand for their papers by lowering their prices or advertising. A cut in price should cause an extension in demand. An advertising campaign, if successful, should cause an increase in demand.

Activity 4

a.

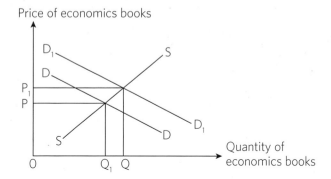

A successful advertising campaign will increase demand.

b.

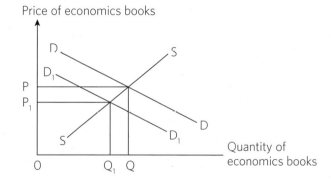

Fewer students studying economics will result in a decrease in demand.

Activity 5

a. a contraction in demand
b. an increase in demand
c. a decrease in demand – fewer people to eat fish.
d. a decrease in demand – some people will switch from eating fish to eating chicken.

Multiple Choice Questions

1. b

   The diagram shows an increasing demand for coffee. A rise in the price of tea may cause some people to switch from drinking tea to drinking coffee. A rise in the price of coffee here is the consequence of demand and not the cause. c and d would be likely to cause a decrease in demand for coffee.

2. d

   An increase in demand moves the demand curve out to the right. a is an extension in demand, b is a contraction in demand and c is a decrease in demand.

3. b

   An inferior good has an inverse relationship with income. As income rises, demand decreases. As people get richer, they buy more of high quality products and less of low quality products.

4. c

   A rise in the price of a product will cause the demand to contract. The demand for a product used with it will decrease – less will be purchased – not because it has risen in price but because a related product has become more expensive.

Unit 7

Activity 1

a.

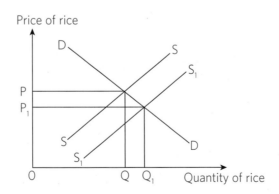

The supply of rice has increased. This would cause the price to fall and demand to contract.

b. The supply of rice can decrease as a result of bad weather, disease, an increase in production costs or an imposition of a tax on rice.

Activity 2

a. (i) Unit cost is total cost/output. In this case, this is $500/100 = $5.
   (ii) The new unit cost is $600/200 = $3.

b. Supply will increase as costs of production have fallen.

Activity 3

a.

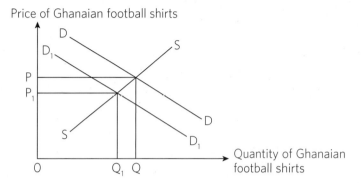

Price of Ghanaian football shirts

A football shirt is a normal good. Demand would decrease, causing a fall in price and a contraction in supply.

b.

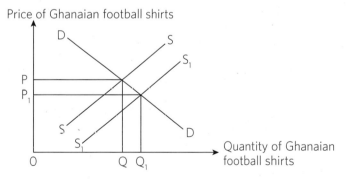

Price of Ghanaian football shirts

A rise in workers' productivity would reduce costs of production. This, in turn, would cause price to fall and demand to extend.

c.

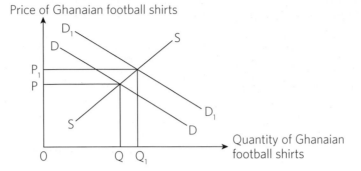

Price of Ghanaian football shirts

If Ghana wins the world cup, their shirts will become more popular. This will increase their demand. Higher demand will raise price, which would cause the supply to extend.

d.

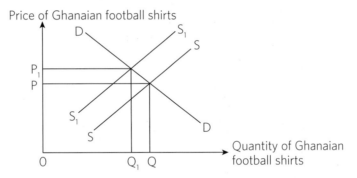

Price of Ghanaian football shirts

A tax placed on a product causes a decrease in supply. This results in a rise in price and a contraction in demand.

e.

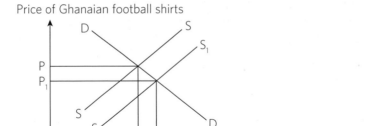

More efficient machinery will decrease the cost of production, causing an increase in supply. This, in turn, will cause a fall in price and an extension in demand.

Activity 4

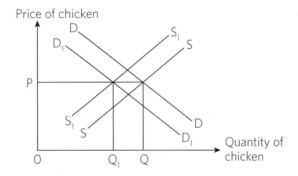

The slaughter of chicken will reduce the supply of chicken. Also, the disease is likely to discourage the consumption of chicken and hence demand will decrease. These changes will cause the quantity bought and sold to fall. The effect on price will depend on the relative size of the two shifts. Price may rise, fall or if (as in the diagram) supply and demand decrease by an equal amount, remain unchanged.

Multiple Choice Questions

1. d

    An increase in supply results in a shift to the right of the supply curve. a is a contraction in supply, b an extension in supply and c a decrease in supply.

2. c

A subsidy will provide an incentive for farmers to produce more milk. a, b and d would decrease supply.

3. c

A reduction in the cost of raw materials would cause an increase in supply.

4. c

A decrease in supply would raise price and cause demand to contract.

Unit 8

Activity 1
a.   75%/-25% = -3
b.   -10%/20% = -0.5
c.   40%/-50% = -0.8

Activity 2
a.   -60%/10% = -6
b.   6%

Activity 3
a.   elastic – a luxury
b.   elastic – a luxury
c.   inelastic – it is addictive
d.   inelastic – it is necessary for commuters to get to work at specific time
e.   inelastic – a necessity

Activity 4
a.   25%/-25% = -1 = unity
b.   -20%/5% = -4 = elastic
c.   40%/-10% = -4 = elastic
d.   0%/100% = perfectly inelastic
e.   -25%/12.5% = -2 = elastic

Multiple Choice Questions
1.   b

PED is %☐QD/%☐P.

2. c

Demand will rise by a smaller percentage than the change in price, causing total revenue to fall. In the case of products with inelastic demand, price and total revenue move in the same direction.

3. d

If a product has close substitutes, a rise in price is likely to result in demand falling by a greater percentage as consumers switch to rival products. A decrease in price will cause demand to rise by a greater percentage, as consumers switch away from rival products. a, b and c would make demand inelastic.

4. b

PED = –25%/50% = –0.5, i.e. inelastic.

Unit 9

Activity 1

a. –60%/–20% = 3
b. 5%/40% = 0.125
c. 12.5%/10% = 1.25

Activity 2

a. 40%/25% = 1.6
b. 1.6%

Activity 3

a. elastic – cheap and quick to produce and can be stored
b. elastic – again cheap and quick to produce and can be stored
c. inelastic – takes a relatively long time to be made
d. elastic   for the same reasons as in (a) and (b)
e. inelastic – takes time to breed and mature and cannot be stored for long

Multiple Choice Questions

1. b

PES is a relative measure of the responsiveness of supply to a change in price.

2. d

A figure less than 1, but greater than zero, indicates inelastic supply.

3. c

If a product can be stored, it should be relatively easy to alter its supply. a, b and d would be likely to make supply inelastic.

4. c
> Elastic supply is usually illustrated by a shallow supply curve. d shows inelastic supply, a and b show the suply curve sloping the wrong way.

Unit 10

Activity 1

a.

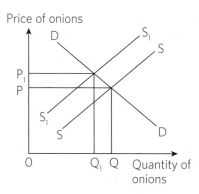 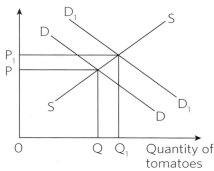

b. The market for onions responded to the shortage caused by the poor crop by an increase in price. The higher price rationed out the onions and restored the market to equilibrium. The higher demand for tomatoes raised their price and encouraged the producers to supply them in greater amounts.

Activity 2

a. Higher wages.

b.

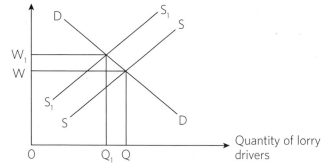

The emigration of lorry drivers to the US would reduce the supply of lorry drivers in India. This would be expected to raise the wages of lorry drivers in India.

Activity 3

a. A fall in demand would be likely to lower the price.

b. The evidence is that resources moved out of the crisps industry, in response to a decrease in demand.

Activity 4

a. Dyson becoming market leader in vacuum cleaners in the US and achieving record profits.

b. Consumers may benefit from Dyson spending more on research and development and investment, as this would improve the quality and quantity of its existing products and also stimulate the introduction of new products.

Multiple Choice Questions

1. a

    Firms are motivated by profit. To earn high profits, firms seek to keep costs low and revenues high. Firms would not try to encourage rivals to enter the market, as their entry would make it more difficult for the existing firms to earn high profits.

2. b

    Supply is exceeding demand. The surplus will cause the price to fall. A lower price will result in a contraction in supply and an extension in demand.

3. a

    In a competitive market, firms have to keep costs down to retain their customers.

4. c

    Production points C and D are both inefficient but C is less efficient than D. D is closer to the production possibility curve and hence closer to productive efficiency. The movement from production point B to C and from A to D, both represent a reduction in productive efficiency. Points A and B are equally efficient.

Unit 11

Activity 1

a   Among the private costs are the costs of buying the land and the building materials and the wages of the workers.

b. Pollution is an external cost, as it harms those who are not directly involved in the production and consumption of the products involved. For example, those living near the factories may keep bad health as a result of carbon dioxide emissions from the factories.

Activity 2

a. The merit good and equity arguments.

b. Education is likely to be under-consumed, if left to market forces as people underestimate its value to themselves. Also, while making their consumption decisions, they do not take into account the associated benefits to others.

Activity 3

a. Alcohol is a demerit good, as it is more harmful to drinkers than they realise and causes harmful effects on third parties including rowdy behaviour and road accidents.

b. Among the ways, the UK government can adopt to reduce the drinking of alcohol, are placing or increasing a tax on the product, providing information about its harmful effects and banning its consumption. A tax would raise the price of alcohol, which would cause a contraction in demand (although demand may be relatively inelastic). The provision of information may reduce demand. A ban would be designed to stop the consumption of alcohol, but it might be difficult to enforce.

Activity 4

a. The profit motive. More airlines would fly a particular route, if they think that they will make a profit on the route.

b. Consumers may benefit from lower prices and increased quality.

Multiple Choice Questions

1. b

    If firms are producing above the lowest possible cost, they are failing to achieve productive efficiency. a refers to consumer sovereignty, which should result in allocative efficiency. c and d refer to markets adjusting to changes in market conditions. They should result in equilibrium being restored, eliminating shortages and surpluses.

2. b

    One of the characteristics of a merit good is that it is more beneficial than those consuming it realise. A merit good does have external benefits. c refers to a demerit good and d to a public good.

3. c

    Demerit goods will be over-consumed and hence over-produced, as their harmful effects on the consumers and others are not appreciated. a and b are likely to be under-produced and public goods may not be produced at all.

4. b

Information failure is a major cause of market failure. a, c and d should all promote efficient working of markets. Competition provides a 'carrot' and a 'stick' for firms to be efficient. Differences in pay between skilled and unskilled workers provide an incentive for workers to be productive. Mobility of resources makes it easier and quicker for markets to respond to changes in consumer demand.

Unit 12

Activity 1

a. If the price of oil rises, it may make it profitable to search for alternatives. The fear of such an occurence may make OPEC increase the supply of oil to lower its price.

b. OPEC may want to restrict the supply of oil to conserve it, to ensure a stream of income in the long term.

Activity 2

a. Pollution (air and noise) and accidents.

b. It is likely to reduce the number of flights, as it will make travelling more expensive. Of course, the effect will depend on the size of tax and the price elasticity of demand for air travel.

c. An external benefit is a beneficial effect that third parties enjoy, as a result of the production or consumption decisions of others. In this case, a new airport may create work for taxi drivers in the area and may boost other local businesses also. They may be able to enjoy high profits not as a result of their own actions but because of people travelling to and from the airport.

Multiple Choice Questions

1. b

Placing a limit on the quantity of fish, that can be caught, should conserve fish stocks for the future.

2. c

Private costs plus external costs equal social costs.

3. d

People travelling on the train benefit car drivers, as their action reduces the volume of traffic on the roads.

4. c

Installing new equipment will increase a firm's costs but it should reduce costs on third parties, including those households who live close to the firm.

Unit 13

Activity 1

a. From tax revenue.

b. It may want to spend money on education, as it may be concerned that everyone should have access to this vital service. It may be worried that if left to market forces, it will be under-consumed. Improved education may also help to raise labour productivity and increase productive capacity of workers.

c. Spending more on education should, in the long run, raise productivity. This should increase economic growth. If the country does grow, income and expenditure will increase and hence the government will receive more direct and indirect tax revenue.

Activity 2

a. The government will benefit in terms of high corporation tax revenue. There will also be a probable reduction in the amount of unemployment benefit paid by the government. This is because profitable firms are likely to expand and take on more workers.

b. Private sector firms may be more efficient than state owned enterprises, as the market provides both a 'carrot' and a 'stick' for them to produce at a low cost and to make the products desired by consumers. If firms are efficient, they are rewarded with high profits and if they are not, they are punished by going bankrupt.

Multiple Choice Questions

1. d

Private sector firms do not have the financial incentive to produce public goods, as they cannot stop non-payers from consuming the product. This means that either state-owned enterprises have to produce them or the government has to provide the incentive for private sector firms to make them (by paying them). Either way, the government finances their production.

2. b

    A transfer payment is a payment to someone, not in return for providing a good or service. In the case of a government transfer payment, the government does not decide the use of resources – this is done by the recipients. In the case of a, c and d the government decides the allocation of resources.

3. c

    All the members of the country can benefit from the education of the poor, since they should become more productive workers and hence would help increase the output of the country.

4. b

    The government may be seeking to achieve full employment. When households and firms spend their money, they are not taking into account the effect it will have on employment.

Examination Practice

Multiple Choice Questions

1. Who decides, what is produced in a market economy?
    a. Consumers
    b. Managers
    c. Shareholders
    d. The government

2. The table shows demand and supply schedules for bread.

Price of a loaf of bread ($)	Number of loaves demanded per week	Number of loaves supplied per week
0.80	500	180
1.00	400	240
1.20	320	320
1.40	240	500

What will be the equilibrium price for a loaf of bread?
    a. $0.80
    b. $1.00
    c. $1.20
    d. $1.40

3. Price is initially set above equilibrium. Market forces then move it towards equilibrium. As price falls, what will happen to demand and supply?

	Demand	*Supply*
a.	contracts	contracts
b.	contracts	extends
c.	extends	extends
d.	extends	contracts

4. Which of the following is likely to cause the price of the lamb to decrease?
    a. A decrease in the number of sheep farmers
    b. An increase in the price of beef
    c. A subsidy given to sheep farmers
    d. A successful advertising campaign for lamb

5. What effect is an increase in advertising expenditure likely to have, on the demand and supply curves of a product in the short term?

	Demand	Supply
a.	decreases	decreases
b.	decreases	increases
c.	increases	increases
d.	increases	decreases

6. The table shows the demand and supply of a book published by a Japanese firm.

Price per book ($)	Quantity demanded per week	Quantity supplied per week
a. 10	5 000	2 000
b. 15	4 000	3 000
c. 20	3 000	4 000
d. 25	2 000	5 000

When the price rises from $10 to $15 per book, what is the price elasticity of demand for the book?
a. −0.4
b. −0.8
c. −1.0
d. −2.5

7. What could make demand for a product become more elastic?
a. A fall in its price
b. A fall in the proportion of income spent on the product
c. A decrease in the time period under consideration
d. An increase in the number of close substitutes

8. What is meant by inelastic supply?
a. When a fall in price causes a greater percentage fall in supply
b. When a fall in price causes a smaller percentage fall in supply
c. When a rise in price causes a fall in supply
d. When a rise in price causes no change in supply

9. Which profit making enterprise will not harm the environment?
a. Intensive farming using chemical fertilisers
b. Recycling waste paper into newspapers

c. Steel manufacturing, which generates the emission of carbon dioxide

d. Deforestation in tropical rainforests to obtain timber for furniture production

10. Which government measure is designed to increase external benefits?
    a. A decision to reduce spending on education
    b. A subsidy given to bus companies
    c. A reduction in the tax on alcohol
    d. The removal of fines on companies that pollute

Structured Questions

1. In Japan persistent worries about job security, high unemployment and a steady fall in income have caused a reduction in the consumer expenditure. This has lead to a decrease in prices of some products.
   a. Explain how the price of a good is determined by market forces. (4)
   b. Use demand and supply analysis and diagrams to explain how the reasons given in the above extract could cause a fall in the price of a product. (6)

   (Cambridge 0455 Paper 2 Q2a and b May/June 2002)

2. a. Explain the difference between an equilibrium price and a disequilibrium price. (4)
   b. Many more people travel by aeroplane today than ten years ago. With the help of a demand and supply diagram, explain what might have happened in the market for air travel to cause this increase. (6)
   c. Define price elasticity of demand and suggest why different goods have different price elasticities. (5)
   d. Discuss whether knowledge of price elasticity of demand is of use to a company selling holiday tours. (5)

   (Cambridge 0455 Paper 2 Q2 Oct/Nov 2007)

3. In the UK, the Royal Society for the Protection of Birds (RSPB) has recently bought land around the coast to prevent construction on the breeding area for rare birds. It has received donations from the public towards the cost. The RSPB plans to set up special visitor centres in the area.
   a. Explain what factors of production are involved in the above action by the RSPB. (4)
   b. Discuss whether the local area might be more likely to gain/lose from the action of the RSPB. (6)
   c. Define the following terms and identify an example of each in the above passage:
      (i) private cost
      (ii) social benefit. (4)
   d. The RSPB is a private charity. Do you think the protection of rare birds should be the responsibility of a government, rather than private charities? (6)

   (Cambridge 0455 Paper 2 Q3 Oct/Nov 2003)

The Individual as Producer, Consumer and Borrower

UNIT 14

Specialisation, Exchange and Money

Countries, firms and workers may choose to specialise. Such specialisation means that they will have to exchange some of what they produce with other products they make. Money makes such exchange easier. This unit examines the effects of specialisation and explores the importance of trade and money in encouraging specialisation.

The Meaning of Specialisation

Specialisation means the concentration on particular products or tasks. Instead of making a wide range of products, a firm may specialise in manufacture of one or a few products. A doctor may concentrate on treating patients with heart problems rather than on treatment of patients suffering from a number of illnesses.

Key Point

Specialisation: the concentration on particular products or tasks.

Specialisation of Countries

What countries are good at producing is influenced by the quantity and quality of their resources. For instance, a country with a good climate, good beaches and a good supply of labour may decide to concentrate on tourism.

If countries specialise in what they are best at producing, the output should be higher and hence their citizens should enjoy higher living standards. Producing a relatively narrow range of products will mean that countries will have to export some of their output. This is necessary for them to gain revenue for spending on imports of products that their citizens want to buy but their countries are not producing.

Countries should benefit from specialisation and trade, but there are risks involved. Concentrating on a few products is fine if demand for these products remain high and costs of production do not rise. If, however, demand suddenly falls or costs rise, the countries can run into difficulties. Producing a wider range of products spreads risks.

Activity 1

Clothing is a major industry in Bangladesh and, in 2012, it accounted for 69% of its exports. Nearly a third of its exports go to USA. Clothing is also an important industry in Turkey but accounts for only 19% of its exports.

a. On the basis of information provided, decide which country is more specialised.

b. Identify the other piece of information that could help you decide the answer to (a).

Specialisation of Firms

Firms that specialise in a narrow range of products can get to know their markets well and build up a reputation. It is also easier to control a firm that makes only a few products. The nature of resources available to producers may influence their decision on what to specialise in. For instance, in very hilly conditions, the only possibility open to a farmer may be keeping goats or sheep. Location and the demand in that location, also play a role in firms' decisions. A food shop in a rich area will be more likely to stock expensive items than the one in a poor area.

Some firms, however, choose not to specialise. They diversify to spread their risks across a number of products. If demand for one product is falling, it is likely that demand for at least one of its other products will be rising.

Specialisation of Workers

This is also referred to as **division of labour**. Instead of producing the whole good or service, a worker carries out one particular task. The key advantage claimed for specialisation of workers is lower cost per unit produced.

There are a number of reasons why this may occur. One is that workers can specialise on the task they are best at and by doing this task over and over again, they become very good at it – *practice makes perfect*. This should mean that output per worker increases.

Concentrating on a particular task means that workers can be trained more quickly and knowledge about handling a full range of equipment may not necessarily be imparted to them. Time may be saved as workers will not have to move from one job to another and breaking down the production process into a number of tasks may also make it easier to design machinery, enabling the use of workers alongside.

There is no guarantee, however, that specialisation of workers will reduce unit costs. In fact, there is a risk that specialisation may result in higher unit costs. Workers may get bored doing the same task each day. This may lead to workers not taking care of their work and as a result making more mistakes. Boredom may also result in workers taking more days off due to sickness and staying in jobs for shorter periods of time. Having specialised staff may make it difficult for other workers to cover up for those absent, due to both sickness and training.

Key Point

Division of labour: workers specialising in particular tasks.

Rank the following educational workers, starting with the most specialised and finishing with the least specialised:
a.   a teacher of nineteenth century French history
b.   a supply teacher who covers for absent teachers
c.   a teacher of nineteenth century history
d.   a teacher of history
e.   a teacher of history and geography.

Specialisation and the Individual

Individuals can be affected by specialisation in their roles as entrepreneurs, workers and consumers.

An entrepreneur starting a new firm may find it easier to concentrate on manufacture of one or two products. If the firm is successful and grows, additional staff can be employed with expertise in different areas and a greater range of products can be produced.

Workers who are specialised can become very skilled and, if their skills are in high demand, can earn high wages. Concentrating on a particular task or job can enable workers to pursue their specific interests. For instance, doctors who are interested in brain disorders and injuries may seek to specialise in neuroscience. Specialising in less demanding jobs can reduce the pressure on workers. Some factory workers who have undertaken the same task for some years may be able to do it, almost without thinking.

There are, however, possible disadvantages to workers being specialised. One is that demand for their services may fall and if they are trained or practised in only one job, they may encounter problems getting another job. For instance, if demand for coal falls, coal miners may not find it easy to gain jobs if the jobs on offer require different skills. Also, as previously mentioned, concentrating on a particular task or job may be boring and may not make full use of a worker's talents.

Consumers can receive a number of benefits from specialisation, including lower prices and better quality. There is a risk, however, that consumers may lose out in terms of variety. For example, a builder may concentrate on building flats of the same design and a car firm may make only a narrow range of models.

The Extent of Specialisation

The key influence on the extent to which countries, firms and workers specialise is the size of the market. If a firm is selling in a large market, the size of its output will be large and it will probably be employing a higher number of workers. In this case, its workers can specialise. For instance, in a large building firm, one worker may concentrate on wiring, one on plumbing, one on brick laying and so on. In contrast, in a small building firm employing two workers, each of the workers will have to carry out a number of tasks.

Good transport links increase the size of the market. Being able to sell to different parts of the country or more number of countries, increases the number of potential consumers. This, in turn, is likely to increase the size of firms and the number of workers employed by them.

Money also facilitates specialisation. This is because when workers and firms specialise, trade becomes imperative. Some of the products produced have to be exchanged for other products. For example, if I concentrate on writing books I will have to sell the books for money and use the money I earn to buy food, clothes, housing and other items.

The Functions of Money

Money allows people to buy and sell products. In carrying out this function, money is said to act as a *medium of exchange*. Products are exchanged for money and that money is used to buy other products.

Products $\longrightarrow$ Money $\longrightarrow$ Products

Enabling people to exchange products is money's most important function. It has three other functions which are – to act as a store of value, a unit of account and a standard for deferred payments. Acting as a store of value means that money can be saved. It would be silly to save eggs, for example, as eggs go bad over time and hence no one will be prepared to accept them a few weeks after they have been laid. Money, however, does not deteriorate with time and hence will be acceptable in the future.

Money can also be used to place a value on an item. Prices are expressed in monetary terms. A newspaper may be priced at $2 and a book at $30. This function of acting as a unit of account, or measure of value (as it is sometimes called), enables buyers and sellers to agree on what items are worth, relative to each other. In the example above, one book is worth fifteen newspapers. With $60 to spend, a person can either buy two books or thirty newspapers.

The fourth function of money is to act as a standard for deferred payments. This means that money allows people to borrow and lend. Someone who wants to buy something now can get it by borrowing money from someone who does not want to use it now. They can strike an agreement about the amount to be repaid in the future.

 # Types of Money

The main forms of money used in most countries are **coins, notes** and **bank accounts**. Coins are often used to make small purchases and are given in change. Notes are used to buy more expensive items. It is interesting to note, however, that in most countries the main form of money is bank accounts. These account for the largest proportion (in terms of value) of payments made. There are a number of ways of transferring money from one bank account to another. These include *direct debits* and *cheques*.

Although bank accounts are the most important form of money, they are not legal tender whereas coins (up to a certain value) and bank notes are. Legal tender is any form of payment which, by law, has to be accepted in settlement of a debt. So a person has to accept bank notes in payment but they have the right to refuse, for instance, a cheque. In practice, however, most people and firms find payment from bank accounts convenient and hence are willing to accept it.

To act as money, an item does not need to have intrinsic value. This means that it does not have to be worth something in its own right. For instance, both silver and bank notes can act as money but whereas silver is wanted for a variety of purposes, bank notes have no intrinsic value. An item does have to possess a number of characteristics for it to serve as money. The most important one is that it should be generally acceptable. If people are not prepared to accept the item as payment, it will not be able to carry out the functions of money. To achieve generally acceptability, the item has to be in limited supply. Why, for instance, should people accept twigs as payment in a country with many trees?

The other characteristics an item needs are – that it is durable (will last some time), portable (can be carried around easily), divisible (can be divided into units of different values), homogeneous (every note or coin of the same value should be exactly the same) and recognisable (people can easily see that the item is money).

Key Point

Money: an item which is generally acceptable as a means of payment.

Activity 3

Discuss how many characteristics of money, each of the following items possesses.

a. Leaves
b. Sea shells
c. Gold

 **Summary**

- Countries, firms and workers can specialise.

- Countries and firms that specialise can increase their output but they face the risk that demand or costs may suddenly change.

- Division of labour can reduce cost per unit produced, as workers can concentrate on what they are best at, training costs are reduced, money spent on equipment is decreased, workers' time can be saved and the production process can be mechanised.

- Firms may experience certain disadvantages due to specialisation of their workers. One is that workers may get bored due to the monotonous nature of their job and as a result make more mistakes, take time off work and possibly even resign. Another is that firms may find it difficult to cover for the workers who are off sick or under training.

- The extent to which firms and countries can specialise depends on the size of the market.

- Specialisation creates the need to trade and money makes it easier to trade.

- The four functions of money are - medium of exchange, store of value, unit of account and standard for deferred payments.

- To act as money, an item has to be generally acceptable, limited in supply, durable, portable, homogeneous, divisible and recognisable.

 Teacher's Tip

Do not confuse the functions and characteristics of money. Remember the functions concern the transactions/operations that money helps to make possible whereas the characteristics are the features which an item needs to possess to act as money.

Multiple Choice Questions

1. What is the term used to describe workers, specialising in particular tasks?
   a. Division of labour
   b. Labour turnover
   c. Flexibility
   d. Rationalisation

2. What is a disadvantage of a firm specialising?
   a. Demand for its products may suddenly fall.
   b. It will have to buy more equipment.
   c. The productivity of its workers may rise.
   d. Training its workers may take longer.

3. Money enables people to save. Which function of money does this describe?
   a. Medium of exchange
   b. Store of value
   c. Unit of account
   d. Standard for deferred payments

4. What would make an item unsuitable to act as money?
   a. It is easy to carry.
   b. It is generally acceptable.
   c. It is perishable.
   d. It is recognisable.

Banks

Banks play an important role in economics. In this unit, the functions of both commercial banks and central banks are explained. Two other types of banks are briefly explored and the issue of independent banks is discussed.

 ## Banking

Banking is a major industry in a number of countries. It helps people to borrow and lend and carry out a range of other financial activities. By doing this, it enables more efficient use of resources and encourages the growth of output of economies.

 ## Commercial Banks

Commercial banks are also called **joint stock banks, retail** or **high street** banks. All four names tell us something about them. Commercial indicates that they are business organisations which seek to make a profit. Joint stock means that they have limited liability and are in the private sector. In most countries, the majority of banks are public limited companies but there is usually a number of private limited banks also. Retail suggests that they are selling the public something – in this case banking services. High street tells us that these banks are found in most of the towns and cities. They are the banks we are most familiar with.

Key Point

Commercial banks: private sector banks which aim to make a profit by providing a range of banking services.

The Main Functions of Commercial Banks

The three main and traditional functions of commercial banks are to accept deposits, to lend and to enable customers to make payments. The first function enables customers to keep their money in a safe place. Deposits can be made into two types of bank accounts. One is a **current account**, sometimes called a demand account. There is easy and immediate access to money in this type of account but usually interest is not paid on money held in such an account. Customers use current accounts mainly to receive and make payments. The other type of account is a **deposit** or **time account**. A period of notice usually has to be given before money can be withdrawn from this account. Interest is paid on any money held in a deposit account and customers use deposit accounts as a way of saving.

Banks make most of their profit by charging higher interest from borrowers than that paid on the money held with the banks. There are two main ways of borrowing from a bank. One is in the form of an *overdraft*. This enables a customer to spend more than what is in her or his account, up to an agreed limit. Interest is charged on the amount borrowed. This can be a relatively expensive way of borrowing and is mainly used to cover short term gaps between expenses and income. The other way of borrowing is by taking a *loan*. This is usually for a particular purpose and for a particular period of time. Interest is charged on the full amount of the loan but the rate of interest is likely to be lower than that on an overdraft. A customer may be asked to provide some form of security, known as *collateral*, when taking a loan. This is to ensure that if the loan is not repaid, the asset given as collateral can be sold and the money recovered. In practice, though, banks try to avoid doing this by checking very carefully whether the person seeking a loan will be able to repay it. In the case of a firm, this is likely to involve a scrutiny of the firm's accounts and business plan.

The first two functions of banks, effectively borrowing from their customers and lending to them, means that they act as financial intermediaries. They accept deposits from those with more money than they currently want to spend and lend it to those with an immediate desire to spend more money than they have at hand. In other words, they channel money from lenders to borrowers.

Lenders ⟶ Banks ⟶ Borrowers

The third main function that banks carry out is to enable their customers receive and make payments. This is referred to as acting as agents for payments and providing money transmission services. There is now a range of ways in which people can receive money and make payments out of their accounts. These include cheques, standing orders, direct debits, debit/credit cards and online banking.

Other Functions of Commercial Banks

Over a period of time, commercial banks have built up a range of other services that they offer their customers. Most commercial banks now provide travellers cheques and change foreign currency. Customers can leave important documents, such as house deeds and small valuables with their banks and the banks are also likely to be willing to help with the administration of customers' wills. They can provide advice and help with a number of financial matters, such as completion of tax forms and the purchase and sale of shares. Many banks also now sell insurance and offer a wide variety of savings accounts, with a range of conditions and interest rates. Some now offer mortgage loans, which are loans to buy houses.

Activity 1

In 2005, the biggest commercial bank in Brazil, *Banco Bradesco*, made a record profit of $5.5 billion reais. It was criticised, however, for charging a very high rate of interest on its loans. The average monthly interest rate on an overdraft at the bank was 8.19%, equivalent to a compound annual rate of 157% and 10.24% a month (or 222%) on a credit card.

a. What is an overdraft?

b. Discuss whether Banco Bradesco is likely to continue to earn high profits.

The Aims of Commercial Banks

The key aim of a commercial bank is to make a profit for its shareholders. The main way it does this, is by giving loans (which bankers often refer to as advances). Another aim which can conflict with the key aim is what is known as liquidity. Banks have to ensure that they can meet their customers' requests to withdraw money from their accounts. To do this, banks have to keep a certain amount of, what are called, *liquid assets*. These are items which can be turned into cash quickly and without incurring loss. Banks earn most of the interest by giving long term loans. However, if they tie up all their money in such loans, they would not be able to pay out cash to the customers requesting it. They have to balance profitability and liquidity – having some assets earning high interest but being illiquid and having others earning low or no interest but being liquid.

Banking and Islam

In a number of Muslim countries, commercial banks are not allowed to charge interest on bank loans. This is because many Muslims regard charging of interest, sometimes called usury, as a sin. Traditionally, Muslim banks have provided finance for firms by lending to them in return for a share in their profits. In recent years, more US and European commercial banks have sought to expand existing branches and open up new branches in Muslim countries in the Middle East and Asia. Most employ Islamic sharia scholars and experts who can issue religious edicts (fatwas) that approve financial products including loans. The US based bank *Citigroup*, for instance, has created an independent sharia advisory board of Islamic scholars to offer it advice and the German based bank,

Deutshe Bank, is a majority shareholder in the Dar Al Istithmar sharia consultancy, which launched the world's first dedicated training programme to create financially qualified Islamic scholars.

Other Banks

Two other types of banks are **investment banks** (sometimes called merchant banks) and **savings banks**. Merchant banks act as bankers, mainly to large firms. They accept deposits from them and lend to them. They manage the issue of new shares and buy and sell shares and other financial securities on behalf of their customers. They also give advice on, and help with, mergers and takeovers.

Savings banks are found across the world. As their name suggests, their aim is to encourage savings. They particularly try to encourage people with relatively low incomes to save. They make it easy to withdraw cash with few penalties. A large proportion of the money lent by savings banks goes to the government.

 Activity 2

India's largest private sector bank is ICICI Bank. In recent years, it has been expanding into other countries, including the UK. In 2012, it had branches or subsidiaries in twelve countries. These overseas concerns aim their services mainly at Indian communities. They are, however, attracting a high number of non-Indian customers. The main reason why they have been so successful is largely because they have often paid a higher interest rate on deposits than rival banks.

a. What function of a commercial bank is mentioned in the extract?
b. Explain one other function of a commercial bank.

 Central Banks

 A central bank is the single most important and influential bank in the country or, in the case of the European Union, the region. The three most well-known central banks in the world are probably the *Federal Reserve Bank of the USA* (often called the Fed), the *European Central Bank* (ECB) and the *Bank of England*. Central banks are owned by governments and are responsible to them.

Key Point

A central bank: a government owned bank which provides banking services to the government and commercial banks.

The Functions of a Central Bank

The functions of a central bank include:

- **Acts as a banker to the government.** Tax revenue is paid into the government's account at the central bank and payments by the government for goods and services are made out of this account.

- **Operates as a banker to the commercial banks.** Holding accounts at the central bank enables commercial banks to settle debts between each other and to draw out cash, if their own customers are taking more cash from their branches than usual.

- **Acts as a lender of last resort.** This means it will lend to banks which are temporarily short of cash.

- **Manages the national debt.** The national debt is the total amount the government owes. Over time, government debt tends to build up. The central bank carries out borrowing on behalf of the government by issuing government securities, for instance government bonds, pays interest on these and repays them when they fall due.

- **Holds the country's reserves of foreign currency and gold.** The central bank keeps foreign currency and gold to influence the exchange rate. (see Unit 50)

- **Issues bank notes.** The central bank is responsible for printing notes and destroying notes which are no longer suitable for circulation. It also authorises the minting of coins.

- **Implements the government's monetary policy** with the prime aim of keeping inflation low and steady. This involves controlling the money supply and influencing interest rates throughout the economy, by changing the interest rate it charges on its loans. The government may instruct the central bank to increase or decrease the money supply. In some cases, central banks implements interest rate changes decided by their respective governments. In other cases, central banks have been given the responsibility to set interest rates.

- **Controls the banking system.** Many central banks play a key role in regulating and supervising the banking system.

- **Represents the government** at meetings with other central banks and international organisations such as the World Bank and the International Monetary Fund.

Activity 3

The Reserve bank of India (RBI) is the central bank of India. It is based in Mumbai and has twenty two regional offices across India. One of its functions is to implement and monitor monetary policy. Another is to ensure that the country's commercial banks follow sound policies, including sensible lending policies.

a. Identify one way in which a central bank differs from a commercial bank.

b. What is the key feature of a sensible lending policy?

c. Explain one other function of a central bank.

Independence of Central Banks

A number of governments have given their central banks the authority to decide the rate of interest. The governments still decide the aims of their central banks and give them a target for inflation. The Bank of England, for instance, is instructed to use the rate of interest to achieve an inflation target of 2%. If it thinks that there is a danger that the price level will increase by more than 2%, it will raise the rate of interest whereas if it thinks it will fall below 2%, it will lower the rate of interest.

There are a number of advantages in allowing the central bank to decide the rate of interest for banking. Unlike a national government, a central bank is unlikely to be tempted to lower the rate of interest to win public support. Most central banks also have extensive knowledge of the banking system and the appropriate rate of interest to set.

 **Summary**

- The three main functions of commercial banks are – to accept deposits, lend and to enable their customers to make payments.

- Other functions of commercial banks include dealing in foreign currency, holding important documents and small valuables, helping with wills and tax, selling insurance and providing mortgage loans.

- Investment banks provide banking services to large firms including loans, issuing shares, providing advice and help with mergers and takeovers.

- Savings banks seek to encourage savings, particularly among those with low incomes.

- A central bank is owned by the government. Its functions include acting as the banker to the government and commercial banks, managing the national debt, holding reserves of foreign currency, acting as lender of last resort, issuing bank notes, controlling the money supply, implementing interest rate changes, supervising the banking system and meeting with other central banks and international organisations.

 Teacher's Tip

In answering a question on banking, check very carefully, the type of bank focussed in the question. It is a common mistake to confuse a commercial and a central bank.

Multiple Choice Questions

1. In which way do commercial banks earn profit?
    a. By charging more to lend money than they pay to borrow it
    b. By paying more to borrow money than they charge for lending it
    c. By minting coins
    d. By printing notes

2. Which type of bank is responsible for supervising a country's banking system?
    a. A central bank
    b. A commercial bank
    c. An investment bank
    d. A saving bank

3. What is a function of a central bank?
    a. Controlling the money supply
    b. Deciding on the amount of government expenditure
    c. Issuing shares
    d. Raising taxes

4. What is the main aim of a commercial bank?
    a. To act as banker to the government
    b. To issue bank notes
    c. To make a profit
    d. To manage the national debt

Stock Exchanges

Apart from raising finance by borrowing, public limited companies can sell shares to generate finance. These shares, also called *equities*, are traded on stock exchanges. Governments also raise finance by selling securities on stock exchanges. In this unit, the functions of stock exchanges will be examined, the relationships between share prices, dividends and yields will be explained, the reasons why shares are bought will be outlined, the factors influencing share prices will be examined and the ways of financing investment will be assessed. The role of profit will also be touched upon.

The Nature of Stock Exchanges

A stock exchange, also called a *bourse* in some countries, is an organisation which enables shares and other financial assets to be bought and sold. It is mainly a market for second hand shares and securities, that is existing shares and securities, although some newly issued shares are also traded on the stock exchange. Those who trade on stock exchanges are referred to as **stock brokers**.

It is only the shares of public limited companies which have been approved by the authorities of the stock exchanges, sometimes called the *Council*, which can be traded. These companies are referred to as **listed** or quoted companies.

Stock exchanges have a physical location. For instance, the Deutsche Bourse is in Frankfurt, India's main stock exchange is in Mumbai and the Tokyo Stock Exchange's, London Stock Exchange's and New York Stock Exchange's names indicate their location. These are the main stock exchanges in Germany, India, Japan, the UK and USA but most countries have a number of stock exchanges. For instance, India has 22 stock exchanges including the ones in Bangalore, Calcutta and Delhi. In the UK, there are stock exchanges in Birmingham, Liverpool and Manchester. These stock exchanges provide a physical location for trading but nowadays most business takes place via electronic networks.

Key Point

A stock exchange: an organisation for the sale and purchase of shares and other securities.

Functions of Stock Exchanges

Stock exchanges carry out a number of functions. These include:

- providing a market for the purchase and sale of shares in public limited companies and sale of bonds and other securities for the government and local authority. This helps both public limited companies and the national and local government authorities to raise finance, since buyers of shares and bonds know that the shares can be sold further, at a higher price.

- enabling companies to grow externally by merging or taking over another company. A merger occurs when the managers of two companies agree to form one new combined company. A takeoever involves the management of one company buying enough shares in another company to gain control of it. In practice, it can sometimes be difficult to distinguish between a merger and a takeover.

- mobilising savings for investment. Savings are channelled towards firms and governments which can use them to finance projects.

- influencing the use of savings. Demand for shares in successful companies is higher than for those in the firms, which are seen to be struggling. This makes it easier for successful firms to sell their shares and gain a high price for them. Consequently, this makes it easier for them to raise finance and expand.

- protecting those who buy shares. Any company which wants to be quoted on the stock exchange has to meet certain requirements such as publishing a range of information for prospective share buyers.

- providing an indication of economic performance. Share prices tend to rise when the economy is performing well and expected to continue to do well. Such conditions create what is called a **bullish market**. In contrast, a **bearish market** is one where share prices are falling.

General indices of share prices are also compiled. These are based on a number of representative shares. For instance, the FTSE 100 index (Financial Times/Stock Exchange 100 index) shows movements in the average share price of the UK's one hundred largest public limited companies.

 Key Points

A bull: someone who buys shares expecting their price to rise.

A bear: someone who sells shares expecting their price to fall.

Activity 1

The Cairo Stock Exchange has a modern trading floor, equipped with the latest technology. One of its main functions is to protect the buyers.
a. Identify one way in which stock exchanges protect shareholders.
b. Explain one other function of a stock exchange.

 # Dividends and Yields

A dividend is a share in the profit of a company that has been distributed to a shareholder. Dividends can be expressed as a percentage of the nominal price or the market price of a share. The *nominal price*, also called the face value, is the price at which the share was issued. This price is printed on the share certificate. In contrast, the *market price* is the current price of the share. A share may be issued for $10, for example, but if the company is doing very well its price may rise to $25.

If a company states that it is paying a 10% dividend, this means that it will pay out $1 on a share with a nominal value of $10. In this case, someone holding shares that had been issued for $200 in total, would receive extra $20.

Of greater concern to the shareholder, is the **yield**. This is the dividend expressed as a percentage of the market price and represents the return on the money paid for a share.

$$\text{Yield} = \frac{\text{Dividend per share}}{\text{Market share price}} \times 100$$

In the example above, the yield would be:

$$\frac{\$1}{\$25} \times 100 = 4\%$$

 # Reasons Why Shares Are Bought

There are four main reasons to account for the purchase of shares by people and firms. One is for the *dividend* paid. People and firms, including insurance companies, which want a steady income will buy shares in companies that pay out a good dividend regularly. Another reason is to make a *capital gain*. Some people and firms buy shares, speculating that their market price will rise. If this happens, they can sell their shares and make a profit. Of course, someone may hold a range of shares – some for the dividend they pay and some in the expectation that their price will rise.

A third reason for buying shares is to influence the running of a company. For instance, shareholders can put pressure on managers to follow more environmentally friendly policies. Shares are also bought by those intending to takeover a company.

Influences on Share Prices

Share prices are determined by demand and supply (see unit 5). Among the specific factors, that can influence share prices, are:

- **Interest rates**. A rise in interest rates is likely to reduce share prices. This is for two reasons, which are related to each other. One is that it increases the opportunity cost of holding shares – people may now earn more by placing their money in a deposit account in a bank than by holding shares. The other is that people may expect share prices and dividend payments to fall. Higher interest rates will encourage people to save more and borrow less. This means they will spend less. Lower expenditure is likely to reduce firms' revenue. Their costs may also rise, if they have borrowed in the past. Both effects will reduce firms' profits.

- **Profit record**. The profits earned and expected to be earned by firms directly influence share prices. A firm with high and/or rising profits is likely to see its share prices increase.

- **Government policy**. A cut in corporate taxes is likely to raise share prices as people will expect firms to be able to pay out larger dividends.

- **The issue of new shares**. When a firm issues new shares, it increases their supply usually resulting in a fall in their price.

- **Takeovers and rumours of takeovers**. Buying up shares to gain control of a firm will usually drive up their price as will thesuggestion, that a takeover is about to occur.

Activity 2

In May 2006, the UK based British Telecommunications (BT) announced a rise in profits and expressed confidence that it could deliver even higher profits in 2007. It attributed this success to an increase in revenue from broadband and from the sale of IT to big companies. The company also announced a 14% dividend.

a. Explain the meaning of a 14% dividend.
b. What would you expect to have happened to the price of BT shares in June 2006? Explain your answer.

Investment Finance

Firms wanting to buy capital goods in order to expand can borrow, use retained profits and, in the case of limited companies, they can issue shares. Selling shares, however, has two main disadvantages. One is that (as noted above) issuing more shares will tend to reduce their price. This is unlikely to be popular with existing shareholders. To overcome this problem, firms may give a portion of their new shares or sell them at a reduced rate to the existing shareholders. The other disadvantage is that in the case of a public limited company, it increases the risk of being taken over. Anyone can buy shares, including another rival company with ambitions to gain greater control over the market.

Borrowing from a bank involves a commitment to make regular interest payments, which may be difficult if a firm's revenue does not come in at regular intervals. It also runs the risk that the bank may seek to influence the firm's decisions, especially if it appears that the firm is experiencing difficulties.

These drawbacks to issuing of shares and borrowing (which can be referred to as external finance) help to explain why **retained profits** (internal finance) are the main source of investment finance. Another key reason for relying mostly on retained profits, is that firms are more likely to expand when they are making a profit. In fact, profit provides both the incentive and the finance to buy capital goods.

 **Activity 3**

In June 2005, the Chinese Bank of Communications issued new shares on the Hong Kong stock exchange. People rushed to buy these, some even borrowing from banks to get the necessary money. A year later the shares had risen in price by 98%.

a. Explain two reasons why people may have wanted to buy shares in the Chinese Bank of Communications.

b. What effect may a rise in share price have on the yield on shares?

 # The Role of Profit

In the private sector, profit is the driving force. As noted in Unit 2, it is the reward for risk bearing and organising the other factors of production. Public limited companies make profits in order to pay dividends to shareholders and to reward managers. Those firms which just break even or make a loss will find it difficult to sell any more shares, keep good managerial staff and ensure the happiness of existing shareholders. Discontented shareholders may seek to vote off the directors at an annual general meeting.

As discussed above, profit also provides finance for investment. Profit which is not distributed to shareholders but kept back for spending on capital goods, is referred to as retained profit.

Summary

- Shares and government bonds are bought and sold on stock exchanges.

- Stock exchanges allow public limited companies and governments to raise finance, enable companies to manage and takeover other companies, mobilise saving for investment, provide protection for those who buy shares and give an indication of economic performance.

- A dividend is often expressed as a percentage of the nominal price of a share whereas the yield is the dividend expressed as a percentage of the market price of the share.

- People and firms buy shares to earn interest, to make a capital gain, to influence the functioning of a company and to takeover companies.

- Share prices will fall if interest rates rise, firms' profits fall, the government raises corporate taxes and new shares are issued.

- The three main sources of investment finance are issuing shares, borrowing and using retained profits. The most popular source is retained profits.

- Profits reward entrepreneurial skills, provide payments for shareholders and funds for investment.

Teacher's Tip

In analysing the reasons for changes in share prices, it is important to use demand and supply analysis.

Multiple Choice Questions

1. In which type of business organisation are shares sold on the stock exchange?
   a. Sole proprietor
   b. Partnership
   c. Private limited company
   d. Public limited company

2. Which of the following is a function of a stock exchange?
   a. To accept deposits of cash
   b. To help raise finance for public limited companies and the government
   c. To supervise the banking sector
   d. To enable companies to exchange unsold stocks of consumer goods

3. What is a dividend?
   a. The difference between the issue and the sale price of a government bond
   b. The difference between the nominal price and the market price of a share
   c. A payment of interest on a government bond
   d. A payment to shareholders out of profit

4. Under which circumstance, is the price of a share in a public limited company most likely to fall?
   a. An announcement of record profits
   b. A fall in the rate of interest
   c. A report that a takeover of the company is about to occur
   d. A rise in corporate taxes

Choice of Occupation

The previous section was concerned with demand and supply and price determination. The next three units of this section focus on the demand and supply of labour and wage determination. This unit looks at the factors that affect an individual's choice of occupation.

 Key Factors

There is a wide range of factors that influence the choice of jobs. These can be divided into wage factors (also called monetary or pecuniary factors), non-wage factors (also referred to as non-monetary or nonpecuniary) and limiting factors.

Wage Factors

An important influence on what jobs a person decides to do, is the pay on offer. The total pay a person receives is known as his **earnings**. In addition to the basic wage, earnings may also include overtime pay, bonuses and commission.

Key Point

Earnings: the total pay received by a worker.

Wages

Generally the higher the wage rate on offer, the more attractive the job. For instance, a person would expect to be paid more as a doctor than as a cleaner.

Some economists distinguish between a salary and a wage. They define a **salary** as a payment made on a monthly basis, calculated on the basis of a fixed annual rate, irrespective of the number of hours actually worked. In contrast, they consider a **wage** to be a payment made weekly, based on the number of hours worked in a week. Nowadays, however, the distinction has become somewhat blurred and sometimes both terms are used to describe the standard payment for a worker's labour.

Pay of many workers is based on a standard number of hours. Some workers pay, however, varies according to number of hours for which they work (a time rate system) or the amount they produce (a piece rate system). The former benefits the employers as they can easily estimate their labour costs and also the workers as they can bargain collectively about the rate paid. However, a time rate system does not reward hard work by paying lazy and industrious workers the same.

This problem is overcome by a piece rate system, which pays workers according to their output. This system can only be used, if a worker's output can be easily measured and the product is standardised. This is why, though it is sometimes found in the primary and manufacturing sectors, it is very uncommon in the services sector. For instance, it could not be applied to doctors. One doctor may carry out three operations while another may perform eight operations in a day. The three operations, however, might have been more complex operations. Less supervision may be needed with a piece rate system but workers may focus on quantity at the expense of quality. Also the health of some workers' may suffer, if they feel pressurised to produce a high output.

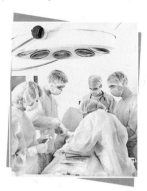

Key Point

Wage rate: a payment which an employer contracts to pay a worker.

Overtime Pay

Overtime pay may be paid to the workers who work in excess of the standard working week. It is usually paid at a higher rate.

Overtime can benefit both employees and employers. Workers with young families, for instance, are often anxious to increase their pay and may be attracted by jobs that offer regular overtime. It enables employers to respond to higher demand without taking on new workers, until they are sure that the higher demand will last. It is easier, less costly and less disruptive to reduce overtime than to sack workers if demand declines.

There is a risk, however, that workers may become tired as a result of working for longer hours. If this does occur, the output they produce over the day may not increase and even its quality may fall. In fact, some employers have found that when workers are aware that they are going to be working for longer hours, they pace themselves accordingly and put less effort into each hour.

Bonuses

A bonus is an extra payment. It can be paid to workers who produce above a standard amount, finish a project ahead of time, secure a profitable contract or contribute to higher profits in some other way. Bonuses can provide an incentive for workers to produce both a high and a good quality output and to stay with a firm. However, care has to be exercised while awarding them. Resentment may be caused if it is thought that they are awarded unfairly. This resentment can lead to those workers, who do not receive a bonus, becoming demotivated. As a result, the quantity or quality of their output may fall and some workers may resign.

Those people who welcome a challenge and have confidence in their own ability may be attracted to the jobs which pay bonuses. In recent years, there have been instances when very large bonuses have been paid to some workers in the financial sector, particularly in merchant banking.

Commission

Commission is often paid to the sales people. It involves them receiving a proportion of the value of the sales they make. Sometimes, this is in addition to a standard wage and sometimes it makes up their total payment.

 **Activity 1**

> Chinese airlines are carrying more and more passengers. The country's aviation industry is expanding more rapidly than the rate at which pilots can be trained. As a result, it is seeking to recruit foreign pilots. In 2005, China paid its pilots $5 000 a month which was only three quarters of the average pilot's pay in India and a third of the amount paid, on average, in the UK.
>
> a. How much were pilots paid, on average, in India and the UK in 2005?
> b. Explain what would be expected to happen to pilots' pay in China.

Non-wage Factors

People do not always choose the highest paid job on offer. They take into account a range of other factors including job satisfaction, type of work, working conditions, holidays, pensions, fringe benefits, job security, career prospects, size of firm and location.

Job Satisfaction

Nursing and teaching are not particularly well paid occupations and a number of those undertaking them can earn more in other occupations. These jobs, however, can provide a high degree of job satisfaction. Nurses and teachers can derive considerable satisfaction from improving people's health and educating students.

Of course, some jobs provide both high pay and a high level of job satisfaction. Brain surgeons, TV presenters and top football players all have interesting, challenging and well paid jobs.

Type of Work

Most people would rather do non-manual than manual work. This is because it is physically less tiring and generally offers more mental stimulation. Non-manual work also tends to be better paid. People also like to do jobs which enjoy a high status and most of these tend to be non-manual. For example, university professors tend to be held in higher regard than masons. Some people are prepared to undertake dangerous work including deep sea diving and bomb disposal but most people prefer to work in a safe environment.

Working Conditions

Working conditions are an important determining factor. People like to work in pleasant surroundings, with friendly colleagues and enjoying regular breaks.

Working Hours

Occupations vary in terms of the number of hours expected from workers and the timing of those hours. Managers and senior officials tend to work for longer hours than shopkeepers.

Some occupations offer workers, the opportunity to work part-time, say 16 hours a week. A number of them also offer flexible working hours, where workers alter the hours they work from week to week. This is sometimes to suit the employer, with workers working longer hours when demand for the product is high, and sometimes to suit the worker. An example of the latter case is parents engaging in term-time working.

Nurses, emergency plumbers and catering staff often work in unsociable hours i.e. they often have to work at nights and in the evenings when other people are resting or enjoying themselves. Some nurses and other workers, including factory workers, work in shifts. This involves working at different periods of the day and night. There may be day and night shifts or three eight hour shifts during the day.

Holidays

In a number of countries, the law sets down a minimum length of holiday entitlement for full time workers. Even in these countries, however, the length of holidays varies. Teaching is one occupation, well known for the length of holidays on offer. In fact, one reason for people preferring to go for teaching is the benefit of long holidays. Having time off when children are on holiday is an advantage for parents.

Pensions

With people living longer in most countries, occupational pensions are becoming an important influence. There is considerable variation in the provision of occupational pensions. Some jobs provide their workers with generous pensions whilst others do not provide any financial help post retirement. In many countries, for instance, the police can retire relatively early on good pensions whereas casual agricultural workers are unlikely to receive a pension. Generally, workers in the public (state) sector receive more generous pensions than those in the private sector.

Fringe Benefits

Fringe benefits are the extra benefits provided to workers by their employers. These may include free or subsidised meals, health schemes and social and leisure facilities. Playing for a major football club, such as Real Madrid or Manchester United, will bring a wide range of fringe benefits. The club may, for instance, buy a player a house, arrange insurance for him and get his car repaired.

Job Security

Many workers are attracted by occupations which offer a relatively high degree of job security. A high degree of job security means that workers are unlikely to be made redundant. Such a situation is more likely to occur in occupations, where there is a high demand for the product and workers are given long term contracts. High demand for the product would mean that employers would not want to get rid of the workers and a contract would restrict their ability to do so. Civil servants often have a high degree of job security but casual workers, including agricultural and building workers, have little job security and can be sacked at short notice.

Career Prospects

People are often prepared to accept low wages at the start of their careers, if they think that there is a good possibility that they will gain promotion to a well paid and interesting post. Trainee accountants, barristers and doctors are not usually highly paid and often work for long hours at the beginning of their careers. They will expect, however, that as they pass examinations and gain experience, their pay will rise to a relatively high level and their work will become more challenging.

Size of the Firms

People are often attracted to occupations in large firms and organisations. This is because such firms and organisations often pay more and offer better career prospects, job security and fringe benefits than smaller ones. For instance, a number of people are attracted to work for the country's civil service for such reasons.

On the other hand, some people prefer to work for smaller firms. This is because they believe that the atmosphere will be more friendly than that in a large firm. Studies have found that labour relations are indeed better in small factories and offices.

Location

People may choose an occupation, which they can undertake close to their home. This will mean that they do not have to spend much money or time for travelling to and from work.

 **Activity 2**

In 2005, in the UK the four most popular occupations for new graduates were accountancy, the civil service, public sector health care (the National Health Service NHS) and public sector broadcasting (BBC). A record number of graduates applied for the NHS's schemes in management, finance and human resources. It is thought that they were attracted mainly by the good career opportunities provided by the country's largest employer.

a. How many of the top four occupations for new graduates in UK are in the public sector?

b. Apart from good career opportunities, explain two possible reasons for a graduate to opt for a job in public sector health care.

Limiting Factors

Most people would obviously like a well paid, satisfying job with good working conditions, long holidays, generous fringe benefits, good career prospects and a convenient location. In practice, however, people's choice of occupation is limited by a number of factors including the qualifications they have, the skills they possess, the experience they have and the place where they live.

The more occupationally mobile and the more geographically mobile people are, the wider the choice of occupation available to them.

Occupational Choice and Opportunity Cost

Choosing to take up one occupation involves rejecting other occupations. Workers have to decide what is important to them. A worker may be prepared to give up a well paid job or the opportunity to undertake such as job, in favour of a less well paid job that offers more job satisfaction. For example, a merchant banker may resign to take up a job as a teacher.

 **Activity 3**

    a.   Identify three reasons why a person may want to be a pilot.

    b.   Explain three reasons why a person, despite wanting to be a pilot, may not succeed in becoming a pilot.

 **Summary**

- A person's choice of occupation is influenced by both wage and non-wage factors.

- High wages tend to attract more workers.

- Some workers may receive earnings above the basic wage or salary rate because of overtime pay, a bonus or commission.

- People are likely to be attracted to occupations which offer high job satisfaction, good working conditions, short working hours, long holidays, generous pensions, good fringe benefits, job security, good career prospects and a convenient location.

 Teacher's Tip

Remember if you are asked a question about *non-wage factors* influencing a person's choice of occupation it is NOT relevant to include a discussion on wages, overtime, pay, bonuses or commission.

Multiple Choice Questions

1. What is a non-wage factor that may influence a person's choice of occupation?
   a. Bonuses
   b. Fringe benefits
   c. Overtime payments
   d. Salary

2. Piece rates are a method of payment to workers based on:
   a. How many hours they work
   b. When they work
   c. The output they produce
   d. The output they sell

3. What would increase a woman's choice of occupation?
   a. An increase in her qualifications
   b. An increase in transport costs
   c. An increase in gender discrimination
   d. An increase in housing costs

4. Which of the following would encourage someone to take up an occupation?
   a. An absence of fringe benefits
   b. Job security
   c. Long hours
   d. Short holidays

Differences in Earnings

In the previous unit it was mentioned that doctors are paid more than cleaners. This unit examines why some group of workers are paid more than others.

 ## Wage Determination

The key factors that determine the amount of pay received by workers are the demand for and supply of their labour. Other influencing factors include the relative bargaining power of employers and workers, government policies, public opinion and discrimination.

Demand and Supply

The higher the demand for and the lower the supply of workers in an occupation, the higher the pay is likely to be. Fig. 1 shows the markets for doctors and for cleaners.

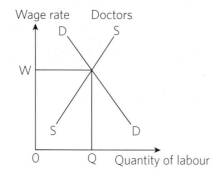 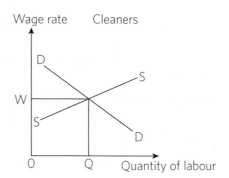

Fig. 1 The market for doctors and cleaners

The supply of doctors is low, relative to demand for their services. There is only a limited number of people with requisite qualifications and the willingness and ability to undertake a long period of challenging training to become doctors.

It might also be expected that the supply of cleaners would be low and their pay high, as few people would want to work as cleaners. Cleaning is not a particularly interesting job as it can involve unsociable hours, not very pleasant working conditions and does not usually offer good career prospects. The supply of cleaners, nevertheless, is often high relative to their demand. This is because although some people may not be keen to work as cleaners, they do so because the job does not require any qualifications or special skills and only a minimum amount of training is sufficient. This often results in the supply of cleaners being high relative to their demand.

Unskilled workers are generally paid less than skilled workers. Demand for skilled workers is high whilst their supply is low. There are two main influences on the demand for workers. One is the amount of output they can produce and the other is the price, for which that output can be sold for. Skilled workers are usually highly productive, producing both a high quantity and a high quality of output per hour. Also, the supply of skilled workers is usually lower than that of unskilled workers.

Supply also explains why some workers, who are involved in dangerous jobs, are well paid. There is a limited supply of people who are willing to work as steeplejacks. To try to overcome this reluctance a number of employers pay workers undertaking this job, a higher rate than that paid to other building workers.

The supply of workers in the agricultural and manufacturing sectors vary. In a number of countries, including some Asian and African countries, there is a surplus of agricultural workers which results in lower agricultural wages. The demand for and price of products made by manufacturing industries tend to increase at a more rapid rate than those made by primary sector industries. This helps to keep the  demand for manufacturing workers high, relative to agricultural sector workers.

Demand and supply of workers in the private and public sectors vary amongst countries. In some countries the public sector is expanding whilst in others it is contracting. A number of people like working in the public sector because of greater job security, longer holidays and better pensions than those offered in the private sector.

Activity 1

Under which circumstance is an occupation likely to be well paid?
a.   Demand is high/low.
b.   Supply is high/low.
c.   Workers have strong/weak bargaining power.
d.   Workers are skilled/unskilled.

Relative Bargaining Power of Employers and Workers

Wages are likely to be higher in occupations where workers have strong bargaining power relative to employers. This is more likely to be the case if most of the workers are members of a **trade union** or professional organisation which can bargain collectively on their behalf. (See unit 20)

Most doctors and lawyers, for instance, belong to their professional organisation which represents their interests. This bargaining position is strengthened by the knowledge that they would be difficult to replace with other workers and any industrial action taken by them would have serious consequences. In contrast, most cleaners and waiters do not belong to a workers' organisation. Their bargaining strength is further reduced by the fact that they are usually widely dispersed and hence are not organised as a strong union. Also, they can be replaced by other workers relatively easily.

Public sector workers in many countries, including the UK and India, are more likely to belong to a trade union or professional organisation than private sector workers. In some cases, this can be attributed to the fact that the governments are more willing to negotiate with trade unions than private sector employers. In other cases, it is because public sector workers find it easier to get together to operate as one bargaining body.

Public sector workers also tend to be affected by government labour market policies more than their counterparts in private sector. These policies may or may not raise wages. A government is, for instance, likely to ensure that all its workers are paid at or above a national minimum wage (see next section) whereas some private sector firms may seek to find ways round such legislation. If, however, a government introduces a policy to hold down wage rises in a bid to reduce inflationary pressure, it is in a stronger position to restrict the wage rises of its own workers.

Government Policies

Government policies affect wages in a variety of ways. A government clearly influences the wages of those workers, whom it employs in the public sector. Its policies also influence wages in the private sector. Those policies, which promote economic growth, tend to push up wages throughout the economy as they increase demand for labour.

Specific government policies may have an impact on particular occupations. For example, if a government introduced a law requiring car drivers to take a test every ten years – demand for driving instructors is likely to rise, pushing up their wages.

Government labour market policies, of course, directly affect wages. One of the best known labour market policies is a **national minimum wage** (NMW). Such a policy imposes a wage floor, making it illegal to pay a wage rate below that. The aims behind a NMW are to raise the pay of low-paid workers and reduce poverty.

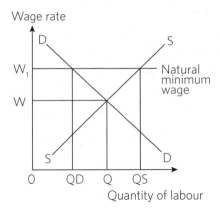

Fig. 2 A national minimum wage causing unemployment

To have any impact on wages, however, a NMW must be set above the market equilibrium wage rate. This has led some economists and politicians to argue that it may cause unemployment.

Fig. 2 shows a NMW raising the wage rate from W to W1 but causing unemployment since the supply of people wanting to work at this wage rate exceeds demand for workers' labour.

Other economists argue that a NMW can raise both the wage rate and employment. They think that paying a higher wage to workers will raise their motivation and hence their productivity. This, combined with higher demand for products arising from higher wages, can increase demand for labour. Fig. 3 shows that if demand for labour does increase, the equilibrium wage rate may the equal to NMW.

The introduction of a NMW may provoke some workers, who were previously being paid a wage at or just above that level, to press for a wage rise to maintain their wage differential.

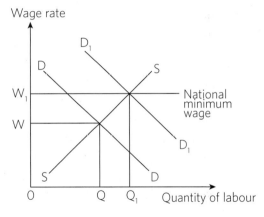

Fig. 3 A national minimum wage with rising employment

Key Points

National minimum wage: A minimum rate of wage for an hour's work, fixed by the government for the whole economy.

Wage differential: The difference in wages.

Public Opinion

Public opinion tends to consider that jobs which involve long periods of study and training should be highly rewarded. There are variations in how some occupations are regarded in different countries. For example, engineers are more highly regarded in Scandinavian countries than they are in the UK. A number of occupations are generally held in high esteem, like doctors and nurses.

Public opinion can influence wage rates in a number of ways. One is through the wage claims made by the workers. For instance, firefighters tend to regard their labour as being worth as much as that undertaken by the police. So if the police get a pay rise, firefighters are likely to seek an equivalent pay rise.

In most countries there is usually a league table of wage rates, with workers trying to maintain their position in the table and challenging it only occasionally. So, for example, a hotel porter is unlikely to expect to be paid as much as a veterinary doctor.

Public opinion can put pressure on a government to revise the wages it pays to the public sector workers. The public may, for instance, believe that nurses should be more highly rewarded. A government seeking to gain or maintain popular support, may feel compelled to raise nurses' pay.

There are a relatively high number of women working in the nursing profession. In some countries social attitudes are against working women. In these countries, it is harder for women to find employment and they may be receiving significantly less pay than their male counterparts.

Activity 2

Factory workers in the garment industry in Mauritius are among the lowest paid in the country, earning less than the workers in mining, transport and construction industries. Most work on 'piece rates' and are paid a productivity bonus if they exceed their production targets. As their pay is so low, they are heavily dependent on both bonuses and overtime. These extra payments take their earnings above the national minimum wage.

a. Define:
    (i)   piece rates
    (ii) national minimum wage.

b. Explain three possible reasons why factory workers in the garment industry may receive lower pay than construction workers.

Discrimination

Discrimination occurs when a group of workers is treated unfavourably in terms of employment, the wage rate, the training received and/or promotional opportunities. For example, some employers may be reluctant to have female workers. The lower demand will result in lower pay, as shown in Fig. 4.

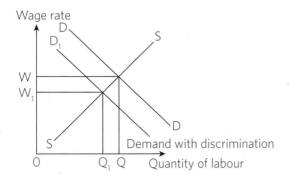

Fig. 4 The effect of discrimination

Increasingly, governments are making such discrimination illegal. Nevertheless, throughout the world, women are (on average) still paid less than men.

One reason for this is that women tend to work for fewer hours than men. Even when hourly wage rates are considered, however, women still get paid less than men.

There are a number of reasons for this:

- women tend to be less well qualified than men

- they tend to be more heavily concentrated in low paid occupations

- they are less likely to belong to trade unions and professional organisations

- they are still discriminated against.

Activity 3

In 2011, female workers in Chile earned 10% less than male workers. A smaller proportion of women are working in Chile, as compared to any other Latin American country. To encourage more women to enter the labour force and to generate greater wage equality, the Chilean government introduced a new labour code for the public sector. This forbids pregnancy tests, removes the need for mention of a candidate's gender from job applications and requires training during normal working hours. The government is encouraging the private sector to adopt the code as well.

a. Identify two possible reasons for a smaller proportion of working women in Chile than in other Latin American countries.

b. What evidence is there in the extract that suggests about female workers being discriminated against in Chile?

Summary

- The main reasons for some occupations receiving higher earnings than others is because demand for their labour is higher whilst supply of their labour is lower.

- Demand for workers is likely to be high, if they are productive and the price, for which their output can be sold, is high.

- The supply of labour can be limited by the need for high qualifications, long periods of training and special skills.

- Other reasons for higher earnings include workers having strong bargaining power, favourable government policies, workers being held in high public esteem and absence of discrimination.

- A national minimum wage is likely to raise the wages of the low paid but its effect on unemployment are uncertain.

- Skilled workers are paid more than unskilled workers because they are more productive and are in shorter supply.

Teacher's Tip

It is crucial that you apply demand and supply analysis for analysing the differences in earnings between different occupations.

Multiple Choice Questions

1. What might explain payment of low wages in a particular occupation?
    a. A strong trade union
    b. A low price paid for the products produced
    c. A limited supply of labour
    d. Short holidays

2. Which worker is likely to receive the lowest earnings?
    a. A chief executive
    b. A dentist
    c. An IT specialist
    d. A street cleaner

3. What could explain why some entertainers earn high wages?
    a. Some enjoy the job more than others.
    b. There is a high demand for their skills.
    c. There is a high number of people wanting to be entertainers.
    d. There is not much training required to be an entertainer.

4. Why are bus drivers paid less than pilots?
    a. They are less qualified.
    b. They work for longer hours.
    c. Their training takes longer periods of time.
    d. They travel shorter distances.

Changes in Earnings

Earnings change with time and between occupations and sectors, as market forces and other influencing factors undergo a change. This unit examines the main reasons responsible for change in earnings.

Changes in the Earnings of Individuals Over Time

The earnings of most individuals change over the course of their working life. For most of the workers, their earnings increase as they get older. This is because the longer people work, the more skilled and productive they tend to become. Their productivity increases because they gain experience and, in some cases, undertake training. Becoming more skilled increases a worker's chances of being promoted and achieving higher pay.

Some workers may switch employers in pursuit of higher pay. Others may agree to take on more responsibility for more pay.

There is a chance, however, that earnings may fall with passage of time. Some older workers may decide to give up working overtime and some may switch to less demanding work. The firm or organisation, that people work for, may experience financial difficulties and as a result it may reduce wages and cut bonuses.

Why Earnings of Occupations Change

The main reason for a rise or, less commonly, fall in earnings is a change in demand and/or supply of labour. Other reasons include changes in bargaining power, changes in government policies and changes in public opinion.

Changes in the Demand for Labour

If demand for labour increases, earnings are likely to rise. The wage rate may be pushed up and bonuses increased. In addition, more overtime may become available and it may be paid at a higher rate too.

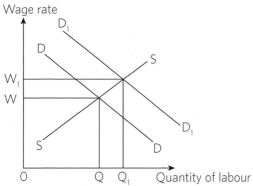

Fig. 1 The effect of an increase in the demand for bricklayers' labour

Fig. 1 shows the wage rate for bricklayers being driven up by an increase in demand for their labour.

What can cause demand for labour to increase? There are three main causes.

These are:

- An increased demand for the product. Demand for labour is a *derived demand*. Higher the demand for products, greater is the number of workers employed.

- A rise in labour productivity. Higher productivity increases the return from hiring workers.

- A rise in the price of capital. In some occupations, it is possible to substitute labour for capital in the production process.

In recent years, the pay of pilots has been rising throughout the world. More and more people are travelling by plane for both business purposes and holidays and hence the demand for the services of pilots is increasing. In contrast, in many countries the wages of agricultural workers have been falling relative to the wages of other workers. Demand for their labour has been declining, in part, because it has become easier to replace it with capital.

Changes in the Supply of Labour

A decrease in the supply of labour for a particular occupation or sector would be expected to raise the wage rate. Among the factors that could cause a decrease in the supply of workers are:

- a fall in the labour force. If there are fewer workers, in general, it is likely that an individual business will find it more difficult to recruit workers.

- A rise in the qualifications or length of training required to do the job. This will reduce the number of people eligible for the job.

- A reduction in the non-wage benefits of a job. If, for example, the working hours or risks involved in doing a job increase, fewer people are likely to be willing to do it.

- A rise in the wage or non-wage benefits in other jobs. Such a change would encourage some workers to switch from one occupation to another.

Consider the situation depicted in Fig. 2. One of the reasons the pay for accountants, for instance, has risen is that the qualifications to do the job has increased. The figure shows the wage rate of accountants being driven up by a decrease in the supply of their labour.

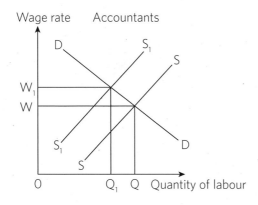

Fig. 2 The effect of a decrease in the supply of accountants' labour

![Activity 1]

Activity 1

India has one of the fastest growing air travel markets in the world. It started to expand in the mid 1990s when the monopoly of state run Indian Airlines ended and Jet Airways and Air Sahara were launched. Its rate of expansion accelerated in 2003 with the founding of Air Deccan, a 'no-frills' carrier. In 2005 Spice Jet, Go Air and Kingfisher Airlines were launched. This expansion has resulted in an increase in the number of pilots and air cabin crew employed in India.

a.   Explain what is likely to have happened to the wages of air cabin crew in India in recent years.

b.   Explain two reasons for pilots receiving a higher remuneration than the air cabin crew.

The Extent to Which Earnings Change

The magnitude of the change in the wage rate due to a change in demand for, or supply of, labour is influenced not only by the size of the change but also by the elasticity of demand for labour and the elasticity of supply of labour. Fig. 3 shows demand for labour increasing by the same amount in both cases, but the impact on the wage rate is much greater in the first case where both the demand for and supply of labour are inelastic.

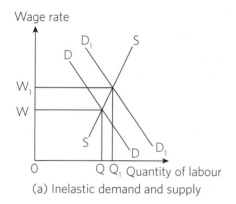

(a) Inelastic demand and supply

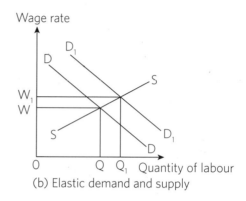

(b) Elastic demand and supply

Fig. 3 The influence of elasticity on the effect of an increase in demand for labour

The main determinants of elasticity of demand for labour are:

- **The proportion of labour costs in total costs.** If labour costs form a large proportion of total costs, a change in wages would have a significant impact on costs and hence demand would be elastic.

- **The ease with which labour can be substituted by capital.** If it is easy to replace workers with machines, demand would again be elastic.

- **The elasticity of demand for the product produced.** A rise in wages increases costs of production which, in turn, raise the price of the product. This causes demand for the product to contract and demand for labour to fall. The more elastic the demand for the product is, the greater the fall in demand for it and hence for workers – making demand for labour elastic.

- **The time period.** Demand for labour is usually more elastic in the long run as there is more time for firms to change their methods of production.

There are also a number of determinants of elasticity of supply of labour. These are:

- **The qualifications and skills required.** The more qualifications and skills needed, the more inelastic supply will be. For instance, a large increase in the wage paid to brain surgeons will not have much effect on the supply of labour. This is especially true in the short run, as it will take years to gain the requisite qualifications and experience.

- **The length of training period.** A long period of training may put some people off the occupation. It will also mean that there will be a delay before those who are willing to take it up are fully qualified to join the labour force. Both effects make the supply of labour inelastic.

- **The level of employment.** If most workers are employed already, the supply of labour to any particular occupation is likely to be inelastic. An employer may have to raise the wage rate quite significantly to attract more workers and encourage the workers employed in other occupations to switch jobs.

- **The mobility of labour.** The easier workers find it to change jobs or to move from one area to another, the easier it will be for an employer to recruit more labour by raising the wage rate. Thus, higher mobility makes the supply elastic.

- **The degree of vocation.** The stronger the attachment of workers to their jobs, the more inelastic supply tends to be in case of a decrease in wage rate.

- **The time period.** As with demand, supply of labour tends to become more elastic over time. This is because it gives workers more time to notice wage changes and to gain any qualifications or undertake any training needed for a new job.

Key Points

Elasticity of demand for labour: a measure of the responsiveness of demand for labour to a change in the wage rate.

Elasticity of supply of labour: a measure of the responsiveness of the supply of labour to a change in the wage rate.

Activity 2

In which of the following occupations is the demand for labour likely to be elastic?

a. An occupation in which technical progress is continually developing inexpensive labour saving techniques.

b. An occupation which produces a product with inelastic demand.

c. An occupation belonging to a labour intensive industry.

d. An occupation where labour costs form a small proportion of total costs.

Other Influencing Factors

A change in unions' bargaining power or willingness to take industrial action can affect earnings. If, in the future, Pakistan removes its ban on agricultural workers forming unions and bargaining collectively, the wage rate of agricultural workers would be expected to rise. In recent years, the greater willingness of UK NHS workers to threaten industrial action is perceived as one reason inducing a pay rise for them.

Another reason for the higher pay – now enjoyed by UK doctors, nurses and other health care workers; is the government's decision to expand the NHS. This decision has increased the demand for health care workers.

A government decision to reduce road building, in contrast, may reduce the wages of those working for private sector road construction firms.

Governments can change wage rates in a number of ways.

- Raising the national minimum wage will increase the pay of low paid workers.

- Despite the rise in supply, improved education may actually raise the wages of skilled workers as it may increase their demand more than the supply. This is because employing more skilled workers should reduce costs of production and increase international competitiveness. If this is the case, demand for products produced by the country's firms should increase and more MNCs may be attracted to set up their franchises in the country.

- Government policies on immigration can also affect wages. Making it easier for foreign people to live and work in the country should increase the supply of labour. If a country is short of, for instance, information and communication technology (ICT) workers, giving more permits to foreign workers should increase the supply of such workers and may hold down wage rises too.

- The introduction of government anti-discrimination laws may help to increase the career prospects and wages of disadvantaged groups. Such legislation works, in part, by changing public opinion. In many countries attitudes to working women have become more favourable and the capabilities and services of women workers are being valued more. This, combined with a rise in the educational performance of women, has raised women's wages.

- Advances in technology can alter wage rates. In some cases, it can put downward pressure on wage rates by reducing demand for workers. For instance, new technology in the banking industry has reduced the number of banking staff in a number of countries. In other cases, however, new technology can increase wages. For example, the development of products such as DVD players and PCs in recent years has increased demand for the services of electricians.

Activity 3

In October 2006, the UK government introduced a legislation, making it illegal for employers to discriminate against workers on the grounds of age. Now, employees who feel that they are being treated differently by their employer or by their co-workers purely because of their age, can make a claim against firms.

a. Explain three reasons which may explain payment of lower wages to workers, who are discriminated against.

b. How may a payment of higher wages to both older and younger workers reduce labour costs?

Summary

- An increase in demand for labour will increase the wage rate.

- The main causes of an increase in demand for labour are an increased demand for the product produced, a rise in labour productivity and a rise in the price of capital.

- A decrease in the supply of labour will increase the wage rate.

- Among the causes of a decrease in the supply of labour are a fall in the labour force, a rise in the qualifications or length of training required, a reduction in the non-wage benefits of a job, a rise in the wage or non-wage benefits of other jobs.

continued····>

- Extent of change in wage rates, as a result of a change in the demand for and supply of labour, is influenced by the elasticity of demand for and supply of labour.

- The main determinants of elasticity of demand of labour are the proportion of labour costs in total costs, ease of substitution of labour by capital and the elasticity of demand for the product produced.

- The main determinants of elasticity of supply of labour are the qualifications, skills and length of training required, the level of employment, the mobility of labour and the degree of vocation.

- An increase in bargaining strength, more favourable government policies and more favourable public opinion can increase the wage rate.

Teacher's Tip

If you are commenting on the PED and PES of labour in a particular occupation, ensure that the slope of the demand and supply curves are consistent with your comments.

Multiple Choice Questions

1. Which combination is most likely to cause a rise in pay rates?

	Productivity of workers	*Supply of workers*
a.	falls	falls
b.	falls	rises
c.	rises	falls
d.	rises	rises

2. Point X in the diagram shows the market for electricians in a country. There is an increase in the number of people who train as electricians. What is the new equilibrium point?

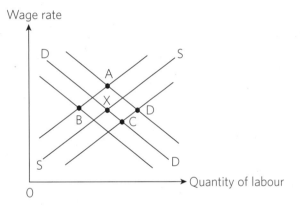

3. What may cause the wages of factory workers to fall?
   a. An increase in the national minimum wage
   b. An increase in the employment opportunities in the country
   c. A reduction in the supply of factory workers
   d. A reduction in the workers' bargaining power

4. The diagram shows that the wage rate of nurses was originally W. It then changed to W_1. What could have caused this change?

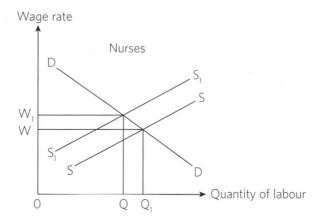

a. An increase in nurses' pay
b. An improvement in nurses' working conditions
c. A rise in the qualifications needed to become a nurse
d. An increase in demand for health care

Trade Unions

As mentioned in two previous units, trade unions can influence the wages paid to the workers. This unit examines the various types of trade unions, their aims and their actions.

 Types of Trade Unions

Trade unions are associations of workers formed to represent their interests and improve their pay and working conditions. There are four main types of trade unions. These are:

- **Craft unions.** These represent workers with particular skills e.g. plumbers and weavers. These workers may be employed in a number of industries.

- **General unions.** These unions include workers with a range of skills and from a range of industries.

- **Industrial unions.** These seek to represent all the workers in a particular industry, for instance, those in the rail industry.

- **White collar unions.** These unions represent particular professions, including pilots and teachers.

Unions in a country, often belong to a national union organisation. For example, in India, a number of unions belong to the All India Trade Union Congress (AITUC). This is the oldest and one of the largest trade union federations in the country.

A number of them also belong to international trade union organisations such as the International Confederation of Free Trade Unions, which has more than 230 affiliated organisations in 150 countries.

 Key Point

A trade union: an association which represents the interest of a group of workers.

 **Activity 1**

Decide what type of union the following Indian and UK unions are:

a. Andhra Pradesh Auto Rickshaw Drivers and Workers' Union
b. The National Union of Teachers
c. Transport and General Workers' Union
d. Pondicherry Textile Labour Union
e. Punjab Breweries Workers' Union
f. Sheffield Wool Shears Workers' Union

 # Role of Unions

Unions carry out a number of functions. They negotiate on behalf of their members on pay scales, working hours and working conditions. These areas can include basic pay, overtime payments, holidays, health safety, promotion prospects, maternity and paternity rights and job security. Depending on the circumstances, unions may try to protect or improve workers' rights. They also provide information on a range of issues for their members, for instance on pensions. They help with education and training schemes and may also participate in measures designed to increase demand for the product produced and hence for labour. Some also provide a range of benefits to their members including strike pay, sickness pay and unemployment pay. In addition many get involved in pressurising their governments to adopt a legislation, which will benefit their members or workers in general, such as fixing a national minimum wage.

Collective Bargaining

An individual worker may not have the skill, time or willingness to negotiate with her or his employer. A worker is also likely to have limited bargaining power. If she or he presses for a wage rise or an improvement in working conditions, the employer may be able to dismiss her or him and take on someone as a replacement. Unions enable workers to press their claims through collective bargaining. This process involves negotiations between union officials, representing a group of workers, and representatives of employers.

 Key Point

Collective bargaining: representatives of workers negotiating with employers' associations.

The Basis of Wage Claims

There are a number of arguments, a union can put forward while asking for a wage rise. One is that the workers deserve to be paid more because they have been working harder and have increased productivity. Another argument is that an industry whose profits have risen can afford to pay higher wages to its workers. This argument may be linked to the first one as the workers are likely to have contributed to the higher profits. A third argument is known as the *comparability argument*. A union may argue that the workers it represents, should receive a pay rise to keep their pay in line with similar workers. For instance, a union representing nurses may press for a wage rise if doctors are awarded higher pay. The nurses' union is unlikely to ask for the same pay as doctors. What is more likely is that they will seek to maintain their wage differential. So, if before the rise of doctors' pay, nurses received a wage that was 60% of the doctors' earnings, they are likely to demand a rise that will restore this differential.

A fourth argument that is often put forward is that workers need a wage rise to meet the increased cost of living. If the price level is rising by 6%, workers will need a wage rise of at least 6% to maintain their wage's purchasing power. This is sometimes referred to as maintaining their **real income** (income adjusted for inflation).

 **Activity 2**

In 2006 university lecturers in UK went on strike, refusing to set and mark examinations. The lecturers wanted higher pay, claiming that their pay had fallen behind similar workers.

a. What type of argument were the university lecturers advancing?
b. What type of union is likely to represent university lecturers?

 # Factors Affecting the Strength of a Trade Union

Among the factors which empower a union are:

- **A high level of economic activity.** If output and income in a country are increasing, most industries are likely to be doing well and so should be able to improve the pay and conditions of workers. When output reaches high levels and most people who want to work are employed, firms will be competing for workers. To retain their existing workers and to recruit more workers, firms are likely to be more willing to agree to union requests for higher pay and better working conditions.

- **A high number of members.** The more members a union has, the more funds it is likely to have to finance its activities. Also, the employers will find it difficult to replace union labour by non-union labour in such a scenario.

- **A high level of skill.** Unions representing skilled workers are in a relatively strong position as it can be difficult to replace their workers with other skilled workers and expensive to train unskilled workers.

- **A consistent demand for the product** produced for the workers. Unions that represent workers making goods and services that are essential to consumers are in a strong position to bargain.

 ## Industrial Action

If negotiations break down on wage claims or disputes occur over working conditions, there is a range of industrial actions that can be initiated by a union in support of its claim. There could be an overtime ban, with workers refusing to work longer than their contracted hours. Workers may also 'work to rule'. This involves workers undertaking the tasks required by their contracts only.

The most well known form of industrial action, however, is a **strike**. This involves workers withdrawing their labour. A strike can be official or unofficial. An official strike is one which is approved and organised by the union. In contrast, an unofficial strike is one which has not been approved by the union. This can occur when the strike is called by local union representatives and is over before the union has the time to approve it or in the cases when the union does not agree with the action. Strike action can be measured in three main ways. These are:

- the number of strikes

- the number of workers involved

- the number of working days lost.

The last measure gives the clearest indication of the impact of the strike on the economy. Governments often try to prevent strikes by encouraging unions' and employers' representatives to go to arbitration, in case negotiations break down. Arbitration concerns the involvement of a third party seeking to reach an agreement. The arbitrator may be a government body or an independent third party chosen by both the parties.

Activity 3

In each case decide which union is likely to be more successful, if it pursues strike action:

a. a union representing fire fighters or a union representing flower sellers
b. a union representing skilled workers or a union representing unskilled workers
c. a union striking during a period of high unemployment or a union striking during a period of low unemployment.

Influence on the Supply of Labour

Besides negotiating and taking industrial action, unions can seek to raise the wages of its members by restricting the entry of new workers into the industry, occupation or craft. Unions may seek to do this by insisting that new recruits have high qualifications or may operate a closed shop. The latter occurs when employers can only employ only those workers who are members of the union or who agree to join the union. (In contrast, an open shop occurs when an employer is free to employ members or nonmembers of the union).

 Trade Unions, Firms and Workers

Firms can be harmed by industrial action undertaken by trade unions. The amount of revenue lost and damage done to the reputation of a particular firm by a strike will be influenced by the effect on rival firms and the length of the strike. A firm's costs and flexibility will also be adversely affected by overtime bans and 'work to rule' action.

Unions, however, can provide benefits to the firms. It is less time consuming, less stressful and hence cheaper to negotiate with workers as a group than to negotiate with each worker individually. Unions also provide a useful channel of communication between employers and workers. They often encourage workers to engage in education and training which raises productivity and promote improved health and safety. They also provide an outlet to vent workers' discontent and channel their grievances to the employers, thereby reducing conflict.

Unions can also benefit non-unionised labour as any improvement in pay and working conditions usually applies to non-members also.

Unions Around the World

The role and importance of trade unions varies across the world. In fact in some countries, including the Maldives and Saudi Arabia, trade unions are illegal.

Industrial workers in Pakistan have the right to form trade unions but a number of laws restrict their actions and hence their effectiveness. The government can, for instance, ban any strike that may cause 'serious hardship for the community', endanger the national interest or has continued for 30 days or more. The law is even more restrictive in the case of agricultural workers who are prevented from forming any unions.

Union membership, as a percentage of the labour force, is high in Mauritius. Approximately a quarter of workers are in a union. The rate is, however, lower in the country's Export Processing Zones (EPZs). In these areas, managers often make it difficult for workers to join a union by threatening to close down their factories if workers join unions.

Unions are more powerful in European countries. They are particularly strong in the Nordic countries of Finland and Sweden, where union membership is high. Union membership fell in the UK in the 1980s and 1990s for two main reasons. One was legislation which reduced trade union rights and the other was a rise in unemployment, particularly in sectors that had been heavily unionised. In more recent years, membership has grown amongst women workers. It continues to be higher among public sector workers than private sector workers. France has one of the lowest union densities in Europe, with approximately only 8% of workers belonging to trade unions (in comparison to 30% in UK). French unions do, however, exert considerable power. This is because the unions enjoy public support, are willing to take strike action and French laws secure the importance of their role. For instance, in France, unemployment benefit is set by an independent body which has to negotiate with unions and union representatives have the right to seat on firms' works councils.

Summary

- There are four main types of trade unions. These represent workers with particular skills, from particular industries, from particular professions and from a diverse background.

- Trade unions seek to protect and enhance workers' pay, working hours and working conditions.

- Trade unions allow workers to bargain more effectively through collective bargaining.

- Trade unions can argue for a wage rise on a number of grounds including appropriate returns for hard work, apportionment of higher profits earned, relatively higher wages of similar workers and increased cost of living.

- A trade union will be stronger the more members it has, the higher the level of economic activity the firm/industry enjoys, the more skilled the workers are, the more public support it enjoys, the lower the contribution of wage costs to total costs are and the fewer substitutes there are for the product produced.

- Industrial action includes overtime bans, work to rule and strikes.

- Trade unions may seek to raise wages by restricting the supply of labour through demanding high qualifications and restricting the employment to union members (closed shop).

- Trade unions may also lower firms' costs by making it easier for the employers to communicate with workers and by encouraging the workers to participate in schemes which raise productivity.

- The role and importance of trade unions vary in different countries. Some countries do not allow trade unions to operate whereas in other countries trade unions are relatively powerful.

Teacher's Tip

In discussing trade unions, it is useful to refer to the role of trade unions (if any) in your country.

Multiple Choice Questions

1. In which circumstance is a trade union most likely be able to raise the wages of its members?
    a. It is easy to replace workers with machines.
    b. It is easy to replace unionised labour with non-unionised labour.
    c. The profits of the firms in the industry are low.
    d. The share of labour costs in total costs in low.

2. Which measure of strike activity indicates workers' sentiment about the strike?
    a. The number of strikes
    b. The number of workers involved
    c. The amount of working time lost
    d. The amount of revenue lost by firms

3. Which of the following is not a function of a trade union?
    a. Improving working conditions
    b. Increasing shareholders' dividends
    c. Raising members' wages
    d. Representing members' interests

4. A trade union is pressing for a wage rise for its members. Which of the following would increase its chances of being successful?
    a. An increase in productivity
    b. An increase in unemployment
    c. A decrease in profitability
    d. A decrease in union membership

Motives for Spending, Saving and Borrowing

In previous units, differences and changes in earnings were discussed. The income earned by people is a major factor influencing the size of their expenditure. It can also influence the amount borrowed by them. This unit examines the reasons for people to spend, save and borrow and the main influences governing their decisions.

Expenditure

People spend in order to buy goods and services and to maintain a given standard of living. Among the main items involving expenditure are food, clothing and footwear, housing, gas, electricity, water, consumer durables, transport, entertainment and leisure goods and services.

Influences on Spending

The main influence on the amount spent by a person or household is disposable income. As income rises, people usually spend more in total but less as a percentage of their disposable income. Among the other factors influencing the magnitude of expenditure are wealth, confidence, the rate of interest, the distribution of income and advances in technology.

Wealth is linked to expenditure in four main ways. One is that wealth generates income, for instance, dividends from shares and this income can be spent. Wealth can also be cashed in by, for instance, withdrawing money from a bank account or selling a car, and then spent. People can use their wealth as security for loans. Wealth also affects confidence. If, for example, the value of people's housing rises, people will feel richer and are likely to spend more.

Confidence is an important influence on consumption. If people feel more optimistic about their future career prospects and income, they are likely to spend more. In contrast, if they become pessimistic about economic prospects they will tend to spend less.

Expenditure may also fall if the **rate of interest** rises. This is because, it will make borrowing more expensive, encourage saving and reduce the amount spent by people who have borrowed in the past. Of course, those people who have savings will gain more income and consequently, they may spend more. Their higher spending, however, will be more than offset by reduced expenditure of others. This is because savers tend to be richer than borrowers and hence tend to spend a smaller percentage of their income.

The difference that exists between the average propenvity to consume (APC – *see* Unit 22) of high and low income groups means that a more even distribution of income and transfer of income from the rich to the poor, is likely to increase expenditure in a country. Advances in technology may also increase expenditure. This is because new products, such as DVDs and ipods, encourage people to replace existing products.

Key Point

Wealth: a stock of assets including money held in bank accounts, shares in companies, government bonds, cars and houses.

Forms of Saving

There are a number of forms of saving. Some forms are *contractual*. This means that people sign a contract, agreeing to save a certain amount on a regular basis. The main forms of contractual saving are insurance policies and pension schemes.

Non-contractual saving includes placing money in bank and building society accounts, buying government securities, shares and property. By its very nature, non-contractual saving varies more with time and is more heavily influenced by changes in interest rates than contractual saving.

Reasons for Saving

People save for a variety of reasons. Some people are, what are called, **target savers**. This means that they save to gain a particular sum of money for a particular purpose. This may be, for instance, to buy a car or a home.

People also save for their retirement, for their children's future, for precautionary reasons and to provide an income or capital gain. When people retire, their income from their work stops. Even if they receive a state pension and an occupational pension, income from savings can make their retirement more comfortable.

Some people save in order to help finance their children's education or to leave them a inheritance, when they die.

Most people like to have some savings to cope with emergencies and unexpected problems and take advantage of any unforeseen opportunities. For example, people may lose their jobs, their drains may become blocked or they may see a car for sale (at what they regard to be a bargain price).

Some people also save to increase their current income. The more people save, the more interest they tend to receive not only in total but also per unit saved. This is because financial institutions usually reward those disproportionately, who save large amounts. Those who hold their savings in the form of shares, government bonds or a house, may also hope that they will benefit from a rise in the value of their assets.

Influences on Saving

Among the influences on saving we have:

- **income.** As with consumption, the main influence on saving is disposable income. As disposable income rises, the total amount saved and the proportion saved (the savings ratio) increases.

- **wealth.** The wealthier people are, the easier they will find it to save.

- **the rate of interest.** A rise in the rate of interest may reduce some target saving as people can now attain their target amounts by saving less. Overall it is likely to increase non-contractual saving as it pushes up the reward for saving.

- **the tax treatment of savings.** Tax concessions on the income earned from saving will encourage people to save. In a number of countries there are some free schemes where no tax is charged on the interest earned.

- **the range and quality of financial institutions.** The greater the variety of saving opportunities on offer, the more likely people will find a scheme that will suit them. Confidence in the ability of institutions to pay an interest and repay the amount saved, is also important.

- **age structure.** The young and the old tend to save less than middle-aged people. The old, especially the very old, draw on their savings to ensure a reasonable living standard during retirement.

- **social attitudes.** The attitude to saving varies between countries. In some it is held in high esteem while in others people prefer to spend most of their income when they receive it.

Activity 1

National savings ratios 1990–98

Country	%
Bangladesh	6.3
Chile	28.4
Haiti	–6.1
India	24.2
Pakistan	15.8

Source: World Bank Database

a. Explain how Haiti could have had a negative savings ratio.
b. What was the rate of expenditure in Bangladesh, in the period shown?
c. What do Chile's and Bangladesh's savings ratios suggest about the relative income levels in the countries in this period?
d. Explain the possible reasons, other than differences in disposable income, which may be responsible for the savings ratio of India being higher than that of Pakistan.

Borrowing

Borrowing moves income from people who do not want to spend it now to those who need more money than they currently have. Some people who run into financial difficulties borrow in a bid to maintain their living standards. These people hope that their income will soon rise, so that they can repay the loans and overdrafts. Other people borrow in order, for instance, to buy a car or to go on a foreign holiday. Most people who buy a house have to borrow some of the money to finance their purchase.

The influences affecting the amount of money borrowed by people include:

- **the availability of loans and overdrafts.** The easier it is to borrow, the more likely people are to borrow.

- **the rate of interest.** A rise in the rate of interest will increase the cost of borrowing, which is likely to reduce borrowing.

- **confidence.** The more confident people are about the future, the more they will anticipate earning in the future. They may adjust their spending patterns now, financing some of their extra expenses by borrowing with an expectation that their higher income will enable them to repay their loans.

- **social attitudes.** Some countries and some groups within countries are more concerned about the risks of people getting into debt by borrowing, than others.

Activity 2

The savings ratio in Japan fell from 23% in 1975, to 14% in 1990, to 5% in 2010. Two reasons given for this by Japanese economists were a fall in inflation and a rise in the number of retired people in relation to the number of workers.

a.   Define the savings ratio.

b.   Explain why the savings ratio may fall due to a rise in the number of retired people in relation to the number of workers.

Summary

- The influences on expenditure include the level of disposable income, wealth, confidence, the rate of interest, the distribution of income and advances in technology.

- Some forms of saving are contractual and some are non-contractual.

- People save to buy certain products, to make their retirement more comfortable, to help their children, to cope with unexpected expenses and opportunities and to earn income.

continued ⋯>

- The main influences on saving are disposable income, the rate of interest, the tax treatment of saving, the range and quality of financial institutions, age structure and social attitudes.

- The key influences on borrowing are the availability of loans, the rate of interest, confidence and social attitudes.

Teacher's Tip

Remember that a rise in disposable income enables people to both spend and save more.

Multiple Choice Questions

1. Interest rates rise. How is this likely to affect household savings and expenditure?

	Saving	Expenditure
a.	rise	rise
b.	rise	fall
c.	fall	fall
d.	fall	rise

2. What is most likely to cause a rise in expenditure in an economy?
    a. A rise in confidence
    b. A rise in income tax
    c. A reduction in wealth
    d. A more uneven distribution of income

3. What can cause a fall in saving?
    a. A rise in the range of financial institutions
    b. A fall in the rate of interest
    c. A rise in disposable income
    d. A fall in the rate of tax imposed on earnings from saving

4. What is the main influence on consumption?
    a. Disposable income
    b. Social attitudes
    c. The rate of inflation
    d. The rate of interest

Differences in Expenditure Patterns

Besides influencing the amount spent by people, income also influences consumer choices. This unit examines how and why different income groups have different expenditure patterns.

 Income

Gross income is the total income received by a person before deductions from his or her salary or wage, principally income tax. What is important, however, in determining people's expenditure patterns, is their **disposable income**. This is their income after the deduction of direct taxation, including income tax. Even more significant is **real disposable income**. This is disposable income *adjusted for inflation*. If real disposable income rises, it means that people's purchasing power will rise and they will be able to buy more goods and services.

Key Point

Disposable income: income after the deduction of direct taxes.

Sources of Income

There are three main sources of income. These are:

- **Earned income.** The main source of most people's income is their earnings from employment.

- **Investment income.** This is income in the form of profits, interest and dividends. Entrepreneurs can earn profits, people who lend money receive interest and shareholders can receive dividends.

- **State benefits.** Some people depend on income from the state. These include the unemployed, the elderly and those who are too disabled or sick to work.

Income and Consumption

People can either spend or save their disposable income. When people are very poor, they cannot afford to save. All of their disposable income will be spent on buying basic necessities to survive. In fact, some may have to spend more of their income in order to be able to buy enough food and clothing and pay for housing. When people spend more than their income, they are said to be *dissaving*. This is because they are either drawing on their past saving or more likely, borrowing other people's savings.

As income rises people are able, to both spend and save more. As people become richer they buy more and better quality products. It is interesting to note, however, that whilst the total amount spent rises with income, the proportion spent tends to fall. A top class footballer in Italy may earn a disposable income of $80 000 a week whilst an unemployed person in Italy may live on benefits of $120 a week. The unemployed person may spend all of the $120. The footballer can clearly afford to spend more and is likely to do so. However, even if he has a very luxurious lifestyle, it is unlikely that he will spend all of the $80 000. If he spends $60 000 (a huge amount) he will only be spending 75% of his disposable income, whilst the unemployed person is spending 100% of his income.

The proportion of income which people spend is sometimes referred to as the **average propensity to consume (APC)**. It is calculated by dividing consumption by disposable income. Table 1 shows that as income rises, expenditure increases but the APC falls. For instance, at an income of $300 people spend 90% of their income.

Table 1 The relationship between disposable income and consumption.

Disposable income ($)	Consumption ($)	APC
100	120	1.2
200	200	1.0
300	270	0.9
400	320	0.8
500	350	0.7

The relationship between disposable income and consumption can also be shown graphically. Fig. 1 shows that at very low levels of income, there is dissaving. At Z level of income, all income is spent. Then as income rises past Y, saving occurs. Over the complete range of income, expenditure continues to rise but it rises at a slower rate.

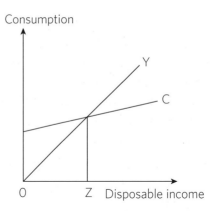

Fig. 1 The relationship between disposable income and consumption

Key Points

Consumption: expenditure by households on consumer goods and income.

Average propensity to consume: the proportion of household disposable income which is spent.

Pattern of Expenditure

Different income groups tend to have different patterns of spending. The poor tend to spend a higher proportion of their income and total expenditure on food and clothing than the rich. This is not because they eat more and wear more than the rich! Indeed the rich are likely to spend more in total on food – as they tend to buy a greater variety and higher quality of food and more on clothes – as they buy more clothes and clothes of a higher quality. The amount they spend is, however, usually a smaller proportion of their income and total expenditure. A rich US family may spend $400 a week on food and clothing out of a disposable income of $2 000 and a poor family may spend $40 out of a disposable income of $100. This would mean that 40% of the disposable income of the poor family goes on food and clothing, as against 20% of the disposable income of the rich one.

The rich spend more, both in total and as a proportion, on luxury items, consumer durables, entertainment and services. For instance, the rich spend more on cars, jewellery, theatre trips and foreign holidays. This difference in spending patterns also occurs between countries, with spending, as a proportion of disposable income and total expenditure on food and other necessities, being higher in poor countries while spending on luxuries forming a greater share of disposable income and total expenditure in rich countries.

Spending patterns vary within income groups in a country, according to differences in household composition, tastes and age. Households without children are likely to spend a higher proportion on recreation and eating out than households with children. Some households may value cultural activities more than others whilst others may be keener to spend more on medical care. The retired tend to spend a higher proportion, than average, on heating and a lower proportion on transport and entertainment. On the other hand, people in their late teens and twenties often spend a higher proportion on clothing and entertainment.

 **Activity 1**

Table 2 shows how three people spend their disposable income.

	Person A	Person B	Person C
Food and clothing	35%	45%	15%
Consumer durables	35%	35%	45%
Leisure goods and services	30%	20%	40%

Place the three people in the most likely order of disposable income from the richest to the poorest.

 **Saving**

Saving is disposable income which is not spent. As already noted, it is not possible to save below a certain income level. As disposable income rises, both the total amount saved and the proportion of disposable income saved increases. Table 3, using the same disposable income and consumption figures, as in Table 1, shows this. The **average propensity to save (APS)** is calculated by dividing saving by disposable income. The APS is also sometimes referred to as the *savings ratio*.

Table 3 The relationship between disposable income and saving

Disposable income ($)	Consumption ($)	Saving ($)	APS
100	120	–20	–0.2
200	200	0	0.0
300	270	30	0.1
400	320	60	0.2
500	350	150	0.3

At an income of £500, people save 30% of their disposable income. It is useful to note that APS plus APC add upto 1, since disposable income is either spent or saved.

Fig. 2 shows the usual relationship between disposable income and saving.

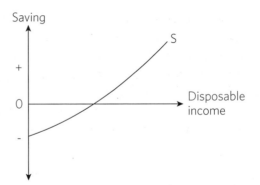

Fig. 2 The relationship between disposable income and saving

Key Point

Average propensity to save/savings ratio; the proportion of household disposable income that is saved.

Activity 2

Table 4 The relationship between disposable income, consumption and saving.

Income ($)	Consumption ($)	Saving ($)	APC	APS
100	100			
200	180			
300	240			
400	280			
500	300			

Complete the above table.

Borrowing

Borrowing enables people to spend more than their current disposable income. It does, however, involve a cost in the form of interest which has to be paid. It is also usually a temporary situation as loans and overdrafts have to be repaid. The poor, whilst sometimes having a greater need to borrow, are likely to experience greater difficulty in borrowing. This is because they will have less security to offer for any loan and lenders may be more worried about their ability to keep up interest payments and repay any loan.

Summary

- Income can be obtained from employment, financial investment and state benefits.

- Disposable income can be spent or saved.

- As disposable income rises, people spend more in total but less as a percentage.

- Saving rises in total and as a percentage of disposable income, as people get richer.

- The poor spend a higher proportion of their total expenditure and disposable income on food and other basic necessities than the rich, but a smaller proportion on luxuries.

- By borrowing, people can spend more than their disposable income.

Teacher's Tip

It is important to distinguish between the absolute amount spent and percentage of expenditure spent on a particular item or category of items.

Multiple Choice Questions

1. Which group spends the highest proportion of their total expenditure on food?
   a. The poor
   b. The middle income group
   c. The rich
   d. The very rich

2. Which statement about different income groups is true?
   a. Low income groups save more, in percentage terms, than high income groups.
   b. Low income groups find it easier to borrow than high income groups.
   c. High income groups spend less, in percentage terms, than low income groups.
   d. High income groups do not borrow money.

3. What must be occurring, if consumption is less than disposable income?
   a. Borrowing
   b. Income levels are falling
   c. Income is being redistributed to the poor
   d. Saving

4. A woman having a gross income of $200 and a disposable income of $150 spends $100. What is her APS?
   a. 0.25
   b. 0.33
   c. 0.50
   d. 0.75

Answer Key

Unit 14

Activity 1

a. Bangladesh appears to be specialising to a greater extent than Turkey. A higher proportion of its exports are accounted for by clothing.

b. Proportion of Bangladesh's output and Turkey's output, accounted for by clothing.

Activity 2

a, c, d, e and b.

Activity 3

a. Leaves are reasonably portable and they are recognisable. They are, however, not limited in supply and hence are unlikely to be generally acceptable. Also, they are not durable or homogeneous.

b. Seashells are durable, portable and recognisable. They are also divisible as sea shells come in a variety of sizes. They are, however, not perfectly homogeneous and may not be that limited in supply in countries with coastlines. Hence, they may not be generally acceptable, although sea shells have acted as money in some countries in the past.

c. Gold possesses all the characteristics of money. It has been used as money before and is still acceptable in most countries. Its use as money, however, involves an opportunity cost as it has intrinsic value. Gold can be used for jewellery and industry. In contrast, notes, coins and bank notes essentially have only one purpose.

Multiple Choice Questions

1. a

   A straightforward definition question. Labour turnover is concerned with the length of time for which workers stay in a job. Labour flexibility refers to how flexible workers are in terms of the tasks they do, the hours they work for and the geographical location at which they work. Rationalisation is the process of reducing wasteful duplication in a firm.

2. a

   If a firm is producing one or a few products, a fall in demand for its product (or products) will have a significant impact on its income. A firm that specialises will have to buy less equipment and will be able to train its workers more quickly. A rise in productivity is an advantage and not a disadvantage of specialisation of workers.

3. b

    Money enables people to save, as it can be stored.

4. c

    To act as money, an item must be durable. a, b and d are all desirable characteristics of money.

Unit 15

Activity 1

a. An overdraft is a way of borrowing money from a commercial bank. It is the permission given to a bank's customer to spend more money than what is present in her or his account.

b. Banco Bradesco is charging a high rate of interest. This may discourage people from borrowing from the bank and consequently threaten its profitability. The extent to which this occurs, of course, will depend on the rate of interest charged by other banks in Brazil and the quality of their service.

Activity 2

a. The extract mentions interest paid on deposits, so it is referring to the function of accepting deposits.

b. Another function of a commercial bank is lending. The bank charges a higher interest rate from borrowers than it pays to those depositing money with it. Bank customers can borrow by taking a loan or by arranging an overdraft. A lower rate of interest is charged on a loan but it is charged on the full amount of the loan.

Activity 3

a. A central bank is owned by the government whereas a commercial bank is owned by its shareholders.

b. The key feature of a sensible unding policy is to lend only to those who will be able to repay the loan.

c. Another function is to act as banker to the commercial banks. The commercial banks keep accounts at the central banks. These are like the current accounts kept at commercial banks and are used for the same two main purposes. One is to make and receive payments, but this time the commercial banks are transferring money from and into their accounts from other commercial banks. The other is to withdraw cash, when needed.

Multiple Choice Questions

1. a

   Commercial banks' interest rate for borrowers is higher than the rate paid to depositors. c and d are functions carried out by central banks.

2. a

   Supervising the country's banking system is one of the functions of a central bank.

3. a

   Controlling the money supply is another key function of a central bank. b and d are functions carried out directly by the government. c is undertaken by private sector financial institutions.

4. b

   Commercial banks are in the private sector and their key aim is to make a profit. a, c and d are functions of a central bank.

Unit 16

Activity 1

a. Stock exchanges protect shareholders by selling shares only in those companies, which are listed. To be listed, companies have to provide a wealth of information and fulfil certain specified requirements.

b. One of the functions carried out by a stock exchange is to make use of savings for investment. Companies and the government can use people's savings to buy capital goods.

Activity 2

a. A 14% dividend means that the amount of profit paid per share is 14% of the nominal price. So if, for instance, a share has a face value of $10, the owner will receive a payment of $1.40.

b. I would have expected the price of BT shares to rise, as the company had experienced a rise in profits and was expected to earn even higher profits in the next year.

Activity 3

a. Some people buying shares in the Chinese Bank of Communications might have been hoping to make a capital gain. Others might have bought them in an expectation to earn a high yield.

b. A rise in share price may reduce the yield on shares. For instance, if the share price was $10 and the dividend was $1, the yield would be 10%. Then if the share price rose to $20, the yield would fall to 5%.

Multiple Choice Questions

1. d

    Sole proprietors and partnerships do not issue shares. Private limited companies do, but they are not sold on the stock exchange.

2. b

    a is a function of a commercial bank and c is a function of a central bank. d is a specific function of a stock broker.

3. d

    A dividend is a proportion of the profits earned by a company, paid out to shareholders of the company. Profits earned by a company can either be distributed to shareholders and/or retained for future investment.

4. d

    A rise in corporate taxes would mean that firms would retain less proportion of profits earned. This would reduce the dividends paid by public limited companies and so would be likely to lower their share prices. a, b and c are likely to raise the price of a share in a public limited company.

Unit 17

Activity 1

a. $5 000 is three quarters of $6 667 and a third of $15 000. So, pilots in India were paid $6 667 and pilots in the UK were paid $15 000.

b. The shortage of pilots in China would be expected to push up the wages of pilots in the country.

Activity 2

a. Three of the top four were in the public sector – the civil service, public sector health care (the NHS) and public sector broadcasting (the BBC).

b. Two possible reasons for a graduate to desire working in public health care sector are that he or she may think the job may provide a high level of job satisfaction and job security.

Activity 3

a. Three possible reasons why a person may want to be a pilot are the high pay offered, the high status attached to the profession and the good occupational pensions.

b. There are a number of reasons to account for a person's failure in becoming a pilot. These include a lack of qualifications, poor health and a lack of vacancies.

Multiple Choice Questions

1. b
Bonuses, overtime payments and salary are all wage factors.

2. c
Piece rates are a method of payment based on the output produced by workers. The higher the output a worker produces, the higher the amount paid to him.

3. a
The more qualifications a person has, the more choice of occupation she or he will have. b and d would reduce geographical mobility and hence reduce a person's choice of occupation. c would decrease a woman's choice of occupation.

4. b
Most people would find job security an attractive feature of an occupation. a, c and d may discourage a person from taking up an occupation.

Unit 18

Activity 1

a. Demand is high.
b. Supply is low.
c. Workers have strong bargaining power.
d. Workers are skilled.

Activity 2

a. (i) Piece rates are a method of paying workers on the basis of their output.
   (ii) A national minimum wage is a floor, set by the government, below which wages cannot be reduced.

b. Factory workers in the garment industry may receive lower pay than construction workers because they are in higher supply relative to demand, have less bargaining power and are less favoured by government policy.

Activity 3

a. Among the possible reasons, accounting for a smaller proportion of working women in Chile than in other Latin American countries may be, lower pay for women workers in Chile, discrimination against women workers in Chile, social attitudes against working women and less availability of child care.

b. The extract notes that female workers earned nearly a fifth less than men. It also mentions that the government introduced a new labour code to curb unfavourable treatment of female workers.

Multiple Choice Questions

1. b

   Demand for labour is a derived demand. Workers are employed to produce products. The lower the demand for products, the lower the demand for labour. Hence, the wages paid are likely to be less. a and c may result in higher wages. d may reduce the supply of workers and hence may raise wages.

2. d

   To be a street cleaner, one does not require qualifications or any special skill. As a result, supply of street cleaners tends to be high relative to their demand. In contrast, the demand for chief executives, dentists and ICT specialists tends to be high relative to supply and consequently, the workers involved in these occupations are usually paid higher wages.

3. b

   Demand for the services of some entertainers is very high and this enables them to command high earnings. c and d would tend to lower the pay. Those who enjoy the job more than others may be willing to work for lower wages.

4. a

   The lower qualifications required to be a bus driver than a pilot means that the supply of bus drivers (relative to demand) is higher.

Unit 19

Activity 1

a. The wages of air cabin crew in India is likely to have increased, as demand for their services has risen.

b. Pilots are paid more than cabin crew as their supply is lower, relative to demand. This is because more qualifications and skills required to become a pilot and airlines can possibly reduce the number of cabin crew but not the number of pilots. This gives stronger bargaining power to the pilots than cabin crew.

Activity 2

a. and c. – in both cases, a rise in wages is likely to result in a greater percentage contraction in demand for labour. In the case of (a) some workers would be replaced by machines. In the case of (c) a rise in wages would raise costs and hence prices, by a relatively large amount. This, in turn, would reduce demand for the product and the number of workers significantly.

Activity 3

a. Workers who are discriminated against may be paid less than other workers because they are offered lower wages, may be given less training and may not be promoted.

b. Paying higher wages to older and younger workers may increase their motivation, reduce labour turnover and persuade employers to train them to get a better return. All of these effects would increase labour productivity and reduce labour costs per unit.

Multiple Choice Questions

1. c

   Higher productivity increases the returns from employed labour and reduces unit labour costs. A reduction in the supply of labour would result in a shortage of workers which, in turn, would push up the wage rate.

2. c

   An increase in the number of people, who train as electricians, would increase the supply of electricians – shifting the supply curve to the right, reducing the wage rate and causing the demand to extend.

3. d

   Lower bargaining power may reduce the wages of factory workers. a, b and c are all likely to raise wages. Factory workers tend to be low-paid, so they are likely to benefit from a rise in the NMW. An increase in employment in the country should result in greater competition for hiring labour and hence may push up wages. A reduction in the supply of workers would probably have the same effect.

4. c

   The diagram shows that the wage rose as a result of a decrease in the supply of nurses. A rise in the qualifications required to become a nurse would reduce the number of people who are eligible to work as nurses. a and d would increase demand for nurses and b would increase their supply.

Unit 20

Activity 1

a. craft or industrialised union
b. white collar union
c. general union
d. industrial union
e. industrial union
f. craft union

Activity 2

a. The university lecturers were advancing the comparability argument – comparing their pay with that of a head teacher and that of a doctor.

b. University lecturers are in a white collar union.

Activity 3

a. A union representing fire fighters. They provide an essential service. People can do without flowers for a period of time.

b. A union representing skilled workers. It is more difficult to replace skilled than unskilled workers.

c. A union striking during a period of low unemployment. In such a situation, it would be difficult to replace the workers on strike.

Multiple Choice Questions

1. d
   If labour costs form a small proportion of total costs, a rise in wages will not increase the total costs substantially. As a result, the price of the products produced will not rise much and so demand will not fall significantly. a, b and c would all reduce a trade union's strength. a and b would be likely to mean that a union would be reluctant to press for a wage rise as it may fear that such a move may result in some of their members losing their jobs. c would mean that the firms would not be able to afford significant wage rises.

2. c
   If workers feel strongly about an issue, they are likely to be prepared to strike for a long period of time.

3. b

    Trade unions seek to protect and improve workers' pay and conditions. Their role is not concerned with helping shareholders, although both workers and shareholders have an interest in firms doing well.

4. a

    A rise in productivity is likely to increase output, revenue and profits of a firm. Unions can argue that such an increase justifies a wage rise and is likely to provide the money to pay for such a rise.

Unit 21

Activity 1

a. A negative savings ratio means that people in Haiti were spending more than their income by borrowing from others.

b. 93.7% i.e. 100% - 6.3%.

c. Chile has a higher savings ratio than Bangladesh which suggests that income is higher in Chile.

d. The Indian savings ratio may be higher than that in Pakistan because the income levels may be higher, the interest rate may be higher, the tax treatment of savings may be more favourable, a greater range of good quality financial institutions may be available and social attitudes may be more favourable to saving.

Activity 2

a. The savings ratio is the proportion of disposable income saved.

b. Retired people draw on their savings to maintain their living standards whilst workers tend to build up their savings.

Multiple Choice Questions

1. b

    A rise in the rate of interest increases the returns on savings. To save more, people will have to spend less.

2. a

    People spend more when they are confident. They will expect things to improve, including their disposable income and hence their ability to spend. b would reduce disposable income and as a result expenditure. c would mean that people's ability to spend is reduced. d would mean that income would transfer from the poor, who spend a higher proportion of their income to the rich, who spend a lower proportion of their income.

3. b

    a, c and d would all tend to encourage saving. A lower rate of interest would reduce the money earned from saving.

4. a

    b, c and d can all influence consumption. The main influence, however, is disposable income. Higher the income of the people, more is their expenditure.

Unit 22

Activity 1

c, a and b. The rich spend more (in percentage terms) on consumer durables and leisure goods and services whilst the poor spend a higher proportion on food and clothing.

Activity 2

Disposable income ($)	Consumption ($)	Saving ($)	APC	APS
100	100	0	1.0	0.0
200	180	20	0.9	0.1
300	240	60	0.8	0.2
400	280	120	0.7	0.3
500	300	200	0.6	0.4

Multiple Choice Questions

1. a

    As income rises, the percentage of income spent on food declines. More income can be spent on other items, including luxuries.

2. c

    High income groups spend more in total than low income groups, but less as a percentage. This is because they can afford to save some of their income. Low income groups have a smaller savings ratio than rich income groups and find it harder to borrow. High income groups do borrow money. The rich may borrow, for instance, to buy more luxurious housing.

3. d

    Disposable income minus consumption equals saving. Borrowing enables people to spend more than their income. Income levels could be rising or falling and there may or may not be a redistribution of income.

4. b

    The woman is saving $150 – $100 = $50. Her APS is saving/disposable income.

Examination Practice

Multiple Choice Questions

1. 'Money enables people to borrow and lend'. Which function of money does this describe?
   a. Measure of value
   b. Medium of exchange
   c. Standard for deferred payment
   d. Store of value

2. What is a function of a commercial bank?
   a. To control the money supply
   b. To decide on the amount spent by the government
   c. To lend to individuals and firms
   d. To manage the national debt

3. Which combination of events is likely to increase the price of shares?

	Firms' profits	*Interest rates*
a.	decrease	decrease
b.	decrease	increase
c.	increase	increase
d.	increase	decrease

4. Under what circumstances, are the wages paid to an occupation likely to be high?

	Demand for labour	*Supply of labour*
a.	high	high
b.	high	low
c.	low	low
d.	low	high

5. The diagram shows the market for lawyers in a country. The original equilibrium is at X. What would be the new equilibrium, if the qualifications needed to be a lawyer are increased?

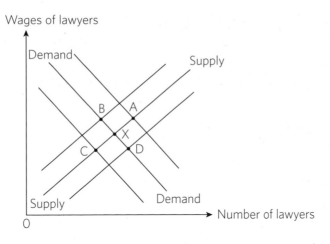

Wages of lawyers

Demand

Supply

B   A

X

C   D

Supply

Demand

0   Number of lawyers

6. More people throughout the world visit the cinema. What impact is this likely to have on the demand for actors and their wages?

	Demand for actors	Wages of actors
a.	decreases	decrease
b.	decreases	increase
c.	increases	increase
d.	increases	decrease

7. Which combination of events would increase a trade union's ability to negotiate a wage rise for its members?

	Labour productivity	Unemployment
a.	decreases	decreases
b.	decreases	increases
c.	increases	increases
d.	increases	decreases

8. In which circumstance will a strike be most damaging to a firm?
   a. The firm has large stocks of the product.
   b. The firm has no competitors.
   c. The strike involves most of the workers.
   d. The strike is short-lived.

9. Which government measure is most likely to increase the proportion of income saved by people?
   a.   A decrease in interest rates
   b.   A decrease in wages paid to government employees
   c.   An increase in income tax
   d.   An increase in the number of tax-free saving schemes

10. When a country's living standard improves, what is likely to happen to the percentage of household income spent on entertainment and food?

   Percentage of household income spent on:

	Food	Entertainment
a.	decreases	decreases
b.	decreases	increases
c.	increases	increases
d.	increases	decreases

Structured Questions

1.   Some workers work for long hours but earn little because the hourly wage received by them is very low.

   a.   Why do you think a worker would be prepared to work for very low wages? (5)

   b.   What reasons might make a worker decide to move to another job at the same scale of pay? (5)

   c.   Some workers belong to a trade union. Explain how membership of a trade union might be beneficial to a worker. (5)

   d.   An older skilled worker's pattern of expenditure and saving is likely to be different from that of a younger unskilled worker. Discuss. (5)

   (Cambridge 0455 Paper 2 Q4 May/June 2005)

2.   a.   Explain three things, other than wages, that might influence a person's choice of occupation. (6)

   b.   Discuss which factor of production might be most significant in the operation of a luxury hotel. (4)

   c.   A hotel will offer a variety of job opportunities. Workers in some of them will be paid more than workers in others. Discuss the reasons. (10)

   (Cambridge 0455 Paper 4 Q7 Oct/Nov 2005)

3. It was reported that in a country, the poorest households spent 30% of their income on food while the richest households spent 13% on food.

   a. Do these figures indicate that the actual amount that the richest households spent on food is lower than that spent by the poorest households? Explain your answer. (4)

   b. Ali has started his first job. Faizal is now in a senior position in his company. Describe the differences in the expenditure pattern of the two. (4)

   c. Analyse the motives that might cause a person to save rather than spend. (6)

   d. What might be the result of a general increase in the level of consumers' expenditure in an economy? (6)

   (Cambridge 0455 Paper 4 Q6 May/June 2004)

The Private Firm as Producer and Employer

UNIT 23

Types of Business Organisations

Previous units discussed different types of economic systems and mentioned public limited companies, private limited companies, state-owned companies and foreign-owned companies. In a market economy, most firms are in the private sector whereas in a planned economy, they are in the public sector. In a mixed economy, they are in both the private and public sectors. In this unit, the types of business organisations which exist in the two sectors are examined.

The Level of Production

Industries consist of firms producing the same product. The car industry, for example, includes firms such as Volvo, General Motors and Toyota.

A firm is a business entity, also sometimes referred to as a business organisation. Firms can have a number of plants. A plant is a production unit or workplace such as a factory, farm, office or branch. A firm may own several plants. The major car firms have factories throughout the world. Fig. 1 shows the level of production in the banking industry.

Banking industry

↓

Bank

↓

Branch

Fig. 1 Production in the banking industy

Key Point

An industry: a group of firms producing the same product.

The Stages of Production

Industries and their firms and plants, operate at different stages of production. The

primary sector is the first stage of production. It includes industries, such as agriculture, coal mining and forestry, involved in the extraction and collection of raw materials. The **secondary sector** is involved with the processing of raw materials into semi-finished and finished goods – both capital and consumer goods. It covers manufacturing and construction. The building, clothing and steel industries are in this sector.

The third stage of production is called the **tertiary sector**. Industries producing services such as banking, insurance and tourism, come into this sector.

Some economists identify a fourth sector also, the **quaternary sector**. This is really a sub-section of the tertiary sector. It covers those service industries which are involved with the collection, processing and transmission of information – essentially information technology.

As economies' income grows, their industrial structure usually changes. Poor countries often have a large proportion of its output accounted for and its labour force employed in industries in the primary sector. As they develop, the secondary sector becomes more important and gradually the tertiary sector accounts for most of its output and employment. Table 1 shows the contribution to output of the three sectors in six selected countries.

Table 1 Percentage contribution to the output of different industrial sectors.

Country	Primary %	Secondary %	Tertiary %
Pakistan	22	25	53
India	18	27	55
China	10	47	43
UK	1	21	78
USA	1	18	81
Hong Kong	0	8	92

Activity 1

The following is a list of industries. Decide the sector to which each industry belongs:

a. chemicals   b. education   c. fishing

d. retailing   e. telecommunications   f. transport

 # Business Organisations

In each stage of production, there is a variety of types of business organisations. Some of these are in the private sector. This means that they are owned by individuals and groups of individuals. Others are in the public sector which means that they are state-owned and controlled. Of those in the private sector, some business organisations have limited liability whereas others do not. Limited liability considers a firm and its shareholders (those who put their money into a company in return for a share of ownership of the firm) to be separate. A firm has limited liability when it is fully liable for any debt it incurs but the liability of its shareholders is limited to the amount that they have agreed to pay for their shares. They can lose what they have paid for (or are due to pay for) their shares, if the business gets into difficulties, but they cannot lose any more. They cannot, for example, be required to sell their home to meet the debts of the firm.

Limited liability encourages people to buy shares as they know that they are not putting their personal assets at risk. This helps to finance firms and allows them to expand.

Key Point

Limited liability: shareholders' liability for the business is limited to the value of the shares they have agreed to buy.

Sole Proprietors

A sole proprietor, also called a sole trader, is a 'one-person business'. This means it is owned by one person. This person carries out both the functions of the entrepreneur, bearing the uncertain risks and organising the factors of production. She or he is said to be self-employed. A sole proprietor can employ any number of people. In practice, sole proprietors tend to be relatively small. This is because one person is unlikely to be able to control a very large firm. Also the amount of finance the business has is limited to the amount, one person – the owner is prepared to put into the business.

A sole proprietor has unlimited liability. If the business fails, the owner can lose not only the money she or he has put into it but some or even all of her (or his) personal assets, depending on the size of the business debts. If, on the other hand, the business is a success, the sole proprietor will receive all the profits.

Although sole proprietors are small, they are the most common type of business organisation in most countries. This is because they are relatively easy to set up. Table 2 lists the main advantages and disadvantages of this type of firm.

Table 2 The main advantages and disadvantages of a sole proprietor.

Advantages	Disadvantages
* Flexible – quick to respond to changes in demand as one person makes the decisions * Incentive to be efficient as owner will get all the profit * Personal contact with consumers can promote sales * Personal contact with employees can motivate them * Low start up costs	* Unlimited liability * Limited finance available to expand the business * The sole proprietor may lack the full range of skills needed * The success of the business is dependent on the health of one person * Lack of continuity. The business ends if the sole proprietor goes bankrupt, dies or is no longer willing to run the business

Key Point

A sole proprietor: a business owned by one person.

Partnerships

Most partnerships, like sole proprietors, have unlimited liability and partners are self-employed. The partners are the owners of the business. There have to be at least two partners and the maximum number is usually limited to twenty, although in some cases more than twenty members are allowed. Again, as with sole traders, partnerships can employ any number of workers.

Also, partnerships are relatively easy to set up. Having more than one owner means that partnerships are likely to be able to raise more finance and have more expertise at hand in running the business. In fact, some of the partners may possess specialist skills. Even if one of the partners is on leave (say due to illness), it will hamper the functioning of the firm as significantly as in the case of a sole proprietor.

Partnerships, however, lack continuity since if one partner leaves, the whole partnership is automatically dissolved and a new one would have to be set up by the remaining partners. A partnership's access to finance, whilst greater than a sole proprietor's, is still limited. Partnerships are particularly common in professional services such as accountancy, architects, dentists and solicitors.

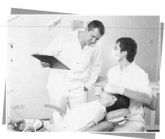

Key Point

A partnership: a business organisation of two or more people who are personally responsible for its debts and share its profits.

Activity 2

Decide which of the following apply to a:
(i)   a sole proprietor
(ii)   a partnership
(iii) a sole proprietor and a partnership
    a.   one owner
    b.   limited finance
    c.   some scope for specialisation
    d.   unlimited liability.

Private Limited Companies

Private limited companies, sometimes referred to as *limited companies*, are a form of joint stock company. This means that a number of people can jointly own the business. The financial capital of the company is divided into shares. Information about the company has to be provided to the shareholders on an annual basis. The company has a continuous existence i.e. it carries on even if a major shareholder dies or sells her or his shares.

As the name suggests, private limited companies have limited liability. They must have at least two members. Most are relatively small firms with many of them being owned by families. This is because these companies cannot invite the general public to buy their shares. It is necessary to get the consent of the other shareholders before any shares are sold and they have to be sold to known individuals. This restriction on who the shares can be sold to helps to keep the control of the firm in few hands, with those owning the shares usually managing the business. It does, however, limit the amount of finance which can be raised. For this reason, some private limited companies convert to public limited companies.

Key Point

A private limited company: a business organisation with limited liability which can only sell its shares with the approval of existing shareholders.

Public Limited Companies

Public limited companies often have 'plc' at the end of their names whereas private limited companies usually have 'ltd'. They are, however, similar to private limited companies as both are joint stock companies, have limited liability and a continuous existence. They can, however, sell their shares to the general public. This increases the number of potential shareholders and the ability of their shareholders to sell their shares on the stock exchange. This also increases people's willingness to buy them. This means that this type of business organisation can raise a considerable amount of finance through the sale of its shares. This, together with bank loans and reinvested profits, can enable them to grow to a large size.

To be able to sell their shares to the general public, public limited companies have to provide more information than private limited companies. First, they are required to issue a prospectus describing the company and its plans and explaining the offer of shares. After that, they have to send a copy of their accounts and a report each year to every shareholder.

In industrialised countries, whilst sole traders are usually the most common type of business organisation, public limited companies account for the largest proportion of output. However, there are two main risks attached to public limited companies. One is that their shares are available on the stock exchange, hence they may be subject to a take over. The other is that the shareholders may be too concerned with gaining high dividends (share of profits) at the expense of the long term development of the companies.

Key Point

A public limited company: a business organisation with limited liability which sells its shares to the general public.

The Separation of Ownership and Control

In a public limited company, there is a separation between ownership and control of the company. The role of the entrepreneur is divided between shareholders and the directors. The shareholders are the owners but most of them do not take an active part in the running of the company. The control of the company is in the hands of a board of directors, elected by shareholders at an annual general meeting (AGM). If the shareholders are not satisfied with the way the business is being managed by the directors, they can vote them out although in practice not many shareholders turn up for the AGM.

Activity 3

Decide whether the following statements are most relevant to a sole proprietor, a partnership, a private limited company or a public limited company.
a. Quoted on the stock exchange
b. Easy to set up
c. Dissolved on the death of one of the owners
d. Shares can only be sold with the agreement of existing shareholders

Multinationals

A multinational company (MNC) is a business organisation, that produces in more than one country. For instance, the US based MacDonalds has outlets in many countries, the UK based Lloyds TSB Bank has branches in a range of countries and the Japanese based Toyota has factories in a number of countries. Most MNCs are public limited companies but an increasing number of SOEs are now producing internationally. For instance, the chinese state-owned oil giant, the China National Offshore Oil Company (CNOOC) operates in a number of countries. There are a number of benefits MNCs hope to gain by spreading their operations in more than one country. Producing in countries where products are sold rather than exporting to those countries will reduce the MNCs' transport costs and enable them to keep in close contact with the market. It may also enable them to get around any restrictions on imports, to gain access to cheaper labour and raw materials. They may also receive grants from the governments of the countries in which they set up their franchises.

MNCs can have a number of effects on the countries in which they are located, some beneficial and others harmful. They can increase employment, output and tax revenue, bring in new technology and management ideas and help in development of infrastructure. They may, however, be more prone to pollute and willing to close down plants in foreign countries. Their size and their ability to shift production may mean that they can put pressure on the governments of the countries, in which they have plants, to give them tax concessions and not to penalise them for poor safety standards. In addition, although MNCs may increase employment, there is a risk that they may drive domestic firms out of business. The profits they earn may be paid to shareholders in other countries rather than being reinvested in the host country.

Recent years have seen the growing importance of MNCs. These companies are increasingly seeing countries, throughout the world, as their markets and possible locations for production. Besides setting up the operating plants abroad which produce the complete finished good, they are also spreading different parts of the production process in different countries. For instance, an MNC producing cars may base its design in a country with a strong tradition in design, its assembly in a country with a skilled but low cost labour force and its administration and marketing in other countries. In fact, the production process of some products is spread over more than fourteen countries.

Key Point

Multinational company: a company which produces in a number of countries.

Activity 4

Which of the following would attract a MNC to set up in a country?
a.   Low corporate taxes
b.   Government grants
c.   Strict employment laws
d.   A good educational system
e.   Cheap land

Co-operatives

Co-operatives are owned jointly by their members and are run for the benefit of those members. There are a number of types of co-operatives. In the case of worker co-operatives, the people who work in the business own it, make the decisions and share the profits. The main aim of consumer co-operatives is to help the buyers of the product. They buy in bulk and so are able to sell at relatively cheap prices. The general public can buy shares in these co-operatives. They receive interest on their shares which can only be sold back to the co-operative. Each shareholder (called member) has only one vote at shareholders' meetings, irrespective of number of shares they possess. Any profits made are distributed to shoppers, based on the amount spent by them.

The other types of co-operatives include housing and trading co-operatives. Housing co-operatives buy and manage low-cost housing. Trading co-operatives are formed by small businesses joining together to share techniques, capital equipment and workers and to be able to buy raw materials in bulk. In India, they are important in the primary sector. The Indian government encourages farmers of some products, including cotton, edible oils and sugar, to join together in co-operatives.

Co-operatives can bring a number of benefits to members including the benefits of size and give important decision-making power to those involved. There is a risk, however, that there may be a lack of management skill.

Key Point

A co-operative: a firm that exists for the benefits of its members.

Public Corporations

Public corporations, also called *state-owned enterprises* and *nationalised* industries, are owned by the government. The chairman and board of managers are appointed by the government. They are responsible for the day to day management but are accountable to the government. There are no shareholders in public corporations. The funds come from the government, from government approved loans and from the private sector. Public corporations do not seek to make a profit. Their aim is to work in the public interest.

There are a number of advantages that can be claimed for public corporations. Some of them are as follows:

- They base their decisions on the full costs and benefits involved.

- They can be used to influence economic activity. To boost the country's output, public corporations can be directly encouraged to increase their output.

- In cases where it is practical to have only one firm in the industry, such as rail infrastructure, a public corporation would not abuse its market power.

- Ownership of a whole industry by the government makes planning and coordination easier. For instance, if the state runs the train system, it can ensure that train timetables are coordinated.

- It is important to ensure that basic industries, such as electricity and transport survive, charge low prices and produce good quality as other domestic industries depend on them.

There are, however, a number of disadvantages associated with public corporations.

- They can be difficult to manage and control. The large size of the organisations may mean that time has to be spent on meetings and communicating with staff, slowing down decision making.

- They may become inefficient, produce low quality products and charge relatively high prices, due to a lack of competition and the knowledge that they cannot go bankrupt.

- They will need to be subsidised if they are loss making. The use of tax revenue to support them has an opportunity cost – it could be used to spend on, say, training more teachers and nurses.

Key Point

Public corporation: a business organisation owned by the government which is designed to act in the public interest.

Privatisation

Concern about the performance of public corporations and increased confidence in market forces has led a number of countries to sell their public corporations, or part of their public corporations, to the private sector. Those supporting this move argue that private sector firms are likely to produce the comodities, desired by consumers, at a low cost and offer them at low prices. This is because market forces provide an incentive for firms to be efficient in the form of profit and a threat of bankruptcy if they are in efficient. Besides low prices and high quality, privatisation may result in greater choice. Freedom from government regulation may reduce administration costs and enable managers to respond more quickly to changing conditions. There may, also, be less risk of under-investment in the private sector. The funds available to a public sector firm for investment will depend on the profits it earns and its ability to convince shareholders and lenders of its success. Public corporations may be kept short of funds for investment, however successful they are, if the government wants to spend the money elsewhere.

Privatisation, however, is itself criticised. There is no guarantee that private sector firms will face the full pressure of market forces. Some private sector firms may not face competition – they may be monopolies (i.e. the only firm selling the product). In this case they can be inefficient, charge high prices and produce low quality products without compromising on profits. They may not take into account the total costs and benefits to the society due to their actions. For instance, they may cause pollution. Privatisation also reduces government's control of the economy.

Key Point

Privatisation: the sale of public sector assets to the private sector.

Activity 5

It is important not to confuse public corporations and public limited companies. Complete table 3 which compares the two.

Table 3 A comparison of a public corporation and a public limited company

	Public corporation	*Public limited company*
Ownership Sector Aim	The government Acts in the public interest	Private

Summary

- Industries consist of many firms producing the same products and firms may have a number of plants.

- The three main stages of production are – primary (collecting and extracting raw materials), secondary (manufacturing and construction) and tertiary (services).

- A sole proprietor is a one-person business with unlimited liability.

- Partnerships have at least two members and have unlimited liability.

- Private limited companies have limited liability but their shares can only be sold with the consent of existing shareholders.

- Public limited companies can become large because they have both limited liability and can sell their shares to the general public on the stock exchange.

continued····>

- MNCs are growing in importance. MNCs operate in other countries for a variety of reasons including reduced transport costs, getting round import restrictions, obtaining government grants and access to cheaper labour and raw materials.

- MNCs can have a number of effects on the countries in which they are based. They may raise output, employment and tax revenue and bring in new technology and management ideas but may generate pollution, drive out domestic producers, may shift production to other countries and unduly influence the government.

- Co-operatives are owned by their members. These may by the workers, consumers or producers.

- Public corporations do not have shareholders as they are owned by the government. They should be run in the public interest, can be used to influence economic activity, do not abuse market power, can make planning easier and can ensure the survival of important industries.

- A number of governments have sold off some of their public corporations to the private sector and others are in the process of doing so. They hope that the businesses will operate more efficiently in the private sector.

Teacher's Tip

Try not to confuse public limited companies and public corporations (state owned enterprises).

Multiple Choice Questions

1. Which of the following is a characteristic of a sole proprietorship?
   a. The business employs only one worker.
   b. The business has limited liability.
   c. The profits of the business go to the sole proprietor.
   d. Shares in the business are sold on the stock exchange.

2. The government sells off a state owned enterprise to thousands of shareholders who can sell their shares on the stock exchange. How has the state of the organisation changed?
   a. From a public limited company to a private limited company
   b. From a public limited company to a public corporation
   c. From a public corporation to a private limited company
   d. From a public corporation to a public limited company

3. Which of the following is an advantage to a country, of having a multinational company producing in that country?
   a. The company employs local people.
   b. The company depletes non-renewable resources rapidly.
   c. The company sends its profits back to the country in which its headquarters is based.
   d. The company reduces its costs by lowering its health and safety standards.

4. What is meant by 'the separation of ownership and control' in public limited companies?
   a. Consumers both own and control the companies.
   b. Workers both own and control the business.
   c. The companies are owned by shareholders but managed by the state.
   d. The companies are owned by shareholders but managed by directors and managers.

Demand for Factors of Production

Firms employ factors of production in order to produce products. They constantly review the factors to be employed and their most suitable combinations. This unit examines the factors that influence firms' decisions on choice of factors to be employed.

 ## What Factors of Production are Employed

The type of factors of production employed is influenced by the type of product produced, the productivity of the factors and their cost. A firm producing a standardised model of car is likely to be very capital intensive whereas a beauty salon is likely to be labour intensive.

When factors of production are substitutes, a rise in the productivity or fall in the cost of one of them may result in a change in the combination of resources being employed. A fall in the price of capital goods, for example, might lead to the replacement of some workers with machines. In other cases where factors of production are complements, a fall in the price of one or a rise in its productivity may increase the employment of all factors in a firm. For instance, a fall in the price of aircraft may make it possible for an airline to fly to more destinations. If so, they will also employ more pilots, more cabin crew and obtain more take off and landing slots at airports.

 ## Altering Factors of Production

If a firm wants to change the quantity of resources employed by it, it will find it easier to do this with some factors than others. In the short run, there is likely to be at least one fixed factor of production. This means the quantity cannot be altered quickly. The most obvious example is the size of the factory or office. It will take time for a firm desiring expansion, to extend its buildings or build new ones. Similarly, one wanting to reduce output is unlikely to be able to stop renting or sell off its buildings quickly. In contrast, it is likely to be easier to change the quantity of labour. Even in the very short run, it may be possible to alter the quantity of labour by changing the amount of overtime available. It may also be possible to change orders for raw materials and capital equipment but it will depend on the length of contracts and, in the case of increasing demand, the availability of spare capacity in firms producing them.

Combining the Factors of Production

It is important to achieve the right combination of factors of production. For instance, it would not make sense for a hairdressing salon to have ten hair dryers and two hairdressers or a farmer to have a large amount of land and only a few cattle. In the first case, labour would be underutilised and in the second case, there would be an insufficient number of livestock to make full use of land. While deciding the combination of resources, firms seek to achieve the highest possible productivity. For instance, table 1 shows that the most appropriate number of workers to be employed (in terms of productivity) with five machines is seven, since this is where output per worker is highest. It is interesting to note that the combination is not always one machine per worker. This is because workers may work in shifts, some workers may be undertaking training and, of course, in some cases one worker may use more than one piece of machinery.

Table 1 Combining labour with machines.

No. of machines	No. of workers	Total output (units)	Output per worker (average product) (units)
5	1	50	50
5	2	120	60
5	3	210	70
5	4	320	80
5	5	450	90
5	6	600	100
5	7	770	110
5	8	800	100
5	9	810	90

Activity 1

From the following information, calculate the average product of labour and decide the most efficient combination of workers and machines.

No. of machines	No. of workers	Total output (units)
4	1	10
4	2	24
4	3	45
4	4	72
4	5	100
4	6	108
4	7	112

Factors Influencing Demand for Capital Goods

Among the key factors influencing demand for capital goods are the price of capital goods, price of other factors of production, profit levels, corporation tax, income, interest rates, confidence levels and advances in technology.

A rise in the price of capital goods will cause a contraction in demand for capital goods whereas an increase in the price of another factor of production, particularly labour, may increase the demand for capital goods. This will occur, if the factors are substitutes and the rise in price of another factor makes the production of a unit of output more expensive than that involving a rise in capital. If another factor is a complement, an increase in its price would cause a decrease in demand for capital. If profit levels are high, firms will have both the ability and the incentive to buy capital goods. A cut in corporation tax would also mean that firms would have more profit available to plough back into the business and greater incentive to do the same. Rising real disposable income will lead to an increase in consumption. This, in turn, is likely to encourage firms to invest as they will expect to sell a higher output in the future.

A cut in interest rates would also tend to raise consumption and thereby encourage firms to expand their capacity. In addition, lower interest rates would increase investment because they would reduce the opportunity cost of investing and lower the cost of borrowing. Firms can use profits to buy more capital goods instead of depositing them in bank accounts. With low interest rates, firms would be sacrificing less interest by buying capital goods. Borrowing to buy capital goods would also be less costly.

Another key influence on investment is firms' expectations about the future. If they are confident that sales will rise, they will invest now. In contrast, a rise in pessimism will result in a decline in investment.

Advances in technology will increase the productivity of capital goods. If new and more efficient machinery is developed, firms are likely to invest more.

Key Point

Corporation tax: a tax on profits of a company.

 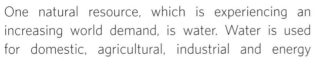

Demand for Land

Productivity is a key factor influencing demand for land. In terms of agricultural land, the most fertile land will be in highest demand and receive the highest rent. City centre sites are also very productive as firms have the potential to attract a high number of customers.

If a shop in the centre of New York becomes vacant, it is likely that a number of retail firms would compete for it in the expectation that they could earn a high revenue there. The competition pushes up the rent, that can be charged for a favourable site.

One natural resource, which is experiencing an increasing world demand, is water. Water is used for domestic, agricultural, industrial and energy production purposes. As countries become richer, they make heavier demands on scarce water supplies. Global use of water has increased six times in the last hundred years and is predicted to double again by 2050.

Activity 2

Rising living standards in China and India are increasing the demand for water, which in turn is affecting the price of water.

a. Explain how improving living standards would increase the demand for water.

b. Using a demand and supply diagram, explain what is likely to happen to the price of water in the future.

Factors of Production and Sectors of Production

The demand for factors of production can alter as an economy changes its industrial structure. As mentioned in Unit 23, the distribution of resources among different sectors changes with economic development. In most cases, agricultural reform permits resources to move to low cost manufacturing. Then, resources move to higher value added manufacturing and then finally the service sector becomes the most important one. This is the case with, for instance, China where currently most of its resources are concentrated in the secondary sector and where the secondary sector is the main engine of economic growth. Not all economies, however, conform to this pattern. India's service

sector has expanded before it has built up a sizeable manufacturing sector. In fact, in 2012, India's service sector accounted for 55% of the country's output.

Different industries make use of different factors of production. The chemical industry, for instance, is very capital intensive and agriculture is land intensive (along with being water intensive).

Activity 3

The broadband revolution is revolutionising the mode of working for many. It is enabling more people to work from home and effectively introducing a new piece work model. The more flexible a country is, in creating new employment relationships, the better it will be at getting the most of the new technologies.

a. What is meant by a 'piece work' model?
b. Explain how having workers working form home may affect a firm's:
   (i) output
   (ii) costs of production.

 **Summary**

- The key factors that influence the factors of production employed are the type of products produced, the productivity of the factors and their cost.

- In the short run, there is likely to be at least one fixed factor of production, most commonly capital.

- The average product of labour (productivity) is total output divided by the number of workers.

- Demand for capital goods is influenced by the price of capital goods, the price of other factors of production, profit levels, income, interest rates, confidence and advances in technology.

- City centre sites command a high rent because they are in high demand.

- The factors of production, used in an economy, are influenced by the economy's industrial structure.

 Teacher's Tip

Remember that whilst production is output, productivity is output per worker or output per factor of production.

Multiple Choice Questions

1. The table shows the distribution of the workforce of a country between two years.

	Employment in millions	
	Year 1	*Year 2*
Agriculture	10	8
Mining	4	5
Manufacturing	20	20
Retailing	10	12
Education	5	5

How did the distribution of employment change between year 1 and year 2?

Primary industry	*Secondary industry*	*Tertiary industry*
a. fell	unchanged	rose
b. rose	fell	unchanged
c. unchanged	rose	fell
d. rose	unchanged	fell

2. A doctor and an operating theatre are:
    a. complementary factors of production
    b. substitute factors of production
    c. an example of labour and land
    d. an example of enterprise and capital.

3. Which of the following would cause an increase in demand for capital goods?
   a. A decrease in corporation tax
   b. A fall in disposable income
   c. A rise in interest rates
   d. A rise in pessimism

4. Twenty five workers produce a total output of 300. What is the average product per worker?
   a. 12   b. 25
   c. 300   d. 7 500

Costs of Production

The previous unit mentioned rises in productivity and advances in technology. Both would be likely to reduce a firm's average cost of production. This unit explores the concepts of total cost, average cost, fixed costs, average fixed cost, variable costs and average variable costs and examines the effect of changes in output on these costs.

 ## Total and Average Cost

Total cost (TC), as its name implies, is the total cost of producing a given output. The more the output is produced, the higher the total cost of production. Producing more units requires the use of more resources. Average cost (AC) is also referred to as unit cost and is given as total cost divided by output. Table 1 shows the relationship between output, total cost and average cost.

Table 1 Total and average cost.

Output	Total cost ($)	Average cost (4)
0	10	–
1	30	30
2	48	24
3	60	20
4	88	22
5	125	25

Key Point

Total cost: the total cost of production.

Fixed Costs

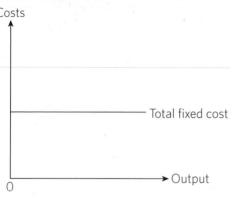

Costs

Total fixed cost

Output

0

Fig. 1 Total fixed cost

Table 1 indicates that there is a cost even when output is zero. In the short run, some factors of production are in fixed supply. When a firm changes its output, the costs of these factors remain unchanged – they are *fixed*. For instance, if a firm raised its output, the interest it pays on past loans would remain unchanged. If it closed down during a holiday period, it may still have to pay for security and rent for buildings. Fig. 1 shows that total fixed cost (TFC) remains unchanged as output changes.

Fixed costs (FC) are also sometimes referred to as **overheads** or **indirect costs**.

Key Point

Fixed costs: costs which do not change with output in the short run.

Average Fixed Cost

Average fixed cost (AFC) is total fixed cost divided by output. As fixed cost is constant, average fixed cost is divided by higher output. Table 2 and Fig. 2 show how average fixed cost falls as output increases.

Table 2 Average fixed cost.

Output	Total Fixed cost ($)	Average Fixed cost ($)
0	10	–
1	10	10
2	10	5
3	10	3.33
4	10	2.5
5	10	2

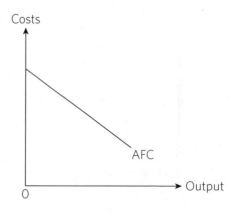

Costs

AFC

Output

0

Fig. 2 Average fixed cost

Variable Costs

Variable costs (VC), also sometimes called **direct costs**, are the costs of the variable factors. They vary directly as output changes. Production and sale of more cars will involve an increased expenditure on component parts, electricity, wages and transport for a car firm.

As output increases, total variable cost rises. It usually tends to rise slowly at first and then rise more rapidly. This is because productivity often rises at first and then begins to decline after a certain output.

Fig. 3 shows the change of total variable cost (TVC) with output.

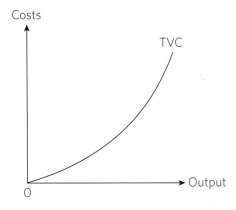

Fig. 3 Total variable cost

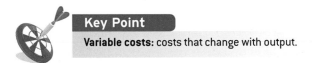

Key Point

Variable costs: costs that change with output.

Average Variable Cost

Average variable cost (AVC) is total variable cost divided by output. As output increases in the short run, average variable cost tends to fall and then rise. This is for the same reason which accounts for an increase in total variable cost at different rates with increase in output. Table 3 and Fig. 4 show the change in average variable cost with output.

Table 3 Average variable cost

Output	Total Variable cost ($)	Average Variable cost ($)
1	40	40
2	70	35
3	90	30
4	120	30
5	175	35

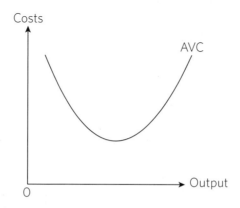

Fig. 4 Average variable cost

A bakery is faced with the following costs: flour, yeast, rent, business rates, insurance, overtime pay, depreciation and energy costs. Decide which are fixed and which are variable costs.

Fixed and Variable Costs

In practice, it is not always easy to decide whether a cost is fixed or variable. This is particularly true of *payments to workers*. It is clear that overtime payments and the wages of temporary workers are variable costs as they vary directly with output. The basic wage or salary paid to workers, however, may be regarded as a fixed cost since it has to be paid irrespective of the amount of output.

Sum of total fixed cost and total variable cost equals total cost. For instance, if fixed costs are $800 and variable costs are $4 200 a week, the total cost of production would be $5 000 a week.

Fig. 5 depicts the constitution of total cost including fixed and variable costs.

In the long run, however, all costs are variable. This is because all factors of production can be altered, if sufficient time is available. For instance, a firm can increase the size of its factory, office or farm. Therefore its rent and business rates would rise and it can hire more workers, pushing up the wage bill.

Fig. 6 depicts total cost in the long run.

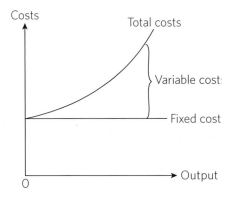

Fig. 5 The composition of total cost

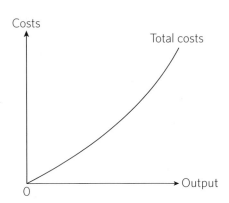

Fig. 6 Long-term total cost

 Average Cost

In the short run, average cost consists of **average fixed cost** and **average variable cost**. The shape of the short run average cost curve is usually U-shaped. The long run average cost curve is also usually U-shaped. This can be explained as follows. As a firm alters its scale of production, it first experiences economies of scale and then, after reaching a certain output, it may encounter diseconomies of scale (see unit 29 for an explanation of economies and diseconomies of scale).

Key Point

Long run: the time period when all factors of production can be changed and all costs are variable.

Table 4 Costs of production

Output	TC	TFC	TVC	AC	AFC	AVC
0	60					
1	110					
2	150					
3	180					
4	200					
5	230					
6	300					

 Summary

- Total cost rises with output.

- In the short run, firms incur both fixed and variable costs.

- Fixed costs do not change with output in the short run.

- Average fixed costs fall as output rises.

- Variable costs increase as output rises.

- Average variable cost tends to fall and then rise, as output increases.

- In the short run, total cost consists of fixed and variable costs.

- In the long run, all costs are variable.

- The shape of the long run average variable cost is influenced by economies and diseconomies of scale.

 Teacher's Tip

While deciding whether costs are fixed or variable, remember to consider whether the costs will change with output in the short run. Remember that **all** costs change with output in the long run.

Multiple Choice Questions

1. Which of the following is a fixed cost to a manufacturing firm?
    a. Insurance on buildings
    b. Overtime payments to workers
    c. The cost of energy
    d. The cost of raw materials

2. A firm produces 50 units of output. The total variable cost of this output is $200 and the total fixed cost is $300. What is the average cost of production?
    a. $2
    b. $4
    c. $6
    d. $10

3. A firm in the short run has only fixed costs. Which diagram shows the total cost?

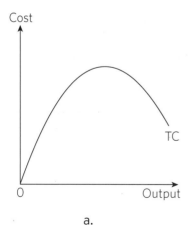

a.

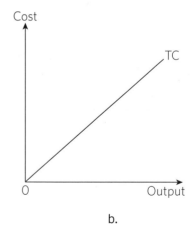

b.

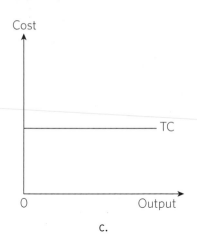

c.

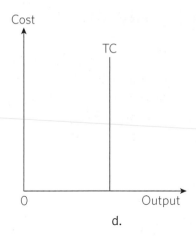

d.

4. Which statement about variable costs is correct?
   a. They are equal to total cost minus fixed costs.
   b. They exist only in the short run.
   c. They fall with output.
   d. They have to be paid even when nothing is produced.

Principle of Profit Maximisation

Profit is made when the revenue earned by a firm is greater than the costs incurred by it. Profit maximisation is a goal pursued by most private sector firms. This unit explores profit and revenue in more detail, focussing particularly on profit maximisation.

 ## The Nature of Profit

Total profit is the positive difference between total revenue and total cost. Profit per unit (sometimes referred to as the profit margin) is the positive difference between average revenue (revenue per unit) and average cost (unit cost).

 ## Revenue

The money received by firms from selling their products is referred to as revenue. Total revenue is, as its name suggests, the total amount of money received by firms receive through sale of their products. Average revenue is found by dividing total revenue by the quantity sold and is the same as **price**.

A rise in the sales of perfectly competitive firms has no effect on price. In this case, total revenue rises consistently as more quantity is sold. Table 1 shows the change of total revenue with sales.

Table 1 Average and total revenue of a perfectly competitive firm.

Quantity sold	Average revenue (price per unit) ($)	Total revenue ($)
1	10	10
2	10	20
3	10	30
4	10	40
5	10	50
6	10	60
7	10	70

Fig. 1 shows the same information graphically.

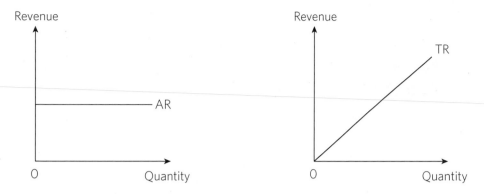

Fig. 1 The average and total revenue curves of a perfectly competitive firm

In most markets, however, firms are price makers and need to lower price to sell more. Table 2 and Fig. 2 depict the change in total revenue and average revenue in this case.

Table 2 Average and total revenue in an imperfectly competitive market.

Quantity sold	Average revenue (price per unit) ($)	Total revenue ($)
1	10	10
2	9	18
3	8	24
4	7	28
5	6	30
6	5	30
7	4	28

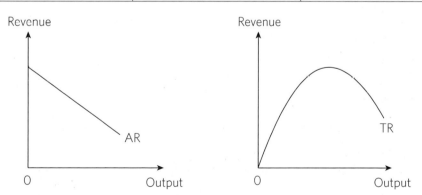

Fig. 2 The average and total revenue curves of an imperfectly competitive firm

Average revenue falls as the quantity sold rises. Total revenue rises at first, reaches a peak and then falls beyond a certain level of sales.

Goals of Firms

Firms may pursue a range of goals including sales revenue maximisation, growth, profit satisficing, improvement of the environment, social responsibility and profit maximisation.

Sales revenue maximisation occurs when a firm makes as much revenue as possible. In table 2, this occurs when the quantity sold is 5. High and expanding sales revenue tends to make it easier for firms to raise finance and cheaper to sell in bulk. Of course, in deciding the quantity to be produced and sold, firms have to consider their costs also. Those who run firms – the managers, directors and chief executives, may have the growth of the firm as their key objective, and hence they may try to maximise sales. This is because managers, directors and chief executive's pay and status is more closely linked to the size of the firm they run. Those in charge of large firms are usually paid more than those running smaller firms and also tend to be held in higher esteem. They may also have greater job security as the larger the firm they run, the more difficult it will be for any other firm to take it over and replace them with their own managerial team.

In recent years, firms have been showing a greater concern about the environmental and social effects of their actions. A number of firms have sought to clean up their production processes and ensure that they source their raw materials from firms that do not employ child labour.

While seeking to maximise sales revenue and growth, improve the environment, assume socially responsibility or achieve any other objective, the managers, directors and chief executives of limited companies need to keep their shareholders happy. Achieving enough profit to pay out high enough dividends to keep them happy is called profit satisficing.

Traditional theory, however, suggests that firms seek to maximise profits. This means that they try to earn the largest profit possible over a period of time. It is interesting to note that whilst some of the other goals may appear to conflict with profit maximisation, pursuit of them may actually increase profits in the longer term. For instance, increasing the size of the firms may involve reducing the number of competitors and increasing the scale of operation may reduce average costs.

Both of these outcomes would increase profits. Seeking to pursue environment friendly policies and being socially responsible may raise costs of production but may also increase demand and revenue, as consumers are becoming increasingly concerned that firms should act in an ethical manner. Government run concerns, of course, may have other goals including providing a service to the community and maintaining high employment.

Key Points

Profit maximisation: making as much profit as possible.

Profit satisficing: sacrificing some profit to achieve other goals.

Profit Maximisation

Profit is maximised when the positive gap between revenue and cost is greatest. Table 3 shows that profit would be maximised at 40 units of output.

Table 3 The relationship between total revenue, total cost and profit.

Output	Total revenue ($)	Total cost ($)	Total Profit ($)
10	200	220	-20
20	380	380	0
30	500	480	20
40	600	540	60
50	660	620	40
60	700	710	-10

Besides calculating total profit, the profit per unit can be found by deducting average cost from average revenue, as shown in Table 4. In this case, profit is maximised at three units.

Table 4 The relationship between average revenue, average cost and profit.

Output	Average revenue ($)	Average cost ($)	Total Profit ($)
1	15	15	0
2	14	12	2
3	12	9	3
4	9	8	1
5	5	10	-5

From the information in Table 4, it is possible to calculate total revenue (by multiplying average revenue with output), total cost (by multiplying average cost with output) and total profit (by multiplying profit per unit with output). These figures are shown in Table 5.

Table 5 Total Revenue, total cost and total profit.

Output	Average revenue ($)	Average cost ($)	Profit per unit
1	15	15	0
2	28	24	4
3	36	27	9
4	36	32	4
5	25	50	−25

If information is given on output, costs and revenue, it is possible to work out revenue as shown in table 6. This is because it is known that

$$profit = revenue - cost.$$

so revenue = profit + cost. Similarly from information on output, revenue and profit, cost can be calculated.

$$Cost = revenue - profit.$$

Table 6 The relationship between total cost, total profit and total revenue.

Output	Total cost ($)	Total profit ($)	Total revenue ($)
10	400	0	400
20	700	100	800
30	900	300	1 200
40	1 200	400	1 600
50	1 700	300	2 000

Activity 1

a. From the following information, determine what is the profit maximising output.

Output	Total revenue ($)	Total cost ($)
10	80	90
20	150	150
30	210	190
40	260	210
50	300	260

b. From the following information, complete the column for total cost.

Output	Total revenue ($)	Total profit ($)	Total cost ($)
10	80	−20	
20	150	0	
30	210	30	
40	260	20	
50	300	−40	

Effects of Changes in Profits

Profits provide an incentive for entrepreneurs to undertake production. An increase in profit will encourage more firms to enter a competitive market. It will also provide firms with more finance to update their capital equipment and expand their business.

A profitable firm will also find it easier to obtain external finance. Shareholders are more likely to want to buy shares in profitable firms and banks are usually willing to give them loans. These firms may also find it easier to recruit top managers and directors, attracted by their success.

The effect of a fall in profit may vary with time. At first it may have little impact on the behaviour of firms, if they think that it will only be short lived. After a while if profits remain low, or fall further, some firms will cut back on production and others will cease production.

Ways of Increasing Profit

The two fundamental ways of increasing profit are to

- reduce costs of production, and

- raise revenue.

There are a number of ways of reducing costs of production. One is by reducing any wastages and inefficiency. Another is by increasing the productivity of **factors of production.** In the short run the second strategy may actually raise costs but in the long run it may lower average costs and raise revenue by improving quality. For instance, a firm may spend more on training workers and may replace existing equipment with more technologically advanced version. In the longer run, these measures should increase output per worker and per machine and therefore reduce average cost. A third way is by increasing the size of the firm through merger or takeover. A larger firm may be able to take advantage of economies of scale (see unit 29).

It will be likely to have higher total revenue. It may also have a higher total profit and profit per unit, due to its greater market share. Firms with considerable market power often have inelastic demand for their products. When demand is inelastic, a firm can increase its revenue by raising price. In contrast if demand is elastic, the revenue may be raised by cutting down price.

Besides trying to raise revenue by changing price, firms may seek to increase demand for the products. There is a variety of ways in which this can be done. They may seek to improve the quality of their products, diversify and be more responsive to changes in consumer demand by improving their market research. Another method that firms may employ is advertising. A successful advertising campaign is one which increases demand by more than the cost and hence raises profit.

Activity 2

In the first half of 2006, the US firm Wal-Mart – the world's largest retailer, announced a rise in sales revenue but a fall in profit. A company spokesperson said the firm was seeking to reduce stock levels and expected the demand to increase in the future.

a. How can sales revenue rise but profits fall?

b. Explain:

   (i)   how a reduction in stock levels could increase profit

   (ii) one way a firm could increase demand.

Activity 3

In 2005, Marks & Spencer, a well-known UK clothes retailer received a total revenue of £7 035m and earned a profit of £588m. 'Next', a smaller clothes retailer earned £2 585m in total revenue and a profit of £380m.

The way that clothes retailers seek to raise demand for their products varies. Some spend a lot on advertising while others concentrate on buying good sites and window displays.

a. Calculate Marks & Spencer's total cost in 2005.

b. Compare Marks & Spencer's and Next's profits in 2005, in percentage terms.

c. Explain how buying good sites and window displays can increase profits.

Summary

- Average revenue (price) is total revenue divided by the quantity sold.

- In a perfectly competitive market, average revenue stays the same as the quantity sold rises. In most markets, however, firms have to lower the price to sell more.

- Firms may seek to maximise sales revenue, grow, improve the environment and their social image, earn enough profit to satisfy shareholders or make as much profit as possible.

- Profits are maximised when the positive gap between revenue and cost is greatest.

continued····>

- Total profit is total revenue minus total cost whilst profit per unit is the difference between average revenue and average cost.

- A change in profit may affect the number and size of firms in the industry.

- Profit can be increased by raising revenue or cutting costs.

- Costs can be cut by reducing wastages and inefficiency, raising productivity and increasing the scale of operation.

- Revenue can be raised by altering price, improving the product, adapting more quickly to changes in consumer demand and advertising.

Teacher's Tip

Remember that profit is not the same as revenue. Revenue might increase but profit would fall, if costs rise by more than revenue.

Multiple Choice Questions

1. A firm sells 100 units at a price of $4 per product. From this information, calculate the firm's total revenue (TR) and average revenue (AR).

	Total revenue ($)	Average revenue ($)
a.	100	4
b.	100	25
c.	400	4
d.	400	25

2. A firm achieves profit maximisation. What does this mean?
   a. It cannot increase its profit by changing its output.
   b. It makes more profit than the other firms in the industry.
   c. It maximises its total revenue.
   d. It produces at the lowest possible cost.

3. Which group is most concerned with profit maximisation?
   a. Consumers
   b. Shareholders
   c. The government
   d. Workers

4. The table shows the total cost and profit of a firm making cameras.

Sales of cameras	Total cost ($)	Total profit ($)
10	500	-100
20	800	0
30	1 000	200
40	1 560	40

   What is the average revenue generated from the sale of cameras?
   a. $33.33
   b. $39
   c. $40
   d. $50

Pricing and Output Strategies

The previous unit discussed profit. One key determinant of the size of profit earned by a firm is the level of competition it faces. In fact the level of competition in a market influences the behaviour and performance of firms. In this unit, the two extremes of competition are examined and a distinction is made between normal and supernormal profits.

 ## Market Structure

Market structure is a term for the conditions which exist in a market. There are four main categories of market structure, two of which are perfect competition and monopoly. Perfect competition is the highest degree of competition possible between the firms in the same industry. In contrast, a monopoly may face no direct competition.

Characteristics of Perfect Competition

For perfect competition, a number of conditions need to exist. These are:

- There must be many buyers and sellers. In such a situation, a single buyer or supplier will not be significant enough to influence the price. If one firm increases its output, the change it would make to the industry's supply would not be enough to have any impact on the price. Similarly, if one buyer stopped purchasing the product, the fall in demand would be too small to have an impact on the product's price. In fact price is determined by the market demand and supply and an individual firm is a price taker, unable to influence price.

- There must be a low degree of market concentration. This means that each firm has a tiny share of the market. It follows on from the previous condition, since if there are many firms in the industry, each one will only contribute a small amount of the total market supply.

- There must be free entry into and exit from the market. This means that there must not be anything which makes it difficult for the firms to enter or leave the industry, that is to start or stop producing the product.

- The product must be homogeneous, that is identical. There is no branding or advertising. With identical products on offer, consumers will not be concerned about the source of the product.

- Buyers and sellers must be perfectly informed. Buyers will know about where the suppliers are and about their products. Sellers will have knowledge about the activities of the rivals production techniques, the availability and price of resources.

Key Point

Perfect competition: a market structure with the highest level of competition. There are no barriers or restrictions on the entry into and exit from the market.

 **Activity 1**

a. Identify three reasons accounting for consumer preference for one firm's products over that of rival firms.

b. If a firm's products become more popular than that of its rivals, what will happen to its market share?

The Behaviour of Perfectly Competitive Firms

An individual firm will not raise the price of its product, as it will lose all of its sales to rival firms if it does. There is no incentive for a firm to cut its price since at the market price, it can sell any quantity it wishes. As a result, firms are price takers. They have to accept the market price.

Firms will be constantly seeking to gain a competitive advantage by improving their products. They will also respond quickly and fully, to any changes in demand.

Free entry and exit and perfect information will mean that in the long run firms will only earn enough profit to keep them producing the product. In the short run, they may earn more or less than this level of profit which is referred to as **normal profit**. If demand for the product rises, the firms in the industry will make higher than normal profit. This level of profit, called **supernormal** or abnormal profit, will attract new firms into the industry. Their entry will increase supply which, in turn, will lower the price and return profit to the normal level. If, on the other hand, demand falls, firms would initially make a loss. This will force some firms out of the industry. The exit of the firms will reduce supply, cause price to rise and restore normal profits.

> **Key Point**
>
> **Normal profit:** the minimum level of profit required to keep a firm in the industry in the long run.

Performance of Perfectly Competitive Firms

The high level of competition is usually expected to promote efficiency. It provides firms with both an incentive and a threat to produce according to consumers' wants at the lowest possible cost. Any firm that can respond more quickly to consumers' demands or can cut its costs should gain a competitive advantage and earn higher profits. The threat arises because any firm that is not efficient, produces at a higher cost or does not respond to changes in consumer tastes, will be driven out of the market.

Besides the possibility of low prices and good quality, perfect competition provides consumers with a wider choice. There is no guarantee, however, that perfect competition will produce the best outcome for consumers. The high level of competition will drive the price down to a level which just covers the cost. That price, however, may not be that low. This is because perfectly competitive firms are likely to be small and often production on a larger scale reduces unit costs (see unit 29). In addition whilst consumers have a choice of sellers, they do not have a choice in terms of variations of the product.

Definition of Monopoly

The usual meaning of a monopoly is a 'sole supplier of a product having 100% share of the market'. This is often referred to as a pure monopoly and we would concentrate on the same only. Some governments define a monopoly as a firm that has 25% or more share of the market and a dominant monopoly, when a firm has a 40% share of the market.

> **Key Point**
>
> **Monopoly:** a market with a single supplier.

Characteristics of a Monopoly

* The firm is the industry. It has a 100% share of the market.

* There are high barriers to entry and exit, making it difficult for other firms to enter the market.

* A monopoly is a price maker. Its output is the industry's output and so changes in its supply affect the market price.

Occurrence of Monopolies

It may be worthwhile to consider the causes which lead a firm to have total control of a market. In some cases, a monopoly may develop over time. One firm may have been so successful in cutting its costs and responding to changes in the consumer tastes in the past, that it has driven out rival firms and captured the whole of the market. Also, mergers and takeovers may result in the number of firms being reduced to one.

Alternatively a monopoly may exist from the start. One firm may own, for instance, all the gold mines in a country or it may have been granted monopolistic powers by a government which makes it illegal for other firms to enter the market. A patent would also stop other firms from producing the product.

Why Do Monopolies Continue?

Another important question to be asked is 'What stops new firms from breaking into the market and providing competition to a monopoly?' It is the existence of **barriers to entry** and exit. One type of barrier is a *legal barrier*. As mentioned above, this may be in the form of a patent or a government act.

Another important barrier to entry is the *scale of production*. If the monopoly is producing on a large scale, it may be able to produce at a low unit cost. Any new firm, unable to produce as much, is likely to face higher unit cost and hence will be unable to compete. It can also be expensive to set up a new industry, if large capital equipment is required. Other barriers to entry include the creation of brand loyalty through branding and advertising and monopoly's access to resources and retail outlets.

Barriers to exit can also stop new firms from entering the market. One barrier to exit may be a *long-term contract* to provide a product. Some firms may be reluctant to undertake such a commitment. A significant barrier to exit is the existence of *sunk costs*. These are the costs, such as advertising and industry specific equipment, which cannot be recovered if the firm leaves the industry.

Activity 2

In each case, consider what type of barriers to entry and exit may exist in the following markets:

a. airlines
b. film production
c. steel production
d. window cleaning.

The Behaviour of a Monopoly

The **existence of barriers to entry**, means that a monopoly can earn supernormal profits in the long run. Firms outside the industry may not be aware of the high profits being earned. Even if they do know about the high profits and want to enter the industry, they are kept out by the high barriers to entry and exit.

A monopoly has control over the supply of the product but though it can seek to influence the demand, it does not have control over it. In fact, a monopoly has to make a choice. It can set the price, but then it has to accept the level of sales, consumers are prepared to buy at that price. If, on the other hand, it chooses to sell a given quantity, the price will be determined by what consumers are prepared to pay for this quantity. Fig. 1 shows that if a firm sets a price P, the demand curve determines that it will sell amount Q. If itdecides to sell amount Q_1, it will have to accept a price of P_1.

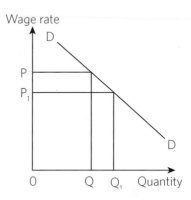

Fig. 1 The choice facing a monopolist

The Performance of a Monopoly

Monopolies are often criticised. This is because there are concerns that the absence of competition may lead to inefficiency. A monopoly may restrict the supply to push up prices and may produce a poor quality product, knowing that consumers cannot switch to rival products. It may also fail to respond to changes in consumer tastes and develop new products.

It is possible, however, that a monopoly could be relatively efficient and actually benefit consumers. If it produces on a large scale, its unit cost and price may be lower than that in a more competitive market. In fact in some cases a monopoly would definitely be more efficient than competition. This would be the case when it prevents the wasteful duplication of capital equipment. For instance, it would be expensive and possibly unsafe to have a number of different firms laying and operating rail tracks.

A monopoly's high profits would also enable it to spend on research and development and therefore, it may introduce new, improved variations. Although it does not have direct competitive pressure to do this, it knows that it will receive all the profits resulting from any successful introduction of new methods and products. In addition, the need to overcome barriers to entry and break the monopoly may encourage firms outside the industry to try and develop a better product.

Occurrence of Perfect Competition and Monopoly

In practice, it is difficult to find markets which have the characteristics of perfect competition. In most markets, buyers and sellers do not have perfect information, there is often some product differentiation and brand loyalty and existence of frequently barriers to entry and exit. Among the markets which come closest to perfect competition are foreign currency and some agricultural products such as carrots and wheat. There are many buyers and sellers of dollars on foreign exchange markets. Each dollar is similar throughout the world and it is easy to find out information about the market. Even in this case, however, some traders have more power than others.

The number of firms that can be defined as monopolies depends, in part, on the way markets have been defined. The more narrow the definition, in terms of the product and geographical area, the more examples will be found. For example, a country may have only one firm supplying gas but several firms in its energy industry. There may be a relatively high number of food retailers in a town but only one food shop on an estate, making it a local monopoly.

 **Activity 3**

Complete the following table:

Comparison of perfect competition and monopoly

	Perfect Competition	*Monopoly*
Level of competition		none
Number of producers	many	
Barriers to entry		high
Type of long term profit	normal	
Influence on price	price taker	
Number of substitutes		none

 **Summary**

- The key characteristics of perfect competition are presence of many buyers and sellers, low degree of market concentration, free entry and exit, homogeneous product and perfect information.

continued····>

- Perfectly competitive firms are price takers who can earn only normal profit in the long run.

- Perfect competition may promote efficiency, keep prices low and quality high. However, low scale production may mean that prices are not as low as possible and also there may be a lack of choice of types of products.

- The key characteristics of a monopoly are dominance of the market by one firm and high barriers to entry and exit.

- A monopoly is a price maker which can earn supernormal profits in the long run due to barriers to entry and exit.

- A monopoly can arise because one firm captures the market, one firm is formed by mergers and takeovers or the law protects a firm's monopolistic power.

- Barriers to entry include legal barriers, scale of operation, high set up costs, brand loyalty and monopolistic access to resources and retail outlets.

- A monopoly can determine price or the quantity it sells, but not both.

- A monopoly may raise price, reduce quality and fail to innovate. However, it is also possible that it may produce at a low cost and hence charge a low price. It may also innovate due to the availability of finance and sense of security.

Teacher's Tip

Identify a monopoly in your country and evaluate its performance.

Multiple Choice Questions

1. Which of the following is a feature of a perfectly competitive market?
   a. A differentiated product
   b. Few buyers and sellers
   c. Imperfect information
   d. No barriers to entry and exit

2. Network Rail is a monopolistic UK firm. What does this mean?
   a. The firm is a price taker.
   b. The firm has no competitors.
   c. The firm has a small share of the market.
   d. The firm is not protected by barriers to entry.

3. In which type of market structure can supernormal profits be earned in the short run?
   a. Monopoly
   b. Perfect competition
   c. Monopoly and perfect competition
   d. Neither monopoly nor perfect competition

4. Which of the following is a barrier to entry?
   a. Brand loyalty
   b. Lack of advertising
   c. Low set up costs
   d. Perfect information

Different Size of Firms and Integration

This unit examines the factors that influence the size of firms, the growth of firms and the main types of integration. It also explores the reasons behind existence of small firms despite the advantages of producing on a large scale.

 The Factors Influencing a Firm's Size

There are three main measures of the size of a firm. These are the number of workers employed, the value of the output it produces and the value of the financial capital it employs.

The size of a particular firm is influenced by a number of factors. These include:

- The **age of the firms**. Most firms start small. Every year new firms are set up but not all of them survive. Those that do, may take some time to grow in size.

- The **availability of financial capital**. The more financial capital a firm has to draw on to finance its expansion, the larger it is capable of growing.

- The **type of business organisation**. Public limited companies are usually larger than private limited companies which, in turn, are larger than partnerships and partnerships are usually larger than sole traders. This is mainly due to the availability of financial capital. Public limited companies can use retained profits, borrow and sell shares to raise the finance to expand. A sole trader cannot sell shares and it is likely to find it more difficult and more costly to borrow.

- **Internal economies and diseconomies of scale**. If a firm is experiencing lower average costs as it expands, it can lower the price for its products and capture more market share. The reluctance to experience internal diseconomies of scale may limit a firm's growth.

- The **size of the market**. This is the key factor in determining the size of a firm. If there is a large demand for the product, it is possible for a firm to grow to a large size.

 **Growth of Firms**

There are two ways a firm can increase in size. One is called **internal growth**. This is also sometimes referred to as natural or organic growth. It involves a firm increasing the market for its current products or diversifying into other products. This type of growth may occur through increasing the size of existing plants or by opening new ones. For example, MacDonalds – the US fast food chain, has grown to a large size by opening more and more outlets throughout the world.

The other way through which a firm can grow is through **external growth**. This involves the firm joining with another firm/firms to form one firm through a merger or a takeover. Such joining together is known as integration. The three main types of integration are **horizontal integration, vertical integration** and **conglomerate integration**.

External growth allows a firm to increase its size more quickly than internal growth. With internal growth, however, there is more control over the size of the firm. There is a risk that external growth may take a firm past its optimum size.

 **Activity 1**

> Pantaloon, India's largest food retailer, operates a number of Bazaar hypermarkets and Food Bazaar grocery stores. In 2006, it started to expand outside its city locations.
> a. What type of growth was experienced by Pantaloon in 2006?
> b. Explain two influences on the size of a firm.

Horizontal Integration

Horizontal integration is the merger of two firms at the same stage of production, producing the same product. For example, the merger of two car producers or two TV companies. There are two key motives behind horizontal integration. One is to take greater advantage of economies of scale. The new firm will be larger and hence may be able to produce at lower average cost. The other is to increase the market share. By merging with another firm producing the same product, a direct competitor is eliminated. Another possible benefit that may arise from horizontal integration is *rationalisation*. If the two firms had not been using all their resources fully, merging could enable them to sell off the redundent resources, for instance, one office block. The new firm may also be able to save on managerial staff. There is a risk, however, with horizontal integration that the merged firm may experience diseconomies of scale. Also, a large firm can be difficult to control. It may also be difficult to integrate the two firms if they initially had different management structures or are located some distance apart.

Vertical Integration

Vertical integration occurs when a firm merges with another firm involved with the production of the same product but at a different stage of production. It can take the form of vertical integration backwards or vertical integration forwards.

Vertical integration backwards is when a firm merges with a firm that is the source of its supply of raw materials, components or the products it sells. For example, a supermarket chain may takeover a bakery and a tyre manufacturer merger with a producer of rubber. The main motive behind such an integration is to ensure an adequate supply of good quality raw materials at a reasonable price. Another aim might be to restrict the access of the rival firms to the supplies.

Vertical integration forward is when a firm merges with, or takes over, a market outlet. For instance, an oil company may buy a chain of petrol stations and an airline may merge with a tour operator. The two key motives behind this form of vertical integration are to ensure that there are sufficient outlets and the products are stored and displayed well in high quality outlets. A firm may also hope that such a merger may help in the development and marketing of new products.

As with horizontal integration, problems may be encountered with vertical integration also. Again there may be management problems. The managers of the merged firms may not be familiar with running, for instance, a market outlet. The two firms may also have been of different sizes and this may require some adjustment or the buying in of some supplies from other firms or the selling of supplies to other firms.

Conglomerate Integration

A conglomerate merger involves the merger of two firms making different products. For example, an electricity company may merge with a travel company and an insurance company may merge with a chocolate producer.

The main motive behind a conglomerate merger is diversification. Such a merger spreads a firm's risks and may enable it to continue its growth, even if the market of one of its products is declining.

Coordinating a firm producing a range of products can, however, prove to be very challenging. In fact, after a number of years, some firms demerge, i.e. they divide into two or more firms.

Key Point

Conglomerate merger: a merger between firms producing different products.

The Effect of Integration on Consumers

Integration can bring advantages and disadvantages to consumers. If it leads to greater economies of scale, consumers may enjoy lower prices. They may also benefit from high quality products and innovation, if the merger increases the efficiency of the firm.

However, if the integration results in diseconomies of scale, consumers may experience higher prices and poorer quality. There is also a risk, in the case of horizontal integration, of reduced choice for consumers and use of greater market power by the merged firm to push up prices.

Activity 2

In August 2006, Banca Intesa and Sanpaola IMI, Italy's second and third largest banks merged. Take overs and mergers occur frequently in the banking industry throughout the world.

a. Identify two reasons to explain merger of banks.

b. Explain two advantages gained by bank customers from a bank merger.

Advantages of Small Firms

Despite the benefits of growth, a large proportion of the firms in any country are small. There are a number of reasons for this.

- The small size of the market. As suggested earlier, this is probably the key influence. If demand for the product is small, a firm producing it cannot be large. Demand for very expensive items, such as luxury yachts, may be small as it may be for individually designed items, such as designer dresses and suits and for repair work.

- Preference of consumers. For some personal services, such as hairdressing, consumers prefer small firms. Such firms can cater to their individual requirements and can provide a friendlier and more personal service.

- Owner's preference. The owner (or owners) of a firm may not want it to grow. People who own and run firms have various motives. Some may want to avoid the stress of running a large firm and may be worried that expansion the firm may lead to loss of control.

- Flexibility. Despite the advantages of large firms, small firms may survive because they may be able to adjust to changes in market conditions more quickly. A sole trader, in particular, is likely to be in regular touch with his or her customers and should be able to pick up on changes in their demand. He or she can also take decisions more quickly as there is no need to consult with other owners.

- Technical factors. In some industries, little or no capital is needed. This makes it easy for new firms to set up. It also means that technical economies of scale are not important and small firms do not suffer a cost disadvantage. The lower the barriers to entry, the more small firms there are likely to be, in the industry.

- Lack of financial capital. Some firms may want to expand but they may lack the finance required to do so. As mentioned in the beginning, it may be difficult for sole traders to raise financial capital.

- Location. If a product is relatively heavy in relation to its value, transport costs can form a high proportion of total costs. This can lead to emergence of local, rather than national markets and such markets can be supplied by small firms.

- Cooperation between small firms. For example, small farmers may join together to buy seeds, foodstuffs and equipment such as combine harvesters.

- Specialisation. Small firms may supply specialist products to, and distribute the products of, larger firms. For instance, a relatively small firm may provide training services for a large accountancy firm.

- Government support. Governments in many countries provide financial help and advice to small firms. This is because small firms provide a high number of jobs, develop the skills of entrepreneurs and have the potential to grow into large firms.

Activity 3

Decide which of the following circumstances are likely to explain the existence of a number of small firms in an industry.
a. The need for high expenditure on research and development.
b. The existence of diseconomies of scale at a low level of output.
c. Low barriers to entry and exit.
d. High start up costs.
e. A global market.
f. Discounts given for bulk buying.

Summary

- The key factors influencing the size of a firm are its age, the availability of financial capital, the type of business organisation, output over which it will experience economies of scale, and (most significantly) the size of the market.

- Firms can grow internally by increasing their output or externally by merging with, or taking over, another firm.

- The three main types of integration are horizontal, vertical and conglomerate.

- Horizontal integration increases market share and may enable the new firm to take greater advantage of economies of scale.

- Vertical integration backward secures supplies whilst vertical integration forward secures outlets.

- The key motive behind a conglomerate merger is diversification.

continued····>

- Despite the advantages of a large size, small firms continue to exist because of limited demand, consumers preference for personal attention, the owner's disinclination to expand, flexibility, low or no barriers to entry, a lack of financial capital required for expansion, role of suppliers of specialist goods or services to larger firms and government assistance.

Teacher's Tip

Find information on a merger in your own country. Analyse the reasons for the merger and consider whether it has benefited the consumers.

Multiple Choice Questions

1. Which of the following is an advantage, a small firm may have over a large firm?
   a. It can adapt more quickly to changes in demand.
   b. It can raise finance more easily.
   c. It can hire specialist staff.
   d. It can spread its risks.

2. What is most likely to be supplied by small firms?
   a. Banking
   b. Film production
   c. Shoe repair
   d. Steel

3. A toy manufacturer merges with a chemical company. What type of integration is this?
   a. Conglomerate
   b. Horizontal
   c. Vertical integration backward
   d. Vertical integration forward

4. In May 2005, Cadbury Schweppes – a UK chocolate and soft drinks producer, took over Green and Black – a chocolate producers pecialising in organic chocolate. This is an example of:
   a. Conglomerate integration
   b. Horizontal integration
   c. Vertical integration backward
   d. Vertical integration forward.

Economies of Scale

Unit 26 mentioned that firms' average costs are influenced by economies of scale and diseconomies of scale. This unit explores the concept in detail and elaborates on the distinction between internal and external economies and diseconomies of scale.

 ## The Meaning of Economies of Scale

Economies of scale are the advantages, in the form of lower **long run average costs (LRAC)**, of producing on a larger scale. When economists and entrepreneurs talk about economies of scale, they are usually referring to internal economies of scale. These are the advantages gained by an individual firm by increasing its size i.e. having larger or more plants. They come in a variety of forms – see below.

The other type of economies of scale are external economies of scale. These are the advantages available to all the firms in an industry, resulting from the growth of the industry.

 Key Points

Internal economies of scale: lower long run average costs resulting from a firm growing in size.

External economies of scale: lower long run average costs resulting from an industry growing in size.

 ## The Meaning of Diseconomies of Scale

Diseconomies of scale are essentially the disadvantages of 'being too large'. A firm that increases its scale of operation to a point where it encounters rising long run average costs is said to be experiencing internal diseconomies of scale. External diseconomies of scale arise from an industry being too large, causing the firms within the industry to experience higher long run average costs.

Key Points

Internal diseconomies of scale: higher long run average costs arising from a firm growing too large.

External diseconomies of scale: higher long run average costs arising from an industry growing too large.

Internal Economies and Diseconomies of Scale

As a firm changes its scale of operation, its average costs are likely to change. Fig. 1 shows the usual U-shaped LRAC curve. Average costs fall at first, reach an optimum point and then rise.

In very capital intensive industries, such as oil refining, long run average costs may fall over a considerable range of output as shown in Fig. 2.

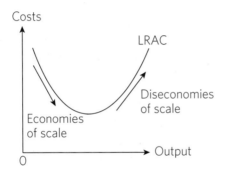

Fig. 1 Internal economies and diseconomies of scale

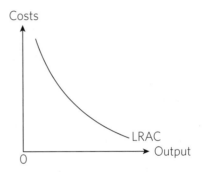

Fig. 2 Downward sloping LRAC curve

In other cases, average costs may fall relatively quickly to their lowest point (the minimum efficient scale) and then remain constant over a large range of output. This would give an L-shaped LRAC curve as shown in Fig. 3.

External economies and diseconomies of scale have a different effect on a firm's LRAC curve. In the case of external economies of scale, a firm's average costs will be reduced not by the changes in its own output but by the changes in the industry's output. Fig. 4 shows how external economies of scale result in a downward shift of a firm's LRAC curve.

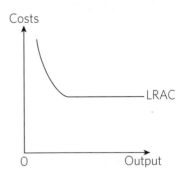

Fig. 3 L-shaped LRAC curve

In contrast, external diseconomies of scale will raise a firm's LRAC curve at each and every level of output as shown in Fig. 5.

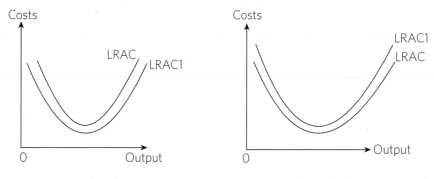

Fig. 4 The effect of external
economies of scale

Fig. 5 The effect of external
diseconomies of scale

Types of Internal Economies of Scale

As a firm increases its scale of operation, there are a number of reasons responsible for a decline in its average cost. These include:

- **Buying economies**. These are probably the best known type. Large firms that buy raw materials in bulk and place large orders for capital equipment usually receive *discount*. This means that they pay less for each item purchased. They may also receive better treatment than small firms in terms of quality of the raw materials and capitale quipment sold and the speed of delivery. This is because the suppliers will be anxious to keep such large customers.

- **Selling economies**. The total cost of processing orders, packing the goods and transporting them does not rise in line with the number of orders. For instance, it costs less than twice as much to send 10 000 washing machines to customers than it does to send 5 000 washing machines. A lorry that can transport 40 washing machines does not cost four times as much to operate as four vans which can carry 10 washing machines each. A large volume of output can also reduce advertising costs. The total cost of an advertising campaign can be spread over more units and, again, discounts may be secured. A whole page advertisement in a newspaper or magazine is usually less than twice the cost of a half page advertised. Together, buying and selling economies of scale are sometimes referred to as **marketing economies**.

- **Managerial economies**. Large firms can afford to employ specialist staff as they can spread their pay over a high number of units. Employing specialist buyers, accountants, human resource managers and designers can increase the firm's efficiency, reduce costs of production and raise demand and revenue. Large firms can also engage in division of labour amongst their other staff. For example, car workers specialise in a particular aspect of the production process.

- **Financial economies**. Large firms usually find it easier and cheaper to raise finance. Banks tend to be more willing to lend to large firms because such firms are well known and have valuable assets to offer as collateral. Banks often charge large borrowers less, per $ borrowed, in order to attract them and because they know that the administrative costs of operating and processing large loans are not significantly higher than the costs of dealing with small loans. Large firms can also raise finance through selling shares which is not an available option for sole traders and partnerships. Public limited companies can sell to the general public. The larger and better known the companies are, the more willing people are to buy their shares.

- **Technical economies.** The larger the output of a firm, the more viable it becomes to use large, technologically advanced machinery. Such machinery is likely to be efficient, producing output at a lower average cost than small firms.

- **Research and development economies**. A large firm can have a research and development department, since running such a department can reduce average costs by developing more efficient methods of production and raise total revenue by developing new products.

- **Risk bearing economies**. Larger firms usually produce a range of products. This enables them to spread the risks of trading. If the profitability of one of the products it produces falls, it can shift its resources to the production of more profitable products.

Activity 1

Decide the type of internal economies, each of the following may be an example of:
a. a farmer using a combine harvester
b. a chemical company setting up a laboratory to develop anti-AIDS drugs
c. a supermarket chain employing an expert in chocolate to place its orders with suppliers
d. a book publisher buying a large quantity of paper
e. a soap manufacturer buying a two minute advertisement on national television
f. a car manufacturer issuing new shares.

Internal Diseconomies of Scale

Growing beyond a certain output can cause a firm's average costs to rise. This is because a firm may encounter a number of problems including:

- **Difficulties controlling the firm**. It can be hard for those managing a large firm to supervise everything that is happening in the business. Management becomes more complex. A number of layers of management may be needed and there may be a need for more meetings. This can increase administrative costs and make the firm slower in responding to changes in market conditions.

- **Communication problems**. It can be difficult to ensure that everyone in a large firm has full knowledge about their duties and available opportunities (like training etc.). Also, they may not get the opportunity to effectively communicate their views and ideas to the management team.

- **Poor industrial relations**. Large firms may be at a greater risk from a lack of motivation of workers, strikes and other industrial action. This is because workers may have less sense of belonging, longer time may be required to solve problems and more conflicts may arise due to the presence of diverse opinions.

External Economies of Scale

A larger industry can enable the firms in that industry to reduce their average costs in a number of ways including developing:

- **A skilled labour force**. A firm can recruit workers who have been trained by other firms in the industry.

- **A good reputation**. An area can gain a reputation for high quality production. For example, the Bordeaux region of France is well known for its high quality wine production and Maldives has a reputation of being a popular holiday joint.

- **Specialist suppliers of raw materials and capital goods**. When an industry becomes large enough, it can become worthwhile for other industries, called *subsidiary industries* to set up for providing for the needs of the industry. For instance, the tyre industry supplies tyres to the car industry.

- **Specialist services**. Universities and colleges may run courses for workers in large industries and banks and transport firms may provide services, specially designed to meet the particular needs of firms in the industry.

- **Specialist markets**. Some large industries have specialist selling places and arrangements such as corn exchanges and insurance markets.

- **Improved infrastructure**. The growth of an industry may encourage a government and private sector firms to provide better road links, electricity supplies, build new airports and develop dock facilities.

External economies of scale are more likely to arise if the firms in the industry are located in one area. This is why they are sometimes referred to as **economies of concentration**.

External Diseconomies of Scale

Just as a firm can grow too large, so can an industry. With more and larger firms in an area, there will be an increase in transport with more vehicles bringing in workers and raw materials and taking out workers and finished products. This may cause congestion, increased journey times, higher transport costs for firms and possibly reduced workers' productivity. The growth of an industry may also result in increased competition for resources, pushing up the price of key sites, capital equipment and labour.

Activity 2

The US mining firm, Phelps Dodge, has been expanding its production of copper in the Congo in recent years. In 2006 it produced 80 000 tonnes of copper and expected, with more investment, to produce 800 000 tonnes by 2020.

Mining currently contributes 25% of the Congo's total output and the mining industry is still growing.

a. Explain two types of internal economies of scale that can been be enjoyed by a mining company.

b. Explain two types of external economies that may be experienced by firms in the mining industry.

Summary

- Increasing output can reduce long run average costs. The savings made are referred to as economies of scale.

- Internal economies of scale are falling long run average costs resulting from the growth of a firm.

continued····>

- Examples of internal economies of scale include buying economies, selling economies, managerial economies, financial economies, technical economies, research and development economies and risk bearing economies.

- Internal diseconomies of scale are rising long run average costs, resulting from a firm growing too large.

- Examples of internal diseconomies of scale include difficulties controlling the firm, communication problems and poor industrial relations.

- External economies arise from the growth of the industry and include a skilled labour force to draw on, a good reputation, specialist supplies of raw materials and capital equipment, specialist services, specialist markets and improved infrastructure.

- External diseconomies of scale are caused by an industry growing too large and experience disadvantages like congestion and a rise in the cost of factors of production.

- Internal economies and diseconomies of scale explain the usual U-shape of the long run average cost curve.

- If the increasing size of the industry gives rise to external economies of scale, a firm's long run average cost curve will shift downwards. The creation of external diseconomies of scale will cause the long run average cost curve to move upwards.

Teacher's Tip

Economies of scale result from the growth of a firm or industry – they do not cause it. The type of economy of scale, that is defined incorrectly by the students, most frequently, is financial economies.

Multiple Choice Questions

1. What is meant by internal economies of scale?
    a. A fall in short run average costs arising from the growth of a firm
    b. A fall in long run average costs arising from the growth of a firm
    c. A fall in short run average costs arising from the growth of an industry
    d. A fall in long run average costs arising from the growth of an industry

2. What is meant by financial economies of scale?
    a. Lower average costs experienced by large banks and other financial institutions
    b. Lower average costs arising from a large firm operating its finance department more efficiently
    c. Lower average costs due to the ability of large firms to borrow more cheaply
    d. Lower average costs occurring because of the use of larger capital equipment

3. A firm's long run average cost curve shifts upwards. Which of the following could have caused this?
    a. Internal economies of scale
    b. Internal diseconomies of scale
    c. External economies of scale
    d. External diseconomies of scale

4. Why might the growth of an industry reduce a firm's costs of production?
    a. It may cause a decrease in subsidiary industries.
    b. It may create greater competition for resources.
    c. It may lead to the development of specialist markets.
    d. It may reduce the supply of infrastructure.

Answer Key

Unit 23

Activity 1

a. secondary
b. tertiary
c. primary
d. tertiary
e. tertiary or quaternary
f. tertiary

Activity 2

a. (i)
b. (iii)
c. (ii)
d. (iii)

Activity 3

a. public limited company
b. sole proprietor
c. a partnership
d. a private limited company

Activity 4

(a), (b), (d) and (e).

Activity 5

	Public corporation	Public limited company
Ownership	the government	shareholders
Sector	public	private
Aim	act in the public interest	to make a profit

Multiple Choice Questions

1. c

   In a sole proprietorship, the owner bears the uncertain risks, organises the factors of production and receives all of the profit made. The business may employ any number of workers. It has unlimited liability and does not issue shares.

2. d

   A state owned enterprise is also known as a public corporation. A company which can sell its shares on the stock exchange is a public limited company.

3. a
   Employing local people will create jobs and may raise incomes. b, c and d are all possible disadvantages of having an MNC producing in a country.

4. d
   In a public limited company, shareholders bear the uncertain risks and directors and managers organise the factors of production.

Unit 24
Activity 1

No. of machines	No. of workers	Output per worker (average product)
4	1	10
4	2	12
4	3	15
4	4	18
4	5	20
4	6	18
4	7	16

The most efficient combination of workers and machines is 4 machines and 5 workers.

Activity 2

a. Rising living standards tend to increase demand for water significantly. More water is demanded for a variety of purposes including washing, watering gardens, cleaning cars, filling swimming pools, processing food and other industrial uses.

b. As living standards in most countries should rise in the future, demand for water is likely to increase which will cause its price to rise as shown in Fig. 1. Supply will extend as water companies will have a financial incentive to collect more rain in reservoirs, dam more rivers and desalinate sea water.

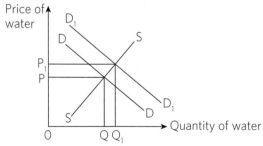

Fig. 1 The effect of an increase in demand for water

Activity 3

a. A piece work model is a method of paying workers on the basis of amount of output produced by them.

b. (i)   It may increase output as workers will spend less time travelling to and from work. Thus, they may start working earlier and finish later. However, there is some risk that, without supervision, they may reduce their effort and output but a piecework model may overcome this limitation.

    (ii) Costs should be reduced as the firm will not need much space to accommodate workers. Some rooms may be required for meetings and key staff but considerably less factory or office space and car parking space would be required. This saving should be greater than any rise in communication costs which, given advances in technology, should be low.

Multiple Choice Questions

1. a

    Agriculture and mining are in the primary sector and their employment fell from 14m to 13m. Manufacturing is in the secondary sector and employment stayed constant at 20m. Retailing and education are in the tertiary sector and employment in these two industries rose from 15m to 17m.

2. a

    Doctors and operating theatres are used together. They are not substitutes – an operating theatre cannot be used without a doctor. A doctor is an example of labour and an operating theatre is an example of capital.

3. a

    A decrease in corporation tax would provide an incentive for firms to buy more capital goods. They would know that they would be able to keep more of any profits made. b, c and d would also be likely to reduce demand for capital goods. Less disposable income would be likely to reduce demand for the capital goods. Higher interest rates would have the same effect besides increasing the cost of investment. A rise in pessimism would be likely to make the entrepreneurs expect a lower return from investment.

4. a

    Average product per worker is total product divided by the number of workers. In this case, it is 300/25.

Activity 1

Fixed costs = rent, business rates, insurance, and depreciation.

Variable costs = flour, yeast, overtime pay and energy costs.

Activity 2

Output	TC	TFC	TVC	AC	AFC	AVC
0	60	60	0	—	—	—
1	110	60	50	110	60	50
2	150	60	90	75	50	45
3	180	60	120	60	20	40
4	200	60	140	50	15	35
5	230	60	170	46	12	34
6	300	60	240	50	10	40

Multiple Choice Questions

1. a

    In the short run, insurance on buildings will not change with firm's output, as the size of the building will not alter. b, c and d are all variable costs.

2. d

    The total cost is $500 ($200 + $300). Average cost is total cost divided by output. In this case, $500/50 = $10.

3. c

    In the unusual case of a firm having only fixed costs, its total cost would not change as output changes.

4. a

    Fixed costs plus variable costs equal total cost. b and d apply to fixed costs. c applies to average fixed costs and may apply to average variable cost over a given range.

Activity 1

a.

Output	Total profit ($)
10	–10
20	0
30	20
40	50
50	40

The profit maximising output is 40 units, since this is where profit is highest.

b.

Output	Total profit ($)
10	100
20	150
30	180
40	240
50	340

Activity 2

a. Sales revenue could rise and profits fall, if costs rise by more than revenue.

b. (i) A fall in stock levels will reduce costs. Less staff time and less space will be required for storage of products. These resources could then be put to alternative uses or the number of workers employed and the building space used could be reduced.

(ii) A firm could seek to increase demand for its products by advertising. This might be on television, in newspapers or through direct mailing. For instance, a successful advertising campaign is one which increases revenue by more than the cost of the campaign.

Activity 3

a. Marks & Spencer's total cost in 2005 was £7 035m – £588m = £6 447m.

b. In terms of its costs, Marks & Spencer's earned a profit of 9.12%. Next's costs were £2 585m – £2 205m and its profit as a percentage of its costs was 17.23%. Hence, whilst Marks & Spencer's profit was greater in absolute amount, it was smaller in percentage terms.

c. Good sites for a retailer are in city centres, where there are many potential buyers and hence an increased potential revenue. Good window displays should attract more customers into the shops and turn potential into actual revenue.

Multiple Choice Questions

1. c

   Total revenue is price multiplied by quantity sold i.e. $4 x 100 = $400. Price is the equivalent of average revenue, so in this case average revenue is $4.

2. a

   Profit is maximised when profit is at its highest.

3. b

   One of the key reasons shareholders buy shares is to earn a high share of profit.

4. c

Sales of cameras	Total revenue ($)
10	400
20	800
30	1 200
40	1 600

Average revenue is total revenue/quantity sold. Throughout the range of sales, this is $40 e.g. $1 200/30.

Unit 27

Activity 1

a. A consumer may prefer to buy one firm's products over that of rival firms if the products are cheaper, have better quality or enjoy a better brand image.

b. If a firm's products become more popular than those of its rivals, it will attract more customers and gain a higher market share.

Activity 2

a. Airlines – barriers to entry include take off and landing slots at airports, safety requirements and brand loyalty.

b. Film production – possible barriers include brand loyalty and monopoly ownership of retail outlets.

c. Steel production – barriers to entry include high set up costs and scale of production.

d. Window cleaning – there are few barriers to entry into this market. It is cheap to enter and leave, start up costs are low, large scale production does not lower unit costs significantly and branding and advertising are not particularly significant.

Activity 3

	Perfect competition	*Monopoly*
Level of competition	high	none
Number of producers	many	one
Barriers to entry	none	high
Type of long run profit	normal	supernormal
Influence on price	price taken	price maker
Number of substitutes	many	none

Multiple Choice Questions

1. d

   A perfectly competitive market has free entry and exit. Its product is homogeneous, there are many buyers and sellers and perfect information.

2. b

   A monopoly, in the sense of a pure monopoly, has no competitors. It is a price maker, has a 100% share of the market and is protected by barriers to entry.

3. c

   In the short run, many firms under conditions of both monopoly and perfect competition can earn supernormal profits, provided demand is high. In the long run, however, supernormal profit can be earned only by a monopolist and not by perfectly competitive firms. This is because perfectly competitive firms' profits are not protected by barriers to entry.

4. a

   If consumers become attracted to a particular brand, they become reluctant to switch to a product made by a new firm. b, c and d would all make it easy for a new firm to enter the market.

Unit 28

Activity 1

a. Internal growth.

b. One influence is the size of the market. A firm selling a product in an expanding market has the potential to grow in size. Another influence is the age of a firm. A new firm is likely to be of relatively small size.

Activity 2

a. To take greater advantage of economies of scale and to gain a greater market share.

b. If the merger enables the new firms to take greater advantage of economies of scale and work more efficiently, bank customers may be able to enjoy lower bank charges and improved banking services such as internet banking.

Activity 3

(b) and (c) would tend to favour small firms.

(a), (d), (e) and (f) would all be likely to encourage the emergence of large firms in the industry.

Multiple Choice Questions

1. a

An owner of a small firm tends to be in close contact with consumers and does not have to hold meetings before making choices.

2. c

Shoe repair is not a standardised product that can be mass produced. Each repair is likely to be slightly different. There are no real barriers to entry into the market and economies of scale are not significant. a, b and d are industries dominated by large firms.

3. a

In this case, the firms are in different industries.

4. b

The firms were producing the same product at the same stage of production.

Unit 29

Activity 1

a. technical economies
b. research and development economies
c. managerial economies
d. buying economies
e. selling economies
f. financial economies

Activity 2

a. A mining company could exploit, for example, technical economies of scale. Large capital equipment can be used in the industry as the more the amount of coal mined, the more viable the employment of the equipment becomes. It can also take advantage of financial economies of scale. A large mining company is likely to be able to borrow more easily and more cheaply than a small firm.

b. Firms in the mining industry may be able to take advantage of a skilled labour force and specialist suppliers of capital equipment. New mining firms can hire workers trained by other firms in the industry. Subsidiary industries will set up, if the mining industry is large enough to supply it with goods and services including capital equipment.

Multiple Choice Questions

1. b

    Economies of scale occur when a firm alters its scale of production by changing all its factors of production. d defines external economies of scale.

2. c

    A definition question.

3. d

    External diseconomies of scale raise a firm's average costs, independent of its own output. c would shift the average cost curve downwards. a would cause a movement down the average cost curve and b will lead to a movement up the average cost curve.

4. c

    c is an example of external economies of scale. a and d are unlikely to occur but a, b and d would all increase a firm's costs of production.

Examination Practice

Multiple Choice Questions

1. The following information shows the cost and revenue of a firm producing coats.

Total output of coats	Total costs ($)	Total revenue ($)
100	2 000	2 400
200	3 600	4 200
300	4 500	5 000
400	5 200	5 600

   At what output, does the firm maximise profits?
   a. 100
   b. 200
   c. 300
   d. 400

2. A business has many owners. They have limited liability and are able to sell shares on the stock exchange. What type of business is this?
   a. A partnership
   b. A private limited company
   c. A public corporation
   d. A public limited company

3. The table shows the demand for a chocolate bar. Which price gives maximum revenue?

	Price per bar of chocolate ($)	Demand for chocolate (thousands of bars)
a.	4	10
b.	3	15
c.	2	20
d.	1	25

4. The diagram shows the fixed costs, variable costs and the total cost of a firm.

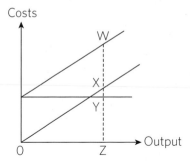

Costs

Which distance represents the firm's variable costs at Z units of output?
a. WX
b. XY
c. WY
d. YZ

5. A firm sells 200 units at $9 each. Its average fixed cost is $2 and its average variable cost is $4. How much profit does the firm make?
a. $400
b. $600
c. $800
d. $1 800

6. Which diagram represents the average revenue curve of a perfectly competitive firm?

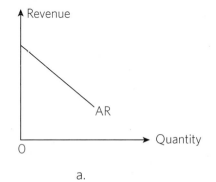

a.

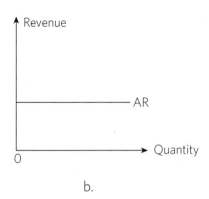

b.

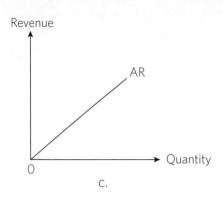

AR

Quantity

c.

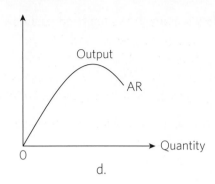

Output

AR

Quantity

d.

7. The diagram shows a firm's total variable cost

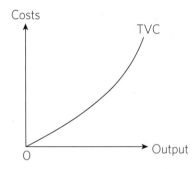

Which one of these curves represents its average variable cost curve?

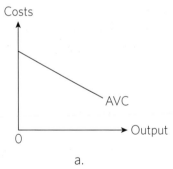

a.

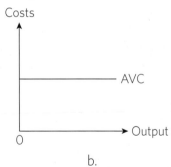

b.

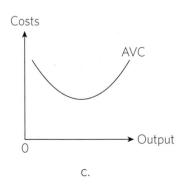

c.

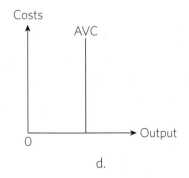

d.

8. How is average fixed cost calculated?
   a. By adding average variable cost and average cost
   b. By deducting average cost from total cost
   c. By dividing total fixed cost by output
   d. By multiplying average cost by total fixed cost

9. Which of the following will benefit a small firm?
   a. Bulk buying
   b. Easy access to finance
   c. Flexibility
   d. Specialist managers

10. What is meant by vertical integration backwards?
   a. A firm merging with a less profitable firm
   b. A firm merging with one of its outlets
   c. A firm merging with one of its suppliers
   d. A firm merging with a smaller firm

Structured Questions

1. Sometimes in an industry, a firm buys a smaller competitor which uses similar factors of production. At other times, a firm buys another firm which supplies it with the raw materials and other inputs for its production.
   a. Explain what is meant by the factors of production. (4)
   b. Discuss the reasons supporting the decision of some firms to remain small. (6)
   c. Identify the types of integration in the two situations described above. (3)
   d. Discuss whether such integration is always beneficial. (7)

   (Cambridge 0455 Paper 4 Q2 May/June 2006)

2. In 2004, the price of shares of Manchester United, a well-known British football club, fell. The club revealed that in the financial year 2003/4, it made payments to the football players' agents mounting to £5 million. This was equal to 20% of its profits before tax. It announced a fall in profits (before tax) of £11.4 m, relative to the financial year 2002/3.
   The club said that in the next financial year, income from the televising of football matches would be reduced by £14 millions, partly because the team was no longer at the top of the Premier League. It would also not have the benefit of the large sum it received in the previous year from selling one of its players – David Beckham, to a Spanish club.

Manchester United also planned to add another 7 800 seats to its ground at a cost of £39m. This building work meant that there would be no special dividend for shareholders, as there had been in the previous year.

a.   Calculate the profits, before tax, for Manchester United Football Club in the financial year 2003/4. Show how you calculated your answer. (2)

b.   Why do firms need to make profits? (4)

c.   With reference to the data and with the help of a demand and supply diagram, analyse the reasons for a fall in the price of shares of Manchester United Football Club. (6)

d.   Imagine you are on the board of directors of the club. In view of the information in the above extract, discuss whether you would be concerned about the fall in profits in the year 2003/4. (8)

e.   You are in charge of a business, whose shareholders wish for higher profits. Explain the proposals you would put forward to them. (8)

(Cambridge 0455 Paper 6 Q1 May/June 2006)

3.   A major computer company announced that its profits in 2003 had fallen.

a.   Explain the reasons behind a fall in profits. (5)

b.   There are some very large computer companies. How might a firm become large? (5)

c.   Some companies are often believed to be benefitted from economies of scale. Briefly describe three types of economies of scale, that a computer company might experience. (6)

d.   Discuss the considerations that may lead a company to change its use of different factors of production. (4)

(Cambridge 0455 Paper 4 Q3 May/June 2005)

Role of Government in an Economy

The Government as a Producer and an Employer

The previous section concentrated on firms. In this section, the focus switches to the role of the government, with the first unit discussing the government as a producer and an employer.

 The Government as a Producer

A government may produce products which it believes are of national importance or the products that are produced by a natural monopoly, or those which it thinks are essential and hence should be available to all. Also, it may produce those commodities which the private sector may under-produce or not produce.

Key Industries

Most countries seek to ensure that their key industries survive and do well. Some of these industries may be considered to be world-beaters or potential world-beaters. These particular key industries are often called **national champions**. In China and France, for instance, such industries are run by the government as nationalised industries. In Italy, they receive favoured loans from banks. In a number of countries, the government also stops foreign companies from taking them over or merging with them.

Natural Monopolies

Natural monopolies, such as rail infrastructure, may be run by the government. This is, in part, to prevent consumers being exploited by a private sector firm charging a high price. Also to produce at a low average cost a high output may be required and at such an output, a loss may be incurred.

Essential Products

Most governments produce at least some goods and services that they think are essential. In some countries, governments provide affordable housing to rent. Besides housing, education and health care are also seen as essential services and some governments produce them and provide them to people free of cost or at subsidised prices.

Merit Goods

Besides being essential products, education and health care are also merit goods. As explained in unit 11, a merit good is one whose benefit to consumers and others is undervalued by them. As a result, they would under-consume it and so private

sector firms would under-produce it. This is why some governments produce educational and health care services and other merit goods such as library services. To stimulate the consumption of merit goods, governments also pay private sector firms to produce them, provide information about their benefits and in some cases make their consumption compulsory.

Key Point

A merit good: a product which the government considers as beneficial and which will be under-consumed if left to market forces.

Public Goods

There are some products that private sector firms have no incentive to produce. This is not because people do not want them but because they know that if they are provided, they can consume them without paying. For example, it is not possible to exclude someone from enjoying the benefits of defence and street lighting even if they are not prepared to

pay for them directly. This is why governments produce them or pay private sector firms to make them and raise finance through taxation. It is also interesting to note that public goods are non-rival. This means that a person enjoying the product does not reduce someone else's enjoyment. An additional family moving into a town protected by sea defences, does not reduce the defence experienced by other families.

Key Point

Public good: a product which is non-rival and non-excludable and hence needs to be financed by taxation.

The Government as an Employer

The government employs workers and managers to operate its state owned enterprises. Employing people helps a government to achieve some of its aims for the economy. To reduce unemployment, the government can employ more workers. To control rises in prices, the government can limit wage rises of its own workers and the prices charged by its enterprises. It can also set an example in terms of employment practice by, for instance, providing its workers with good quality training, preventing discrimination and ensuring good pensions to its workers.

Activity 1

In 2005, 95% of mail in the UK was delivered by the Royal Mail. In that year the Royal Mail made a profit, reinvesting some of it and distributing some of it to its employees as bonuses. The UK government has liberialised the postal market and an increasing amount of mail, particularly bulk mailing business, is being delivered by the private sector firms such as DHL (a German owned company).

a. Explain one argument for:
   (i) the state delivering mail
   (ii) private sector firms delivering mail.
b. Explain two advantages of working for a state-owned enterprise.

Activity 2

In August 2006, the Government of Bahrain announced that government departments, schools, universities and other state institutions would have weekend holidays of Friday and Saturday instead of Thursday and Friday. The change was designed to bring Bahrain in line with other countries in the region, including Libya, Iraq and Syria which had also changed their weekends. It was also designed to make it easier for Bahrain's private sector firms, the majority of which work from Sunday to Thursday, to do business with the government.

a. Explain two reasons why a government may run hospitals.
b. Identify three products that may be supplied by private sector firms to government schools.

Summary

- A government may seek to ensure the survival of key industries by running them as state owned enterprises.

- A government may run a natural monopoly and may produce essential products.

- Governments produce, or at least finance, the output of public goods and may produce merit goods.

- Employing workers can help a government achieve its aims for the economy including reducing unemployment, keeping inflation low and raising the standard of employment practices.

Teacher's Tip

It is important not to confuse merit and public goods. At this stage, it would be useful to draw a spider diagram for each one of them.

Multiple Choice Questions

1. A government decides to increase the wages paid to the employees of state owned enterprises. What will increase immediately, as a result of this decision?
   a. Government expenditure
   b. A budget surplus
   c. Unemployment
   d. Unsold goods and services

2. What type of product is education?
   a. An inessential good
   b. An inferior good
   c. A merit good
   d. A public good

3. In what type of economy, are most workers employed by the government?
   a. Free enterprise
   b. Market
   c. Mixed
   d. Planned

4. A government decides to limit the wage increase of state employees. What is it most likely trying to achieve?
   a. A reduction in employment
   b. A reduction in intlationary pressure
   c. An increase in the wages paid to private sector employees
   d. An increase in the attractiveness of public sector employment relative to private sector employment

UNIT 31

Aims of Government

The previous unit mentioned that a government can help achieve some of its aims by employing workers. This unit focuses on the main aims governments have for their economies.

Government's Macroeconomic Aims

Macroeconomics is concerned with the whole economy. The main government aims for the economy are full employment, price stability, economic growth, redistribution of income and stability of balance of payments. A government can operate a range of policy measures to achieve these aims and it is judged on their success or otherwise. Performance of the economy, however, is influenced not just by government policies. In a market, which is becoming increasingly global, one economy's macroeconomic performance is being affected more and more by the dynamics of other economies.

Full Employment

Most governments try to achieve full employment. This means that people who are willing and able to work can find employment. Of course, not everyone wants to work or is

able to work. These people are not in the labour force. They are said to be economically inactive and are dependent on those in the labour force. They include children, the retired, those engaged in full time education, home makers and those who are too sick or disabled to work. Those who are in work or are unemployed but actively seeking work, form the labour force and are said to be economically active.

The unemployment rate is calculated as a percentage of the labour force, i.e.:

$$\frac{\text{Unemployment}}{\text{Labour force}} \times 100$$

So if 5 million people are unemployed out of a labour force of 40 million, the unemployment rate is:

$$\frac{5m}{40m} \times 100 = 12.5\%$$

Most economists think that full employment is not actually 0% unemployed. They usually put the figure at approximately 3%. This is because they think that even in a strong economy with demand for labour equalling the supply of labour, there will always be some workers changing jobs and being unemployed for short periods.

Key Point

Unemployment rate: the percentage of the labour force who are willing and able to work but are without jobs.

Price Stability

Governments aim for price stability because it ensures greater economic certainty and prevents the country's products from losing international competitiveness. If firms, households and workers have an idea about future level of prices, they can plan with greater confidence. It also means that they will not act in a way that will cause prices to rise in the future. Firms will not raise their prices because they expect their costs to be higher, households will not bring forward purchases for fear that items will be more expensive in the future and workers will not press for wage increases just to maintain their real disposable income.

In seeking to achieve price stability, most governments are not aiming for a zero percentage change in price. A common target is a stable inflation rate of 2%. They do not aim for unchanged prices, for two main reasons. One is that measures of inflation tend to overstate rises in prices. A price index (see unit 36), for instance, might indicate that the general price level has risen by 1% but in practice, prices might not have changed and might have even fallen slightly. Some of the prices paid by people are lower than those appearing in the official price level indices, as people buy some products at reduced prices in sales and also make second hand purchases. Price rises can also hide the improvements in products. A car may cost $100 more this year than last year, but it may incorporate a number of new features such as satellite navigation. So the question arises, is the car actually more expensive or is it a different car?

A second reason is that a slight rise in prices can provide some benefits. It can encourage producers to increase their output, as they may think that higher prices will lead to higher profits. It can also enable firms to cut their wage costs by not raising wages in line with inflation. The alternative to such a move might be a cut in employment.

Economic Growth

When an economy experiences economic growth, there is an increase in its output in the short run. This is sometimes referred to as actual economic growth. In the long run, for an economy to sustain its growth, the productive potential of the economy has to be increased.

Such an increase can be achieved as a result of a rise in the quantity and/or quality of factors of production.

The difference between actual and potential economic growth can be shown on a production possibility curve. On Fig. 1, the movement from point A to point B represents actual economic growth – **more capital and consumer goods are made**. The shift outwards of the production possibility curve from YY to ZZ represents potential economic growth – **the economy is capable of producing more**.

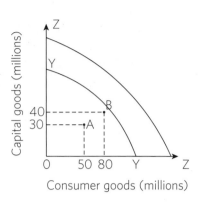

Fig. 1 Actual and potential economic growth

In analysing economic growth and other macroeconomic issues, economists also make use of aggregate demand and aggregate supply diagrams. **Aggregate demand** (AD) is the total demand for an economy's products and consists of consumption (C), investment (I), government expenditure (G) and exports minus imports (X-M). **Aggregate supply** is the total output of producers in an economy. Aggregate supply is perfectly elastic if the economy has a significant number of unemployed resources, as then more can be produced without a contingent rise in costs of production and prices. The curve becomes more inelastic as the economy approaches full employment since then the firms will be competing for resources and this will push up their costs and, as a result, the price level. At full employment of resources, aggregate supply becomes perfectly inelastic, since at this point further increase in output is not possible.

Fig. 2 shows actual economic growth. The rise in AD has resulted in a rise in the country's output (see unit 40 on real GDP) and a small rise in the price level.

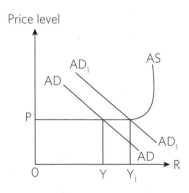

Fig. 2 Actual economic growth

Fig. 3 shows potential economic growth. The maximum amount, that the economy can produce, has increased.

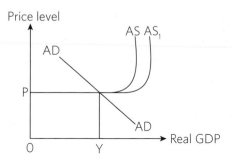

Fig. 3 Potential economic growth

In this case, the rise in the quantity and/or quality of resources has no impact on output. If, however, an increase in productive potential occurs when an economy is operating close to full employment, it can cause a rise in the country's output and a fall in the price level as shown in Fig. 4.

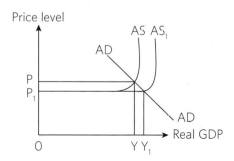

Fig. 4 Potential economic growth causing a rise in national output

Governments want to achieve economic growth because producing more goods and services can raise people's living standards. Economic growth can indeed transform people's lives and enable them to live longer because of better nutrition, housing and health care.

The determinant of a country's possible economic growth rate is its level of output, in relation to its current maximum possible output and its growth in productive capacity. If, for instance, an economy is growing at 2% below its maximum possible output and its productive capacity is expected to increase by 3% this year, its possible economic growth rate is 5%. Most governments would like their economies to be working at full capacity and their actual economic growth rate to coincide with their potential economic growth rate.

Key Point

Economic growth: an increase in the output of an economy and in the long run, an increase in the economy's productive potential.

Activity 1

Table 1 Mexico's industrial structure by output and employment in 2005.

	% share of output	% share of employment
agriculture	4	18
manufacturing	27	24
services	69	58

In 2005, Mexico had an economic growth rate of 4.1%, an unemployment rate of 3.2% and an underemployment rate of 25%.

a. What is meant by an 'economic growth rate of 4.1%'?

b. In which sector is underemployment likely to have been the highest in 2005? Explain your answer.

c. From the information given, explain whether Mexico had the potential to grow at a faster rate than 4.1% in 2005.

Redistribution of Income

A government may seek to redistribute income from the rich to the poor. The more money someone has, the less they tend to appreciate each unit. A rich person with an income of $10 000 a week is unlikely to miss $100 but that sum would make a huge difference to someone currently struggling on $20 a week.

Governments redistribute income by taxing and spending. The rich are taxed more than the poor. Some of the money raised is spent directly on the poor by means of benefits such as housing benefit and unemployment benefit. Other forms of government expenditure, such as that on education and health, particularly benefit the poor. Without the government providing these services free of cost or at subsidised prices, the poor may not find them accessible.

Governments are unlikely to aim for a perfectly equal distribution of income. This is because taxing the rich too heavily and providing too generous benefits may act as a disincentive to effort and enterprise.

Balance of Payments Stability

Over the long run, most governments want the value of their exports to equal the value of their imports. If expenditure on imports exceeds revenue from exports for a long period of time, the country will be living beyond its means and will get into debt. If export revenue is greater than import expenditure, the inhabitants of the country will not be enjoying as many products as possible.

Governments also seek to avoid sudden changes in other parts of the **balance of payments**. This is because they can prove to be disruptive for the economy. For instance, there may be a sudden and unexpected movement of money out of the country's financial institutions into financial institutions of other countries. Such a movement can have an adverse effect not only on the banks of a country but also on the country's exchange rate and eventually on the price of the country's imports (see units 50 and 51).

Key Point

Balance of payments: a record of a country's economic transactions with other countries.

 Activity 2

Table 2 Selected economic indicators in July 2006

Economy	Economic growth rate %	Unemployment %	Inflation rate %
Germany	1.4	10.9	2.0
Japan	3.8	4.0	0.6
Poland	5.2	19.0	1.2
Pakistan	6.6	9.0	7.7

a. Did any of the countries shown, achieve all of their macroeconomic aims in July 2006? Explain your answer.
b. Which country is likely to have had the highest number of unemployed workers in July 2006? Explain your answer.

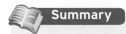

Summary

- The main macroeconomic aims of the government are full employment, price stability, economic growth, redistribution of income and stability of balance of payments.

- Full employment is usually considered to be an unemployment rate of 3%.

- Price stability implies low and stable inflation.

- Low and stable inflation creates certainty and avoids a loss of international competitiveness.

- Measures of inflation tend to overstate rises in prices.

- Economic growth can improve people's living standards by increasing the availability of goods and services.

- For economic growth to continue in the future, a country's productive capacity has to increase.

- Governments redistribute income from the rich to the poor by means of taxation and government expenditure.

- Most governments aim for a match between export revenue and import expenditure in the long run.

Teacher's Tip

Find out the unemployment rate, inflation rate, economic growth rate and current account position of your own country and compare them with the figures for three major economies. In answering questions about macroeconomic performance, it is useful to show an awareness of the events in your economy and other economies.

Multiple Choice Questions

1. Which of the following is a macroeconomic aim of the government?
    a. A fall in national output
    b. High unemployment
    c. Imports exceeding exports
    d. Price stability

2. A country has a population of 120m and a labour force of 50m. 6m of its labour force are unemployed. What is the unemployment rate?
    a. 3.53%
    b. 5%
    c. 10.71%
    d. 12%

3. Which of the following could increase a country's productive potential?
    a. An improvement in education
    b. A reduction in the retirement age
    c. Retention of worn out machinery by firms
    d. Migration of workers to other countries

4. What is meant by potential economic growth?
    a. An increase in the total demand in the economy
    b. An increase in productive capacity of an economy
    c. The economy's export revenue being greater than its import expenditure
    d. The economy operating at full employment

The Government's Influence on Private Producers

Governments influence private producers in a number of ways, including through the policies they implement to achieve their macroeconomic aims, their policies which affect particular industries and products, the contracts they give to private sector producers and the partnerships they form with private sector producers.

 ## Government Macroeconomic Policies

The three main types of government macroeconomic policies are fiscal policy, monetary policy and supply-side policy.

Other government policies including industrial, competition and environmental policies, price controls, exercised by government, also affect private sector producers.

Fiscal Policy

Fiscal policy refers to changes in government expenditure and taxation. Government expenditure, also called *public expenditure*, and taxation occur at two main levels – national and local. Governments spend money on a variety of items including benefits (for the retired, unemployed and disabled), education, health care, transport, defence and interest on national debt.

A government sets out the amount it plans to spend and raise in tax revenue in a **budget** statement. A budget *deficit* is when the government's expenditure is higher than its revenue. In this case, the government will have to borrow to finance some of its expenditure. In contrast, a budget *surplus* occurs when government revenue is greater than government expenditure. *A balanced budget*, which occurs less frequently, is when government expenditure and revenue are equal.

A government may deliberately alter its expenditure or tax revenue to influence economic activity. If a government wants to raise aggregate demand in order to increase economic growth and employment, it will increase its expenditure and/or cut taxation by lowering tax rates, reducing the items taxed or raising tax thresholds. For example, a government may cut income tax rates. This will raise people's disposable income, which will enable them to spend more. Higher consumption is also likely to raise investment.

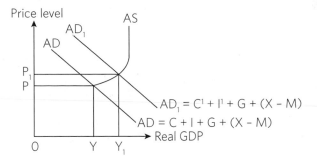

Fig. 1 The effect of a reflationary fiscal policy

Fig. 1 shows the effect of a **reflationary fiscal policy** (also called an **expansionary fiscal policy**).

A government may implement a **deflationary fiscal policy** (also called a **contractionary fiscal policy**) to reduce inflationary pressure. A cut in government expenditure on, for instance, education would reduce aggregate demand. Such a reduction may lower the rise in the general price level.

Key Points

Reflationary fiscal policy: rises in government expenditure and/or cuts in taxation designed to increase aggregate demand.

Deflationary fiscal policy: cuts in government expenditure and/or rises in taxation designed to reduce aggregate demand.

Monetary policy

Monetary policy includes changes in the money supply, the rate of interest and the exchange rate, although some economists treat changes in the exchange rate as a separate policy.

The main monetary policy measure, currently used in most countries, is changes in the rate of interest. A rise in the rate of interest helps implement a deflationary monetary policy. It will be likely to reduce aggregate demand by lowering consumption and investment. Households will spend less due to availability of less discretionary income, expensive borrowing and greater incentive to save. Firms will invest less as they will expect consumption to be lower. Also the opportunity cost of investment will have risen and borrowing will have become expensive. A higher interest rate may also reduce aggregate demand by lowering net exports (see unit 51).

Changes in the money supply, as with changes in interest rates, are implemented by Central Banks on behalf of governments. If the money supply is increased by the Bank printing more money, buying back government bonds or encouraging commercial banks to lend more, the aggregate demand increases. On the other hand, a decrease in the money supply reduces aggregate demand.

Activity 1

In 2006, China's economy was growing rapidly at an annual rate of 11.3%. The government was concerned that inflation might rise. To prevent aggregate demand rising too quickly, China's Central Bank – the People's Bank of China, raised the rate of interest in August 2006.
a.   What is meant by 'aggregate demand'?
b.   Why might a rise in the rate of interest slow down economic growth?

Supply-side Policy

Supply-side policy measures are measures designed to increase aggregate supply and hence increase productive potential. Such policies seek to increase the quantity and quality of resources and raise the efficiency of markets. These include improving education and training, cutting direct taxes and benefits, reforming trade unions and privatisation. Improving education and training is designed to raise labour productivity. The intention behind cutting direct taxes and benefits is to make work more attractive, relative to living on benefits. If successful, this will make the unemployed search for work more actively and will raise the labour force by encouraging more people (including for instance married women and the disabled) to seek employment. Reforming trade unions may make labour more productive and privatisation may increase productive capacity, if private sector firms invest more and work more efficiently than state owned enterprises.

Microeconomic Policies

Some supply-side policy measures seek to increase aggregate supply by focusing on particular industries. For example, a privatisation programme may involve the selling of one or two industries. In this way, supply-side policy measures are also having an impact on the microeconomy. There are a range of policy measures which are specifically microeconomic in nature, that is they concentrate on particular industries and products.

These include subsidies, indirect taxes, competition policy, price controls, environmental policies and regulation.

Subsidies and taxes

A government can seek to build up its industries in a number of ways. It can provide subsidies to infant industries and research grants to innovative firms. It might also protect its industries by imposing taxes and restrictions on rival imported products (see unit 52).

Government subsidies affect the output of some firms only. In contrast, all firms are likely to be affected by taxes in some way. Government tax firms' profits which has an impact on the ability and willingness of firms to invest. Indirect taxes raise firms' costs of production whilst income tax lowers consumers' disposable income, and as a result demand for firms' products.

The effect of a subsidy given to producers is influenced by the size of the subsidy and the price elasticity of demand. As explained in unit 7, a subsidy being an extra payment to producers, shifts the supply curve to the right. The larger the subsidy, the more increase there is in supply. On a diagram, the size of the subsidy is represented by the distance between the two supply curves. In Fig. 2, the subsidy per unit is SY. If all the subsidy is passed on to consumers, prices would fall to P_2. As demand is inelastic, producers have to pass on most of the subsidy to encourage an extension in demand. Price actually falls to P_1, with consumers receiving most of the benefit ($PSXP_1$) and the producers keeping the rest (P_1XYP_2).

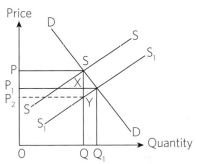

Fig. 2 The effect of a subsidy in the case of inelastic demand

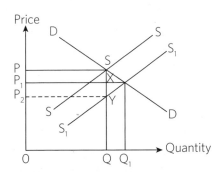

Fig. 3 The effect of a subsidy in the case of elastic demand

If demand is elastic, a subsidy will have more impact on the quantity sold and less on the price. In this case, the producers can keep more of the subsidy as shown in Fig. 3.

In deciding whether to grant a subsidy, a government has to consider the opportunity cost as the money which could have been used for another purpose.

The impact of a tax is again influenced by the size of the tax and the price elasticity of demand. The higher the tax, the greater is its impact. A tax on a product with inelastic demand would have a greater effect on price than the quantity sold. In the case of a product with elastic demand, it is the other way round (see unit 35). If a government wants to raise revenue, it should tax products with inelastic demand. This is because the quantity sold will not fall by much. For example, a tax of $2 per product may be placed on a product that initially has sales of 2,000 a day. If the tax causes sales to fall to 1,800, the government will receive $3,600 in revenue. However, if the demand had been elastic and sales had fallen to 900, the government tax revenue would have been $1,800 only.

In contrast, if the government's aim is to discourage the consumption of a product (in particular a demerit good) it will be more successful if demand is elastic. This is one of the problems in using taxation to discourage smoking, as demand for tobacco products is inelastic.

Competition policy

Competition policy seeks to promote competitive pressures and prevent firms from abusing their market power. There are a number of ways a government might be able to do this, including prevention of mergers that it thinks will not be in the interest of consumers, removal of barriers to entry and exit into markets, regulation of monopolies and prohibition of uncompetitive practices. Uncompetitive practices may include, for example, predatory pricing and limit pricing. Predatory pricing involves a firm charging a price below the cost to drive a rival firm (or firms) out of the market. Limit pricing is setting the price low enough to discourage the entry of new firms into the market.

Environmental policies

Firms can be affected by a range of policies, designed to improve environmental conditions. A government may place restrictions on the amount of pollutants emitted by firms into the air, sea and rivers. It may then fine any firms which exceed these limits. Another policy, which has become more popular in recent years, is **tradable permits**. This involves a government issuing permits to firms, allowing them to pollute up to a certain

limit and to sell part of their allocated limit, if they pollute less. The idea is that the cleanest firms will be able to sell most of their permits, whilst those who pollute the most will have to buy more of other firms' permits. This will reduce the costs of the cleanest firms, whilst raising the costs of the worst polluting firms. As a result the cleanest firms should capture a higher market share and consequently, pollution should fall.

Activity 2

The European Union, an economic bloc of European countries, runs an emissions trading scheme. Companies in certain energy-intensive sectors are issued with permits to produce a certain tonnage of carbon dioxide. If they produce less than their allowance, they can sell the excess.

a. What is meant by an energy intensive sector?

b. Explain how an emissions trading scheme may reduce pollution.

Price controls

A government may limit firms' ability to set their own prices by imposing price controls. A government may set a maximum ceiling on the price in order to enable the poor afford basic necessities. To have any impact, a maximum price has to be set below the equilibrium price. Fig. 4 shows a maximum price being set at P_x, below the equilibrium price of P. Some people will now be able to purchase the product at a lower price. The problem is, however, that a **shortage** will be created as at this lower price the quantity demanded exceeds the quantity supplied. To prevent the development of an illegal market in the product, some method of its allocation will have to be introduced. This might be through queuing, rationing or even a lottery.

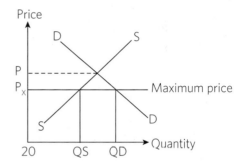

Fig. 4 The effect of setting a maximum price

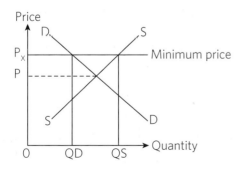

Fig. 5 The effect of setting a minimum price

To encourage production of a product a government may set a minimum price (P_x). To have an impact on a market, this will have to be set above the equilibrium price as shown in Fig. 5.

This time the problem created is a **surplus**, with the quantity supplied being greater than the quantity demanded. To prevent the price being driven down, the surplus will have to be bought up by the government or some other official body.

A minimum price may also be set on the price of labour in the form of a minimum wage. The motives for such a move and its impact were discussed in unit 18.

Activity 3

China has removed price controls on most consumer goods. Their prices are now determined by the market. The prices of a number of services, however, remain under the control of the National Development Reform Commission – the chief economic planning body in the country. These include, water, oil, power, cable TV fees and parking fees for cars. The price controls are designed to protect people against monopolies and to keep inflation low. There is some evidence, however, that price controls are distorting the market and damaging the economy. Petrol stations in Southern China, for instance, run out of oil quite regularly.

a. How are prices determined by the market?

b. How price controls distort the market?

c. Does the extract suggest that the Chinese National Development Reform Commission sets maximum or minimum prices on the products mentioned? Explain your answer.

Regulation

Regulation includes rules and laws which place restricions on the activities of firms. Besides setting price controls, outlawing uncompetitive behaviour and limiting the amount of pollution emitted by a firm, a government may regulate the target audience for the product, the quality of products and mode of staff management by firms. For instance, a government may pass a law banning the sale of cigarettes to children. It may require firms to ensure that the products produced by them meet certain standards and that it needs to provide its workers a specified number of regular holidays. It may also place restrictions on timing for opening/closing of shops and control the routes that buses must follow.

As a measure to correct market failure, regulations have the advantages of being backed up by law and easily understood. The government does, however, have to check that the rules and laws are being followed and this may be difficult and expensive. Also, a regulation works only if most people agree with it. For instance, it would be difficult to enforce a law that everyone wears a helmet, when riding a motorcycle if such a move is opposed by most of the riders. This is because too much time and money would need to be spent for prosecuting the offenders and the government may become very unpopular.

There are a number of other problems with imposing regulations. They do not directly compensate those who suffer as a result of market failure. Regulations may be too restrictive – reducing market flexibility and creating barriers to entry.

Public Sector Contracts and Partnerships between the Public and Private Sectors

Private sector firms provide a range of products and services for the public sector. For example, private sector road building firms construct and maintain roads for the government in many countries and private pharmaceutical firms supply state health care systems with medicines.

In recent years, in more and more countries, the government is forming partnerships with private sector firms. A common form of partnership is where the private sector initially provides the finance for a state project, such as the building of a hospital. The private sector firm, then, builds it and maintains it for a number of years. The government rents it and operates it, buying it back over time.

In other cases, the public and private sectors provide part of a service. For instance, private sector firms may run train operating companies whilst the government builds and maintains the infrastructure.

 Summary

- The main types of macroeconomic policies are fiscal policy, monetary policy and supply-side policy.

- Fiscal policy influences aggregate demand in the economy by changing taxes and government expenditure.

- The main monetary policy measures include changes in interest rates. A cut in interest rates will raise aggregate demand.

- Supply-side policy is designed to increase aggregate supply.

- Subsidies and taxes influence firms' output and the price they charge for their products.

- The impact of a subsidy/tax depends on their size and price elasticity of demand.

- Other types of polices which influence private sector firms are industrial, competition and environmental policies.

continued····>

- Maximum prices are set below the equilibrium price. They lower prices but lead to shortages.

- Minimum prices are set above the equilibrium price. They can help producers but lead to surpluses.

- Regulations are backed up by law, but it can be expensive to implement them and difficult to check their violation by people. Their effectiveness is influenced by their acceptance by the people.

Teacher's Tip

In answering questions on subsidies, check whether the question is asking about subsidies to producers (which would shift the supply curve) or subsidies to consumers (which would shift the demand curve). If the question just refers to a subsidy, presume it is a *subsidy to a producer* as this is the most common form of subsidy.

Multiple Choice Questions

1. Which of the following is most likely to increase demand in the economy?
    a. A reduction in government expenditure
    b. A reduction in the rate of interest
    c. A rise in a budget surplus
    d. A rise in income tax

2. When does a budget deficit occur?
    a. When imports exceed exports
    b. When government expenditure is greater than government revenue
    c. When interest rates are falling
    d. When the money supply is rising

3. Which type of government policy would include reform of trade unions?
    a. Competition policy
    b. Fiscal policy
    c. Monetary policy
    d. Supply-side policy

4. A government is keen to reduce unemployment. Which measure would not increase public expenditure?
    a. A cut in income tax
    b. A reduction in the retirement age
    c. A rise in the school leaving age
    d. A subsidy to firms to encourage their expansion

Conflicts between Government Aims

Unit 31 explained the main government macroeconomic aims and the previous unit discussed some of the policies it can employ to achieve these aims. This unit explores some of the conflicts that can arise between these aims.

 ## Unemployment and Inflation

Some of the policy measures designed to reduce unemployment may increase inflation. For example, an increase in government expenditure on pensions would raise consumption. This rise would encourage firms to expand their output and take on more workers. The higher aggregate demand may, however, raise the price level.

 ## The Balance of Payments and Economic Growth

Policy measures to reduce expenditure on imports may reduce the economic growth. A rise in income tax, designed to reduce households' expenditure on imports, would also reduce spending on domestically produced products. This fall in demand will reduce the country's output or at least slow down the economic growth.

 ## Government Aims and Aggregate Demand

Unemployment and economic growth tend to benefit from expansionary fiscal and monetary policies. In contrast, deflationary fiscal and monetary policies are more likely to be used to reduce inflation and expenditure on imports.

Priority

If the aims appear to conflict, a government may have to decide between, for instance, reducing inflation and reducing unemployment. Its choice will be influenced by the relative scale of the problem, the consequences of the problem and which problem the country's citizens are most concerned about.

 **Activity 1**

In the 1990s, New Zealand had price stability but relatively low economic growth and high unemployment. In the period from 2000 to 2005, inflation rose above the government's target from 1% to 3% and its trade position worsened but economic growth and employment improved.

a. According to the New Zealand government, what is price stability?

b. Why might a rise in employment be accompanied by a rise in inflation?

 # Government Aims and Supply-side Policy

In the long run, all the government macroeconomic aims have the potential to benefit from supply-side policy. Increasing aggregate supply enables an economy to continue to grow in a non-inflationary way. Fig. 1 shows aggregate supply rising in line with aggregate demand. Such a combination enables output and employment to increase without inflation.

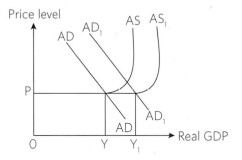

Fig. 1 Aggregate supply increasing with aggregate demand

Improving education and training is likely to increase aggregate demand, as it will probably involve an increase in government expenditure. Also, it will be likely to reduce unemployment by making workers more productive and occupationally mobile.

Increasing productive potential and efficiency can improve an economy's balance of payments position. Producing better quality and cheaper products can increase exports and reduce imports.

It has to be remembered that besides a time lag before the effect of some supply-side policy, some of the measures can be expensive while some might not work. For instance, the government may spend more on education but if subjects taught are not in demand in the future, it may reduce employment.

Activity 2

South Africa's income is spread very unevenly. Whilst the country has a number of millionaires, 50% of the population is living below the poverty line.

To try and reduce inequality the government is trying to boost investment levels, improve infrastructure, cut business costs, expand public works and create more jobs. In 2006, the unemployment rate was officially recorded at 28%.

a. What is meant by an unemployment rate of 28%?

b. Explain how a government can boost 'investment levels'.

Increasing the Effectiveness of Macroeconomic Policies

Besides using supply-side policy measures in the long run to improve macroeconomic performance, there are a number of other ways through which a government can try to ensure that it achieves all its macroeconomic aims.

One is by using a number of policies. A Nobel Prize winning economist, *Jan Tinbergen*, suggested that a government needs to use one policy measure for each of its objectives. So, for instance, if a government wants to stimulate economic growth and reduce imports, it may provide investment grants to firms and place a tax on imports. Another way, to try to ensure that all of its aims are achieved, is to have as much and as accurate information, as possible. One vital piece of information is the size of the multiplier effect of any increase in aggregate demand. For example, if a government raised its expenditure by $20m, the final rise in the country's income, expenditure and output would be greater. This is because those who benefit from the $20m extra expenditure, may themselves spend $16m (saving $4m). In turn those who receive the $16m may spend $13m and so on. If expenditure continues to rise at this rate, total spending, income and output will rise by $100m. In this case, the final increase in expenditure is five times greater than the initial rise.

Governments also try to decide and implement their policies relatively quickly. If there is a delay in introducing policies, there is a danger that economic activity undergoes a change and the policy measures may actually harm the economy. For instance, a period of high unemployment may lead the government to cut income tax, to raise aggregate demand and employment. If, however, by the time the measure is introduced, aggregate demand is increasing anyway, it may increase inflationary pressure.

Key Point

The multiplier effect: the final impact on total expenditure being greater than the initial change.

Recent Developments

In some economies, most notably USA and the UK, changes in recent years appear to have made it possible for economies to experience full employment and high economic growth, without encountering inflation. The key changes are advances in technology and increased global competition. As economies grow, aggregate demand rises and shortages of labour can occur. With advances in technology more can be produced even with full employment of workers. Increased global competition also puts pressure on the firms to keep their costs low.

Activity 3

In 2004 Latin America's economies grew at an average rate of 5.9%, the fastest since 1981. Poverty and inequality, however, were still a significant problem. Poverty itself can hold back economic growth. Unlike in many countries, public expenditure in Latin America does not always reduce inequality as much of it favours the rich (for example, subsidising university students). Recently, however, a number of Latin American countries, including Brazil, Colombia and Mexico, have been adopting measures to reduce poverty including increasing access to primary and secondary education.

a. How may poverty impede economic growth?
b. Explain, how increasing access to primary and secondary education may reduce poverty.
c. Discuss whether an increase in public expenditure always help a government to achieve its macroeconomic aims.

 **Summary**

- Economic growth and employment are likely to benefit from measures designed to increase expenditure but these measures may result in higher inflation and a rise in imports.

- Governments may have to prioritise their aims, selecting to concentrate on the most serious problem.

- Macroeconomic aims may be helped by supply-side policy measures in the long run.

- The effectiveness of macroeconomic policy measures, can be increased by using a number of policies, accurate information and an absence of a time lag.

- Advances in technology and increased global competition are increasing economic growth and keeping inflation down in some countries.

 Teacher's Tip

You may find it useful to draw up a table, comparing the effects of particular policy measures such as a cut in income tax on unemployment, inflation, economic growth and the balance of payments.

Multiple Choice Questions

1. What is most likely to conflict with a government's aim of full employment?
   a. Lower income tax
   b. Lower spending on imports
   c. Higher government expenditure
   d. Higher interest rates

2. What is most likely to happen due to economic growth?
   a. A fall in the standard of living
   b. A fall in tax revenue
   c. A rise in employment
   d. A rise in government expenditure on unemployment benefits

3. What combination of macroeconomic aims is most likely to benefit from a decrease in government spending?
   a. A fall in imports and price stability
   b. Economic growth and full employment
   c. Full employment and a fall in imports
   d. Price stability and economic growth

4. Which of the following may reduce the effectiveness of a government policy measure?
   a. Accurate information
   b. An absence of economic problems in other economies
   c. An absence of policy conflicts
   d. A time lag

Types of Taxation

Unit 32 mentioned that the two instruments of fiscal policy are government expenditure and taxation. This, and the next unit, examine taxation in more depth.

 Aims of Taxation

Most people think that taxes are used to raise revenue for government expenditure. This is, indeed, a key aim of taxation but there are other aims as well, including:

- redistribution of income from the rich to the poor. Higher income groups pay more in tax than the poor and some of the revenue raised is used to pay benefits to the poor.

- discouraging the consumption of what are called **demerit goods**. These are products that the government considers more harmful to consumers than they realise, for example, cigarettes and alcohol.

- raise the costs of firms that impose costs on others by, for instance, causing pollution.

- discouraging the consumption of imports and hence protect domestic industries. By placing tariffs on rival imported products, the country's inhabitants may buy less foreign and more domestic products.

- influence economic activity. As discussed in unit 32, fiscal policy can be used to change aggregate demand. If an economy is experiencing rising unemployment, its government may cut taxes to stimulate an increase in consumption and investment.

Direct and Indirect Taxes

Taxes are either direct or indirect. Direct taxes are taxes levied on a person's or a firm's income or wealth. They are called direct taxes because the people or firms responsible for paying the tax have to bear the burden of the tax. Indirect taxes, which can also be called expenditure or outlay taxes, differ from direct taxes in two key ways. One is that they are levied on spending. The other is that the firms that actually make the tax payment to the government may pass on, at least some of the burden of the tax, to other people. For instance, most of the tax that governments impose on petrol is passed on by petrol companies to the customers in the form of higher prices.

The Main Types of Taxes

The type of taxes imposed vary from country to country. There are some taxes, however, which are levied in most countries. Among the most common type of direct taxes are:

- **Income tax.** This is a tax on income that people receive from their employment and investment income. People are given a tax allowance, which is an amount of income they earn free of tax. Income above this level is referred to as taxable income.

- **Corporation tax.** This is also referred to as corporate tax and as mentioned in unit 26, it is a tax on the profits of firms.

- **Capital gains tax.** This is a tax on the profit made on assets when they are sold for a higher price than what they were bought for. A capital gain may be made, for instance, by shareholders selling shares for more than what they paid for them. When a capital gains tax is imposed, exemptions are usually made. These normally include any money made on the sale of people's main residence.

- **Inheritance tax.** This is a tax on wealth above a certain amount which is passed on to other people, when a person dies.

Common types of indirect taxes are:

- **Sales tax.** As its name suggests, this is a tax imposed when products are sold. In an increasing number of countries, the main type of sales tax is VAT (value added tax). This is levied on the value added by firms at the different stages of the production process. Firms can usually get back the VAT paid by them on the products they have purchased.

- **Excise duties.** These are taxes charged on certain domestically produced goods, most commonly on alcoholic drinks, petrol and tobacco. They are charged in addition to VAT.

- **Customs duties.** These are taxes on imports and are also called tariffs.

- **Licences.** A licence may be needed to use a range of products including a television and a car.

Key Points

Direct taxes: taxes on income and wealth.

Indirect taxes: taxes on expenditure.

Activity 1

Ireland taxes supermarket carrier bags. The main reason for this is to cut their use and reduce litter. A number of other governments are considering the introduction of this measure and other green taxes.

a. Is a tax on carrier bags, a direct or an indirect tax? Explain your answer.

b. Identify two reasons for imposing a tax on carrier bags.

c. Using a demand and supply diagram, explain the effect of imposing a tax on carrier bags, on their market.

Local taxes

Most taxes are levied on a national basis but some are levied on a local basis. Local taxes are used to pay for local services such as education, fire services, libraries, roads and refuse collection. There are two main types of local taxes. One is based on the property of local firms and the other is based largely on the value of household property. In the UK and a number of other countries, business rates are levied on local firms. The government collects the revenue and then distributes it to local authorities on the basis of the number of people living in each area. Council tax is based on the value of people's housing and expenditure of each council. It is collected directly by the local authority. Some countries also use local sales tax.

 The Nature of Taxation

Taxes are progressive, proportional or regressive. A progressive tax is one which takes a higher percentage of the income or wealth of the rich. As taxable income or wealth rises, so does the rate of taxation. In the case of a proportional tax, the percentage paid in tax stays the same as income or wealth change. With a regressive tax, the percentage paid in tax falls as income or wealth rises. So in this case, people with higher incomes pay a smaller percentage of their income in tax than the poor do.

In the case of all three types of tax, the total amount of tax paid usually rises with income or wealth but what differs is the percentage paid (this is shown in table 1). For example, a rich and a poor person pay the same excise duty per litre of petrol bought.

The rich person is likely to buy more petrol and so will pay more tax in total. The amount paid, however, is likely to form a smaller percentage of his or her income – making this a regressive tax.

Table 1 Progressive, proportional and regressive taxes.

Progressive tax		
Income ($)	Taxed paid ($)	Tax rate (%)
100	10	10
500	100	20
1 000	400	40
Proportional tax		
Income ($)	Taxed paid ($)	Tax rate (%)
100	25	25
500	125	25
1 000	250	25
Regressive tax		
Income ($)	Taxed paid ($)	Tax rate (%)
100	40	40
500	150	30
1 000	200	20

 **Activity 2**

In Egypt, in 2006, the standard rate of corporation tax was 40%. Petroleum companies, however, were charged a higher percentage whilst firms which exported a high proportion of their output were charged less. Income tax in the country was a progressive tax and in 2006 the top rate was 65% for income above £E200 000.

a. What is meant by a progressive tax?

b. Explain why a government may tax firms which export a high proportion of their output less than the other firms.

 **Summary**

- The aims of taxation are to raise revenue, redistribute income, discourage the consumption of demerit goods, raise the costs of firms that impose these costs on others, discourage the consumption of imports and influence economic activity.

- Direct taxes are levied on income and wealth and include income tax, corporation tax, capital gains tax and inheritance tax.

- Indirect taxes are levied on expenditure and include sales tax, excise duties, customs duties and licences.

- Local taxes include business rates and council tax.

- Progressive taxes take a higher percentage as income or wealth rises, a proportional tax takes the same percentage and a regressive tax takes a smaller percentage.

 Teacher's Tip

Find out examples of direct and indirect taxes in your own country.

Multiple Choice Questions

1. Which of the following is a direct tax?
   a. Excise duty on petrol
   b. Inheritance tax
   c. Sales tax
   d. Tariff

2. What is meant by a regressive tax?
   a. A tax that falls in line with inflation
   b. A tax that reduces government revenue over time
   c. A tax that places a greater burden on the poor than the rich
   d. A tax that is replaced by one which generates more income

3. The following shows the breakdown of a government's tax revenue.

	$ million
Income tax	80
Corporation tax	40
Customs duties	20
Sales tax	70
Inheritance tax	10

   What is the total amount of revenue received from indirect taxes?
   a. $30m
   b. $90m
   c. $130m
   d. $220m

4. One woman earns $1 000 a month and pays $300 income tax. Another woman receives a salary of $9 000 a month and pays $2 700 as tax. What type of tax is this income tax?
   a. Indirect
   b. Progressive
   c. Proportional
   d. Regressive

Incidence and Impact of Taxation

The previous unit outlined the different types of taxes. This unit examines the incidence of taxation, qualities of a good tax, the impact of direct and indirect taxes and the spread of flat taxes.

 Tax Base, Tax Burden and the Incidence of Taxation

The tax base is the source of tax revenue, that is what is taxed. A wide tax base means that a large range of items and people are taxed. There can be a link between tax rates and the tax burden. A wide tax base may enable tax rates to be relatively low. High tax rates, particularly corporate tax rates, can reduce the tax base. This is because they may cause firms to move out of the country.

The tax burden relates to the amount of tax paid by people and firms. It is sometimes expressed as a percentage of the country's total income (GDP – Gross domestic product). The higher the tax burden, the greater the percentage of peoples' and firms' income taken through tax.

The incidence of taxation refers to the distribution of the burden of an indirect tax, shared between consumers and producers. In the case of products with inelastic demand, consumers bear most of the tax. This is because the producers can pass on a high proportion of the tax in the form of a higher price as they know it will not reduce the demand significantly. In contrast, if products have elastic demand it is producers who bear most of the tax. This is because they know that they cannot pass on much of the tax to consumers as such a move would bring down the sales significantly.

Fig. 1 shows the contrasting impact of a tax on a product with inelastic demand and a product with elastic demand.

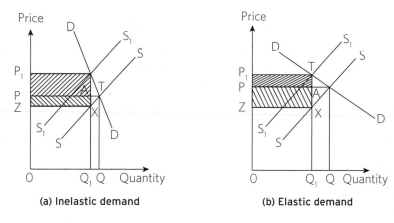

Fig. 1 The influence of PED on the incidence of taxation

The tax shifts the supply curve to the left by the amount of the tax (TAX). The total revenue is P_1TXZ. The proportion of tax borne by consumers is represented by the change in price multiplied by the quantity sold i.e. PP_1TA. The proportion borne by producers, is the amount by which the price producers receive after tax is below the original market price, multiplied by the quantity sold i.e. PAXZ. Elasticity of supply also influences the incidence of taxation. The more inelastic supply is, the more the tax borne by the suppliers. In contrast, if supply is elastic, more of the tax will be borne by consumers.

The Qualities of a Good Tax

Economists have identified a number of qualities that a good tax should possess. These include:

- **Equity.** This means fairness in the sense that the amount of tax people and firms have to pay, should be based on their ability to pay. A rich person has a greater ability to pay tax than a poor person.

- **Certainty.** A tax should be easy to understand and households and firms should be able to calculate the amount of tax required to be paid by them.

- **Convenience.** A tax should be easy to pay.

- **Economy.** The cost of collecting a tax should be considerably less than the revenue it generates.

- **Flexibility.** It should be possible to change the tax if economic activity changes or government aims change. The revenue from some taxes changes automatically to offset economic booms and slumps. For instance, tax revenue rises from income tax and sales tax, without any change in the rates, when there is an economic boom. This is because more people will be employed, incomes will rise and people will spend more. Such a rise in tax revenue may slow down the rise in aggregate demand and prevent inflationary pressure building up.

- **Efficiency.** A tax should improve the performance of markets or at least, not significantly reduce the efficiency of markets. For instance, an extra one-off tax, sometimes called a *windfall tax*, imposed on high supernormal profits of banks may encourage banks to reduce the charges they impose on customers. A tax on pollution may result in a cleaner environment. Income tax rates should not be set so high that they discourage effort.

In practice, it is unlikely that a tax will have all of these qualities. For example, income tax can score high on equity and flexibility but not on certainty if a number of tax allowances are given.

 Activity 1

In most of the countries, small firms are entitled to tax relief for the purchase of capital goods and expenditure on research and development.
a. What type of tax is levied on firms?
b. Why may governments give small firms a tax advantage?

The Impact of Direct Taxes

As suggested above there is a risk that direct taxes, if set too high, may discourage effort, enterprise and saving. High rates of income tax may stop some people from working overtime and taking promotion and prevent some people from entering the labour force. High rates of corporation tax may discourage entrepreneurs from expanding their firms and investing in new markets. On the other hand, high tax rates may encourage some people to work harder. This is particularly likely to be the case with workers who have fixed financial commitments, such as mortgages. In addition, a number of workers cannot alter the hours they work for – they are contracted for a fixed number of hours per week.

The impact of high taxes on income earned from saving is also important. As they reduce the return from saving, they may cause some people to save less but they may encourage target savers to save more. Direct taxes do have the benefits of being able to redistribute income and wealth, act as automatic stabilisers and as a good source of tax revenue in countries with organised labour markets, high literacy rates and high incomes.

The Impact of Indirect Taxes

Whilst direct taxes tend to be progressive, indirect taxes are regressive and therefore proportionately fall more heavily on the poor. Increasing indirect taxes will also raise prices. This increase may stimulate workers to press for wage increases and set off a trend of rising prices, that is inflation. Indirect taxes do, however, have a number of benefits. They are relatively easy and cheap to collect as firms do some of the work. It is believed that they act as less of a disincentive to effort and enterprise than direct taxes. They can be used selectively to achieve particular aims such as reducing the consumption of alcohol. They tend to be harder to evade than direct taxes and easier to adjust. To a certain extent, people also have more choice with indirect taxes. The amount of tax paid by them depends on what they buy. They may decide not to buy products which are highly taxed.

Indirect taxes are also a useful source of income, especially in countries where it is difficult to raise much from income tax because a significant number of workers work in the informal sector. Also in countries with low literacy rates, people might face problems while filling in the tax forms.

Activity 2

In 2006, the French government lowered the top band of income tax from 48% to 40% and reduced the number of tax bands from six to four.

a. Explain whether the changes that the French government implemented in 2006, made its income tax system more/less progressive.

b. Explain one advantage and one disadvantage of using income tax as a source of tax revenue.

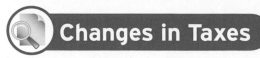 # Changes in Taxes

In recent decades, in a number of countries, governments have become more reliant on indirect taxes and less on direct taxes. This move has been designed to reduce disincentive effects and tax evasion. Even more recently, some countries have been adopting what are called **flat taxes.** A pure flat rate tax system would involve income tax, corporation tax and VAT being set at the same rate with no exceptions. Several of East European economies, for instance, have replaced a number of income and corporate tax rates with one rate. In most of these countries, tax rates have been lowered as they have been flattened. For example, Ukraine has replaced a very progressive income tax system which had a top tax rate of 90% with one rate of 13%.

A number of advantages are claimed for flat taxes. They are simple to administer for governments and firms, there is less incentive to evade paying tax and more incentive for workers and entrepreneurs to earn and produce more. However, concerns have been expressed about the regressive nature of flat taxes although in practice, all existing flat taxes have set the uniform rate above a tax-free level of income.

 ## Summary

- If demand is inelastic, most of an indirect tax will be borne by the consumer whereas if demand is elastic, it will be borne mainly by the producer.

- A good tax is one which is fair, easy to understand, easy to pay, cheap to collect, flexible and efficient.

- Direct taxes may discourage effort, enterprise and saving but they can help to redistribute income and wealth, act as automatic stabilisers and raise a significant amount of revenue.

- Indirect taxes tend to be regressive and may raise prices but these are relatively easy and cheap to collect, do not tend to act as a disincentive to effort, enterprise and saving and are harder to evade.

- Recently a number of countries have moved towards greater reliance on indirect taxes and some have introduced flat taxes.

 ### Teacher's Tip

Consider whether a particular tax in your country fulfils all the requirements of a 'good tax'.

Multiple Choice Questions

1. A government decides to switch reliance from direct to indirect taxes. As a result of this decision, which tax is likely to reduce and which is likely to rise?

	Decrease	Increase
a.	customs duties	capital gains tax
b.	excise duties	corporate tax
c.	income tax	VAT
d.	licences	inheritance tax

2. A government wants to redistribute income from the rich to the poor. Which changes in taxation would help it to achieve this objective?

    a.   A cut in corporate tax and a rise in sales tax

    b.   A cut in VAT and a rise in income tax

    c.   A cut in capital gains tax and inheritance tax

    d.   A rise in customs duties and excise duties

3. In which circumstance will the greatest amount of the tax be borne by the consumer?

	PED	PES
a.	elastic	inelastic
b.	inelastic	elastic
c.	inelastic	elastic
d.	elastic	inelastic

4. The following diagram shows the effect of introducing a tax (TAX). What is the resultant producers' revenue?

    a. $OZXQ_1$

    b. $OPAQ_1$

    c. OP_1TQ_1

    d. $OPYQ$

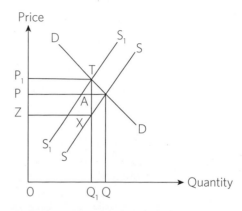

Answer Key

Unit 30

Activity 1

a. (i) The state is likely to be prepared, to deliver to remote communities and it is likely to see the postal service as an essential service.

    (ii) Private sector firms, driven by the profit motive, may cut costs and hence the prices of deliveries to city centres.

b. Working for a state-owned enterprise may provide more job security. This is because it may continue to produce even if it makes a loss, since the state may subsidise it. Those working in a state-owned enterprise may also enjoy good working conditions as the state may seek to set an example.

Activity 2

a. A government may run hospitals to ensure that everyone has access to the essential services. It is likely to provide these services free of cost or at a reduced price, whereas private sector health care providers may charge a higher price. It may also run hospitals to encourage everyone to make sufficient use of these services. Health care tends to be under-consumed, if left to market forces as it is a merit good.

b. Books, computers and furniture.

Multiple Choice Questions

1. a.

    If a government decides to pay its workers more, it will have to increase its expenditure. This may reduce any budget surplus and increase any budget deficit. Unemployment is likely to fall and expenditure on goods and services should rise, which may reduce any surplus.

2. c.

    Education is a merit good as consumers tend to undervalue its benefits to themselves and to others. It is not an inessential product. Demand for it increases as income rises. It is not a public good as non-payers can be excluded from consuming it. In fact, some education is supplied through the private sector.

3. d.

    In a planned economy, most people work for state owned enterprises.

4. b.

    Limiting public sector wages will quench price rises, if products are produced by state owned enterprises. It may also keep down wage rises and hence the prices in the private sector. This is because firms in the private sector will be able to attract workers without having to raise wages significantly. Keeping down public sector pay rises may protect employment. Workers are less likely to be made redundant, in order to keep public expenditure under control.

Unit 31

Activity 1

a. An economic growth rate of 4.1% means that the country has produced 4.1% more output than the year before.

b. Underemployment is likely to have been highest in agriculture. In this sector nearly a fifth of the country's workers were producing only 4% of its output. The number of people working on family firms could be reduced, without any significant fall in agricultural output. Such a reduction would enable the manufacturing and service sectors to expand.

c. Mexico did appear to have the potential to grow at a faster rate than 4.1% in 2005. This was because, although the country appeared to have full employment, it had a high proportion of underemployed workers. If these workers were used more fully, output would have grown more rapidly.

Activity 2

a. None of the economies achieved all their macroeconomic objectives. Germany had price stability but slow economic growth, near full employment but too low a rise in the price level. Poland had high economic growth, rather low inflation but very high unemployment. Pakistan had high economic growth but its unemployment rate and inflation rate were unacceptably high. To make a more informed judgement on the question, it would also be necessary to know whether the countries were experiencing balance of payments stability.

b. Pakistan. Although Germany and Poland have a higher percentage of unemployed workers, they have a smaller labour force.

Multiple Choice Questions

1. d.
    A government would want a rise in output, low unemployment and imports equalling exports in the long run.

2. d.
    The unemployment rate is the number of unemployed workers expressed as a percentage of the labour force. In this case it is, 6m/50m × 100.

3. a.
    An improvement in education would increase labour productivity and so the country's productive potential. b, c and d would all tend to reduce a country's productive

potential. b and d would reduce the quantity of labour and c would reduce the quantity of capital.

4. b.

Potential economic growth is a rise in the maximum output, a country is capable of producing.

Unit 32

Activity 1

a. Aggregate demand is the total demand for a country's products. It consists of consumption, investment, government expenditure and net exports.

b. A rise in the rate of interest may slow down economic growth as it may reduce aggregate demand. A higher interest rate may discourage consumption as the cost of borrowing will rise, the return on saving will fall and people who have taken out loans in the past will have to spend less. Investment may also fall again because not only borrowing will be more expensive but also the opportunity cost of investment will rise and firms will expect lower consumption in the future.

Activity 2

a. An energy intensive sector is an industry that uses a high amount of energy per unit produced.

b. An emissions trading scheme may reduce pollution by rewarding firms which cause little pollution and punish those which generate a high amount of pollution. Permits are issued or sold to firms allowing them to pollute up to a given level. Those which pollute less can sell their leftover allowance to other firms. This should enable them to charge lower prices, gain more market share and reduce the pollution the industry creates.

Activity 3

a. Market forces determine price by the interaction of demand and supply.

b. Price controls may distort the market by creating shortages and surpluses. A maximum price set below the equilibrium price will lead to demand being greater than supply. A minimum price set above the market equilibrium price will result in supply being greater then demand.

c. The extract suggests that Chinese National Development Reform Commission sets maximum price for the products mentioned. This can be concluded from the reference to price controls being designed to keep inflation low and check the shortage of petrol.

Multiple Choice Questions

1. b.

A reduction in the rate of interest is likely to encourage borrowing and discourage saving. This should lead to higher consumption and investment. a, c and d all would be likely to reduce aggregate demand. a would reduce a component of aggregate demand. c would arise from either a fall in government expenditure or a rise in taxation. d would reduce people's disposable income and so would be likely to induce a fall in consumption.

2. b.
    The budget position is concerned with the relationship between government expenditure and government revenue. A deficit occurs when the government spends more than it raises in revenue.

3. d.
    Reform of trade unions is designed to raise the productivity of labour and increase aggregate supply.

4. a.
    A cut in income tax should result in a rise in aggregate demand and hence an increase in the jobs available. d may also reduce unemployment but would cause a rise in public expenditure. The impact of b and c on unemployment is uncertain but both would increase public expenditure – one on pensions and another on education.

Unit 33

Activity 1

a. According to the New Zealand government, price stability is an inflation rate which lies between 1% and 3%. So an inflation rate of e.g. 2%, 1.5% or 2.6%, would be regarded as price stability.

b. A rise in employment may be accompanied by a rise in inflation for two key reasons. One is that as more people are employed, incomes will be higher and so will be the consumption. Higher consumption will increase aggregate demand. If the economy is close to full capacity, this may push up the price level. A rise in employment may also create a shortage of labour and as a result push up wage rates. This would increase the costs for the firms, which in turn will push up the price level.

Activity 2

a. An unemployment rate of 28% means that 28% of the labour force is without jobs.

b. A government could boost investment levels in a number of ways. It could reduce corporation tax. This could provide jobs, with more finance and more incentive to invest. It could lower income tax which may lead firms to invest more, in expectation of higher demand. In addition, it could provide investment grants to firms.

Activity 3

a. Poverty can hold back economic growth in a number of ways. Poor people are likely to have less access to education, especially higher education and health care and consequently they are likely to be less productive workers. High levels of poverty can discourage foreign firms from investing in a country. A significant level of poverty in a country is likely to mean that tax revenue will be low and therefore it will not have much money to spend on developing the economy.

b. Increasing access to primary and secondary education should improve educational standards and raise productivity. It should make it easier for workers to find jobs and better paid employment.

c. An increase in public expenditure would not necessarily enable a government to achieve its macroeconomic aims. The impact will depend crucially on the state of the economy and the use of money. If the economy is operating close to full capacity, an increase in government expenditure may lead to a rise in inflation and a rise in imports. However, if the economy is operating with a high level of unemployment, a rise in government expenditure is likely to be more beneficial. Government expenditure on education and training may provide more long term benefits for the economy than spending on large, prestigious government buildings.

Multiple Choice Questions

1. d.

    Higher interest rates will reduce aggregate demand which may lead to higher unemployment. a, b and c are likely to increase aggregate demand and raise employment.

2. c.

    As output increases, employment is likely to rise. Living standards should rise although it depends on how growth occurs. With higher output and higher employment, tax revenue should increase. As employment is likely to rise, government expenditure on unemployment benefits should fall.

3. a.

    A decrease in government expenditure is likely to reduce aggregate demand and so may reduce inflationary pressure. Lower government expenditure can directly reduce spending on imports since some portion of it goes on imports. Lower government expenditure may also reduce household income which, in turn, is likely to slow down economic growth and reduce employment.

4. d.

    A time lag between deciding and implementing government policies may mean that the policies do not have the desired effect on the economy. a, b and c should all increase the effectiveness of a government policy.

Unit 34

Activity 1

a. It is an indirect tax as it is a tax on expenditure (on carrier bags).

b. To reduce litter and to raise revenue.

c. A tax on carrier bags will cause a decrease in supply, as effectively an extra cost has been placed on suppliers. The decrease in supply will cause prices to rise and demand to extend as shown in Fig. 1. The extent to which price rises and the quantity traded will be influenced by PED.

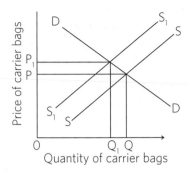

Fig. 1

Activity 2

a. A progressive tax is a tax which takes a higher proportion of the income of the rich than the poor.

b. A government may tax exporters less than the other firms, in order to improve the country's trade position and match import expenditure and export revenue.

Multiple Choice Questions

1. b.
   Inheritance tax is a tax on wealth that is passed on to another persons when someone dies. a, c and d are all indirect taxes.

2. c.
   A regressive tax falls more heavily on the poor.

3. b.
   The indirect taxes are the customs duties and the sales tax. c gives the total for the direct taxes and d gives the total tax revenue.

4. c.
   The tax is on income and so is a direct tax. It is proportional, as the rich person and the poor person pay the same percentage (30%) in tax.

Unit 35

Activity 1

a. Corporation tax.

b. Governments may give small firms a tax advantage, in order to encourage their survival. This is because small firms can innovate, promote competition and employment and develop entrepreneurs.

Activity 2

a. It made it more regressive. It cut the top rate of tax which would have reduced the tax burden on the rich. In addition, it reduced the number of bands. This means that the rise in the percentage of the tax with income would have been reduced.

b. One advantage of using income tax as a source of tax revenue is that it redistributes income from the rich to the poor due to its progressive nature. One potential disadvantage, however, of using income tax is that it may act as a disincentive to workers, savers and entrepreneurs.

Multiple Choice Questions

1. c.

   Income tax is a direct tax and VAT is an indirect tax. Customs duties, licences and excise duties are indirect taxes. Capital gains tax and inheritance tax are indirect taxes.

2. b.

   Cutting VAT would reduce a regressive tax whilst raising income tax would increase a progressive tax. a, c and d would tend to redistribute income from the poor to the rich.

3. c.

   The more inelastic the demand, the more of a tax can be passed on to the consumer. This is because the rise in price will have less effect on demand. Elastic supply will also tend to result in consumers bearing more of the tax burden.

4. a.

   The producer's revenue is OZXQ1. The tax revenue is ZP_1TX. The total amount spent by consumers is OP_1TQ_1.

Examination Practice

Multiple Choice Questions

1. In 2006, output in Indonesia rose by 4.9%. Which of the government objectives does this meet?
    a. Balance of payments stability
    b. Economic growth
    c. Full employment
    d. Price stability

2. Fig. 2 shows the change in government expenditure and tax revenue change with time. What happened over this time period?
    a. The balance of payments moved from deficit into surplus.
    b. The economy moved from a recession into an economic boom.
    c. The government budget deficit moved from surplus into deficit.
    d. The level of inflation exceeded the level of unemployment.

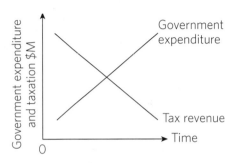

Fig. 2

3. Which government policy measure would be most likely to reduce unemployment?
    a. An increase in income tax
    b. An increase in interest rates
    c. A decrease in government expenditure
    d. A decrease in VAT

4. A government wants to redistribute income from the rich to the poor. Which combination of policy measures would achieve this?

	Progressive taxes	*Welfare payments*
a.	Increase	increase
b.	Increase	reduce
c.	Reduce	reduce
d.	Reduce	increase

5. What is a likely advantage of economic growth?
    a. Government tax revenue falls.
    b. The standard of living falls.
    c. The level of employment rises.
    d. The level of pollution increases.

6. Which government policy measure is most likely to benefit people on a high income?
   a. Increasing housing benefit
   b. Increasing unemployment benefit
   c. Reducing government expenditure on higher education
   d. Reducing income tax

7. Which of the following is an example of a measure that may be used as part of a government's competition policy?
   a. Permitting firms to engage in predatory but not limit pricing
   b. Preventing the merger of two firms which would result in a monopoly
   c. Spending on infrastructure
   d. Shifting the burden of taxation from indirect to direct taxes

8. 'A tax levied on the profit made on selling assets such as second homes and shares' – what type of tax is this?
   a. Capital gains
   b. Corporation
   c. Income
   d. Sales

9. Revenue from a country's income tax rises with income. What does this indicate about the income tax?
   a. It could be a progressive but not a regressive tax.
   b. It could be a proportional tax but not a progressive tax.
   c. It could be a regressive tax but not a proportional tax.
   d. It could be a progressive, proportional or regressive tax.

10. A government decides to stop taxing the profits of firms. This will reduce:
    a. Indirect taxes.
    b. Investment.
    c. The output of firms.
    d. The tax base.

Structured Questions

1. In 2000, the Singapore government's revenue from income tax, motor vehicle tax, betting tax and the tax on goods and services increased. However, the revenue from the tax on goods and services doubled while that from income tax rose by 7%. Singapore depends on its tourist trade for part of its wealth.
   a. Explain the difference between direct and indirect tax and identify one direct and one indirect tax in the above statement. (4)

b. Discuss why governments impose taxes. (6)

c. An increase in revenue from taxes is mentioned in the extract. Discuss whether you can draw conclusions about what might have happened in Singapore to
    (i) the numbers of tourists (4)
    (ii) the level of unemployment. (6)

(Cambridge 0455 Paper 4 Q4 Oct/Nov 2002)

2. From July 2000, Australia had a new tax structure as part of its economic reform. Before the changes were introduced, consumer groups expressed concern about its likely effects. The new system involved a redistribution from direct to indirect taxes through a new tax, charged on goods and services at 10%. However, to compensate for this, income tax was cut and social security benefits were increased. Those in favour of the change insisted that the new system would improve economic efficiency. The new tax covered services, by far the most important sector of the economy and which had previously escaped the tax. As compensation for companies, there were reductions in company tax. Those, who were against the new tax, feared that it would cause a sharp increase in inflation which was already beginning to increase as a result of strong domestic demand and a rise in the price of imported oil.

a. Explain the difference between a direct and an indirect tax. Give two examples of a direct tax based on the above information. (3)

b. If you had to decide whether consumers were disadvantaged by the changes in the tax system, what evidence would you need to investigate? (10)

(Cambridge 0455 Paper 6 Q2 May/June 2002)

3. a. Distinguish, with examples, between:
    (i) direct and indirect taxes (3)
    (ii) progressive and regressive taxes. (3)

b. Explain why governments impose taxes. (6)

c. Discuss what might happen in an economy if a government increases income tax rates. (8)

(Cambridge 0455 Paper 2 Q6 Oct/Nov 2006)

Consumer Prices Index

As noted in Unit 31, one of the main aims of macroeconomic policy is price stability. To assess the extent to which a country is experiencing price stability, changes in prices need to be measured.

 **Price Indices**

Price indices (also referred to as price indexes) show the change in general price level in percentage terms over time. They seek to calculate, the changes in the price of a very large 'shopping basket' of the products, bought by consumers. Two of the main price indices are the **retail prices index (RPI)** and the **consumer prices index (CPI)**. Their coverage is very similar with relatively small differences only. For instance, the RPI includes mortgage interest payments whilst the CPI does not. On the other hand, CPI and not the RPI, includes university accommodation fees.

Constructing a Price Index

There are a number of stages in constructing a price index. These include selecting a base year, finding out how households spend their money, attaching weights to items of expenditure, finding out price changes from a range of trade outlets and then constructing a weighted price index.

Selecting a base year

Government statisticians try to select, a relatively standard year in which there were no dramatic changes, as a base year. The base year is then given a figure of 100 and the price level in other years are compared to this figure. For instance, if the base year is 2007, it would mean that if the price index in 2010 is 123, the general price level had risen by 23% between 2007 and 2010.

Finding out how households spend their money

In calculating the average rise in prices, it is important to know how people spend their money. This is because a price change in an item, that people spend a large proportion of their total expenditure on, will have more impact on the cost of living than on an item on which they spend a relatively small proportion. If, for instance, the price of water rose, it would hit the pockets of most of the population much more than a rise in the price of a trip in an air balloon, something most people will not buy and those who do, will buy infrequently.

To find out the spending patterns of people, government officials carry out surveys of household expenditure. In the UK, a sample of approximately 7 000 households, covering about 16 600 people is used. Every fortnight about 270 of these households are asked to keep a record of their expenditure for fourteen days.

From the information collected, government officials work out the main commodities being bought by the households. This enables them to decide which items to include in the price index and what weights to attach to each of them. If people stop buying a product or their expenditure on it falls to a very small figure, it will be removed from the index. The weights reflect the proportion spent on the items. For instance, if on an average, households spend $120 of their total expenditure of $600 on food – food will be given a weight age of 1/5 or 20%. Table 1 shows the categories of products in the UK's CPI and their respective weights.

Table 1 The weights in the UK's CPI in 2005.

	Category	Weight (%)
a.	Food and non-alcoholic beverages	10.6
b.	Alcohol and tobacco	4.6
c.	Clothing and footwear	6.3
d.	Housing and household services	10.5
e.	Furniture and household goods	6.5
f.	Health	2.4
g.	Transport	14.8
h.	Communication	2.5
i.	Recreation and culture	15.1
j.	Education	1.7
k.	Restaurants and hotels	13.9
l.	Miscellaneous goods and services	11.1

Household spending patterns are reviewed each year with new family expenditure surveys. If these reveal, for instance, that people are spending a greater percentage on recreation and culture and a lower percentage on food and non-alcoholic beverages, the weights of these items in price index will be altered to reflect these changes.

Finding out price changes

Each month government officials find out information about prices. In the UK, about 130 000 price quotations are found for 650 different items. These are obtained from shops, post offices, power companies, train companies and a range of other outlets. From this information, the government estimates the change in prices.

Activity 1

India's CPI covers 260 items. It draws on about 160 000 price quotes from more than 16 500 outlets and selected markets. Most price quotes are collected every week. In the case of products which experience a change in price less frequently, the price quotes are collected every month or every six months.

a. What does a CPI measure?

b. How will the Indian government select the 260 items included in its CPI?

Constructing a weighted price index

Having assigned weights to different items included in the index and measured the change in their prices over time, the final stage is to multiply the weights by the new price index for each category of products and to calculate the change in general price level.

For example, consumers may spend $40 on food, $10 on housing, $25 on transport and $25 on entertainment. This gives a total expenditure of $100. The price of food may have risen by 10%, the price of housing may have fallen by 5%, the price of transport may not have changed and entertainment may have risen in price by 8%.

The information would then be used, to perform the calculation shown in table 2.

Table 2 Weighted price index.

Category	Weight		Price index		Weighted price index
Food	4/10	×	110	=	44.0
Housing	1/10	×	95	=	9.5
Transport	1/4	×	100	=	25.0
Entertainment	1/4	×	108	=	27.0
					105.5

The price index has risen by 5.5%. The change in the price level could also have been calculated rather more directly, as shown in table 3.

Table 3 Weighted price change.

Category	Weight		Price index		Weighted price Index
Food	4/10	×	10%	=	4%
Housing	1/10	×	–5%	=	–0.5%
Transport	1/4	×	0%	=	0%
Entertainment	1/4	×	8%	=	2%
					5.5%

In each case, calculate the inflation rate using the information given.

a. Consumers spend $20 on food, $20 on clothing, $10 on heating and $50 on entertainment. The price of food rises by 5%, the price of clothing falls by 10%, the price of heating rises by 30% and the price of entertainment rises by 20%.

b. Consumers spend $50 on food, $20 on clothing, $60 on transport and $70 on leisure goods and services. The price of food rises by 8%, the price of clothing rises by 10%, the price of transport falls by 10% and the price of leisure goods rises by 5%.

Different Impact of Price Changes

A consumer prices index measures the price of goods and services consumed by the average household. Of course, the expenditure of particular households is likely to differ from the average, in some way. A 2004 study in the US, for instance, found that families with young children had experienced lower inflation than other households, largely due to lower bills for health-care and no expenditure on university fees, which had been increasing in price at a greater rate than the inflation rate.

Summary

- The retail prices index (RPI) and the consumer prices index (CPI) are weighted measures of consumer prices.

- A rise in a consumer prices index indicates inflation.

- Surveys are done of the products bought by households. On the basis of this information, weights are attached to products. The greater the percentage of an average household's total expenditure devoted to a product, the higher its weightage.

- Information on price changes is found from a range of outlets.

- A weighted price index is constructed by multiplying weights by a price index for each category.

- A weighted price change can be found by multiplying weights with price changes.

 Teacher's Tip

In explaining the conception of a consumer price index, it is often useful to give a numerical example.

Multiple Choice Questions

1. What do the weights in a consumer price index indicate?
    a. The change in expenditure on consumer and capital goods.
    b. The extent by which prices of different items have changed.
    c. The items which have been purchased from overseas countries.
    d. The percentage of total expenditure on different items.

2. If a retail price index rises from 150 to 165, what is the inflation rate?
    a. 5%
    b. 10%
    c. 15%
    d. 165%

3. The price of a product rises by 8% in 2007 and its weighted price change is 2%. In 2008, its rise in price falls to 5% but its weighted price change increases to 2 1/2%. What was the weightage of the product in 2007 and 2008?

	2007	2008
a.	1/4	1/2
b.	1/2	1/4
c.	4	2
d.	2	4

4. A family-expenditure survey finds that households spend $20 on clothing and $50 on food in a mouth, out of a total spending of $200. What weights will be attached to the two products?

	Clothing	Food
a.	1/10	1/4
b.	1/5	1/2
c.	1	2
d.	1	21/2

Causes and Consequences of Inflation and Deflation

Inflation is not a one-off increase in the general price level. While examining the causes of inflation, therefore, it is necessary to consider the reasons for a rise in the price level over a period of time. Economists divide the causes into three main categories. These are **cost-push, demand-pull and monetary**.

The consequences of inflation can not only be influenced by its cause, but also its rate, inflation rates of other countries and the action taken by the government to offset its effects.

The price level can fall as well as rise. The consequences of deflation are influenced by similar factors to those of inflation.

Key Point

Deflation: a sustained fall in the general price level.

Cost-push Inflation

Cost-push inflation occurs when the price level is pushed up by increases in the costs of production. If firms face higher costs, they will usually raise their prices to maintain their profit margins.

There are a number of reasons for an increase in costs. One is wages increasing more than labour productivity. This will increase labour costs. As labour costs form the highest proportion of total costs in many firms, such a rise can have a significant impact on the price level. It will also not be a one-off increase. The initial rise in the price level is likely to cause workers to press for even higher wages, leading to a wage-price spiral.

Another important reason is increase in the cost of raw materials. Some raw materials, most notably oil,

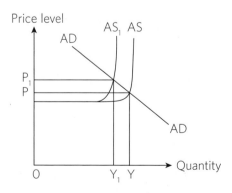

Fig. 1 Cost-push inflation

can change in price by large amounts. Other causes of cost-push inflation are increases in indirect taxes, higher cost of capital goods and increase in profit margins by firms.

Cost-push inflation can be illustrated on an aggregate demand and aggregate supply diagram. Higher costs of production shift the AS curve to the left and this movement forces up the price level, as shown in Fig. 1.

Key Points

Cost-push inflation: rises in the price level caused by higher costs of production.

Wage-price spiral: wage rises leading to higher prices which, in turn, lead to further wage claims and price rises.

 Demand-pull Inflation

Demand-pull inflation occurs when the price level is pulled up by an excess demand. Aggregate demand for a country's products can increase due to higher consumption, higher investment, higher government expenditure or higher net exports. Such an increase in aggregate demand will not necessarily cause inflation, if aggregate supply can extend to match it. When the economy has plenty of spare capacity, with unemployed workers and unused machines, higher aggregate demand will result in higher output but no increase in the price level. If, however, the economy is experiencing a shortage of some resources, for example – skilled workers, then aggregate supply may not be able to rise in line with aggregate demand and inflation occurs. In a situation of full employment of resources it would not be possible to produce any more output. As a result, any rise in demand will be purely inflationary as shown in Fig. 2.

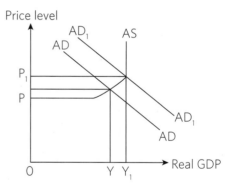

Fig. 2 Demand-pull inflation

Key Point

Demand-pull inflation: rises in the price level caused by excess demand.

Monetary Inflation

Monetary inflation is a form of demand-pull inflation. In this case, excess demand is created by an excessive growth of the money supply. A group of economists, appropriately called **monetarists**, believe that the only cause of inflation is the money supply increasing faster than output. They argue that if the money supply increases, people will spend more and this will lead to an increase in prices.

In explaining their view, monetarists examine the relationship between the money supply and the velocity of circulation on one hand and the price level and output on the other. By definition, both sides must be equal as both represent total expenditure. For example, if the money supply is $100bn and, on average, each dollar changes hands four times, a total of $400bn will be spent. If an output of $200bn products is produced, the average price would be $2 (200bn × $2 = $400bn). If the money supply increases by 50% to $150bn and output and the velocity of circulation remain unchanged, the average price would rise to $3 ($150bn × 4/200bn).

Key Points

Monetary inflation: rises in the price level caused by an excessive growth of the money supply .

Monetarists: a group of economists who think that inflation is caused by the money supply growing more rapidly than output.

Velocity of circulation: the number of times money changes hands.

Activity 1

Inflation rate in Italy fell from 2.8% in 2003 to 1.8% in 2004. This was, in part, because of the rise in the value of the euro (which reduced import prices) and, in part, because of a slowdown in wage rises. However, consumption rose by 1.6% and was expected to rise at a more rapid rate in the next five years. This led some economists to forecast higher inflation in Italy for the period 2005 – 2010.

a.   What is meant by a fall in inflation?
b.   Explain how a slowdown in wage rises may reduce inflation.
c.   Why may a rise in consumption result in inflation?

The Consequences of Inflation

Most of the consequences of inflation are thought to be harmful but some may actually prove to be beneficial. The impact that inflation has, depends on a number of factors. The key ones are the rate of inflation, stability of this rate, its rate relative to the inflation rates of other countries and the reaction of the government.

The Harmful Effects of Inflation

- Inflation causes a fall in the value of money. If prices are rising, each unit of money (e.g. each dollar) will buy fewer products.

The higher the inflation rate, the greater will be the fall in the purchasing power of money. In a situation of **hyperinflation**, the value of money may be falling so rapidly that people may lose confidence in using the country's currency as money.

Key Point

Hyperinflation: a very rapid rise in the price level.

- Inflation redistributes income in an unplanned way. Some people gain from it, while others lose. Workers with strong bargaining power tend to gain, as their income usually rises more than the inflation rate. Normally borrowers also benefit. If the rate of interest is below the inflation rate, borrowers pay back less in real terms than what they borrowed. For instance, a woman may borrow $100. If the inflation rate is 12%, she would have to repay $112 for the lender to just gain back the same amount of purchasing power. If the rate of interest is 8%, she will repay only $108, which has less purchasing power than what she borrowed.

Whilst borrowers are likely to benefit, savers are likely to lose, as they may be repaid less in real terms than what they lent. Workers with low bargaining power and those with fixed incomes also suffer during a period of inflation. The government can seek to protect some vulnerable groups from inflation by index-linking state benefit payments and interest rates on government securities.

Key Point

Index-linking: changing payments in line with changes in the inflation rate.

- The existence of inflation imposes extra costs on firms. Some additional staff time will be taken up, estimating future costs of raw material. There will also be **menu and shoe-leather costs**. Menu costs are the costs involved in changing prices in catalogues, price lists and slot machines etc. Shoe-leather costs arise because money paid to firms will be losing its value as soon as it is received. Even if the firms plan to pay out the money relatively soon, for e.g. wages or raw materials, it would need to protect its value by placing it in a bank or other financial institution, which will pay a rate of interest above the inflation rate. Seeking out good financial returns will involve the time and effort of firms.

- Inflation creates uncertainty. It can make it hard for households and firms to judge the right price to be paid for products now. It can also make it difficult to plan ahead, as households and firms will be uncertain about future prices. This is a particularly grave problem with a high, fluctuating inflation rate. In such an unstable situation, firms may be discouraged from investing which will be harmful for the economy.

- Inflation can harm the country's **balance of payments** position. If a country's inflation rate is above that of its rivals, its products will become less price competitive. This may result in a fall in export revenue and a rise in import expenditure. Such an effect would cause a deterioration in the **current account** position. The fall in demand for the country's products may also result in a rise in unemployment.

- Inflation can cause fiscal drag. This occurs when goverments do not adjust tax brackets in line with inflation. As a result, people's incomes are dragged into higher tax brackets and they are left with lower real disposable income.

Activity 2

Explain in each case, which type of inflation is likely to impose more costs on an economy:

a. a high and fluctuating rate or a low and stable rate

b. a 5% rate with other countries averaging 3% or a 5.2% rate with other countries averaging 6%.

The Beneficial Effects of Inflation

You might be surprised to learn that inflation can have beneficial effects also. These effects are more likely to occur, if the inflation is of a demand-pull, low and stable nature and is below that of rival countries.

- Inflation may encourage firms to expand. A low and stable level of demand-pull inflation may make entrepreneurs optimistic about future sales.

- Inflation reduces the real burden of any debt that households and firms have built up. This may mean that some households and firms will avoid going bankrupt.

- Inflation can prevent some workers being made redundant in a declining industry or region. This is because whilst workers are likely to resist any cut in their money wages, they may accept their money wages rising by less than inflation. In such a case, firms' real wage costs will fall without a resorting to a retrenchment of workers.

Activity 3

In 2004, the Chinese government became concerned about the country's inflation rate. The price level was being driven up mainly by rising raw material and energy prices. Ministers in the Chinese government were anxious to reduce inflation, as they were worried about its possible effects on the country's exports and savings.

a. Was China suffering mainly from cost-push or demand-pull inflation in 2004?

b. Why may inflation have a harmful effect on the country's exports and imports?

c. Explain one other cost imposed by inflation on an economy.

Activity 4

In 2006, Zimbabwe experienced an inflation rate of 1 000%. In May 2006, a one-litre bottle of Coca-Cola was priced at Z$120 000, a pair of jeans at Z$%1.8m and a laptop at Z$300m. Supermarkets were changing the price of some products daily. With money having less worth each day, a bartering system was developing. For instance, some farm workers were paid in produce and people in cities sswapped CDs for food. At this time, the Zimbabwean government was printing an extra Z$60 trillion worth of bank notes to ensure that it could pay the soldiers, police and civil servants and meet other commitments of government spending.

a. What is meant by barter?

b. Explain one cost of inflation, that has been touched on in the extract.

c. From the information given, decide the cause of inflation in Zimbabwe, in 2006.

The Causes of Deflation

Deflation may result from the supply-side or the demand-side of the economy. The price level may be reduced as a result of advances in technology and increases in labour productivity. This is likely to be beneficial as it will means that consumers can enjoy more goods and services and the economy may become more internationally competitive.

In contrast, deflation resulting from a decline in aggregate demand is likely to be harmful. This is because it can lead to a downward spiral in economic activity. Consumers expecting prices to be lower in the future, may postpone their purchase. With lower demand for their products, firms are likely to reduce their output and the number of workers they employ. The reduction in employment will push down aggregate demand further.

The Consequences of Deflation

The effect of deflation will be influenced by whether it is 'good' deflation (caused by an increase in aggregate supply) or 'bad' deflation (caused by a decrease in aggregate demand). Good deflation may reduce a current account deficit or increase a current account surplus if demand for exports and imports is elastic and if the fall in the price level is not offset by a rise the exchange rate. Good deflation can be associated with increases in output and employment.

Bad deflation, however, is likely to cause a rise in unemployment and lower output. It is also likely to discourage investment which will reduce productive capacity and endanger future economic growth. Both bad and good deflation increase the purchasing power of those whose income remains unchanged. It does, however, raise the burden of debt. Any household or firm which has taken out a loan will have to pay back more in real terms. In this situation, borrowers will lose and lenders will gain.

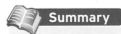

Summary

- Inflation may be caused by increases in the costs of production (cost-push), excess demand (demand-pull) or the faster growth of money supply relative to output (monetary).

- Among the causes of cost-push inflation are - rises in wages and raw material costs.

- Demand-pull inflation is more likely to occur when the economy is at or approaching full employment.

- The effects of inflation will depend on its rate, stability of price rises, its rate relative to other countries and response of the government.

continued····>

- Inflation will cause a fall in the purchasing power of money. Among the other possible harmful effects are – an unplanned redistribution of income, menu costs, shoe leather costs, uncertainty and a worsened position of the balance of payments.

- The possible beneficial effects of inflation include – a stimulus to production, a reduction in debt and reduction of unemployment.

- The effects of deflation are influenced by whether it is 'good' deflation or 'bad' deflation.

Teacher's Tip

It is a common mistake to say inflation is caused by a rise in prices. This shows confused thinking. Inflation is a rise in prices. So the reasons for the rise in the general price level need to be considered.

Also, remember that if inflation falls for example from 8% to 6%, the general price level is still rising.

Multiple Choice Questions

1. Who, among the following, is most likely to benefit during a period of rapid inflation?
   a. Borrowers
   b. Pensioners
   c. Savers
   d. Workers in strong unions

2. Which of the following is a possible cause of demand-pull inflation?
   a. An increase in government expenditure, not matched by a rise in taxation.
   b. An increase in the price of oil, not matched by a fall in the price of other raw materials.
   c. A rise in wages, not matched by an increase in productivity.
   d. A rise in imports, not matched by a rise in exports.

3. The price level rises by 8% as a result of a rise in raw material costs. This is an example of:
   a. cost-push inflation
   b. demand-pull inflation
   c. hyperinflation
   d. monetary inflation.

4. Which of the following must happen as a result of inflation?
   a. A decline in uncertainty.
   b. A fall in the value of money.
   c. An improvement in the balance of payments.
   d. An increase in savings.

Employment

Over time, the pattern of employment in a country is likely to change. There can be alterations in the sectors in which people work, the hours they work for, who they work for, the type of work they do and number of persons employed.

 Industrial Structure

As noted in unit 23, as economies develop, employment moves from the primary to the secondary and then the tertiary sector. In the Netherlands, for instance, most workers (79%) are employed in the tertiary sector whereas in Vietnam, a high proportion of workers (52%) are employed in the primary sector.

Within any country at any particular time, some industries will be expanding and some will be contracting. For instance, in India, employment in textiles is declining whilst it is increasing in ICT and software. This change requires workers to be occupationally and geographically mobile.

Full and Part Time Work

Most workers work full time. Some, however, work part time. Some opt to work part time, as it may fit in with their children's school hours, enable them to look after elderly relatives or pursue other interests. Other people are forced to work part time because they are not able to find full time jobs.

 Employed and Self-employed

In some countries, including the UK, USA and most of Europe, most people work for someone else - i.e. they are employees. The number of self-employed workers is, however, rising. In other countries, including India and Pakistan, a high proportion of people are already self-employed and many of them work in the unorganised sector.

Organised and Unorganised Sectors

The unorganised sector covers workers who do not have the same access to the social security benefits, employment protection and rights as organised labour. For instance, whilst a country may operate a minimum wage, unorganised labour may be paid below it.

The unorganised sector does not include unions and so the workers cannot bargain collectively, to improve their conditions. Some of those working in the unorganised sector are self-employed, some are migratory workers and some are casual workers. Most of them do not pay income tax. Workers in the unorganised sector tend to have lower productivity, lower levels of training and lower wages than workers in the organised sector. A growth in the organised sector tends to raise the quality of employment and labour productivity.

In India, for instance, in 2005 more than 90% of the country's labour force (423m out of 470m workers) were employed in the unorganised sector. In rural areas, mobile casual workers constitute most of the unorganised labour whereas in urban areas, it is contract and sub-contract migratory workers, maids, mechanics in small-scale garages and street stall holders. The average productivity of workers in the private organised sector in the country is six times higher than that of those working in the unorganised sector.

High and Low Quality Employment

High quality employment is skilled work which is interesting and which provides workers with the opportunity to progress, access to training, good working conditions and a relatively high degree of job security. In contrast, low quality employment is unskilled work which often does not require or provides training and does not provide good working conditions.

Private and Public Sector Employment

The proportion of workers employed in the public and private sectors varies from country to country and time to time. In the UK, in 2010, 20% of workers were employed in the public sector while 80% were employed in the private sector. In India (in its organised sector), two-thirds were employed in the public sector and one-third in the private sector.

A major reason for the reduction in the proportion of population, employed in the public sector, in a number of countries in recent years, has been *privatisation*. This involves the sale of state owned enterprises to the private sector. For instance, fewer workers are now employed in the public sector in Poland than twenty years ago.

Workers in the public sector often have more job security and higher non-wage benefits. In some cases, however, their productivity is lower than that of workers in the private sector.

Flexible Employment

Global competition is putting pressure on firms to ensure that their labour force is flexible. A flexible labour force is one which adjusts quickly and smoothly to changes in market conditions. This flexibility can take a number of different forms.

One is in terms of the number of workers employed. The easier it is to hire and fire workers, the more able firms are in adjusting their output in line with consumer demand. Such flexibility, which can be called **numerical flexibility**, can increase workers' sense of job insecurity but it can also raise employment. This is because firms may be more willing to take on more workers when demand for their products rises if they know they can let them go, should demand fall.

Other forms of flexibility are **temporal flexibility** (the ability to change the number of hours, people work), **locational flexibility** (the ability to change the location, where workers work), **functional flexibility** (the ability to change the tasks, workers perform) and **wage flexibility** (the ability to raise or lower wages).

Changes in Employment and Unemployment

A rise in employment may reduce unemployment if it is the unemployed who fill at least some of the extra jobs. It is, however, possible that both employment and unemployment increase. This will occur if the labour force grows faster than the number of jobs available. It is also possible for unemployment to fall without an increase in employment. This is because, finding a job is not the only reason why people stop being unemployed. Some unemployed people may reach retirement age, some may go into full time education, some may emigrate while some may just stop searching for work.

The Labour Force Participation Rate and the Employment Rate

The labour force may grow as a result of an increase in the population of working age, a rise in the labour force participation rate or a combination of the two. The working population may increase due to a rise in the birth rate, a fall in the death rate or net immigration.

The labour force participation rate is the proportion of people who are of working age and belong to the labour force. In other words, it is those who are economically active and form the labour force.

Among the factors that influence the participation rate are:

- The wages on offer. High wages will encourage more people to seek work and will persuade some to stay in the labour force, past the usual retirement age.

- Social attitudes to working women. In countries, where it is acceptable for women to work, there will be a larger labour force and a greater participation rate.

- Provision for the care of children and the elderly. The greater the availability of nursery places and retirement homes, the higher is the labour participation rate.

- Social attitudes and provision for the disabled to work. The greater the number of people willing to accept disabled people working and the easier it is made for the disabled to work (for instance, having ramps installed for wheelchair access), the more potential workers there will be.

- The proportion of school leavers who go for higher education. The more people there are in full time education, the lower the participation rate. Though, it reduces the size of the labour force, a high proportion of people in full time education raises the quality of the labour force.

Another key indicator of labour market activity is the **employment rate or ratio**. This is the percentage of those of working age in employment. The employment rate of a country is again influenced by the attitudes to working women and the disabled labour, participation in post-compulsory full time education, preferred age of retirement, the level of economic activity and the gap between wages and benefits. So, for instance, if there is a high level of demand in the economy, the employment rate is likely to be high. If the gap between wages and benefits increases, there will be more incentive to work and again the employment rate would be expected to increase.

Activity 1

In Sweden, the labour force participation rate in 2005 was 73%, in Poland it was 51% and in Pakistan it was 29%.

a. What is meant by a labour force participation rate of 73%?

b. Explain one reason, for the labour force participation rate of Sweden being higher than that of Pakistan.

Activity 2

In recent years, the UK government has used a series of tax and benefit cuts to help, persuade, and in some cases, force the long-term unemployed, young people, single parents, some of those past-retirement age and some disabled into jobs. In 2006, the UK's employment rate was 75%. The UK government is also keen to increase the quality of jobs and raise labour productivity. One way it is seeking to do this, is by increasing the number of school children progressing into higher education. Such a move reduces the labour force participation rate but raises the quality of labour.

a. What is meant by the 'employment rate'?

b. Explain how 'tax and benefit cuts' could encourage the long-term unemployed to seek work, more actively?

c. How may more school children going for higher education raise labour productivity?

Summary

-   The pattern of employment can vary between sectors and industries over time.

-   Some of those who work part time do so because they want to work for fewer hours but some seek full time employment.

-   The rate of self employment varies amongst countries.

-   A growth in the organised sector usually increases the quality of employment and productivity.

-   High quality employment provides better opportunities and conditions for workers than low quality employment.

continued····>

- A flexible labour market is one which responds quickly and easily to changes in market conditions.

- A rise in employment may be accompanied by a rise or fall in unemployment.

- An increase in the population of working age or a rise in the labour force participation rate increases the size of the labour force.

- Factors affecting the labour force participation rate include the wages on offer, social attitudes to working women and the disabled, the provision for the care of children and the elderly and the proportion of school leavers going for higher education.

Teacher's Tip

Take care whether information on unemployment and employment shows absolute figures or percentages.

Multiple Choice Questions

1. Which of the following are of working age, but do not form a part of the working population?
   a. People past the age of retirement
   b. People who are in full time education
   c. The self employed
   d. The unemployed

2. Which of the following workers experiences the highest quality employment?
   a. A cleaner
   b. A farm labourer
   c. A shop assistant
   d. A solicitor

3. What is likely to reduce a country's labour force participation rate in the short run, but increase it in the long run?
   a. A fall in immigration
   b. A fall in nursery provision
   c. A rise in the birth rate
   d. A rise in the retirement age

4. A move from a planned economy to a market economy is most likely to reduce:
   a. employment in the agricultural sector
   b. employment in the public sector
   c. flexible employment
   d. self employment.

Causes and Consequences of Unemployment

The unemployed are economically active and hence form a part of the labour force. Unemployment has costs both for the unemployed and for the economy. These costs are influenced by the extent of the unemployment, the duration of the unemployment and the cause of the unemployment. The number of people unemployed at any one time is a *stock*. It is influenced by two factors – the rate of flow of people into unemployment and time period for which they are unemployed.

 The Measures of Unemployment

The two major ways of measuring unemployment are

(i) to count those in receipt of unemployment related benefits and

(ii) to carry out labour force surveys.

The first method is known (in the UK) as the **claimant count**. This method has the advantage of being relatively cheap and quick, as the information is gathered any way by the government to know the amount paid out in benefits and its recipients. Its disadvantage, however, is that it tends to understate unemployment. Whilst some people who are actually working fraudulently claim benefits, their number is less than those who are actively seeking employment but not receiving unemployment benefits. People on government training schemes, those staying on at school and some who have been forced to retire early, may actually be searching for employment but they won't be receiving unemployment benefits.

Many countries use a labour force survey, as a way to measure unemployment. This method has the advantage that it can be used to make international comparisons. It also tends to capture the unemployed population more accurately.

The accuracy, though, depends on how the questions are asked and interpreted and whether the sample selected is representative of the labour force as a whole. This method also takes longer, to gather the information than a claimant count.

 ## The Causes of Unemployment

Unemployment can arise due to a number of reasons. One is that workers, who have been fired or voluntarily left one job, have to wait for some time before finding another job. This type of unemployment is called **frictional unemployment**. One form of frictional unemployment is, what is called, **search unemployment**. This arises when workers do not accept the first job offered but spend time looking around for what they regard as an 'acceptable job'. Two other forms of frictional unemployment are **casual** and **seasonal**.

 Casual unemployment occurs when people are out of work between periods of employment. Actors and migrant farm workers are particularly prone to casual unemployment. Seasonal unemployment affects workers, including those working in the building and tourist industries, whose labour is not in demand at certain periods of the year and during periods of bad weather.

Structural unemployment is caused by the decline of industries and particular occupations, arising from long term changes in demand and supply. Industries and occupations can become smaller or cease to exist, as a result of **(i)** another country (or countries) becoming better at producing the product **(ii)** a substitute being found for the product or **(iii)** capital being substituted for labour. Structural unemployment, which is concentrated in one area, can cause particular problems. Such unemployment can be referred to as **regional unemployment**. Another form of structural unemployment is **technological unemployment**. This occurs when workers are made redundant as a result of advances in ICT. For instance, airlines are currently reducing the number of backroom staff they employ, as more people are booking their flights on line.

Structural unemployment is more serious than frictional unemployment as it persists for longer periods and usually affects more workers. In both cases, however, **labour immobility** plays a key role. If workers are more geographically and occupationally immobile, frictional and structural unemployment will be greater and persist for longer time. Measures to reduce frictional unemployment include those which seek to increase labour mobility (including education and training) and those which increase the incentive to work (including cutting income tax and benefits). Measures to reduce structural unemployment also include those which aim to increase labour mobility and encourage firms to move to areas of high unemployment.

Cyclical unemployment may be even more serious than structural unemployment as potentially, it can affect more workers and it is spread throughout the country. It arises from a lack of aggregate demand. It can also be referred to as **demand deficient unemployment**. If an economy goes through a recession, demand for labour is likely to fall and cyclical unemployment will occur. Fig. 1 shows an economy operating below the full employment level of national output.

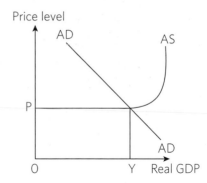

Fig. 1 An economy producing
below full capacity

In such a situation, unemployment is likely to be high. To tackle such unemployment, a government will seek to raise aggregate demand by, for instance, reducing income tax or increasing its expenditure.

Key Point

Recession: a fall in a country's output over a period of six months or more.

Activity 1

In 2012, unemployment in Egypt was 12.4% and in Saudi Arabia, it was 5.4%.

a. Explain one way unemployment may have been measured in the two countries.
b. Why may the unemployment rate be higher in one country than another?
c. Explain what should influence the measures, that the Egyptian government should take, to reduce unemployment in the country.

The Consequences of Unemployment

The existence of unemployed workers makes it easier for firms, wishing to expand, to recruit new workers. It can also keep down inflationary pressure by lowering wage rises. However, it is generally agreed that the costs of unemployment exceed any benefits.

The extent and seriousness of these costs are influenced by the numbers unemployed and the length of time for which they are unemployed. An unemployment rate of nine per cent with people being unemployed, on an average, for three months is less serious than an unemployment rate of six per cent with the average length of unemployment being a year. Those who bear the main burden of unemployment are the unemployed themselves. There are costs for the wider economy also.

The Effects on the Unemployed

Most people who are unemployed suffer a fall in income. In some countries the unemployed do not receive any financial assistance, when they are out of work. In those where unemployment benefits are paid, these are usually noticeably lower than what most of the unemployed were previously earning. Having a job also provides a person with sense of worth. So, losing a job can result in a loss of self-worth. Lower income and the stress of being unemployed can result in a decline in the mental and physical health of the unemployed and may also lead to marriage break-ups in some cases. Lower income may have an adverse effect on the education of the children of the unemployed and hence their employment chances. Those who are unemployed may not be able to afford the school education of their children, past the school leaving age.

Being unemployed can also reduce a person's chances of gaining another job. The longer people are unemployed, the more they lose out on training in new methods and technology. They may also lose the work habit and their confidence may dip.

The Effects on the Economy

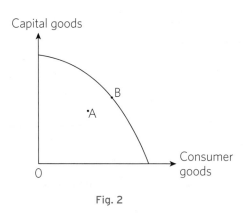

Fig. 2

Unemployment imposes an opportunity cost on an economy. Having unemployed workers means that the economy is not using all of its resources. The economy will not be making as many goods and services, as possible. Fig. 2 shows that unemployment causes an economy to produce at point A. Producing at this point involves the economy forgoing the opportunity to produce more capital and consumer goods. Producing at point B would mean that the economy would be making more products and living standards would be potentially higher.

Unemployment also means that government tax revenue will be lower than possible. When people lose their jobs, their expenditure falls and as a result, indirect tax revenue declines. Income and firms' profits fall and therefore, revenue from income tax and corporation tax decreases.

Besides lowering tax revenue, unemployment puts pressure on government expenditure also. Expenditure on unemployment benefits will automatically rise with unemployment.

If the unemployed suffer from bad health, the government may have to spend more on health care. There is a risk that rising unemployment may lead to rising levels of crime, as some of the unemployed may resort to crimnal activities to gain a higher income. If crime does rise, the government may have to spend more to tackle the problem and ensure the security of its citizens.

Higher government expenditure, resulting from unemployment, involves an 'opportunity cost'. The money spent on benefits, for instance, could have been spent on higher education. Spending on treatment of unemployed people for depression might mean that the government has to spend less on treating people with cancer.

Activity 2

In 2005, the unemployment rate in South Africa was 27%. To try to increase jobs, the government introduced the 'Accelerated and Shared Growth Initiative' in 2006. This involves it, spending more than 370 million rand, over the period 2006 to 2009 on public works (mainly infrastructure) to boost jobs. The long term aims are to raise the growth rate to 6%, by 2010 and to halve unemployment and poverty, by 2014.

Explain:

a. What type of unemployment did South Africa appear to be suffering from, in 2005 and 2006?

b. How may expenditure on infrastructure 'boost jobs'?

c. How will a decrease in unemployment reduce poverty?

Summary

- Unemployment can be measured by counting those in receipt of unemployment benefits or undertaking a labour force survey.

- Frictional unemployment arises when workers are finding new jobs, after leaving the old one.

- Three examples of frictional unemployment are casual unemployment, seasonal unemployment and search unemployment.

- Structural unemployment is caused by long term changes in demand and supply.

continued····>

- Two types of structural unemployment are regional and technological unemployment.

- Cyclical unemployment results from a lack of aggregate demand.

- The unemployed suffer from lower income and possibly from lower self-esteem and bad health also.

- The longer people are out of work, the harder it can be for them to find employment.

- Unemployment is a waste of resources. It results in output and living standards being lower than possible, lower tax revenue and increased government expenditure on benefits and on other costs arising from unemployment.

Teacher's Tip

Remember that the unemployed are included in the labour force and that the unemployment rate is the unemployed as a percentage of the labour force and **not** of the total population.

Multiple Choice Questions

1. Which type of unemployment arises due to a lack of aggregate demand?
   a. Cyclical
   b. Frictional
   c. Seasonal
   d. Structural

2. A country's steel industry is closed down, as buyers switch their purchases of steel to another country. What type of unemployment will occur as a result of this?
   a. Cyclical
   b. Frictional
   c. Seasonal
   d. Structural

3. What is a cost of unemployment?
   a. Higher tax revenue
   b. Lost output
   c. Lower productivity
   d. Reduced inflationary pressure

4. Which policy is most likely to reduce cyclical unemployment?
   a. A reduction in government expenditure
   b. A reduction in interest rates
   c. An increase in direct taxes
   d. An increase in indirect taxes

Gross Domestic Product and Economic Growth

The previous unit discussed unemployment. A rise in a country's output is likely to reduce unemployment. This unit focuses on the method of measurement of country's output, the difficulties involved in measurement, causes of rise in output in the short and long term and the consequences of an increase in output.

 **GDP**

Gross means total, domestic refers to the home country and product means output. So **gross domestic product (GDP)** means the total output produced in a country. There are three methods of measuring this output. These are – the output, income and expenditure methods. All three methods should give the same figure. This is because an output of $20bn will give rise to an income of $20bn which, in turn, will be spent on the output. This relationship is referred to as the circular flow of income and is illustrated in two diagrams in Fig. 1.

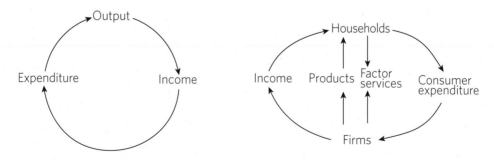

Fig. 1 The circular flow of income

 Key Point

The circular flow of income: the movement of expenditure, income and output round the economy.

The Methods of Calculating GDP

The **output method** measures GDP by adding up the output produced by all the industries in the country. Care has to be taken in using this method to ensure that output is not counted twice. For instance, the value of the output of the car industry includes output produced by the steel and tyre industries also. To avoid this problem, economists include the 'value added' by each firm at each stage of production.

The **income method** includes all the incomes which have been earned in producing the country's output. *Transfer payments*, such as pensions and unemployment benefit, are not included. This is because there is no corresponding output of goods and services.

The **expenditure method** calculates GDP by adding up all the expenditure on the country's finished output. Some of this comes from foreigners when they buy the country's *exports*. Some of the expenditure in the country goes on *imports* which are not produced in the country and which do not generate income for the country's citizens. So, in the expenditure method, it is necessary to add exports and deduct imports. Total expenditure on a country's output, and hence its GDP, includes *consumption, investment, government expenditure and exports minus imports*.

Key Points

Value added: the difference between the sales revenue received and the cost of raw materials used.

Transfer payments: transfers of income from one group to another not in return for providing a good or service.

Nominal and Real GDP

When governments calculate GDP, they usually first measure it in terms of nominal GDP, which is also referred to as **money GDP** or **GDP at current prices**. Nominal GDP is GDP valued in terms of the prices operative at that time. It has *not been adjusted for inflation*. For this reason, nominal GDP figures may give a misleading impression of what is happening to the output of a country, over time. For instance, if prices rise by 20% in a year, there will be a 20% rise in nominal GDP even if output does not change. To get the real picture of a country's output and assess its economic growth, economists adjust nominal GDP by taking out the effects of inflation. They do this by multiplying nominal GDP with the price index in the base year, divided by the price index in the current year. This gives a figure for **GDP at constant prices** referred to as **real GDP**. A rise in real GDP of 5% would mean that the country's output has increased by 5%.

For instance, in 2007, the nominal GDP of a country may be $800bn and its price index may be 100 (base year). In 2008, nominal GDP may increase to $900bn, giving the impression that output has risen by $100bn/$800bn × 100 = 12.5%. If, however, the price index rises to 110, the real GDP in 2006 will be $900bn × 100/110 = $818.18bn.

So the increase in output is $18.18bn/$800bn × 100 = 2.27%, which is considerably below the 12.5% increase in nominal GDP.

Real GDP per head

A rise in real GDP means that more goods and services have been produced. Its impact on the goods and services available to people, will depend on the state of population. If real GDP increases by 5% but population increases by 8%, there will actually be fewer goods and services per head of the population and people's living standards may fall.

To find out, what is happening to people's living standards (see unit 41), economists calculate real GDP per head which is also referred to as **real GDP per capita**. It is found by dividing real GDP by population. If, for instance, real GDP is $80bn and the population is 20m, real GDP per head is $80bn/20m = $4 000. If real GDP rises to $90bn and population rises to 30m, real GDP per head will fall to $90bn/30m = $3 000. In most of the countries, however, real GDP grows more rapidly than population causing real GDP per head to rise.

Activity 1

a. In 2013, a country's nominal GDP is $375bn. In 2014, it rises to $500bn. Between the two years, the price index rises from 100 to 125. What was the percentage increase in real GDP?

b. Table 1 shows a country's real GDP and population over a period of three years. Calculate the real GDP per head in each year.

Table 1 Real GDP and population between 2008 and 2010.

Year	Real GDP ($bn)	Population (millions)
2008	50	20
2009	55	22
2010	45	15

The difficulty of measuring real GDP

GDP figures tend to understate the true level of output. This is because of the existence of an informal economy or sector, which covers unrecorded economic activity. This covers undeclared economic activity and non-marketed goods and services. Economic activity which is not declared is sometimes referred to as the **hidden, shadow** or **grey economy**. There are two reasons for concealing the economic activity. One is, that the activity is illegal such as illegal drug dealing and work undertaken by immigrants, who have not been given permission to work in the country. The other reason is that whilst the activity is legal, the person undertaking it does not want to pay a tax on it. In the UK, it is thought that some workers in building, electrical installation, plumbing and car repairs do not declare all their earnings to the tax authorities.

The size of the informal economy is influenced by a number of factors. These include the number of activities that are declared to be illegal, tax rates, penalties for tax evasion, number of tasks people perform for themselves and the size of the subsistence agriculture.

The existence of an informal economy, besides understating the output produced through GDP figures, has a number of other effects on an economy. It means that tax revenue is below what could be collected. It can also mean that the official inflation rate overstates the rate at which the general price level is rising. This is because prices in the informal economy tend to rise less quickly than in the formal economy.

These are non-marketed goods and services. These are products which are not bought or sold. Family members who help during harvest time, people who clean their own houses and repair their own cars, are all providing products but these are not counted in GDP.

Key Point

Subsistence agriculture: the output of agricultural goods for farmers' personal use.

Activity 2

In 2006, Greece announced a 25% upward revision of its gross domestic product. The revision resulted from government officials recording more service sector activity including some informal sector activity.

a. Did the revision made by Greece in 2006, mean that the economy had produced 25% more output?

b. Why is it difficult to measure the size of the informal sector?

Causes of Economic Growth

In the short term, an increase in aggregate demand may stimulate a rise in output if the economy has unused resources. For instance, a rise in consumption resulting from increased consumer confidence or a cut in income tax may encourage firms to increase their output. In the long term, an economy can continue to experience economic growth only if the quantity or quality of resources increases. The quantity of resources may rise as a result of, for instance, an increase in net investment or the size of the labour force.

The quality of resources may increase due to an improvement in education and training and advances in technology.

 # Consequences of Economic Growth

An increase in output can improve living standards of people. Access to more goods and services can improve their living conditions and increase their life expectancy. In richer economies, people are likely to consume luxury products, have better health care, go for better education than in poor economies. In very poor countries, economic growth is essential to ensure that people have access to basic necessities.

Higher output and incomes increase government tax revenue, making it easier for governments to finance measures to reduce poverty, increase health care provision and raise educational standards, without having to raise tax rates. Poverty can be reduced in a number of ways. Some of the extra tax revenue raised, can be used to increase benefits for the poor, to improve schools in poor areas and provide training to the unemployed.

As an economy grows, its political and economic standing and influence usually increases. Voting power at the **International Monetary Fund (IMF)**, for instance, is influenced by the size of an economy's GDP. Economic growth, however, can involve costs. If the economy is working at full capacity, it may be necessary to shift resources from making consumer goods to capital goods, in order for it to grow. Such a shift will reduce living standards as fewer goods and services will be available for households. This is, however, only a short term cost as in the longer term the extra capital goods will enable manufacture of more consumer goods. Fig. 2 shows the output of consumer goods, initially falling due to the reallocation of resources but then increasing due to the resultant economic growth.

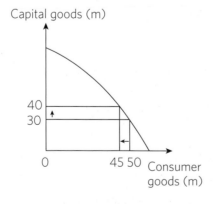 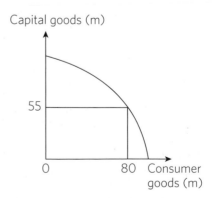

Fig. 2 **The short and long term effects of devoting more resources to capital goods**

Higher output can increase pollution, lead to depletion of non-renewable resources and damage the natural environment. More factories and cars may increase carbon dioxide emissions. Rapid expansion of the furniture and fishing industries, for example, may result in deforestation and depletion of fishing stocks respectively. Construction of more factories, offices, roads and other infrastructure can also destroy wildlife habitats. Due to these risks, economists are increasingly emphasising the need for sustainable economic growth. Economic growth may also lead to greater stress on workers. An increase of output may require some people to work for longer hours, some to learn new skills and some to change their job.

The net impact of economic growth is influenced by its rate, means adopted to achieve it and distribution of its benefits. A very high rate of economic growth may not be sustainable. It may involve non-renewable resources being used up too quickly, before the development of alternate resources.

If productive capacity can be increased in line with increases in aggregate demand, more goods and services can be enjoyed without an increase in prices. Stable economic growth is better than a high economic growth rate, which fluctuates. This is because, it makes it easier for firms and households to plan for the future and hence encourages investment. Some of the extra resources which develop, when productive potential increases, can also be used to reduce levels of pollution. Though there is indeed a risk, that economic growth can generate pollution and cause environmental damage, however, it can lead to improved education and information, pressurise the government and society to care for the environment and provide the resources to do so. Economic growth has the potential to raise living standards, but the extent to which it does so is influenced by the type of products produced and the equality of distribution of extra income (see unit 41).

Key Points

The International Monetary Fund (IMF): an international organisation which promotes international cooperation and helps countries with balance of payments problems.

Sustainable economic growth: economic growth that does not endanger the country's ability to grow in the future.

Economic Growth Rate

It is important to avoid the confusion between a fall in the economic growth rate and a fall in national output. If a country's economic growth rate falls from 5% to 3%, output may still be rising although it may be rising at a slower rate. If output reduces, the economic growth rate would be negative. For instance, an economic growth rate of – 2% would mean that a country has produced 2% less this year than last year. Table 2 shows the change in GDP of Pakistan over a five year period.

Table 2 Pakistan's economic growth rate.

Year	Economic growth rate (percentage change in GDP on a year earlier)
2002	3.1
2003	4.8
2004	6.4
2005	8.4
2006	6.6

Between 2002 and 2006, Pakistan's output grew. Each year, it produced more than the previous year. Between 2003 and 2005, the rate at which output was increasing accelerated. Between 2005 and 2006 its economic growth rate slowed down though it did produce more in 2006 than in 2005.

 **Activity 3**

The graph shows the economic growth rate of Venezuela between 2003 and 2006.

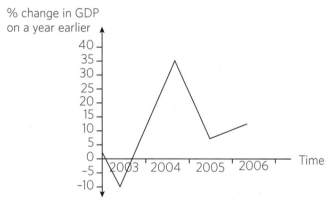

a. Did Venezuela experience a period of stable economic growth between 2003 and 2006? Explain your answer.

b. In which year, did Venezuela experience a fall in output?

c. What happened to the output in 2005?

Recession

A recession occurs when real GDP declines over a period of six months or more. It may be caused by a decrease in aggregate demand and/or decrease in aggregate supply. With lower output, unemployment is likely to rise. The reduction in output and incomes will lower living standards. Investment is likely to be discouraged which will endanger future economic growth.

Summary

- GDP is the total output produced in an economy.

- GDP can be measured by summing up all output produced, all incomes earned from producing that output or the total amount spent on the output.

- Nominal GDP is total output measured in the prices of the year, in question.

- Real GDP is adjusted for inflation.

- Changes in real GDP show changes in output.

- If real GDP per head increases, there will be more goods and services available for people.

- The existence of the informal economy makes it difficult to obtain an accurate figure for GDP.

- High tax rates and a large subsistence agricultural sector may result in a large informal economy.

- In the short term, increases in aggregate demand can lead to an increase in output but in the long term, aggregate supply must also increase for output to continue to rise.

- Economic growth can improve living standards, reduce poverty, raise government expenditure on health care and education and increase the influence of an economy.

- Economic growth may involve a short term opportunity cost, can cause pollution and damage to the environment and may put stress on people.

- Countries aim for stable and sustainable economic growth.

- A recession involves a fall in real GDP over two quarters of a year or more.

Teacher's Tip

In economics, the word 'real' refers to something that has been adjusted for inflation. This includes real GDP, real wages and real disposable income.

Multiple Choice Questions

1. What is meant by economic growth?
   a. An increase in exports
   b. An increase in population
   c. An increase in real GDP
   d. An increase in the price level

2. The diagram shows a country's economic growth over the period 2008 to 2012. What can be concluded from this information?
   a. Output was highest in 2010.
   b. Output was highest in 2012.
   c. Output fell from 2010 to 2012.
   d. Output was unchanged between 2008 and 2009.

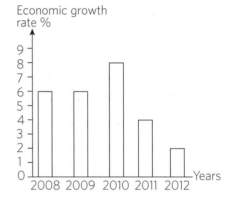

3. If consumer expenditure is $30bn, government expenditure is $10bn, investment is $20bn, exports are $16bn and imports are $20bn, what is GDP?
   a. $56bn
   b. $76bn
   c. $80bn
   d. $96bn

4. What is most likely to cause economic growth?
   a. An increase in capital depreciation
   b. An increase in education and training of workers
   c. An increase in taxation
   d. An increase in unemployment

Living Standards

An increase in real GDP can raise living standards but it is not guaranteed to do so. This unit examines the mode of measurement of living standards, discusses the comparisons of living standards across different countries, outlines the *Human Development Index* and the *Index of Sustainable Economic Welfare* and refers to a couple of other measures.

 ## Measures of Living Standards

There are a variety of indicators that can be used to assess the living standards in a country. These include the number of people or households that own a given consumer good, such as cars, computers, mobile phones and TVs (see Table 1). The number of patients per doctor, enrolment in tertiary education, the adult literacy rate, the average food intake per person and conduct of free elections in the country can also be examined. There are composite indicators such as **Human Development Index** and the **Index of Sustainable Economic Welfare**. The main measure of living standards, however, is still probably real GDP per head.

Table 1 The top ten countries in terms of highest ownership of certain consumer goods.

Cars per 1 000 population		Computers per 100 population		Mobile phone subscribers per 100 people	
Luxembourg	663	Canada	108.6	UAE	232.1
Iceland	659	Netherlands	103.1	Montegegro	207.3
New Zealand	655	Sweden	102.0	Cayman Islands	193.6
Brunei	610	Switzerland	96.3	Macau	192.8
Italy	601	UK	90.7	Hong Kong	179.4
Malta	558	Taiwan	89.0	Bahrain	177.1
Canada	555	USA	84.4	Qatar	175.4
Australia	535	France	82.9	Saudi Arabia	194.4
Guam	531	Denmark	80.9	Panama	164.4
Switzerland	528	Singapore	79.8	Russia	163.6
Austria	500	Luxembourg	62.1		
France	492				

Source: Pocket World in Figures, 2012 edition, The Economist.

Real GDP Per Head as an Indicator of Living Standards

An increase in real GDP per head would suggest that living standards have risen, but it may not necessarily indicate the real situation for a number of reasons.

One is that real GDP is an average. Not everyone may benefit from a rise in the average income level. The extra income may be unevenly spread with a few receiving much higher income and some not receiving any extra income.

Higher output will obviously mean that more goods and services are being produced but not all of these may add to people's living standards. For example, an increase in the output and consumption of tobacco may actually reduce the quality of people's lives by affecting their health and life expectancy adversely. A rise in police services, due to a higher crime rate, is also unlikely to improve most people's living standards.

Increases in real GDP per head figures may understate the products available to people due to undeclared economic activity and non-marketed output. It may, however, overstate it if the quality of output is falling.

Living standards are also influenced by other factors besides material goods and services produced. If output rises but working conditions deteriorate, number of working hours increases, pollution may increase and thus, people may not feel better off.

Comparing Living Standards between Countries

Again one of the main measures is real GDP per head. This measure has the advantage that it takes into account, differences in population size and also incorporates adjustments for inflation.

There are still a number of reasons why it cannot serve as a definite way of ascertaining the quality of living standards of people in a country. (In fact, the citizens of some developing countries enjoy better quality of life than some of those in developed countries.) This is because there can be differences in the distribution of income, the size of the informal economy, working hours and conditions, the composition and quality of output and environmental conditions between countries.

There is also a potential problem in comparing different countries' real GDP per head because countries measure their output in terms of their own currency initially. The comparison, on the other hand, requires to be done in a common unit. There is a risk that if an unadjusted currency is used, the comparison may be distorted. This is because the value of a currency can change on an hour to hour basis. For instance, US dollars may be used. If the real GDP of Kenya was KSh1 200bn and the exchange rate was initially $1 = 100 Kenyan Shillings, the GDP of Kenya would be valued at $12bn. If the exchange rate changed to $1 = KSh80 the next day, the value of its output in dollars would change to $15bn, despite the fact that in that period Kenya would not have risen its output by 25%. It is for this reason that economists make use of *purchasing power parity* exchange rates when comparing countries' GDP. These compare GDP using an exchange rate based on the buying power of currencies in their own countries. If in USA, a given basket of products sells for $5 000 and in Kenya, it sells for KSh45 000, the exchange rate used would be $1 = KSh9. This figure would not be affected by market changes in the price of currencies.

Activity 1

In 2006, the richest self-made woman in the world was a Chinese woman, *Cheung Yan*. She is a paper tycoon with a personal fortune of $3.4bn. She is one of a new breed of super-rich entrepreneurs in a country which, in 2006, had a real GDP per head of $1 470 in comparison with $35 760 in the UK. In that year in China, the disposable income of the top 10% of richest households was more than eight times higher than that for the poorest 10%.

a. Are people in China poorer than people in the UK?

b. Is income evenly distributed in China? Explain your answer.

The Human Development Index

The Human Development Index (HDI) was developed by a team of economists led by *Dr. Mahbub ul Haq*, while he was working for the **United Nations Development Programme** (UNDP). It has been published every year since 1990.

The HDI is a wider measure than real GDP per head. Besides including GDP per head, the HDI considers two other indicators of living standards. One is the length of time for which people can enjoy life, measured as *life expectancy at birth*. The second is education. This is measured by mean years of schooling and expected years of schooling.

On the basis of their HDI values, countries are categorised into very high human development, high human development, medium human development and low human development. The HDI shows that economic growth and human progress may not always match. Some countries such as Namibia and South Africa have recently enjoyed a higher ranking in terms of GDP per head than HDI, whilst others including Costa Rica and Cuba usually score more highly in terms of HDI than GDP per head.

Although the HDI does take into account other factors that influence people's living standards, it has been criticised for what it leaves out. In fact, it has been stated that the index would be high for someone living for a long time in a prison who has been well educated. Among the factors, it does not take into account, are political freedom and the environment. It also does not consider differences in life expectancy, education and differences in income between males and females and between those living in rural and urban areas and other groups.

Table 2 shows the countries with the highest and lowest HDI rankings in 2011.

Table 2 HDI rankings in 2011.

Ranking	Top ten countries	Ranking	Bottom ten countries
1	Norway	178	Guinea
2	Australia	179	Central African Republic
3	Netherlands	180	Sierra Leone
4	USA	181	Burkino Faso
5	New Zealand	182	Liberia
6	Canada	183	Chad
7	Ireland	184	Mozambique
8	Liechtenstein	185	Burundi
9	Germany	186	Niger
10	Sweden	187	Congo (Democratic Republic)

The Index of Sustainable Economic Welfare

The Index of Sustainable Economic Welfare (ISEW), also sometimes referred to as the **Genuine Progress Indicator**, was devised by *Herman Daly* and *John Cobb* in 1989. It starts by adjusting personal consumption for unequal income distribution. Then, it makes a number of deductions and additions. The items deducted are those which reduce economic welfare presently or which may reduce the country's future economic welfare. Examples of such items are social costs and environmental costs. The former include the costs of crime, traffic accidents, time spent on commuting and underemployment. The latter include carbon dioxide emissions, depletion of non-renewable resources and the loss of wetlands and forests. Items which are thought to make a positive contribution to current or future economic welfare are added. These include net capital investment, the value of homework and volunteer work and government expenditure on infrastructure.

Other Measures

There is a wide range of other measures of living standards. Whilst the HDI is the UNDP's best known measure, it also produces several other measures. One is the Multidimensional Poverty Index (MPI). This index is based on deprivations in education, health and standard of living. Household surveys are undertaken to find, for instance, how many households have no member who has completed five years of schooling, someone who is malnourished and who have no access to clean water and no electricity.

Another of the UNDP's measures is the Gender Inequality Index (GII) which considers gender – based disadvantage in terms of reproductive health, empowerment and the labor market. The health dimension is measured in terms of maternal mortality rate and adolescent fertility rate. There are two measures to the empowerment dimension which are the percentage of seats in national parliament held by women and the relative percentage of men and women with at least secondary education. Involvement in the labor market is assessed by comparing the labor force participation rates of men and women.

Economists also calculate the **Happy Life Expectancy Index** (HLEI). This seeks to measure the degree to which people live long and happy lives. It is found by multiplying life expectancy at birth with average life expectancy.

Activity 2

In 2005, the Pakistani economy grew by an impressive 8.4% and the population, by 2.0%. Property prices rose in the country and sales of televisions, mobile phones and cars, including Porsches, boomed. Nevertheless, most of the country's population of 160m remained poor with most people, barely able to afford a motorcycle. The rich/poor divide widened. Only 2m Pakistanis paid income tax, for instance. The government increased its expenditure on health care and education in 2005 but spent even more on military hardware.

a. Identify two different indicators, which would indicate that living standards rose in Pakistan in 2005.

b. Did all Pakistanis enjoy an 8.4% rise in living standards in 2005?

c. Would all the extra government expenditure have increased living standards?

Summary

- There are a number of possible indicators of living standards including consumer goods per head, real GDP per head, the Index of Sustainable Economic Welfare and HDI.

- Real GDP per head gives an indication of material living standards but a rise in average income does not translate into a benefit for everyone. The extra output may not add to the quality of people's lives. Official figures may not capture the total income and and may fail to include other factors – like working conditions, working hours and environmental conditions, which affect living standards.

- One country can have a higher real GDP per head than another but its citizens may still have lower living standards, if they have less leisure time, worse working conditions, lower quality products, worse environmental conditions and a smaller informal economy.

continued····>

- International comparisons in real GDP per head are usually made in terms of purchasing power parity.

- The Human Development Index is based on life expectancy and education, as well as GDP per head.

- Among the other measures of living standards are the Multidimensional Poverty Index, the Gender Inequality Index and the Happy Life Expectancy Index.

Teacher's Tip

For understanding the measures of living standards, it might be useful to discuss (as a group) the change in living standards in your own country in the last five years. You might also want to carry out a survey, asking your friends and relatives, whether they think that the living standards have risen and what leads them to think this (or vice versa).

Multiple Choice Questions

1. What is the most popular measure of the difference in living standards between countries?
    a. Average price level
    b. Gross domestic product per head
    c. The size of the population
    d. The value of the currency

2. What is most likely to cause an increase in a country's standard of living?
    a. A fall in the school leaving age
    b. A fall in the size of the labour force
    c. A rise in the level of pollution
    d. A rise in the number of doctors per head of the population

3. Under which circumstance, would the standard of living of a country be most likely to fall?
    a. A fall of 3% in real GDP and a fall of 6% in population
    b. No change in real GDP and a fall of 3% in population
    c. A rise of 2% in real GDP and no change in population
    d. A rise of 5% in real GDP and a rise of 8% in population

4. In what circumstance, would a fall in working hours be most likely to increase the standard of living?
    a. The average income falls.
    b. The level of output remains unchanged.
    c. The rate of unemployment rises.
    d. The standard of working conditions falls.

Answer Key

Activity 1

a. A consumer price index measures the prices of a range of consumer goods.

b. The Indian government will select the 260 items included in the CPI, by carrying out a family household survey. This will provide it with information about the amount spent by households on different items. Those items, that incur the maximum expenditure, will be included.

Activity 2

a.

Category	Weight		Price change		Weighted price change
Food	1/5	×	5%	=	1%
Clothing	1/5	×	–10%	=	–2%
Heating	1/10	×	30%	=	3%
Entertainment	1/2	×	20%	=	10%
					12%

b.

Category	Weight		Price change		Weighted price change
Food	1/4	×	8%	=	2%
Clothing	1/10	×	10%	=	1%
Transport	3/10	×	–10%	=	–3%
Leisure goods	7/20	×	2%	=	0.7%
					0.7%

Multiple Choice Questions

1. d

    The weights in a weighted price index reflect the distribution of consumer expenditure on different products.

2. b

    The inflation rate is the rise in the retail price index. In this case, it is 15/150 × 100 = 10%.

3. a

    The weighted price change is weight multiplied by price change. In 2007, this would be ? × 8% = 2% i.e. 1/4. In 2008, it would be ? × 5% = 2.5% i.e. 1/2 .

4. a

A weight is calculated by dividing expenditure on a given item with total expenditure. In the case of clothing, this is $20/$200 = 1/10 and in the case of food, it is $50/$200 = 1/4.

Unit 37

Activity 1

a. A fall in inflation means that the general price level is rising at a slower rate.
b. A slowdown in wage rises may reduce inflation, as costs of production will rise more slowly. As a result, firms will not have to push up their prices at the same rate.
c. A rise in consumption may cause inflation, if the resulting higher aggregate demand cannot be met by a rise in aggregate supply. This will occur, if the economy is approaching full employment.

Activity 2

a. A high and fluctuating rate. A high rate may make the country's products uncompetitive and will impose significant menu, shoe leather and administrative costs on firms. A fluctuating exchange rate will increase uncertainty.
b. A 5% rate with other countries averaging 3%. In this case, the country's products are becoming less competitive by international standards.

Activity 3

a. Cost-push inflation. Higher raw material and energy prices would increase firms' costs of production.
b. Inflation, which causes the price of a country's products to exceed that of its trading partners, will be likely to reduce exports and increase imports.
c. Inflation may also lead to an unplanned redistribution of income. Borrowers tend to gain from inflation, as the rate of interest does not usually rise in line with inflation. In contrast, savers tend to lose.

Activity 4

a. Barter refers to the direct exchange of products.
b. The passage refers to supermarkets changing in prices on daily basis. This constitutes menu costs. Changing prices on such a regular basis will involve staff time.
c. The cause of inflation appears to be an excessive growth of the money supply. The Zimbabwean government printed an extra Z$60 trillion bank notes.

Multiple Choice Questions

1. a

Borrowers tend to pay back less in real terms than what they borrowed, during a period of inflation. Pensioners will maintain their real incomes, if pensions rise in line with inflation. Workers in strong trade unions should be able to negotiate wage rises to match the inflation rate. Savers will tend to lose.

2. a

A rise in government expenditure, not matched by taxation, will increase aggregate demand. b and c will be likely to cause cost-push inflation. d may reduce inflation by increasing the number of products in the country, whilst reducing the money supply.

3. a

A rise in raw material costs would cause cost-push inflation. b would result from an increase in aggregate demand, d from an excessive growth of the money supply and c is a 'level' rather than 'type' of inflation.

4. b

A rise in the general price level means that each unit of money, e.g. each $, will buy less.

Unit 38

Activity 1

a. A labour force participation rate of 73% means that 73% of people of working age are employed or seeking employment.
b. One reason is because it is more socially acceptable for women to work in Sweden than in Pakistan.

Activity 2

a. The employment ratio is the percentage of people of working age who are employed.
b. Tax and benefit cuts would increase the gap between paid employment and benefits. This would be likely to create a greater incentive for the long term unemployed to find a job. By remaining jobless, they would be losing more money whilst receiving lower benefits.
c. Going for higher education should make workers more skilled. This will enable them to undertake complex tasks, use complex machinery and enhance their ingenuity.

Multiple Choice Questions

1. b

The working population is the labour force and consists of the employed and the unemployed. c and d are included in the working population. a are not of working age.

2. d

A solicitor has a well paid and interesting job, usually undertaken in good working conditions.

3. c

A rise in the birth rate is likely to result in some parents withdrawing from the labour force for a period of time. The labour force will be increased, when the children gow up and join it.

4. b

In a planned economy, most people are employed by the state.

Unit 39

Activity 1

a. Unemployment might have been measured by conducting a labour force survey. This involves taking a sample of the population and asking people whether they have been actively seeking employment.
b. Unemployment may be higher in one country than another due to lower aggregate demand, declining industries and immobility of workers.
c. The measures should be influenced by the cause of the unemployment, the duration of the unemployment and the likely effectiveness of the measures.

Activity 2

a. It appeared to be suffering from cyclical unemployment, as the government was trying to solve it by raising aggregate demand.
b. Expenditure on infrastructure may boost jobs, as more workers will have to be employed for its development e.g. build roads. These workers will spend more and the higher expenditure will, in turn, increase employment.
c. One of the main causes of poverty is unemployment. Providing workers with jobs gives them a source of income. Most people receive more money from working than from relying on benefits.

Multiple Choice Questions

1. a

A definition question.

2. d

Decline of one industry results in structural unemployment.

3. b

Having unemployed workers means that output is below the maximum, that could be produced. Unemployment will reduce tax revenue. Productivity may rise, as it is likely that less productive workers will lose their jobs first. Reduced inflationary pressure is a benefit rather than a cost of unemployment.

4. b

A reduction in interest rates will increase aggregate demand. In contrast a, c and d would increase aggregate demand.

Unit 40

Activity 1

a. Real GDP = $500bn × 100/125 = $400bn.

Rise in real GDP = $25bn/$375bn × 100 = 6.67%.

b.

Year	Read GDP per head ($)
2008	2 500
2009	2 500
2010	3 000

Activity 2

a. No, the economy had produced the same amount but the revisions meant that more of it was officially recorded.

b. By its very nature, it is difficult to measure the informal economy. This can be attributed mainly to two reasons – some people deliberately try to hide their economic activity and some people do not sell what they produce.

Activity 3

a. The economic growth was unstable. It fluctuated quite significantly – rising at first, then falling and rising again.

b. In 2003.

c. Output rose but at a slower rate.

Multiple Choice Questions

1. c

A definition question. d is inflation.

2. b

More was produced each year so that output must have been highest at the end of the period. The economic growth rate, not the output, was highest in 2010. Output did not fall at any time. Output rose in both 2008 and 2009 – it was the economic growth rate which remain unchanged.

3. a

GDP is C + I + G + (X – M) i.e. $30bn + $10bn + $20bn + $16bn – $20bn.

4. b

An increase in education and training is likely to increase labour productivity. This may raise productive capacity. a, c and d are all likely to reduce output – a would reduce the quantity of capital goods. c would reduce aggregate demand and d is likely to reduce the number of people who are employed.

Unit 41

Activity 1

a. On an average Chinese people are poorer but certain individuals, such as Cheung Yan, are much richer than most people in the UK.
b. No. The passage mentions that the richest group in China have an income eight times more than the poorest.

Activity 2

a. Real GDP per head and the number of televisions per household.
b. No. Some enjoyed a higher rise, including those buying Porsches, while the poor are likely to have experienced a lower rise.
c. The expenditure on health care and education is likely to have raised living standards but the effect of a rise in expenditure on military hardware or social benefit is more debatable.

Multiple Choice Questions

1. b

A straightforward question.

2. d

a, b and c are likely to reduce living standards. b may also reduce living standards if it results in a rise in the dependency ratio.

3. d

This would mean that GDP per head would fall. a, b and c would all result in a rise in real GDP per head.

4. b

In this case, people would be able to enjoy more leisure time and the same amount of income.

Examination Practice

Multiple Choice Questions

1. The graph in Fig. 1 shows a change in consumer prices for a country. What can be concluded from this information?
   a. Consumer prices remained unchanged between 2008 and 2009.
   b. Consumer prices fell from 2009 to 2010.
   c. Consumer prices were higher in 2010 than 2009.
   d. Consumer prices were lower in 2011 than in 2008.

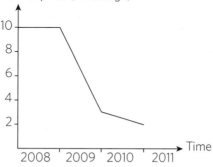

Fig. 1

2. A country experiences a rate of inflation of 5% in 2010. What does this mean?
   a. The consumer price index fell.
   b. The cost of living fell.
   c. The price level rose.
   d. The value of money rose.

3. A country's citizens experience a rise in nominal and real incomes. What combination of events must have occurred?

	Price level	Money income level
a.	fallen	remained unchanged
b.	fallen	risen
c.	risen	remained unchanged
d.	risen	risen

4. India's economy grew by approximately 8.9% in 2006. What must have increased in India in 2006?
   a. Gross domestic product
   b. Labour productivity
   c. The government's budget deficit
   d. The rate of inflation

5. As a result of outsourcing, some call centre workers in the UK have been made redundant. What type of unemployment is this?
   a. Cyclical
   b. Frictional
   c. Seasonal
   d. Structural

6. Which of the following is a cause of cost-push inflation?
   a. An increase in the money supply
   b. An increase in government expenditure on pensions
   c. A rise in the price of housing
   d. A rise in the cost of transporting goods

7. What is a possible disadvantage of economic growth?
   a. A depletion of non-renewable resources
   b. An increase in unemployment
   c. A reduction in the government's ability to reduce poverty
   d. A reduction in the productive capacity of the economy

8. The occupational mobility of labour increases. Which types of unemployment is this likely to reduce?
   a. Cyclical and frictional
   b. Frictional and structural
   c. Structural and cyclical
   d. Cyclical, frictional and structural

9. What measure of living standards is included in HDI but not in real GDP?
   a. Education
   b. Gender equality
   c. Income
   d. Leisure time

10. Why might real GDP per head rise and yet, living standards fall?
    a. Income may be more evenly distributed
    b. Levels of pollution may have risen
    c. the size of the informal economy may have risen
    d. working conditions may have improved

Structured Questions

1. Namibia's inflation rate in January 2001, measured as an annual percentage change in the Consumer Price Index (Retail Price Index), was estimated at 10.6%. Examples of some of the annual increases in prices of the major components that make up the weighted price index were household goods (4.2%), imported goods (10.6%), food (11.7%), housing, power (12.2%), transport and communications (13.8%).

   Examples of increases in prices of some of the minor items in the index were tobacco (9%), recreation and entertainment (4.7%) medical care and health services (20%).

   a. What is meant by inflation? (2)

   b. The information above relates inflation to a weighted consumer price index. How do researchers calculate the rate of inflation? (7)

   c. Study the information above and assess whether it might be a source of concern for the Namibian government. (6)

   (Cambridge 0455 Paper 6 Q2 May/June 2003)

2. Australia's unemployment rate fell to 5.5% in May 2004, the lowest in 23 years. At the same time, total employment decreased to 9.6m. Full-time jobs decreased by 42 600 but part-time employment rose by 1 500. The shift from employment in agriculture and manufacturing has continued.

   a. Calculate the change in total employment. (Show your workings). (2)

   b. Explain why the pattern of employment might change. (8)

   c. The above extract says that the unemployment rate fell yet the numbers employed decreased. Explain how these statements could be valid simultaneously. (3)

   d. Discuss the economic consequences of unemployment. (7)

   (Cambridge 0455 Paper 4 Q4 May/June 2006)

3. The following tables show figures for gross domestic product for some African countries.

   Table 1 Real Gross Domestic Product Millions of US $ Constant 1995 prices.

Country	1995	2000
Botswana	4 899	6 330
Burundi	1 000	946
Egypt	60 159	78 422
Equatorial Guinea	164	731
Ethiopia	5 779	7 451
Namibia	3 503	4 230
South Africa	15 1113	170 568
Zimbabwe	7 117	7 838

Table 2 % annual change in real GDP.

Country	1994-5	1999-2000
Bostwana	5.1	3.4
Burundi	-7.3	-0.9
Egypt	4.7	5.1
Equatorial Guinea	14.3	16.9
Ethiopia	6.1	5.4
Namibia	4.1	3.9
South Africa	3.1	3.1
Zimbabwe	0.2	-4.9

a.   What is meant by economic growth? (3)
b.   What is meant by the use of the word 'real' in table 1? (2)
c.   Consider the figures for Zimbabwe. Do those for the annual change in growth conflict with the figures for real gross domestic product? (2)
d.   You have been told that economic growth brings great benefits and you decide that you would like to live in a country that experienced had the maximum economic growth between 1999 and 2000.
   (i) Which one of the given countries will you choose? (1)
   (ii) What other information would you need, in order to decide whether you would indeed be much better off in this country than any of the others shown? (8)

(Cambridge 0455 Paper 6 Q2 May/June 2004)

Different Stages of Development

This unit examines the meaning of development, the different stages of development, extent of development in these stages, the characteristics of a developing economy and reasons to achieve economic development.

 **Development**

Economic development is wider than economic growth. Besides improved living standards, it also involves reducing poverty, expanding the range of economic and social choices and increasing freedom and self-esteem. As an economy develops, the economic welfare of its population increases. At first, the availability of basic life-sustaining products increases. Then consumption levels rise beyond those needed for survival, and people have more choice vis. a vis. what to consume, where to live and where to work.

The Different Stages of Development

Developed economies are those which have high incomes, high living standards, a high proportion of workers employed in the tertiary sector, high levels of productivity and high levels of investment. These economies are still developing but the term 'developing economies' tends to be applied to those which have lower incomes, lower living standards and a number of other characteristics, as explained in the following paragraphs.

International organisations classify countries in a variety of ways. The United Nations, for instance, divides countries into four levels of development – very high human development, high human development, medium human development and low human development. The World Bank divides countries into high income, middle income and low income.

Measures of development

It is not easy to measure development but a number of ways are used. A common one is *real GDP per head*. This does measure an important aspect of development – material living standards, but it does not measure all aspects of development. A wider measure is the **Human Development Index (HDI)**. As explained in the previous unit, this takes into account life expectancy, educational attainment as well as real GDP per head. A figure of 0 –1 is calculated for each country. Some countries are ranked higher in terms of HDI than real GDP per head—for example, Costa Rica, Vietnam and Zaire. Others have a higher real GDP per head ranking than HDI ranking like Kuwait, Pakistan and Saudi Arabia.

Activity 1

It has been estimated that there are 430m people in Asia, living on less than a $1 a day, compared to about 315m in sub-Saharan Africa. GDP per head is higher in some sub-Saharan African countries than some Asian countries. For instance, it is higher in South Africa, Botswana, Namibia and Gabon than it is in Bangladesh, India and Pakistan. The situation in South Asia, however, is improving whilst in parts of sub-Saharan Africa, it is deteriorating. Whilst those living in extreme poverty fell from 50% to 32% between 1986 and 2006 in South Asia, it rose from 42% to 47% in sub-Saharan Africa over the same period. Other indicators, such as life expectancy, is 65 in India whereas it is only 40 in South Africa and 27 in Botswana.

a.   Identify an indicator of economic development, not referred to in the passage.
b.   Explain two possible reasons why, despite higher real GDP per head, life expectancy is lower in Botswana than India.

Characteristics of Developing Economies

There are a number of characteristics which many developing countries share including:

- **Low incomes per head:** People in developing countries are poorer on an average, than those in developed economies. However, this does not mean that all the people are poor. In fact, some can be very rich.

- **Low levels of saving due to low income:** Poor people cannot afford to save and so the savings ratio (saving as a percentage of disposable income) of a country, where the average income is low, is likely to be low.

- **Low life expectancy and high infant mortality rate:** Someone born in Japan can expect to live up to the age of 85 whereas someone born in Zimbabwe has a life expectancy of 50 years only.

- **High rates of population growth:** In a number of developing countries, the birth rate exceeds the death rate and there is a **high dependency ratio**, with a high proportion of children being dependent on a small proportion of workers.

- **Low levels of education and health care:** These tend to result in low levels of productivity.

- **Low levels of capital goods and poor infrastructure:** These again reduce productivity.

- **Poor housing and sanitation:** A significant number of people may not have access to clean water for drinking and washing.

- **Relatively high number of workers, employed in the primary sector:** Underemployment can be high in agriculture. For instance, ten persons may be doing the work of six. This, again, lowers productivity.

- **Concentration on a narrow range of exports (most of which are primary products):** Developing countries can be subject to, what is known as, the underdevelopment trap or the **vicious circle of poverty**. This is the problem, that a country with low incomes has a low saving rate. This means that most of their resources are used to produce consumer goods. The lack of capital goods keeps productivity and income low, as shown in Fig. 1.

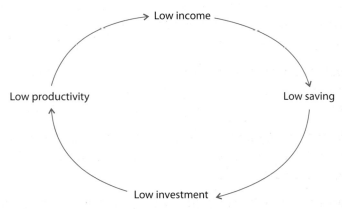

Fig. 1 The vicious circle of poverty

Activity 2

A comparison of Egypt and Singapore in 2005

	Egypt	Singapore
Real GDP per head	$1 070	$24 840
Population under the age of 15	34%	19%
Life expectancy	71	79
Workers employed in agriculture	27%	0%
Doctors per 1 000 of the population	2.2	1.3
Adult literacy rate	56%	93%

Discuss the extent to which the figures in the table suggest that Singapore was a more developed economy than Egypt, in 2005.

Differences between developing countries

No two developing countries are the same and a developing country may not have all the characteristics expected. Brazil, for example, has a real GDP per head, below that of developed countries and has a considerable proportion of population living in poverty. An estimated 35m Brazilians, constituting 20% of the population, live in poverty lacking the resources to proper medical care. Its real GDP, however, is rising and some of the country's population live in considerable splendour. The country's output is moving from low skilled to higher skilled manufacturing. Its financial sector is also growing and it already has a reasonably well developed stock exchange.

Why Governments Seek to Achieve Development

Governments pursue development because they want higher real GDP, higher living standards for their citizens and expansion of range of economic and social choices.

Economic growth has the potential to raise material living standards. If higher real GDP consists of both – more consumer and capital goods, the country's population should be able to enjoy more goods and services, both now and in the future. For development to be achieved, it is important that all people should have access to higher living standards. For this to occur, it is important that the distribution of income does not become too uneven and poverty is reduced.

A reduction in poverty brings benefits both to the poor and to the wider society. Lifting people above poverty, gives them access to (at least) basic necessities, improves their mental and physical health and raises their expectations. People who enjoy better living standards are likely to be more productive, which in turn should lower the country's average costs and make the country more internationally competitive. A reduction in poverty may also reduce pollution. As people become better off, they are more likely to have access to sanitation and environmentally friendly forms of heating.

Expanding the range of economic and social choices, increasing freedom and self-esteem includes increasing access to education, health care and participation in the political process. This should improve the quality of people's lives and enhance future economic performance. Economic development can create a *virtuous circle*. As income, education and health care increase, saving and investment increase and workers become more productive. This raises international competitiveness, which leads to even higher income.

Summary

- Economic development is concerned with improvements in economic welfare. It involves higher real GDP per head, higher living standards, a wider range of choices, more freedom and more self-esteem.

- Development can be measured in terms of real GDP per head, although HDI gives a wider measure of development.

- Among the usual characteristics of developing countries are – low real GDP per head, low savings ratio, low life expectancy, high rate of population growth, low levels of education, health care and investment, a relatively high number of workers employed in the primary sector and concentration on a narrow range of exports.

- Developing countries may experience a vicious circle of poverty that is difficult to break out of.

- Economic development can introduce a range of benefits to people and enhance a country's ability to develop in the future.

Teacher's Tip

Remember that even developed economies are seeking to develop further. No economy is likely to match all the possible characteristics of a developing or developed economy and even in economies with low GDP per head, some inhabitants may be very rich.

Multiple Choice Questions

1. What would be higher in a developed country, relative to a developing country?
   a. Birth rate
   b. Emigration
   c. Gross domestic product per capita
   d. The proportion of the population who are illiterate

2. The table shows information on four countries, A, B, C and D.

	Birth rate	Death rate	Life expectancy at birth
a.	7.0	6.0	82
b.	12.0	9.0	79
c.	14.2	9.6	78
d.	29.2	10.4	60

   Which country is most likely to be a developing economy?

3. What is often found in a developing economy?
   a. A high proportion of the population in higher education.
   b. A high savings ratio.
   c. A low infant mortality rate.
   d. A low investment rate.

4. Most of a country's population is employed in agriculture and its government makes most of the decisions on what is produced. What type of economy is this most likely to be?
   a. A developed, market economy
   b. A developed, planned economy
   c. A developing, market economy
   d. A developing, planned economy

Inequality and Poverty

This unit discusses income and wealth inequality, the nature of poverty and some possible measures to reduce poverty and improve living standards.

Income and Wealth Inequality

Income may be unevenly distributed between households due to uneven holdings of wealth, differences in the composition of households and differences in ability to earn.

Wealth is a stock of assets which have a financial value. Some of these assets, such as shares and government bonds, give rise to income. Some people have a considerable amount of wealth whilst others have none.

Households with a number of workers are likely to have a higher income than those with one or no workers and a high number of dependants.

The wages received by workers is influenced by their skills, qualifications and the number of hours for which they work. High skilled workers with better qualifications are likely to be in high demand and hence are likely to receive high wages. Full time workers usually earn more than part time workers. Some people may be dependant on state benefits or help from relatives and their income is likely to be relatively low.

Wealth is unevenly distributed because there are differences in the assets inherited by people, their savings and entrepreneurial skills. In fact, inheritance is a major reason for some people being wealthy. The more a person can save, the wealthier they will become. Of course, in this sense *wealth creates wealth*. Wealthy people can afford to save more and this makes them wealthier. People with an entrepreneurial flair may be able to build up a business from scratch and become wealthy.

Influence of Government on the Distribution of Income and Wealth

Governments may decide to influence the distribution of income and wealth because of concerns that a very uneven distribution may be socially divisive. It may also want to ensure that everyone has access to a certain standard of living. In influencing the distribution, however, government may be concerned that it does not reduce incentives to entrepreneurs and workers.

Governments can influence the distribution in a number of ways including

- taxation

- the provision of cash benefits

- the provision of free state education and health care, and

- using labour and macroeconomic policies.

Progressive taxes make the distribution of income and wealth more even. The provision of unemployment and other cash benefits can help maintain a reasonable standard of living. Provision of free state education and health care can ensure that everyone has access to these essential services and it may also offer the people, an opportunity to improve their living standards.

Other government policies that can affect distribution of income include minimum wage legislation, regional policy and measures to reduce unemployment.

Activity 1

> 2% of adults own more than half of the world's wealth whilst the least wealthy 50% of the world's adults own only 1% of global wealth. Wealth is heavily concentrated in North America, Europe and affluent Asia-Pacific countries. People living in these countries, together hold almost 90% of total world wealth.
> Wealth is also unevenly distributed within countries. The USA has one of the highest levels of inequality and Japan one of the lowest.
> a. How much of the world's wealth is owned by the wealthiest 50% of adults?
> b. Explain what is meant by Japan having one of the lowest levels of wealth inequality.

 # The Nature and Causes of Poverty

Absolute poverty occurs when people do not have access to basic food, clothing and shelter. People experience **relative poverty**, when they are poor relative to other people in the country. People who are relatively poor are unable to participate fully in the normal activities of the society they live in. Just as a country can be trapped in a vicious circle of poverty, so can be individuals. People who are poor are likely to have worse than average education and health care. This will reduce their productivity, employment opportunities and income and will also affect the prospects of their children.

There are a number of reasons for poverty of people. These include being unemployed, being in low paid work, falling ill and growing old.

Possible Government Policy Measures to Reduce Poverty

There are a number of measures, a government may take in a bid to reduce poverty. Its choice of measures, however, can be restricted by the potential funds raised by it. Among the possible measures, we have:

- **Improving the quantity and quality of education**. In the long term this can be a very effective policy, as it can increase the job prospects and earning potential of the poor and their children.

- **Increasing aggregate demand** to increase employment by, for instance, increasing government expenditure or reducing the rate of interest. Unemployment is a major cause of poverty. Having unemployed and under-employed workers not only lowers their living standards, but also the living standards of others since output will be below potential.

- **Introducing or raising a national minimum wage**. This is designed to tackle the problem of people experiencing low living standards due to low wages.

- **Encouraging more MNCs to set up in the country**. The opening up of new firms in the country should create more employment opportunities.

- **Providing benefits or more generous state benefits**. The elderly and some of the sick and disabled may not be able to work and may not have any savings to support them. Giving them benefits, or raising the benefits they receive, may enable them to avoid absolute poverty. What is more debatable is the effect that raising unemployment benefit will have on poverty. If there is a lack of jobs, it may help in the short term as it will not only raise the living standards of the unemployed but may also reduce unemployment by increasing aggregate demand. If, however, jobs are available and the unemployed are not filling them because they receive a higher income on benefits, raising benefits will reduce the incentive to work.

- **Land reform**. In a number of countries, many agricultural workers work on land owned by a few rich land owners. Those who rent or lease land may be reluctant to improve the fertility of the land. In such circumstances, making ownership of land more equal may increase output and living standards.

Measures to Raise Living Standards

Measures to reduce poverty should also raise general living standards. Improving education and training will enhance the knowledge and earning potential of the people and their ability to participate in the political system of the country. Reducing unemployment, as already mentioned, also raises living standards by increasing the quantity of available goods and services.

Other ways of improving living standards include improving health care, increasing and improving the housing stock, improving the working conditions and reducing pollution.

Economists debate about the extent to which government intervention is needed to achieve these objectives. Some economists argue that government policies will be needed, such as legislation, to give workers holiday entitlement and government provision of housing. Other economists argue that the private sector is better at providing improved living standards. If this is the case, living standards might be increased by reducing government regulation and taxation. For example, if corporation tax is reduced, firms may be encouraged to expand taking on more workers and providing more training.

 Activity 2

In 2007, a survey by the Indian Health Ministry in conjunction with UNICEF – the United Nations children's fund, found that almost 46% of Indian children under the age of three suffer from malnutrition. This is on alarmingly high proportion, compared with about 35% in sub-Saharan Africa and only 8% in China.
In the same year BMW, the German car maker, opened its first factory in India to meet rising demand for western luxury brands.
The factory will make cars for domestic sales only. BMW believes that India could become one of its biggest markets.

a. What evidence is there in the passage, that income is unevenly distributed in India?

b. What type of firm is BMW?

c. How might the opening of factories by firms such as BMW in India reduce the country's child malnutrition?

Measures of Income and Wealth Inequality

To assess the distribution of income and wealth in a country, economist scalculate the percentages of income earned and wealth owned by given proportions of the population. Two common proportions used are – **deciles** (tenths) and **quintiles** (fifths).

The degree of inequality can be illustrated on a **Lorenz curve**. On the vertical axis, the cumulative percentage of income or wealth is plotted and on the horizontal axis, the cumulative percentage of population is indicated. The 45° degree diagonal line shows an equal distribution of income or wealth. The actual distribution is plotted on the diagram. Fig. 1 shows a Lorenz curve based on Table 1. The further the curve is from the 45° line the more unequal the distribution.

Table 1 The distribution of income in a country.

Percentage of the population	Share of income	Cumulative percentage share of income
Poorest 20%	5%	5%
Next poorest 20%	8%	13%
Middle 20%	15%	28%
Next richest 20%	25%	53%
Richest 20%	47%	100%

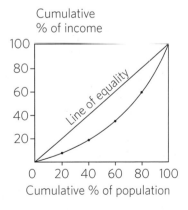

Fig. 1 Cumulative % of population

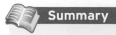 **Summary**

- Some households are rich because they earn high incomes and own assets which generate income.

- The main reasons accounting for wealth of the people are inheritance of wealth, accumulated savings or money earned in business.

- Governments influence the distribution of income and wealth through taxation, the provision of benefits and adoption of macroeconomic policies.

- The main reasons to account for poverty of people are - unemployment and low-paid jobs.

- Among the measures a government may take to reduce poverty and raise living standards include improving education and training, raising aggregate demand, attracting MNCs and improving health care.

- There is a debate amongst economists as to whether the public or private sector is more effective in improving living standards.

 Teacher's Tip

Remember the difference between equity and equality. An equal distribution of income or wealth might be seen as unfair, if people have different needs.

Multiple Choice Questions

1. What may cause a more uneven distribution of income?
   a. An increase in the national minimum wage
   b. An increase in state benefits
   c. A reduction in the top rates of tax
   d. A reduction in unemployment

2. Why does income inequality tend to be associated with wealth inequality?
   a. It is a disincentive for entrepreneurs and workers.
   b. Those with high incomes have higher ability to save than the poor.
   c. Those with high incomes spend a higher proportion of their income than the poor.
   d. Those with low incomes often inherit wealth.

3. What could cause a decrease in absolute poverty but a rise in relative poverty?
   a. The income of the rich rising by less than the income of the poor.
   b. The income of the rich rising by more than the income of the poor.
   c. The income of the rich falling by less than the income of the poor.
   d. The income of the rich falling by more than the income of the poor.

4. Which government measure may reduce absolute poverty?
   a. A cut in government expenditure on state education
   b. An increase in the rate of interest
   c. Granting subsidies to builders of low cost housing
   d. The imposition of a tax on food

Population Growth

Some developing countries have high population growth. This, however, is not true of all developing countries. This unit examines the factors that affect population growth, population structures, the concept of optimum population and the Malthusian theory of population.

 ## Causes of Population Growth

The size of a country's population can grow as a result of a natural increase or net emigration. A natural increase occurs when the birth rate exceeds the death rate. For instance, the crude birth rate in Iran in 2011 was 17.7 per thousand and the death rate was 5.2 per thousand, giving a natural rate of increase of 12.2 per thousand or 1.22%.

The birth rate is influenced by the average age of the population, the number of women in the population and women's fertility rate. The fertility rate (i.e. the average number of children per woman) is in turn affected by:

- the age at which women marry

- the number of women pursuing higher education

- the labour force participation rate of women

- the socio-economic status of women

- the availability of family planning services

- availability of government support for families

- the cost of bringing up children

- provision of benefits for the sick and elderly by the government.

The birth rate is likely to be high when there is a young average aged population in which women marry young, infant mortality rate is high, girl education is poor, women are non-working and it is cheap to bring up children. Other factors leading to a high birth rate are – lack or disapproval of family planning, government cash incentives to have children but a lack of government help to care for the sick and elderly. In contrast, in a country where it is expensive to have children (because there is a legal requirement to send children to school for a number of years and an expectation that some of them will go for higher education) and well paid jobs are open to women – the birth rate is likely to be low. If the government does provide state pensions and sickness and disability benefits, families may not feel that they have to have a large family in order to support them.

The death rate is influenced by nutrition, housing conditions, medical care, lifestyles, working conditions, involvement or non-involvement in military action. A country in which people have healthy diets, enjoy good housing facilities and access to high quality medical care, do not smoke or consume excess alcohol, exercise regularly, enjoy good working conditions and the country is at peace with other countries, is likely to have a relatively low death rate.

Net immigration occurs when more people come into the country to live *(immigrants)* than people who leave it to live elsewhere *(emigrants)*. The rate and pattern of migration is influenced by relative living standards at home and abroad, persecution of particular groups and extent of control on the movement of people. If living standards abroad are better (or perceived as better), there is persecution at home and no restriction to immigration by other countries, some people are likely to emigrate. Most migrants tend to be single people, of working age.

 Activity 1

> Namibia is a high fertility country. It has been found that there is a strong correlation between education and fertility in the country. The more educated a woman is, the fewer children she will have.
> a. What is meant by a 'high fertility country'?
> b. Why would it be expected that more educated women would have fewer children?

Population Structures

The sex distribution of a population indicates the number of males, compared to the number of females. In most countries, more boys are born than girls. However, in a number of countries females outnumber males. This is largely due to women, on an average, living longer than males and higher male infant mortality rates. In some countries, such as Saudi Arabia and China, there are more males in the population than females. This is so because in China, families favour males while in Saudi Arabia more females emigrate than males.

The age distribution is the division of the population into different age groups. In broad terms, the categories are – people under 16, those between 16–64, and those over 65.

Diagrams in the form of bar charts, referred to as **population pyramids** show a more detailed breakdown of the different age groups. The traditional view of the population pyramid of a developing country is a pyramid shape such as that shown in Fig. 1.

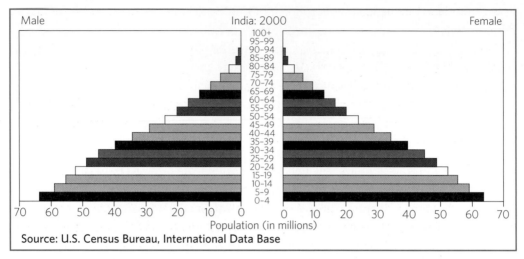

Fig. 1

Such a pyramid reflects a high birth rate and a high death rate. It has a large proportion of young people in its population with only a small percentage of people reaching older age groups. Of course, population structures of all developing countries do not fit this pattern.

The traditional view of the population pyramid of a developed country is reflected in Fig. 2. This is based on a lower birth rate and death rate with more people surviving till they enter old age.

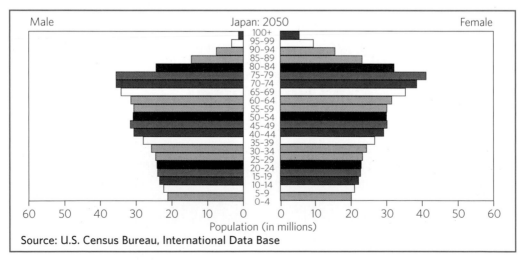

Fig. 2

The age structure of a population influences its *dependency ratio*. This is the:

$$\frac{\text{Number in dependant age groups}}{\text{Number in the labour force}} \times 100$$

The dependant age groups are those below school leaving age and those above retirement age.

 ## The Optimum Population

The term optimum population refers to the number of people which, when combined with the other resources of land, capital and existing technical knowledge, gives the maximum output of goods and services per head of the population.

The concept is not based just on the number of people in a country or per square kilometre. The balance between population and resources is of crucial importance. A country with a large geographical area and a small population may still be considered as overpopulated if there is a shortage of land, capital and technical knowledge, relative to workers' population. In such a case, a government may seek to move towards its optimum population either by introducing measures to reduce its population size or by seeking to increase investment.

A country is said to be under-populated if it does not have enough of human resources to make the best use of its resources. In such a case, its government may encourage immigration. Fig. 3 illustrates the concept of optimum population.

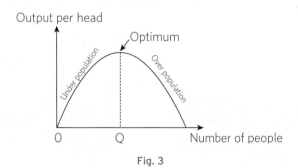

Fig. 3

In practice, it is difficult to determine a country's optimum population and size of actual population relative to it. This is, in part, because the quantity and quality of resources are changing all the time.

The Population Reference Bureau (PRB), forecasted in 2004 that India will overtake China as the world's most populous nation by 2050. It has projected that China's population will rise from 1.3 bn to 1.44 bn whilst India's will increase from 1.08 bn to 1.63 bn. The projections were based on infant mortality rates, life expectancy, fertility rates, age structure, contraception and AIDS rates.

a. Identify a factor influencing the population size, not mentioned in the passage.

b. Explain why India's population may grow, by less than the predicted figure.

 # The Malthusian Theory of Population

Thomas Malthus, a UK economist of the eighteenth century, argued that population pressures would tend to prevent the rise of living standards. He claimed that *population grows at a geometric rate*, that is 1, 2, 4, 8, 16 etc. whilst *food production grows at an arithmetic rate*, i.e. 1, 2, 3, 4, 5 etc. Such a relationship would result in population, doubling every 25 years or so and outstripping food production. He explained that there were two checks which keeps population, within its means of subsistence. One is called **positive checks**. These are the factors which cause a rise in the death rate including epidemics, famine, infanticide and wars. The other are **preventive checks**, including contraception and 'moral restraint', by which he meant delaying marriage.

Improvements in transport and developments in capital goods and technology, including the use of fertilisers and combine harvesters, have enabled food production to rise more rapidly than population. The world has seen both, population and living standards rise. Actually, the Malthusian theory overlooks that people are producers as well as consumers.

 **Summary**

- A country's population can grow as a result of its birth rate exceeding its death rate and/or as a result of net immigration.

- The birth rate is influenced by the average age of the population, the number of women in the population and the number of children they have.

- The age distribution of a population can be illustrated in a population pyramid. The higher the birth rate and death rate, the more pyramid-shaped it will be.

- The death rate is influenced by social conditions, lifestyles, medical conditions and the existence or absence of military conflicts.

- People emigrate in search of better living standards and to escape persecution.

- A country is said to be over-populated, if there is an excess of labour relative to land, capital and technical knowledge.

- The Malthusian theory suggests there is a tendency for the population to increase at a faster rate than the means of subsistence. The experience of the world, however, does not tend to support this.

 Teacher's Tip

While describing differences in the structure of population between developing and developed economies, it is often useful to draw population pyramids. The traditional pyramid shape for a developing economy is *triangular*, showing high birth and death rates and a low life expectancy. The typical pyramid, for a developed economy, is more of an oblong shape with a narrower top and slightly narrower bottom, reflecting an increasing life expectancy and falling birth rate.

Multiple Choice Questions

1. What is meant by the birth rate?
   a. The number of births compared to the number of deaths.
   b. The number of births per thousand of the population per year.
   c. The number of children each woman has on average each year.
   d. The number of children women are expected to have each year.

2. In a country more boys are born than girls and yet, there are more women than men in the population. How can this be explained?
   a. A higher death rate for women than for men.
   b. More women emigrating than men.
   c. The infant mortality rate of females being higher than males.
   d. Women living longer than men.

3. Which of the following is most likely to cause a rise in the average age of a country's population?
   a. A fall in the death rate and birth rate.
   b. A fall in the death rate and a rise in the birth rate.
   c. A rise in the death rate and a fall in the birth rate.
   d. A rise in the death rate and birth rate.

4. What is meant by the sex distribution of a population?
   a. The proportion of females and males in the population.
   b. The proportion of people over retirement age in the population.
   c. Where females and males in the population live.
   d. Where people over retirement age live.

The Effects of Changes in Population

This unit examines a number of issues, relating to the changes in population. These are – the effects of an increase in population, ways of reducing the birth rate, the consequences of an ageing population and emigration.

 Changes in Population

The previous unit mentioned that an increase in population can be caused by the birth rate exceeding the death rate and/or net immigration. A fall in the death rate, for instance, will not necessarily lead to an increase in population if it is offset by a fall in the birth rate. Latvia's population, for example, is declining because its birth rate has fallen at a greater rate than its death rate and it is currently experiencing net emigration.

The Effects of an Increase in Population

The consequences of a growth in a country's population depend on its cause, size of population relative to optimum population and the rate of population growth.

Possible benefits of an increasing population are listed below.

- If the population is below the optimum size, the country will be able to make **better use of its resources**.

- The **size of markets will increase**. This should enable firms to take greater advantage of economies of scale.

- There may be an **increase in factor mobility** if the rise has resulted from an increase in the birth rate or immigration. Expanding industries can recruit new workers to the labour force. These people are likely to be familiar with new ideas and methods. If this is the case, firms' training costs will be reduced.

- **Extra demand will be generated**. This is likely to stimulate investment and this may lead to introduction of new technology.

- A **rise in the labour force** presently due to net immigration and in the future, caused by a rise in the birth rate. Net immigration will bring in more workers. More children being born will increase the dependency ratio in the short term but in the long term, will result in more workers.

Despite the possible advantages of an increasing population, there are a number of reasons for a government to be concerned about population growth. These include:

- **Concerns about famine**. If a country is currently overpopulated and agricultural productivity is low, there is a risk that the country may not be able to feed more dependants.

- **Restrictions on improvements in living standards**. Resources which could have been used to improve living standards may have to be devoted to the provision of goods and services for the extra number of dependants in the population. There may be, for instance, provision of more health care facilities but health care services per head may fall.

- **Overcrowding**. Increases in population may put pressure on housing and social capital and cause traffic congestion.

- **Environmental pressure**. More people in a country may result in a damage to wildlife habitats, water shortages and the depletion of non-renewable resources.

- **Pressure on employment opportunities**. If there is an increase in the number of people of working-age, who lack appropriate skills, the government may have to devote more resources to education and training. It must be remembered, however, that immigration in itself does not cause unemployment. The number of jobs in existence is not fixed. Though immigration will increase the supply of labour, it will also result in an increase in aggregate demand.

- **Balance of payment pressures**. More dependants in the population may result in a rise in imports and some products may need to be diverted from the export to the home market.

Ways of Reducing the Birth Rate

A country, concerned that its population is growing too rapidly, will not want to raise its death rate! It may however, seek, to reduce immigration and try to reduce the country's birth rate. There are a number of ways it could do the latter. An effective way is thought to be improvement of the educational and employment opportunities for women. Educated women tend to be more aware of contraceptive methods, marry later and are likely to restrict their family size, in order to be able to combine raising children with work and also because they have higher hopes for their children's future. Better information and increased availability of family planning services will make it more likely that households will be able to limit their family sizes.

Improvement of health care and nutrition reduces infant mortality and, in turn, the birth rate. One reason which may explain a higher number of children in families is the apprehension and concern over their survival. Another reason for having a large family, is anticipation of social security and support in old age. Setting up pension and sickness insurance schemes will reduce the need for family support. A government can also raise the cost of having children by raising the school leaving age. It can also reduce or stop any financial support, it gives to families for each child they have and instead provide incentives for families who restrict the number of children. The most extreme measure is to make it illegal to have children above a specified number.

 **Activity 1**

China's *one child policy* has resulted in a drop from 5.8 children per couple in the 1970s to 1.8 in 2006. It has been estimated that China's population would have reached 1.5 billion rather than 1.3 billion in 2006, without government intervention. Concern, however, has been expressed that the policy will lead to a smaller number of young workers to support a growing population of pensioners. There has also been, for some time, a concern about the cultural bias towards male heirs. Boys outnumber girls by 15% nationally and by 30%, in the countryside. Girls in China are regularly aborted and abandoned.

Apart from restricting families to one child, the government has also ended free education. Some economists think the latter measure will be more effective in reducing population growth.

a. How successful has China's one child policy been?

b. Explain two reasons why China introduced its 'one-child' policy.

c. Explain how may a reduction of free education lower population growth.

The Consequences of An Ageing Population

A number of countries, including Japan, the USA and many of those in the EU, are experiencing an ageing population. An ageing population is one in which, as its name suggests, the average age is rising. In Japan, for instance, the average age of the population in 2006 was 43 and 26.3% of the population was aged over 60.

An ageing population can be caused by a fall in the birth rate, a fall in the death rate, net emigration or a combination of the three. There are a number of consequences of an ageing population including:

- **A rise in the dependency ratio**: If people are living longer and there are fewer workers because of net emigration, there will be a greater proportion of consumers to workers.

- **A change in the labour force**: Older workers may be geographically and occupationally less mobile. They may, however, be more experienced, reliable and patient.

- **Higher demand for health care**: The elderly place the greatest burden on a country's health service.

- **Greater need for welfare services**, such as caring for the elderly at home and in retirement homes.

- **Rise in cost of state and private pensions**.

- **Change in the pattern of demand**: for example, demand for housing for retired people will rise.

Ways of coping with an ageing population

Having a higher proportion of elderly workers will put pressure on governments to spend more. If they do so, it will involve an *opportunity cost*. The money used, for instance, may have been spent on education instead. An ageing population may also raise the tax burden on workers. There are a number of ways, a government may seek to reduce these effects. One is to raise the retirement age. This will reduce the cost of pensions and increase tax revenue without increasing tax rates. In a country, in which life expectancy is rising, there is some justification for raising the retirement age. Working for a longer period can also increase a workers' lifetime income and, depending on the nature of their work, may keep them physically and mentally healthy for a longer period.

A government may also try to cope with the financial burden of an ageing population, by encouraging or making it compulsory for workers to save for their retirement. It may

try to raise the productivity of workers by means of education and training. This may involve an increase in government expenditure but, if successful, may generate more tax revenue. In addition, it may encourage the immigration of younger skilled workers by issuing more work permits. This will reduce the dependency ratio at least in the short term.

Activity 2

It has been estimated that, in India, the retirement age would have to be raised to 75 and to 85 in China, the UK and US to maintain the ratio of working people to the retired citizens

a. Explain two reasons for an increase in life expectancy.

b. Explain two benefits to workers due to a rise in the retirement age.

Internal Migration

Workers tend to migrate from rural to urban areas in search of better jobs and higher incomes. Such migrants may supply growing industries and result in a better allocation of resources. Their movement may also raise living standards in rural areas if initially there had been underemployment and if they send back money to their relatives. There may, however, be some harmful effects also. If it is the most productive agricultural workers that leave, agricultural productivity may fall. There is also no guarantee that enough jobs will be available in urban areas and a number of external costs, including overcrowding, increased pressure on social capital and congestion may occur as a result of the rapid expansion of cities.

The Effects of Net Emigration

There are a number of possible economic effects of net emigration. This are influenced by the size and the nature of the emigration. Some of these include:

- The size of the working population is likely to be reduced. Most emigrants tend to be of working age.

- The remaining labour force will have a greater burden of dependency.

- The average age of the labour force will increase. This may make it less mobile.

- The sex distribution of the population may be affected. In the case of some countries, more men emigrate than women.

- There may be a shortage of a particular skill if it is mainly workers from one particular category (for instance medical care) who emigrate.

- There may be under-utilisation of resources. The country may become under-populated.

- Those who emigrate may send money home to help their relatives.

Summary

- The effect of an increasing population will depend on its cause, size of the population in relation to the optimum population and the rate of population growth.

- An increase in the size of the population may increase the efficiency of firms, raise factor mobility, increase the demand and make better use of resources.

- A government may be concerned that an increasing population may result in famine, reduced living standards, overcrowding, depletion of resources, environmental problems and unfavourable balance of payments position.

- Ways of controlling the population include raising the educational and employment opportunities for women, increasing availability of family planning services, increasing the cost of having children, providing support for the elderly and providing incentives for limiting the family size.

- An ageing population will raise the dependency ratio, change the labour force, burden the health and welfare services, raise the cost of pensions and alter the pattern of demand.

- Among the possible policies that can be used to cope with an ageing population include – raising the retirement age, promoting workers to save for their pensions, raising productivity and encouraging immigration of skilled workers.

- Internal migration from rural to urban areas may make it easier for firms to recruit labour but may lead to farms losing their most productive workers. Some of those who move to urban areas, may not find jobs and this leads to overcrowding in cities.

- Net emigration is likely to reduce the size of the labour force, increase the dependency ratio, alter sex distribution, reduce the size of the population and increase money sent home.

Teacher's Tip

Remember that both a high rate of population growth and a low rate of population growth can cause problems for an economy, depending on their causes and the state of the economy in relation to its optimum population size.

Multiple Choice Questions

1. What must cause a natural increase in the population of a country?
    a. Immigration exceeding emigration.
    b. Population rising above the optimum level.
    c. Population rising to the optimum level.
    d. The birth rate exceeding the death rate.

2. Why may a government want to reduce the growth of its population?
    a. Capital is not being fully utilised.
    b. The population is below the optimum level.
    c. There are worries about the risk of famine.
    d. There is low population density.

3. What effect is a rise in the birth rate likely to have on the size of the labour force now and in twenty years time?

	labour force now	labour force in twenty years time
a.	decrease	decrease
b.	decrease	increase
c.	increase	increase
d.	increase	decrease

4. Which of the following policies is most likely to reduce the cost to tax payers of an ageing population?
    a. An increase in the number of state retirement homes.
    b. A rise in the retirement age.
    c. A tax placed on private pensions.
    d. Encouragement to net emigration.

Problems of Development

Unit 42 focused on the characteristics of developing economies. This unit examines the conditions necessary for development, the problems faced by developing countries, measures taken by developing countries to promote development, the nature of foreign aid and the impact of the relationship between developing and developed economies.

 ## The Conditions for Development

Most economists agree that for development to occur, there needs to be an improvement in the quantity and quality of resources. More investment, improved education, training and health care can raise, not only real GDP but also the quality of people's lives, their life expectancy and their choices.

 ## The Problems Facing Developing Economies

Developing economies, especially the least developed economies, may face a number of difficulties in seeking to improve their economic performance and living standards. These include:

- **High growth of population**: A high birth rate can result in resources being used, for instance, to feed and educate children. These could have been instead used to increase the country's productive potential and living standards instead.

- **High levels of international debt**: Many poor countries have borrowed heavily in the past. In some cases, a large proportion of the country's income is taken up for repaying (and paying interest on) foreign loans. This means it cannot be used to spend on education, health care and investment. So, the opportunity cost of repaying debt may be economic development.

- **Reliance on the export of primary products**: Over a period of time, the price of primary products tends to fall, relative to the price of manufactured goods and services. This means that some poor countries receive relatively less for their exports whilst having to pay more for their imports. Over the last fifty years, a range of commodity prices, including copper, coffee, cocoa and coal have been falling. A number of primary product markets are dominated by the consuming countries and these developed countries use their buying power to keep down the prices of primary products. There have also been significant fluctuations in the price of some primary products due to climate changes and natural resources.

- **Lack of investment in human capital and capital goods**: Lack of expenditure on education, training and capital goods holds back-increases in productivity, introduction of new technology and international competitiveness.

- **Emigration of key workers**: Doctors, nurses, teachers, managers and other key workers may seek better paid employment abroad. Since 1999, for instance, more medical staff have emigrated from Ghana, than the country has been able to train. Most of these have emigrated to Canada, the UK and USA.

- **Trade restrictions on their products**: Tariffs, other restrictions and foreign government subsidies on their own products, make it difficult for developing countries to sell their products at home and abroad, on equal terms. The steepest tariffs tend to be imposed by developed economies on those products, which developing economies concentrate on, including agricultural produce and labour-intensive manufactured goods. These tariffs also build up as the goods are processed into higher value-added goods, so that developing economies are discouraged from building up their industries.

- **Unbalanced economies**: Certain markets may be underdeveloped such as the financial sector. A lack of a developed financial sector is likely to discourage saving and investment.

 **Activity 1**

Mozambique is heavily dependent on its sugar industry. It has, however, been estimated that it loses more than £20m a year – equivalent to its entire national budget for agriculture and rural development – because of the trade distortions caused by the EU sugar scheme. Production costs of sugar cane are four times lower in Mozambique, than in the EU, but they are prevented from exporting the sugar to the EU and hence benefit from higher prices due to import tariffs charged on their products. In addition, they have to contend with EU export subsidies that further reduce their competitiveness.

a. What is the disadvantage of relying heavily on one product?
b. Explain two ways in which development in Mozambique would be likely to increase, if tariffs were removed from its products.
c. Explain how EU export subsidies on sugar are disadvantageous to Mozambique.

 # Measures to Promote Development

There is some disagreement about the best ways to promote development. For instance, whether it is better to rely on government intervention or market forces, whether developing economies should rely on domestic or foreign sources of investment funds. One strategy, which involves government intervention, is what is called *import substitution*. This involves the protection of new domestic industries against foreign competition by the government. This help is designed to allow the industries to grow and as they do so, imports can be replaced by domestic products. If successful, the strategy can increase domestic output, raise employment and improve the country's 'trade in goods and services balance'. There are risks, however, with this strategy. In the short term, at least, it may raise prices and reduce choice and hence lower economic welfare. Other countries may also retaliate and the domestic industries may become reliant on protection without seeking to increase their efficiency and competitiveness.

An alternative strategy is to try to promote exports by exposing domestic firms to market forces. The idea is that, without government support, firms will be forced to become efficient. The success of this policy, however, depends on the firms being able to compete with foreign firms, some of which may have been established for some time (and as a result may have built up consumer loyalty) and may be taking advantage of economies of scale.

Another strategy is to improve the country's infrastructure, capital stock, education, training and health care systems. As the country may lack the tax revenue to do this, it may seek to attract multinational companies, loans from abroad or foreign aid.

MNCs may promote development in their host countries. They can increase employment and wages, train and educate workers, bring in new technology and improve infrastructure, for example, by building roads and improving dock facilities. MNCs may pay workers in developing countries, less than that in their home countries and may provide them with poorer working conditions. Nevertheless, as long as the wages are higher and the conditions are better than those generally operating in the host countries, the MNCs will be making a positive contribution to development. There are circumstances, however, when MNCs may harm development. MNCs may deplete non-renewable resources, cause pollution and put pressure on host governments to pursue policies which have a detrimental effect on development such as reducing health and safety regulations.

Borrowing from abroad can work, if the funds are used in a way which raises productivity and generates enough income to repay the loans and make a contribution to higher living standards. Interest charged on loans, however, can be high which makes some projects unviable. Also, there is the risk that projects may not be as successful as expected. If this is the case, the developing countries will accrue debt. Some of the money raised may be used for unprofitable prestigious projects, on the military and may be lost due to corruption.

Foreign aid, by its very nature, is on more generous terms. It has the potential to increase development, but it can create economic and political dependency, postpone necessary reforms and bring in inappropriate technology. For example, a gift of complex capital equipment may not be that useful for a country with a high level of unemployed workers who lack education and training. Also, there is a risk that any financial foreign aid may be used for non-profitable projects and these may be corruption in its use.

Foreign Aid

Foreign aid may be given out of a desire to help people, win political support and gain commercial advantage. In the last case, the aid is likely to be in the form of *tied aid*. This means that conditions are placed on what the recipients can spend the aid on – often the requirement is, that it has to be spent on products produced by the donor countries. Foreign aid can be *bilateral or multilateral*. Bilateral aid is aid is from one government to another whereas multilateral aid is channelled through international organisations to developing countries. Such organisations include *the United Nations, the World Bank, the IMF, the EU*, non-government organisations including charities such as Oxfam.

Foreign aid can come in a variety of forms including grants, which do not require repayment, loans charged on favourable terms and the supply of goods, services, technical assistance and guidance. The IMF and World Bank have been criticised for attaching conditions for forgiving past debt. They often require governments to follow, what are known as, structural adjustment programmes. These are designed to increase the quality and quantity of resources but they may, at least in the short term, reduce economic growth and development. For instance, a government may be required to cut its expenditure and this may reduce the provision of education and health care.

It is thought that foreign aid is more likely to promote development if it is more generous, multilateral, untied and is geared towards the needs of the recipients.

 Key Point

The World Bank: an international organisation which provides long term loans on favourable terms, to promote development.

  **Activity 2**

Nigeria faces a number of economic problems including poor infrastructure, emigration of key workers, a relatively high level of corruption and foreign debt. Power and water are not provided for most firms. Firms have to invest in generators. Many professionals, especially doctors emigrate, taking their skills with them. The country is ranked the third most corrupt country in the world. In 2005, GDP per head was $570. In the same year, it was ranked 14th in terms of foreign debt. The Nigerian government is anxious to use the country's revenue on hospitals, roads and schools.

a. Explain how, one of the problems facing Nigeria, could hinder its economic development.

b. Suggest how the aforesaid problem could be overcome.

The Relationship between Developed and Developing Economies

In an increasingly global market, the events in one economy have a greater impact on other economies. For instance, a buoyant UK economy would be likely to benefit Tanzania while an improvement in the Tanzanian economy should bring some advantages to the UK. If the UK economy grows, the UK government will receive more tax revenue and this will enable it to increase its foreign aid, some of which may go to Tanzania. Incomes will be higher in the UK and its people and firms may buy more imports from Tanzania, including more UK people going on holiday to Tanzania. UK firms are likely to earn higher profits and this may encourage some of them to set up units abroad, especially if the UK economy is reaching full capacity.

The UK economy may also develop as a result of an improvement in education. A more educated UK population may be more concerned and interested in the dynamics of other economies. This may result in doling out more foreign aid and tourism to Tanzania.

The development of the Tanzanian economy can also benefit the UK. A more developed Tanzanian economy will need less aid, be able to buy more products from the UK and invest more in the UK.

 **Summary**

- Developing economies face a number of problems including population pressures, international debt, reliance on primary products, lack of investment in human capital and capital goods, emigration of key workers, trade restrictions on their products and unbalanced economies.

- Measures to promote development include import substitution, export promotion, attracting MNCs and applying for foreign aid.

- Foreign aid is more likely to promote economic development if it is multilateral, untied and takes into account the needs and economic conditions of the recipient.

- An improvement in the development of one economy can benefit another, through increased demand for its products, increased investment and, wherever appropriate, increased aid.

 Teacher's Tip

In revising this area, it would be useful to consider the development of the economy of your country and the factors influencing its rate of development.

Multiple Choice Questions

1. Why may a developing country experience difficulties while exporting to a developed country?
    a. It may face trade restrictions on its products.
    b. It may have a high rate of investment.
    c. It may have a low exchange rate.
    d. It may have low labour costs per unit.

2. The table provides information on four countries. Which country is likely to be the least developed?

	Population (m)	Real GDP ($bn)	Life expectancy
a.	100	600	58
b.	200	2 000	70
c.	300	2 100	58
d.	400	3 600	70

3. Why do developing economies, on an average, have a low savings ratio?
    a. Average income per head is low.
    b. Citizens have a range of saving institutions to choose from.
    c. Governments do not promote saving.
    d. Interest rates tend to be high.

4. Which of the following would boost an economy's development?
    a   A rise in expenditure on the police to tackle a higher rate of crime.
    b. A rise in provision of health care per head of population.
    c. A fall in the average number of years of schooling received by children.
    d. A rise of 2% in nominal GDP and a rise of 8% in inflation.

Answer Key

Activity 1

a. Educational accomplishments.

b. Life expectancy may be lower in Botswana than in India due to poor sanitation. This would make the people of Botswana more prone to a range of ailments. It may also be due to the greater spread of AIDS in Botswana.

Activity 2

The evidence does suggest, to a large extent, that Singapore is a more developed country than Egypt. Its income per head is twenty times greater, its life expectancy is higher and its adult literacy rate is better. It also has fewer workers employed in agriculture and a smaller proportion of its population under the age of 15 suggests that it has a lower birth rate. The doctors per 1 000 of the population, however, is lower in Singapore than in Egypt.

Multiple Choice Questions

1. c

    Generally developed countries have higher average incomes than developing countries. a, b and d might be expected to be higher in developing countries.

2. d

    Country D has the highest birth and death rates and the lowest life expectancy.

3. d

    One of the problems in developing countries is a lack of investment. a, b and c are more likely to be found in a developed country.

4. d

    A high proportion of the population working in agriculture is a feature of a developing country. The government makes most of the decisions in a planned economy.

Unit 43

Activity 1

a. The wealthiest 50% of adults own 99% of the world's wealth.

b. Japan having one of the 'lowest levels of wealth inequality' means that wealth is more evenly distributed in Japan than in most of the other countries. In Japan, the gap between those with the maximum wealth and those with the minimal wealth is smaller than that in most countries.

Activity 2

a. The passage indicates that some people in India have the income or wealth to buy luxury products whilst a high proportion of Indian infants suffer from malnutrition.

b. BMW is a multinational company. It has manufacturing units in more than one country.

c. The opening of factories by firms such as BMW in India may reduce the country's child malnutrition by raising incomes, employment and tax revenue in the country. If the factories' output adds to the country's output and does not just replace output produced by domestic firms, employment should also rise in the country.

Multinational companies may pay above the national average wage rate. The extra workers employed and their children should be able to enjoy higher living standards. The impact does not end there. The extra workers, by spending more, will increase demand for other products. This higher demand will generate more employment and higher incomes. As people become richer, they are able to buy more and better quality food and this should reduce malnutrition.

Higher incomes also increase government's tax revenue – both direct tax revenue and indirect tax revenue. The workers will pay more income tax, their expenditure will lead to higher sales tax revenue and MNCs and other firms will pay more corporate taxes. With more tax revenue, the government can spend money on measures to reduce child malnutrition. In the short term, this may involve expenditure on health care and benefits. In the longer term, it may include expenditure not only on health care but also on education and infrastructure.

Multiple Choice Questions

1. c

    A reduction in the top rates of tax would increase the income of the rich and widen the gap between them and the poor. a, b and d would all be likely to raise the income of the poor and hence narrow the gap.

2. b

    As the rich are in a better position to save than the poor, they can build up their assets including shares and property. The possibility of earning high incomes and accumulating wealth is likely to act as an incentive for entrepreneurs and workers. Those with high incomes spend more in absolute terms but a smaller proportion of their income as compared to the poor. Also, those with low incomes do not often inherit wealth.

3. b

    A rise in the income of the poor should reduce absolute poverty. If the income of the rich rises by more than that of the poor, the gap will increase. a would reduce absolute and relative poverty. c would increase absolute and relative poverty. d would increase absolute poverty but reduce relative poverty.

4. c

    Granting subsidies to builders of low cost housing should increase the supply of such housing, reduce its cost and hence make it more accessible to the poor. a would be likely to reduce the quantity and possibly the quality of education available to the poor. b would reduce aggregate demand and employment. d would make food more expensive and would lead the poor to spend a higher proportion of their income on food.

Unit 44

Activity 1

a. A country in which the number of children per woman is high.
b. More educated women are more likely to be informed about family planning. They are also more likely to pursue a career and hence marry later and limit their family size. In addition, they are likely to be better informed about nutrition and hygiene and consequently, it is less likely that their children will die young.

Activity 2

a. Migration.
b. As India develops, its birth rate may fall more than its death rate. The projections may have overestimated the fertility rates also.

Multiple Choice Questions

1. b

    A definition question.

2. d

    If women outlive men, the population may contain more women than men despite more boys being born.

3. a

    A fall in the death rate will mean that people are living longer and a fall in the birth rate will mean there are fewer young people.

4. a

    A definition question.

Activity 1

a. This depends on the mode of measurement of success. It has reduced population growth but it could also be perceived as a setback to development due to the killing and abandonment of girls. It has created gender imbalance.

b. China may have been worried about its ability to feed a rising population. It might also have been concerned that having more children might slow down its development, as more resources would have to be devoted for their care. The opportunity cost of this may, for example, have been improved infrastructure.

c. Reducing free education may lower population growth as it will increase the cost of having children. Parents will have to pay for education of their children. This may dissuade some people from having more children.

Activity 2

a. Life expectancy is increasing due to improved medical care and better nutrition. A greater range of illnesses can now be treated due to more effective medication. Improved nutrition makes it less likely for people to develop a range of illnesses.

b. Workers, who have to work for longer, will have the opportunity to earn more over their working life. They may also be likely to stay mentally and physically fitter for longer.

Multiple Choice Questions

1. d

    Definition question and the key word is 'natural'. b and c can be caused by net immigration.

2. c

    a and b might make a government want to raise the growth of its population and d would reduce a government's concern about the rate of population growth.

3. b

    In the short term, some women will leave the labour force to have children. In the longer term, their children will enter the labour force.

4. b

    Raising the retirement age would automatically reduce the number of pensioners. a, c and d would all be likely to increase the burden on taxpayers.

Unit 46

Activity 1

a. The disadvantage of relying on one product is that there can be sudden changes in conditions of demand and supply. If demand for the product falls or the country experiences problems supplying it, the country's income would fall.

b. If import tariffs were removed on its products, Mozambique would be able to export more. This should raise incomes and employment in Mozambique. As a result, its government would receive more tax revenue which could be spent on education and health care.

c. EU export subsidies make the price of EU sugar cheaper in Mozambique than its own sugar. This reduces the sale of Mozambiquan sugar in its own market and hence lowers its income and employment.

Activity 2

a. The emigration of professional workers will increase the country's dependency ratio, reduce the supply of vital services and will discourage some MNCs from setting up their units in the country.

b. The government may seek a loan from overseas in order to give a higher pay its doctors and other professional and improve their working condition. This may, however, be difficult as the government may have problems repaying the loan due to the burden of existing debt. It may seek to retain professional workers by giving them tax concessions. Even if they pay less tax and stay in the country, the government will still receive more tax revenue than what it would have, if they emigrated. It may also try to attract more MNCs by operating a low corporation tax. These may offer more employment opportunities to professionals.

Multiple Choice Questions

1. a

    b, c and d should make it easier for a country to export. c and d should mean export prices are low. b may mean that export prices are low and the quality of exports is high.

2. a

    Real GDP per head is lowest in country a and its life expectancy is also low.

3. a

    If incomes are low, households have to spend most of it to buy the required goods and services. People on low incomes cannot afford to save.

4. b

    a, c and d are all likely to indicate that development is declining.

Examination Practice

Multiple Choice Questions

1. Which of the following are usually found in a developing economy?
    a. A low average income and a high rate of adult literacy
    b. A high school leaving age and a low life expectancy
    c. A high rate of infant mortality and a high level of labour skills
    d. A low rate of saving and a high rate of adult illiteracy

2. What is most likely to cause an immediate increase in the size of the working population?
    a. A decrease in immigration
    b. A decrease in unemployment
    c. A rise in the retirement age
    d. A rise in the school leaving age

3. What effect is a rise in the birth rate most likely to have?
    a. An increase in the average age of the population
    b. An increase in the dependant population
    c. An increase in labour productivity
    d. An increase in the proportion of females in the population

4. What would reduce the size of the dependant population?
    a. A fall in the death rate
    b. A fall in the retirement age
    c. A fall in the average size of families
    d. Net emigration

5. A country's population is expected to rise and its average age to fall in the future. Which of the following is likely to cause this?

	birth rate	migration
a.	decreases	net emigration
b.	decreases	net immigration
c.	increases	net emigration
d.	increases	net immigration

6. Which policy measure would increase wealth inequality?
    a. A cut in inheritance tax
    b. A reduction in the price of shares
    c. An increase in the tax on savings
    d. A rise in the top rates of income tax

7. For what reason, may a government of a developing country not welcome the presence of a multinational company in its country?
    a. It will speed up the exploitation of non-renewable resources.
    b. It will increase employment in the country.
    c. It will improve the country's infrastructure.
    d. It will bring in new ideas and technology.

8. A developing country registers a rise in its living standards. What is likely to fall as a result?
    a. Adult literacy rate
    b. Employment
    c. GDP per head
    d. Infant mortality rate

9. The table below gives information on four countries. Which country is likely to be least developed?

Country	% of population living in rural areas	% of children attending school	% of population over 60
a.	85	60	10
b.	80	40	5
c.	60	50	15
d.	40	80	18

10. Under what circumstance, will a country register a fall in its population?
    a. When the birth rate is lower than the death rate and there is net emigration.
    b. When the birth rate is lower than the death rate and there is net immigration.
    c. When the birth rate is greater than the death rate and there is net emigration.
    d. When the birth rate is greater than the death rate and there is net immigration.

Structured Questions

1. a. The rate of population growth in developed countries is often different from that in the developing countries. Explain. (5)
    b. Sometimes a government might try to limit the growth of the population of its country. Explain the motivation behind such an action. (4)
    c. As countries become more economically developed, there is a change in the relative importance of different sectors of production. Describe this change. (5)
    d. In many developed countries, there will be a large increase in the proportion of older people during the next 10 to 15 years. Discuss how governments might deal with this situation. (6)

(Cambridge 0455 Paper 4 Q7 May/June 2006)

2. a. In developing countries, the standard of living is often lower than that in developed countries. Identify four indicators that might confirm this. (4)

    b. Sometimes there is much poverty in developing countries. Discuss the reasons for this occurence. (6)

    c. Discuss the measures which may help improve the standard of living in a developing country. (10)

    (Cambridge 0455 Paper 4 Q7 May/June 2005)

3. a. Contrast the occupational distribution of the population of a developing country with that of a developed country. (5)

    b. Apart from the occupational distribution of the population, explain the reason for a country being classified as developing rather than developed. (8)

    c. Multinational companies invest in developing countries. Explain what is meant by a multinational company and discuss whether it is advantageous for a developing country to encourage investment by multinational companies. (7)

    (Cambridge 0455 Paper 4 Q7 May/June 2004)

International Aspects

The Structure of the Balance of Payments

One of the main aims of macroeconomic policy is to achieve stability in balance of payments. This unit examines the structure of the balance of payments, the causes of a financial account deficit and the significance of such a deficit.

 ## The Meaning of the Balance of Payment

The balance of payments is a record of all economic transactions between the residents of a country and the rest of the world in a particular period (over a quarter of a year or more commonly over a year). These transactions are made by individuals, firms and government bodies and include the exchange of goods and services, income, aid, and investment. Money coming into the country is recorded as *credit* items and money leaving the country as *debit* items.

The Sections of the Balance of Payments

The first section of the balance of payments is the best known section. This is the **current account** which covers trade in goods, trade in services, investment income and current transfers. The second section is called the **capital and financial accounts**. This section comprises of three parts. The first part is a relatively small component and is called the **capital account**. The second part, the financial account, can involve substantial sums and for some countries, this section indeed overshadows the current account in terms of the amount leaving and entering the country. The third part is **official reserves**. The last section is an estimate of any mistakes that have been made or items that have been left out while compiling the balance of payments. This is known as net errors and omissions.

The current account

The current account shows the income earned by the country and the expenditure made by it in its dealings with other countries. It is usually divided into four sub-sections.

a. **Trade in goods**. This covers exports and imports of goods including cars, food and  machinery. Such goods are sometimes referred to as **visible exports and imports** or **merchandise exports and imports**. If revenue from the export of goods exceeds the expenditure from import of goods, the country is said to have a *trade in goods deficit*. This can also be referred to as a visible trade deficit. In contrast, *a trade in goods surplus* (visible trade surplus) occurs when export revenue exceeds import expenditure.

b. **Trade in services**. As its name suggests, this part records payments for services sold abroad and expenditure on services bought from foreign countries. It can also be referred to as the **invisible balance**. Among the items included are banking, construction services, financial services, travel and transportation of goods and passengers between countries. A *trade in service surplus* would mean that service receipts exceed payments for services.

Together the first two sub-sections give the balance on trade in goods and services.

c. **Income**. This records two categories of income flow, which are compensation of employees and investment income. Compensation of employees includes wages, salaries and other benefits earned by residents working abroad minus that earned by foreigners working in the home economy. Investment income covers profit, dividends and interest receipts from abroad minus profit, dividends and interest paid abroad. Investment income is earned on direct investment, portfolio investment and loans. If, for instance, a multinational company sends profits out of the country back to its home country, it will appear as a debit item in this section. The receipt of dividends on shares in foreign companies and interest on loans made to foreign firms will be credit items.

d. **Current transfers**. These are transfers of money, goods or services which are sent out of the country or come into the country, not in return for anything else. Items include gifts, charitable donations, money sent to and received from relatives abroad and aid from one government to other governments.

The balances of the four sub-sections are summed up to give the **current account balance** (also sometimes just called the current balance). A current account surplus arises when the value of credit items exceeds the value of debit items. If the value of debit items is greater than the value of credit items, there is a current account deficit.

The Capital and Financial Accounts

The capital account includes funds bought into the country by new immigrants, funds sent abroad by people emigrating, transfers of funds associated with the acquisition or disposal of fixed assets and the purchase and sale of patents. For most countries, the financial account dwarfs the capital account. It records transactions in assets and liabilities. These can involve substantial investment flows. The three main components of this part are *direct investment, portfolio investment and other investment*. Direct investment covers the purchase of businesses or the establishment of new businesses. Portfolio investment includes the purchase of shares and government bonds. Other investment includes trade credits and loans.

When the country's citizens buy assets abroad, the transactions are recorded as debit items as they involve money leaving the country. Of course, later these purchases will generate investment income in the form of profit, interest and dividends, which will appear as credit items in the current account. In contrast, when foreigners buy assets in the country they are recorded as credit items but they are liabilities as they will later generate debit items in the current account.

The last part of this section is changes in official reserves, also called **reserve assets**. These are items held to settle debts with other countries. They include foreign exchange, special drawing rights issued by the IMF, reserve position at the IMF and gold.

 ## Net Errors and Omissions

The balance of payments is a balance sheet. If all items have been recorded and recorded accurately, debit and credit items should be equal. For instance, if the country has a deficit on the current account it would have to be matched by an equal surplus on its capital and financial accounts. In practice, however, because of mistakes and the failure to record all items (in part due to time delay), the balance of payments does not balance. So the net errors and omissions figure (which can also be called the balancing item or *unrecorded transactions*) is included to ensure that debit and credit items are equal. A negative balancing item means that more money has left the country than has been recorded officially. As more information is discovered and errors corrected, balance of payments figures are revised. The 2007 version of the 2004 balance of payments is more accurate than the 2005 version!

Activity 1

a. In 2000, Bangladesh imported $9 057m worth of goods and services and exported $6 585m worth of goods and services. What was its balance of trade in goods and services?

b. From the following information, calculate South Africa's current account balance in 2000.

	Rand millions
Exports of goods	218 507
Imports of goods	189 012
Exports of services	35 297
Imports of services	38 906
Income receipts	15 124
Income payments	37 638
Current transfers (net receipts)	−6 422

c. From the following information, calculate the net errors and omissions figure on the 2003 UK balance of payments.

	£ millions
Current balance	−20 430
Capital and financial accounts	18 698

The Causes of a Financial Account Deficit

A financial account deficit arises when the investment abroad in the year is greater than the foreign investment which has come into the country. Domestic firms may decide to set up in foreign countries because of lower tax rates, lower costs of production, expanding markets, good factors of production and government subsidies. Domestic firms and individuals may buy foreign shares if profit levels and dividends are high abroad. Similarly, high interest rates may encourage them to buy foreign government bonds and lend to foreign companies and individuals.

The Consequences of a Financial Account Deficit

In the short run, a financial account deficit involves money leaving the country. Firms deciding to buy business abroad and firms and individuals investing in foreign firms and lending to them may mean that potential jobs and incomes are lost to the foreign economy. In the longer term, however, investment abroad can generate incomes at home if the businesses acquired and set up and the portfolio investment prove to be profitable.

Activity 2

India usually has a current account surplus largely because of the money that Indians living in and working in other countries send back to their relatives and due to software service exports. In 2005, however, it had a current account deficit mainly because of a deficit on its visible trade balance.

a. What is meant by a current account surplus?

b. Which section of the current account is not referred to in the passage?

 **Summary**

- The balance of payments is a record of a country's trade and investment with other countries.

- The main sections of the balance of payments are the current account and the capital and financial accounts.

- The current account covers trade in goods, trade in services, income and current transfers.

- A current account deficit means that expenditure on imports of goods and services, income paid abroad and transfers abroad are greater than earnings from exports of goods and services, income and transfers received from abroad.

- The financial account includes direct and portfolio investment abroad (assets) and direct and portfolio investment into the country (liabilities).

- A financial account deficit will lead to exit of money from the country in the short term but in the long term, it will generate investment income which will appear in the current account.

 Teacher's Tip

Remember that investment appears in the capital and financial account, whereas the investment income earned on it appears in the current account.

Multiple Choice Questions

1. The table shows a country's exports and imports for the period 2008 to 2011.

Year	Exports ($m)	Imports ($m)
2008	230	220
2009	250	260
2010	280	270
2011	300	290

   In which year, did the country experience a balance of trade deficit?
   a. 2008
   b. 2009
   c. 2010
   d. 2011

2. Which of the following is an invisible import of Indonesia?
   a. French firms selling insurance to Indonesian firms.
   b. Indonesian citizens buying cars from the USA.
   c. Indonesian firms buying land in Germany.
   d. Tourists visiting Indonesia.

3. Mexican firms sell more oil to the USA and buy more banking services from the UK. How do these changes affect the Mexican balance of payments?

	Visible balance (trade in goods)	Invisible balance (trade in services)
a.	improves	improves
b.	improves	worsens
c.	worsens	worsens
d.	worsens	improves

4. Which of the following items is included in the current account of the balance of payments?
   a. The payment of interest on foreign loans.
   b. The purchase of shares in foreign companies.
   c. The sale of government bonds to foreign residents.
   d. The setting up of a branch of a bank in a foreign country.

Changing Patterns of Exports and Imports

The previous unit explained exports and imports of goods and services with regards to the current account of the balance of payments. This unit examines the differences between international trade and internal trade, the pattern of international trade, factors determining changes in exports and imports, the causes of a current account deficit and significance of such a deficit.

The Difference between International and Internal Trade

Trade involves the exchange of goods and services. International trade, which can also be referred to as external trade, is the exchange of goods and services between countries. In contrast, internal trade is trade within a country. Any trade involves risk and effort. A firm based in one part of the country, selling goods to individuals or firms in another part of the country, has to arrange and pay for transport and may have to wait for the payment of goods. International trade enables firms to reach a wider market, take greater advantage of economies of scale, source their products from a wider area and earn higher profits. It may, however, provide additional challenges to those posed by internal trade.

Buying and selling products across national boundaries may involve the products travelling greater distances. Firms may have to deal with buyers and sellers speaking different languages. If, for instance, a Japanese firm is selling cars to South Africa it will have to produce advertisements, manuals and insurance plans in English and Afrikaans. There may be differences in culture in different countries and these will have to be taken into account in the type of products firms seek to sell and the method of marketing adopted. For example, it is not appropriate to try to sell alcohol to Saudi Arabia where the drinking of alcohol is prohibited. Trade restrictions may also make it difficult for firms to sell their product abroad. If foreign governments place tariffs on imports, it will raise the price of the products sold by the firms and prevent consumers from buying them. Selling and buying in foreign markets expose firms to more competition.

Some may respond by becoming more efficient but others may struggle to survive. Firms engaged in international trade also have to deal with foreign currencies. For example, an Indian firm which sells textiles to a US store may be paid in dollars. It is likely to sell these for rupees. If the value of the dollar falls by the time the Indian firm agrees to a price in dollars and receives the payment, it will earn fewer rupees.

Key Point

A tariff: a tax on imports.

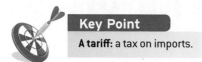 The Pattern of International Trade

There are a number of factors which influence the choice of trading partners of a country. It will usually seek to buy from countries which produce good quality products at low prices and sell to countries which have a high and stable demand for the products it is producing. Most countries, in practice, trade mainly with countries close to them in tastes, development and (sometimes) geography or with whom they share historical links. Much of current world trade takes place between developed countries. Most of this trade is in services and high quality finished manufactured products.

Table 1 shows the main destination of exports and main sources of imports for four countries. It is interesting to note that many of the countries, that are important buyers of a country's exports, are also significant sources of their imports.

Table 1 The trading patterns of four countries (2005).

Argentina	
Main export destinations	*Main source of imports*
a. Brazil	a. Brazil
b. Chile	b. USA
c. China	c. China
d. USA	d. Germany
France	
Main export destinations	*Main source of imports*
a. Germany	a. Germany
b. Italy	b. Belgium
c. Spain	c. Italy
d. Belgium	d. Netherlands

Malaysia	
Main export destinations	*Main source of imports*
a. USA	a. China
b. Singapore	b. Japan
c. Brazil	c. USA
d. Japan	d. Singapore
Nigeria	
Main export destinations	*Main source of imports*
a. USA	a. China
b. India	b. USA
c. Brazil	c. Netherlands
d. Spain	d. UK

 **Activity 1**

Table 2 India's main trading partners in 2005.

Main export destinations	*Main source of imports*
a. UAE	a. China
b. USA	b. USA
c. China	c. UAE
d. Hong Kong	d. Saudi Arabia

India exports a range of products including fruit, meat, minerals, spices, services and wheat. It imports, among other items, capital goods, edible oils, gold, and silver.

a. What proportion of the main countries, that India exports to, also forms its main sources of imports?

b. Explain two reasons for countries to buy spices from India.

Changes in Exports and Imports

There are a number of factors that influence the value of a country's exports and imports. These include:

- **The country's inflation rate:** If the country has a relatively high rate of inflation, domestic households and firms are likely to buy a significant number of imports. The country's firms are also likely to experience some difficulty in exporting. A fall in inflation, however, would increase the country's international competitiveness and would be likely to increase exports and reduce imports.

- **The country's exchange rate:** A fall in a country's exchange rate will lower export prices and raise import prices (see unit 50). This will be likely to increase the value of its exports and lower the amount spent on imports.

- **Productivity:** The more productive a country's workers are, the lower the labour costs per unit and cheaper its products. A rise in productivity is likely to lead to greater number of households and firms buying more of the country's products – so exports should rise and imports fall.

- **Quality:** A fall in the quality of a country's products, relative to other countries' products, would have an adverse effect on the country's balance of trade in goods and services.

- **Marketing:** The amount of exports sold is influenced not only by their quality and price but also by the effectiveness of domestic firms in marketing their products. Similarly, the quantity of imports purchased is affected by the efficacy of the marketing undertaken by foreign firms.

- **Domestic GDP:** If incomes rise at home, more imports may be bought. Firms are likely to buy more raw materials and capital goods, and some of these will come from abroad. Households will buy more products, and some of these will be imported. The rise in domestic demand may also encourage some domestic firms to switch from the foreign to the domestic market. If this does occur, exports will fall.

- **Foreign GDP:** If incomes abroad rise, foreigners will buy more products. This may enable the country to export more.

- **Trade restrictions:** A relaxation in trade restrictions abroad (see unit 52) will make it easier for domestic firms to sell their products to other countries.

Activity 2

UK's invisible exports to China rose by 54% between 2003 and 2005. The country sold a range of invisible exports including private medical insurance, financial services and banking. The biggest growth, however, was in construction services, including those provided on projects for airports, hotels, libraries, offices, motorways, offices, power stations, railways and sports venues.

a. What is meant by an 'invisible export'?
b. Is demand for construction services in China likely to increase or decrease in the future? Explain your answer.

The Causes of a Current Account Deficit

The factors influencing changes in exports and imports give an indication as to what can cause a current account deficit. One is incomes at home and abroad. A deficit arising from low incomes abroad and/or high incomes at home can be referred to as a **cyclical deficit**.

A high exchange rate can also cause a current account deficit. This is because it will mean high export prices and low import prices. There may also be, what can be called, **structural problems**. These can include a problem with the products manufactured by firms in the country, costs incurred to produce them, prices at which they are sold and strategies adopted for marketing them.

The consequences of a current account deficit

A current account deficit may mean that a country is consuming more goods and services than what it is producing. This is sometimes referred to as a *'country living beyond its means'*. A current account deficit can also mean a reduction in inflationary pressure, as there will be a fall in aggregate demand.

A current account deficit does, however, mean that output and employment is lower than possible. If more goods and services were to be produced at home, more workers would be employed.

Significance of a current account deficit depends on its size, duration and cause. A small deficit that lasts for only a short time is unlikely to cause any problem. A deficit that has been caused by the import of raw materials and capital goods, changes in income (domestic and abroad) or a high exchange rate, is likely to be self-correcting over time (irrespective of its size). Imported raw materials and capital goods will be used to produce goods and services, some of which will be exported. Recessions abroad will not last and with a rise in incomes, the country can export more to foreign countries. A deficit on the current account will put downward pressure on the exchange rate. If it does fall, exports will become cheaper and imports will become more expensive – as a result a deficit may be eliminated.

A deficit arising due to a lack of international competitiveness is more serious. This is because it will not be self-correcting. If firms' costs of production are higher due to lower productivity or the quality of the products produced are poor or the products made are not in high world demand, the deficit may persist. In this case, government may have to introduce policies, particularly *supply-side policies,* to improve the country's trade performance.

**Activity 3**

USA has had a large and growing current account deficit, since the 1990s, despite having a surplus on its trade in services balance.

a. Identify:
   (i) two possible causes of a current account deficit
   (ii) a part of the current account other than trade in services.

b. In recent years, did the USA have a deficit or surplus on its capital and financial accounts? Explain your answer.

c. Explain one reason for the growing concern of USA about its current account deficit.

Causes of a Current Account Surplus

A current account surplus may arise for a number of reasons including:

- **A low exchange rate:** This will make export prices cheap and import prices expensive.

- **High quality of domestically produced products.** This will encourage foreign and domestic citizens to purchase the country's output.

- **High incomes abroad.** This will enable foreigners to buy a high volume of the country's exports.

- **Low costs of production.** This may make an economy's products internationally competitive.

Consequences of a Current Account Surplus

An increase in a current account surplus will increase an economy's aggregate demand and so may lead to a rise in real GDP and higher employment. More money will enter the economy than will leave it. It also means that the country is consuming fewer products than it is producing.

If an economy is operating a floating exchange rate, an increase in a current account surplus may result in an appreciation in the exchange rate. This is because demand for the economy's currency will exceed its supply.

Summary

- International trade is the exchange of products across national boundaries.

- International trade may involve relatively long distances, may be with countries with different cultures and languages, may be in a different currency, may face trade restrictions and may involve more competition.

- Main destinations of exports are also the main source of their imports, for many countries.

- Exports and imports are influenced by changes in the inflation rate, exchange rate, productivity, quality, marketing, income and trade restrictions.

- An increase in a current account deficit may be caused by a change in income at home or abroad, a change in the exchange rate or a change in international competitiveness.

- Gravity of a current account deficit depends on its size, duration and cause. A deficit arising from a lack of international competitiveness is the most serious.

- A current account surplus may be caused by a low exchange rate, high quality of domestically produced products, high income abroad and low costs of production.

- An increase in a current account surplus will increase aggregate demand and may raise the exchange rate.

Teacher's Tip

Find out the major trading partners of your country and the reasons for the same.

Multiple Choice Questions

1. The table shows the main source of export earnings with respective product, for four countries.

Country	Product	Percentage of export earnings
W	cars	58
X	copper	63
Y	financial services	70
Z	oil	80

What can be concluded from this information?

a. Countries X and Z specialise in the production of primary products.
b. Country W and Y specialise in the production of tertiary products.
c. Country Z earns most of its export revenue from the sale of secondary products.
d. Country Z earns maximum export revenue.

2. Which of the following would be likely to increase Brazil's exports?

a. A fall in income in Brazil's main trading partners.
b. A fall in the population of Brazil's main trading partners.
c. An increase in the productivity of Brazilian workers.
d. An increase in the rate of inflation in Brazil.

3. Which of the following would cause a rise in Japan's export of services to Malaysia?

a. Japanese airlines carrying more Malaysian passengers.
b. Malaysian firms buying more ships from Japan.
c. More Japanese tourists visiting Malaysia.
d. More Malaysians travellers on Japanese-built trains, in Malaysia.

4. A firm which previously had traded internally, decides to trade externally. What additional risk will it face?

a. Its costs of production may rise.
b. The government may impose a sales tax on its products.
c. There may be a change in demand for its products.
d. Trade restrictions may be placed on its products.

UNIT 49

International Trade

The nature of international trade was discussed in the previous unit. In this unit, the benefits and disadvantages of specialisation of countries are explored and the basis, on which countries specialise, is explained.

The Benefits of Specialisation of Countries

Countries usually concentrate on producing those products, that their resources are best at making. A country with an abundance of fertile land and a small number of workers, for instance, may decide to concentrate on producing arable crops. In contrast, Hong Kong, which has a very limited supply of land and a highly skilled labour force concentrates on financial services. There are a number of advantages, that countries can gain from specialisation. These include:

- **Higher output:** Consumers throughout the world can enjoy more goods and services and hence have higher living standards.

- **Lower costs:** If the firms of a country are good at producing a product, they can specialise in its manufacture. This will enable them to produce on a large scale and hence take advantage of economies of scale. Firms can also buy their raw materials from specialist firms, which are producing at low costs.

- **Spread of ideas and technology:** Specialisation means that countries have to trade. Engaging in international trade can help in the exchange of new management ideas, information about new products and new technology.

- **Increase in competition:** Taking part in international trade can also increase competitive pressure on firms, to be efficient and gives consumers more choice.

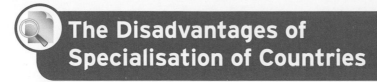

The Disadvantages of Specialisation of Countries

Generally, it is thought that international specialisation and trade increases economic welfare but, nevertheless, there are possible disadvantages including:

- **There can be a decrease in demand.** Firms in another country may become more efficient at producing the product or a substitute product may be developed.

- **There may be supply problems.** This particularly applies to primary products. The supply of rice, for instance, may be hit by bad weather and the supply of gold may be reduced by the collapse of a gold mine.

- **Interdependency.** Specialisation means that firms become more dependent on other firms and consumers rely on firms in other countries for some of their products. A natural disaster or war in one country may mean that domestic firms cannot get their raw materials and consumers may be able to buy particular products only, from other countries.

- **Trade restrictions.** A country's exports may have trade restrictions placed on them, making it difficult for them to be sold abroad.

 Absolute Advantage

It used to be thought that most international trade was based on what is called absolute advantage. This is not actually the case, although it does account for some of international trade.

A country has an absolute advantage in producing a product, if it can produce it using fewer resources than other countries. Table 1 shows that Kenya has an absolute advantage in producing horticultural products, while Hungary enjoys the same in machinery.

Table 1 Output per worker per day.

	Horticultural products (number of plants)	Machines
Kenya	200	1
Hungary	100	5

If Kenya specialises in horticultural products and Hungary specialises in machinery, total output will increase. Kenya can then export horticultural products and import machinery while Hungary can export machinery and import horticultural products. By specialising and trading, the countries improve the international allocation of resources.

 # Comparative Advantage

It is on comparative advantage, rather than absolute advantage, that most of international trade is based. A country is said to have a comparative advantage in producing a product, if it can produce it at a lower opportunity cost.

Comparative advantage explains how two countries can mutually benefit from international trade, even if one is better at producing all products than the other country. Table 2 shows that Germany is better at producing, both cars and chemicals, than the Netherlands.

Table 2 Output per worker per day.

	Cars	Chemicals (units)
Germany	4	400
Italy	1	200

Germany can make four times as many cars as Italy but only twice as many chemicals. The opportunity cost of producing one car is lower in Germany, than in Italy. It is 100 chemicals in Germany whereas, in Italy it is 200 chemicals. So, Germany's comparative advantage lies in cars.

Whilst Italy has an absolute disadvantage in producing both products, it has a comparative advantage in making chemicals. Its opportunity cost of making one unit of chemicals is 1/200th of a car whereas it is 1/100th of a car in Germany.

So, Germany should specialise in making cars and Italy should concentrate on producing chemicals. Germany should export cars and import chemicals and Italy should export chemicals and import cars.

 **Activity 1**

Table 3 Output per worker per day

	Clothing (units)	Fish
Bangladesh	50	200
Vietnam	100	600

Using the information in the table above, answer the following questions:
a. Explain which country has the absolute advantage in producing clothing.
b. Explain which country has the comparative advantage in producing clothing.
c. What will Vietnam export to Bangladesh?

Changes in Comparative Advantage

Comparative advantage changes over time. In the past, USA and the UK had a comparative advantage in producing steel. Now the comparative advantage lies with Brazil and Malaysia.

Comparative advantages changes, as relative costs change. A country may gain a comparative advantage in a product because it discovers new sources of minerals, makes its land more fertile, adopts new technology or increase the productivity of its workers by improving education and training. India, with a labour force having good ICT skills and good command over English, has the comparative advantage in operating call centres. China is currently improving its performance in producing computers and may soon gain a comparative advantage.

Activity 2

India's wine industry is growing. In 2005, it produced 5 million litres a year, compared with a global market of 32 billion. Currently, France is the major producer of wine. Most of India's wineries are in the region of Maharashtra. India's exports of wine are growing at 9 per cent a year. Foreign investment in the Indian wine industry is predicted to grow from $3.5 million (in 2005) to more than $100 million (by 2010).

a. Which country appears to have the comparative advantage in producing wine?

b. Explain one reason, why India may be able to compete in the global wine market in the future.

The Terms of Trade

The terms of trade is the rate at which one country's products are exchanged for those of other countries. It is measured as:

$$\frac{\text{Index of export prices}}{\text{Index of import prices}} \times 100$$

An improvement in the terms of trade occurs, if export prices rise relative to import prices. In this case, a given quantity of exports will be exchanged for a greater quantity of imports. In contrast, an unfavourable movement occurs when export prices fall relative to import prices.

The impact of a change in the terms of trade is not, however, straightforward. It depends mainly on the causes of price change. If export prices rise due to an increased demand for the country's products, the country will be selling more products for a higher price and will be able to afford to buy more imports. If, however, export prices have risen because of inflation, demand is likely to fall. Each export would be exchanged for more imports but fewer exports would be sold. Export revenue would fall and, in total, fewer imports could be bought.

 **Summary**

- Specialisation of countries can increase output, reduce costs and spread new ideas and technology.

- The risks of specialisation of countries include – rival countries' firms may start producing the product, substitute products might be developed, supply problems may be encountered, consumers may become reliant on firms in other countries and trade restrictions may be imposed on their products.

- A country may have an absolute disadvantage in producing a product but may still concentrate on producing it, if it can make it at a lower opportunity cost than other countries.

- A country can gain a comparative advantage in producing a product by discovering new resources or by raising the productivity of capital and labour.

- The terms of trade is the ratio of export prices to import prices.

 Teacher's Tip

In explaining comparative advantage, it is useful to give a numerical example. Keep this simple and make sure that it does show comparative (rather than absolute) advantage.

Multiple Choice Questions

1. Which of the following conditions promote international trade?
   a. Difficulties in communication between countries
   b. Differences in the quantity and quality of resources in countries
   c. High trade restrictions
   d. High transport costs

2. 'Brazil has a comparative advantage in the production of steel.' What does this statement mean?
   a. Brazil buys more steel than other countries.
   b. Brazil produces more steel than other countries.
   c. Steel accounts for a higher proportion of the output of Brazil than other countries.
   d. The opportunity cost of producing steel in Brazil is lower than that in other countries.

3. The table shows the output per worker for two products, in two countries.

   Table 4 Output per worker

	Tractors	Wheat (tonnes)
Country Y	50	500
Country Z	10	250

   What can be concluded from this information?
   a. Country Z has the comparative advantage in producing tractors.
   b. Country Z has the absolute advantage in producing both products.
   c. Country Y will export tractors and import wheat.
   d. It will not be beneficial for the two countries to trade.

4. Saudi Arabia specialises in the production of oil and exports most of its production. What impact, would the discovery of oil in other countries be likely to have, on the Saudi Arabian economy?

	Current account position	economic growth
a.	increased surplus	increase
b.	increased surplus	reduces
c.	reduced surplus	reduces
d.	reduced surplus	increase

Exchange Rates

Unit 48 mentioned that a high exchange rate may cause a current account deficit. This unit explains the meaning of the exchange rate, examines the effect of a change in the exchange rate on export and import prices, compares fixed and floating exchange rates and explores the reasons for purchase and sale of currencies.

The Exchange Rate

An exchange rate is the price of one currency in terms of another currency (or currencies). An exchange rate of £1 = 80 Indian rupees means that it will cost 80 Indian rupees to buy £1 and £1 to buy 80 Indian rupees. An exchange rate index is the price of one currency in terms of a basket of other currencies, weighted according to their importance in the country's international transactions. For example, the *sterling effective exchange rate* measures the value of the pound sterling against a number of currencies, particularly the euro, US dollar and Japanese yen.

The Effect of a Change in the Exchange Rate on Export and Import Prices

In unit 48, it was mentioned that a rise in a country's exchange rate would raise the price of its exports and lower the price of its imports. More precisely, the price of exports rises in terms of foreign currency and the price of imports falls in terms of the domestic currency. For instance, initially 80 Indian rupees may equal £1. In this case an Indian export valued at 800 rupees will sell in the UK at £10. A UK import valued at £20 will sell in India for 1 600 rupees. If India experiences a rise in its exchange rate against the pound sterling, it means that rupees will buy more pounds now. The value of the rupee may rise so that 80 rupees equal £2. This significant rise would mean that the Indian export would now sell for £20 in the UK and the £20 import from the UK would sell for 800 rupees in India. If export prices rise, fewer exports will be sold. The effect on export revenue will depend on price elasticity of demand. If demand is elastic, the rise in price will cause a fall in revenue whereas if demand is inelastic, revenue will rise. In practice, in many export markets, there is considerable competition from firms throughout the world and hence, the demand is elastic.

A Fixed Exchange Rate

A fixed exchange rate is one, whose value is fixed against the value of another currency (or currencies) and is maintained by the government. The value may be set at a precise

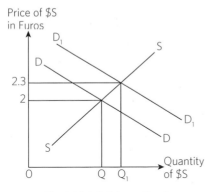

Fig. 1 **Maintaining a fixed exchange rate**

value or within a given margin. If market forces are pushing down the value of the currency, the government will step in and seek to increase its price, either by buying the currency or raising the rate of interest. In Fig. 1, the price of one US dollar is initially two euros. Demand for the dollar rises and, if left to market forces, its price would rise to 2.3 euros. If, however, the government wants to keep the value of the dollar at two euros, it may ask its central bank to sell dollars. If it does so, the supply of dollars traded on the foreign exchange market will increase and price may stay at two euros.

The main advantage of a fixed exchange rate is, that it creates *certainty*. Firms that buy and sell products abroad will know the exact amount they will pay and receive in terms of their own currency, if the exchange rate does not change. A fixed exchange rate can, however, mean that a government has to use up a considerable amount of foreign currency. If the exchange rate is under downward pressure, it may also have to adopt other macroeconomic policy objectives. If a government cannot maintain an exchange rate at a given parity, it may have to change its value. A change in the value of the currency from one exchange rate to a lower one is referred to as **devaluation**. A rise in a fixed exchange rate is called a **revaluation**.

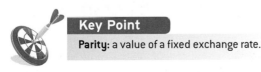

Key Point

Parity: a value of a fixed exchange rate.

A Floating Exchange Rate

A floating exchange rate is one which is determined by market forces. If demand for the currency rises or the supply decreases, the value of the currency will rise. Such a rise is referred to as an **appreciation**. In contrast, a **depreciation** is a fall in the value of a floating exchange rate. It can be caused by a fall in demand for the currency or a rise in its supply. Fig. 2 shows a decrease in demand for pounds sterling, causing the price of the pound to fall.

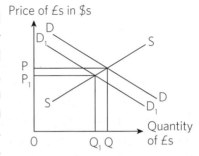

Fig. 2 **A depreciation in the value of £**

A floating exchange rate may help to eliminate a growing current account deficit. If demand for import rises whilst demand for exports falls, supply of the currency will rise (as individuals and firms sell it to buy foreign currency) and demand for the currency will fall. This will lower the value of the currency and hence reduce export prices and raise import prices. Even with a growing current account deficit, however, demand for the currency may rise. Firms and individuals may still buy more of the currency to invest in the country, if they think that economic prospects are good. A floating exchange rate, nevertheless, does allow a government to concentrate on other objectives.

The main disadvantage with a floating exchange rate is that it can *fluctuate*, making it difficult for firms to plan ahead.

Activity 1

The Chinese government has been criticised for maintaining a low value of its currency, in order to keep its products internationally competitive. It has been doing this by selling its currency.

a.   Does it appear that China is operating a fixed or a floating exchange rate? Explain your answer.

b.   How does a low value of its currency help to keep a country's products 'internationally competitive'?

c.   Explain how selling a currency can keep its value down.

The Reasons Why Currencies are Traded

There are a number of reasons for individuals, firms and governments to buy and sell a currency. These reasons can be examined by considering the specific example of demand and supply of Indian rupees.

The demand for Indian rupees will come from:

- Foreigners wishing to buy Indian goods and services.

- Foreign-based Indian firms, sending back profits to India.

- Foreign banks paying interest on money held by Indian residents.

- Foreign firms paying dividends on shares held by Indian residents.

- Indians working abroad, wishing to send money back home to relatives.

- Foreign firms wishing to buy Indian firms and setting up units in India.

- Foreign firms and individuals wanting to buy shares in Indian companies, to save in Indian banks and lend to Indian firms or individuals.

- Foreign governments wanting to hold rupees as reserves.

- Speculators buying rupees in the expectation that the rupee will rise in value in the future. Significant sums of currency can be traded by speculators.

The supply of rupees will come from:

- Individuals wishing to buy foreign goods and services.

- Multinational companies based in India, sending profits home.

- Indian banks paying interest on money held by foreign people living abroad.

- Indian firms paying dividends on shares held by foreigners.

- Foreigners working in India, sending money home to their relatives.

- Multinational companies wanting to buy Indian firms and set up businesses in India.

- Indian firms and individuals wanting to buy shares in foreign companies, save in foreign banks and lend to foreign firms and individuals.

- The Indian government wishing to hold foreign currencies, in its reserves.

- Speculators selling rupees because they expect the price of the rupee to fall.

Fig. 3 shows the effect of a rise in the Indian rate of interest on the market for Indian rupees. This will encourage foreigners to place money in Indian banks and hence, increase the demand for Indian rupees and raise its value.

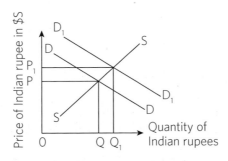

Fig. 3 The effect of a rise in the Indian rate of interest

Activity 2

In each case draw a diagram to show the effect, on the market for Baht (the currency of Thailand) of:

a.   a Japanese multinational company opening up a branch in Thailand
b.   more tourists from Thailand going to India on holiday
c.   Thai banks lending to Ghanaian firms
d.   reduction in demand for Thai exports.

Summary

- An exchange rate is the price of one currency in terms of another currency (or currencies).

- A rise in the exchange rate will increase the price of exports in terms of foreign currency and lower the price of imports in the domestic currency.

- A fixed exchange rate is maintained at a certain rate. Its main advantage is that it reduces uncertainty.

- A floating exchange rate is determined by market forces. If there is a current account deficit, the exchange rate may adjust automatically to make domestic products more competitive.

- Domestic currency may be bought by foreigners wanting to buy the country's products, to invest in the country and due to the expectation of a rise in the value of currency.

- Domestic currency is sold to buy foreign products, to invest in other currencies and for the fear of a decline in its value.

Teacher's Tip

In explaining the method of determining a floating exchange rate, it is useful to draw a diagram. Remember that on the vertical axis of an exchange rate diagram, you should express the price of the currency in terms of another currency.

Multiple Choice Questions

1. 'The Indian rupee fell in value against most major currencies last week.'

   What does this refer to?
   a. India's exchange rate
   b. India's inflation rate
   c. India's interest rate
   d. India's trade position

2. What is meant by 'an appreciation of the currency'?
   a. A fall in value caused by government intervention.
   b. A fall in value caused by market forces.
   c. A rise in value caused by government intervention.
   d. A rise in value caused by market forces.

3. What effect, would a rise in a country's exchange rate have, on its export and import prices?

	Export prices	Import prices
a.	increase	increase
b.	increase	decrease
c.	decrease	decrease
d.	decrease	increase

4. What might have caused the change in the value of the Nigerian currency, shown in the diagram below?
   a. Foreign firms investing in Nigeria.
   b. Foreigners placing more money in Nigerian banks.
   c. Nigerian buying more imports.
   d. Nigerians speculating that the value of the naira will rise.

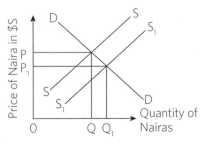

Changes in Exchange Rates

Having touched on the reasons for the purchase and sale of currencies in the previous chapter, this unit examines the reasons for a change in exchange rate, the consequences of changes in the exchange rate, policies employed by the government to correct a current account deficit and the nature of international competitiveness.

Changes in the Exchange Rate

As indicated in the previous unit, an exchange rate may change as a result of a change in the current account balance, direct and portfolio investment, speculation and government action. An increase in a current account surplus would tend to cause the value of the currency to rise. For instance, if export revenue rises relative to import expenditure, demand for the currency will rise. An increase in investment in the country can also cause the price of the currency to rise. If it is generally believed that the currency will rise in value, speculators will act in a way which will help in materialising their expectation. They will buy the currency which, in the case of a floating exchange rate, will push up its value.

A government and its agencies can seek to influence the value of its currency in three main ways. One is by *buying and selling the currency*. If it wants to raise the exchange rate, it will instruct its central bank to buy the currency, using foreign currency to do so. Of course, there is a limit to which it can do this, as it will have a limited supply of foreign currency in its reserves. A central bank may also raise the rate of interest, in a bid to raise the value of the currency. A higher interest rate may attract what are called *hot money flows*. These are funds, which are moved around the financial markets of the world, to take advantage of changes in interest rates and exchange rates. If more people want to place money into the country's financial institutions, it will increase the demand for the currency. In addition, a government may try to raise the value of the currency by introducing measures to *increase exports and reduce imports*.

The Consequences of a Change in the Exchange Rate

A change in the exchange rate, besides affecting exports and imports, may influence economic growth, employment and inflation. A fall in the exchange rate, by lowering export prices and raising import prices, is likely to increase demand for domestic products. This rise in aggregate demand can increase output and employment of the economy, if it is not operating at full capacity initially. Fig. 1 shows real GDP rising from Y to Y_1 as a result of a rise in net exports.

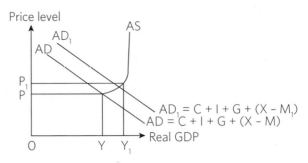

Fig. 1 The effect of a rise in net exports

A fall in the exchange rate can, however, increase inflationary pressure for a number of reasons. Imported raw materials will be more expensive, which will raise the costs of production. Finished imported products will also be more expensive. These appear in the country's consumer prices index and hence a rise in their price will directly boost inflation. It will also increase inflation indirectly, by reducing the pressure on domestic firms to keep price-rise to a minimum, in order to remain competitive.

 Activity 1

The UK operates a floating exchange rate. Between 1996 and 2006, the value of the pound sterling was relatively stable. It was also relatively high, as foreigners wanted to invest in an economy perceived to be well performing.

a.   What is meant by a floating exchange rate?

b.   Identify one benefit of a stable exchange rate.

c.   Explain one advantage and one disadvantage of a high exchange rate.

Measures to Correct a Current Account Deficit

A government may seek to reduce a current account deficit, by reducing the value of its currency. Such a move can be referred to as an *expenditure switching measure*. This is because, it is designed to encourage domestic and foreign citizens to switch their purchases away from foreign products, towards those produced by firms in the country. Import restrictions (see unit 52) are another example of an expenditure switching measure.

A government may also employ *expenditure reducing measures*. These are designed to improve the current account position by reducing demand for products in general, both domestic and foreign. The idea is that this will reduce imports and by making it more difficult for domestic firms to sell on the home market, will force them to increase exports. Expenditure reducing measures include increasing income tax, raising the rate of interest and pushing up rates of indirect taxes.

Expenditure switching and expenditure reducing measures, however, are unlikely to increase exports and reduce imports in the long run. To improve international competitiveness, governments are increasingly using *supply-side* policy measures. For example, improving education and training should raise labour productivity. If this occurs, costs of production should fall and the quality of products produced should improve.

Activity 2

Decide which of the following are expenditure reducing and which are expenditure switching measures.
a.   A rise in sales tax.
b.   Organising a trade exhibition to promote the country's products.
c.   A subsidy given to domestic firms.
d.   A limit being placed on import allowed into the country.
e.   A devaluation of the currency.

 International Competitiveness

A country might be called internationally competitive, if it provides the goods and services desired by consumers at a price acceptable to them. There are a number of indicators of a country's international competitiveness. These include its economic growth rate, its share of world trade, levels of expenditure on research and development, the quantity and quality of education and training and the state of the country's infrastructure. A competitive economy is likely to have a stable economic growth rate, a reasonable share of world trade, high levels of investment and expenditure on research and development, good quality education and training and developed infrastructure.

In the short term, changes in a country's exchange rate and inflation rate can influence its international competitiveness. A fall in both would be likely to make the country's products more attractive to buyers at home and abroad. Changes in productivity, however, will have long-lasting effects. Productivity can be raised by, for instance, investment, education and training and improved working conditions.

Summary

- The value of the exchange rate is influenced by the current account balance, direct and portfolio investment, speculation and government action.

- A fall in the exchange rate would be likely to improve the current account position, boost economic growth and employment but may also tend to increase inflationary pressure.

- A government can seek to improve the current account position by encouraging people to buy more domestic and fewer foreign products or by discouraging people from buying products in general. In the long run, supply-side policies are likely to be most effective.

- An economy will become more internationally competitive, if it can lower its costs of production and raise the quality of what it produces.

- Three important influences on international competitiveness are the exchange rate, inflation rate and productivity.

Teacher's Tip

Think carefully about which curve or curves will shift, when there is a transaction involving foreign exchange. Remember, for instance, that when we buy imports – we sell our own currency and this purchase causes the supply curve to shift to the right.

Multiple Choice Questions

1. Which of the following would cause an increase in the value of the US dollar?
   a. An expectation that the value of the dollar will rise in the future.
   b. A decrease in the US rate of interest.
   c. An increase in US imports.
   d. The sale of US dollars by the US Central Bank.

2. What combination of factors is most likely to cause a fall in the value of a floating currency?

	Demand for the currency	Supply of the currency
a.	increase	increase
b.	increase	decrease
c.	decrease	decrease
d.	decrease	increase

3. If the value of the pound sterling against the US dollar changes from £1 = $2 to £1 = $1.5, what effect will this have?
   a. UK exports to the US will rise in price.
   b. The US will import more UK products.
   c. UK tourists will be able to buy more, for less money, in the US.
   d. The value of the pound sterling has risen in price.

4. Which of the following is most likely to reduce a deficit on the current account of the balance of payments?
   a. A fall in government expenditure on benefits.
   b. A fall in income tax.
   c. A rise in the consumer confidence.
   d. A rise in the value of the currency.

UNIT 52

Free Trade and Protection

Unit 49 discussed some of the benefits of specialisation of countries and trading and mentioned that a risk of specialisation is imposition of trade restrictions. This unit examines the benefits of free trade, the methods of protection and the arguments for protecting a country's industries from foreign competition.

The Benefits of Free Trade

Free international trade occurs when there are no restrictions on the products bought by firms and consumers from abroad or products sold by firms to other countries and no imposition of special taxes.

Such unrestricted trade should allow countries to concentrate on what they are best at producing and hence allow for an efficient allocation of resources. If countries are able to exploit their comparative advantage fully – world output, employment and living standards should be higher, than if resources were less efficiently allocated. Selling freely to a global market should enable firms to take greater advantage of economies of scale, raise competitive forces and give them access to more sources of raw materials and components. These effects should lower prices for consumers, who will also gain from a greater choice of products.

Activity 1

The United States has been accused of hypocrisy by preaching free trade whilst itself imposing trade restrictions and putting up barriers to foreign takeovers of US firms.

a. What is meant by free trade?
b. Identify two trade restrictions.

Methods of Protection

Despite the potential advantages of free trade, every country in the world engages in protectionism, albeit to differing extents. Protectionism is the protection of the country's industries from the competition posed by other countries' industries and hence involves restriction of free trade.

There are a number of methods, a country or groups of countries may employ, to protect their industries. These include:

- **A tariff:** This is a tax on imported products and is also referred to as a *customs duty or import duty*. Sometimes tariffs are used to raise government revenue but most commonly, they are used to discourage the purchase of imports. Placing a tariff on an imported product raises its price. The tariff is likely to be set at a level which will mean that the imported products will sell at a higher price than domestically produced goods.

- **A quota:** This is a limit placed on the quantity of a good that can be imported. For instance, a country may limit the number of cars that can be imported into the country at 40 000.

- **Embargo:** This is a complete ban on the import of a product or trade with another country.

- **Exchange control:** A government may try to stop households and firms from buying imports, by restricting the availability of foreign currency. Those wanting to buy foreign products, travel or invest abroad will have to apply to buy foreign currency.

- **Quality standards:** A country may require imports to reach artificially high standards. This measure will either dissuade other countries from selling to the country or push up their costs and prices, if they do try to sell to the country.

- **Expensive paperwork:** Requiring foreign firms, who wish to sell to the country, to fill out a considerable amount of time-consuming paperwork may persuade them to switch over to other markets.

- **Voluntary export restraints (VERs):** A government may persuade the government of the exporting country to agree to restrict the number of units of a product sold by it. It may do this by agreeing to do the same or by threatening to impose tariffs or quotas, if they do not agree.

- **Subsidies:** A government may protect its domestic industries from cheaper imports by giving them subsidies. Such help may enable domestic firms to sell at lower prices, which may undercut the price of imports.

Besides placing restrictions on imports, a government may impose restrictions on exports also if it is concerned that selling the product abroad will lead to shortages at home. In June 2006, for instance, the Indian government imposed a ban on the export of pulses, including dal, until March 2007. The export ban was introduced to stabilise domestic prices, after the output of pulses in the country was saverely affected by a drought.

Arguments for Protectionism

A number of arguments are presented for protecting domestic industries. Some favour protection of particular domestic industries while some advocate protection of all domestic industries. The strength of the arguments varies.

- **Protection of infant industries:** The argument is that new industries, which have the potential to grow, may be eliminated by foreign competition before they have really started. Giving them some protection may enable them to grow, take advantage of economies of scale and become internationally competitive. It can, however, be difficult to identify the new industries which indeed have such a potential. There is also the risk that the industries will not respond to the opportunity by becoming more efficient but may become dependent on the protection.

- **Protection of declining industries:** These industries are also known as *sunset industries*. In a dynamic economy, some industries are likely to be declining. If other industries are expanding and labour is mobile, this may not be a problem. However, if labour is immobile, the decline of a major industry may lead to a significant rise in unemployment. A government may decide to protect the industry to allow it to decline gradually, in order to avoid this. As workers retire and leave of their own accord, the protection can be removed. Owners of the industry, however, may resist the removal of the protection.

- **Protection of strategic industries:** These are industries essential for the survival of the country. Most governments provide some protection to their agricultural and defence related industries, to ensure consistency of supplies. A country, that is dependent on imports of food and weapons, runs the risk of its supplies being cut off due to wars or natural disasters.

- **Raising employment and improving the trade position:** Reducing imports can enable domestic firms to expand and take on more workers. This would raise employment and income. There is a high risk, however, of *retaliation*. If other countries do respond by imposing trade restrictions, the country will buy fewer imports but will also sell fewer exports. So employment, income and the trade position may not improve. Restricting imports of raw materials may be particularly harmful as it will raise domestic firms' costs of production.

- **Protection of industries from low wage competition:** This is not a strong argument in favour of protectionism. Low wages do not necessarily mean low costs of production. A foreign industry may pay low wages but if the productivity of its workers is low, its average cost of production may be high. If both wages and costs are low, it may mean that a foreign industry has a comparative advantage. If this is the case, then under conditions of free trade, demand for the industry's products is likely to rise and this higher demand will probably push up wages.

- **Protection of industries from unfair foreign competition.** It is generally agreed that trade restrictions can be imposed to prevent *dumping*. This occurs when foreign firms sell products at a price, below costs of production. This makes it very difficult for domestic firms to compete. The foreign firms may be enjoying subsidies by their governments. A common motive behind dumping is to drive domestic firms out of the market, gain a large market share and then raise prices. Firms that do not do this may have problems competing, although their costs may still be competitive due to higher labour productivity.

The strongest arguments for protecting domestic industries are probably the infant industry, strategic industry and protection from unfair competition arguments.

The key arguments against protectionism are that it can result in lower choice, higher prices, inefficiency and retaliation. These arguments are stronger against protecting declining industries, raising employment and improving the trade position and protecting industries from low wage competition.

 **Activity 2**

In August 2006, the EU was debating the introduction of anti-dumping duties on shoes from China and Vietnam. A fifteen month investigation established, that dumping had taken place with the two countries subsidising their shoe producers. Between 2000 and 2005, European footwear production had contracted by about 30% and nearly 40 000 jobs in the industry had been lost.

a. Explain what is meant by dumping.
b. What impact may the imposition of anti-dumping duties on shoes from Vietnam have, on their sales in the EU?
c. What might happen to the EU shoe industry, without protection?

 Summary

- Free international trade can raise output, reduce prices and increase choice.

- The most common method of protecting domestic industries is to place a tariff on imports.

- Other methods of protecting domestic industries include – imposing a quota, imposing an embargo, setting artificially high quality standards, requiring completion of expensive paperwork, persuading the other country to agree to a voluntary export restraint and granting subsidies to domestic industries.

- The arguments for protecting domestic industries include – protecting infant industries, protecting declining industries, protecting strategic industries, raising employment, helping the trade position, protecting industries against low wage competition and protecting industries against unfair competition.

- The strongest arguments for protectionism are probably the infant industry, strategic industry and protecting industries against unfair competition arguments.

 Teacher's Tip

Remember that whilst increasing a *tariff increases* protectionism, increasing a quota *reduces* protectionism.

Multiple Choice Questions

1. Which of the following would reduce trade restrictions in a country?
   a. An increase in tariffs.
   b. An increase in quota limits.
   c. The imposition of exchange control.
   d. Tighter health and safety standards.

2. A government had been allowing manufactured goods to enter its country, without any trade restrictions. It, then, decides to impose a 10% tariff on all imported manufactured goods. What effect will this change have, on the cost of living and government revenue?

	cost of living	government revenue
a.	increases	increases
b.	increases	reduces
c.	reduces	reduces
d.	reduces	increases

3. What is meant by dumping?
   a. The employment of cheap labour
   b. The imposition of tariffs on imports
   c. The removal of health and safety standards
   d. The sale of products below cost price in another country

4. Under what circumstances, would the protection of infant industries be justified?
   a. If their long term costs are higher than the revenue earned by them.
   b. If they generate substantial external costs.
   c. If they have the potential to grow and gain a comparative advantage.
   d. If the number of workers they employ will decline over time.

Answer Key

Activity 1

a. Balance of trade in goods and services = exports minus imports.
$6 585m – $9 057m = –$2 472m.

b.

	R millions
Trade in goods	29 495
Trade in services	–3 609
Income	–22 514
Current transfers	–6 422
	–3 050

c.

	£ million
Current balance	–20 430
Capital account	1 243
Financial account	17 455
Net errors and omissions	1 732
	0

Activity 2

a. A current surplus means that the country has received more from its exports of goods and services, income and current transfers than it has spent on imports and the income and transfers it has sent abroad.

b. Income.

Multiple Choice Questions

1. b

   In 2009, import expenditure exceeded export revenue. In the other three years, there was a trade surplus.

2. a

   Insurance is a service and it is being bought by Indonesia. b is a visible import, c would appear in the financial account as a transaction in assets and d is an invisible export.

3. b

   Mexico is selling a visible export and buying an invisible import.

4. a

   a is investment income. b, c and d would all appear in the financial account.

Unit 48

Activity 1

a. 75%. UAE, USA and China are all important destination of Indian exports and sources of its imports.

b. Countries may buy spices from India because of their higher quality and lower price offered by India, with respect to other countries.

Activity 2

a. An invisible export is a service sold abroad.

b. Demand for construction services in China is likely to increase in the future. This is because China is expected to continue to grow. More businesses are likely to set up and housing and places of entertainment to be built.

Activity 3

a. (i) A rise in the exchange rate and a rise in inflation.
    (ii) Trade in goods.

b. It must have had a surplus on its capital and financial accounts to offset the deficit on the current account.

c. It may be concerned that the products it is manufacturing are not in high world demand. If this is the case, it may continue to have a deficit.

Multiple Choice Questions

1. a

    Copper and oil are primary products and financial services is a tertiary product. From the information given, it is not possible to work out which country earns the maximum export revenue.

2. c

    A rise in the productivity of Brazilian workers is likely to reduce costs of production of Brazilian firms. This should allow them to sell their products abroad, at cheaper rates. a, c and d would all be likely to decrease Brazil's exports.

3. a

    Transporting airline passengers is a service. b would increase Japan's exports of goods. c is an invisible import of Japan and d is internal Malaysian trade.

4. d

    Trade restrictions are a feature of international trade. a, b and c would all occur with internal trade.

Unit 49

Activity 1

a. Vietnam has the absolute advantage in producing both products, as it can produce more clothing and catch more fish.

b. Bangladesh has the comparative advantage in producing clothing. In Bangladesh, 1 clothing unit = 4 fish but in Vietnam, 1 clothing unit = 6 fish. So Bangladesh has a lower opportunity cost in clothing than Vietnam. It can make half as many clothing units as Vietnam but only catch a third as many fish.

c. Vietnam will concentrate on its production of fish and export some to Bangladesh.

Activity 2

a. France appears to have the comparative advantage in wine production, as it is a major producer. Its dominant position, however, might be due to other factors such as government subsidies and trade restrictions.

b. More foreign investment in India's wine industry should enable it to grow. This should enable it to take advantage of economies of scale.

Multiple Choice Questions

1. b

   Differences in resources give rise to differences in efficiencies and opportunity cost ratios. a, c and d would all tend to discourage international trade.

2. d

   b and c may be true but it is d which needs to be satisfied necessarily. A country may have a comparative advantage in a few products.

3. c

   Country Y has the absolute advantage in both products. It has the comparative advantage in tractors. Its opportunity cost is 10 wheat, compared to an opportunity cost of 25 wheat in country Z. Country Z has the comparative advantage in wheat. It has an opportunity cost of 1/25 tractor compared to Y's 1/10.

4. c

   If another country discovers oil, the supply of oil would increase. This may reduce the price of oil. This, in turn, may decrease Saudi Arabia's export revenue and slow down its economic growth.

Unit 50

Activity 1

a. A fixed exchange rate, as the passage refers to the Chinese government 'maintaining a low value of its currency.'

b. A low value of a country's currency would mean that its export prices are low and its import prices are high.

c. Selling a currency would increase its supply. This, in turn, would reduce price. Fig. 1 shows the impact of an increase in the supply of the Chinese currency, the Yuan, on its price.

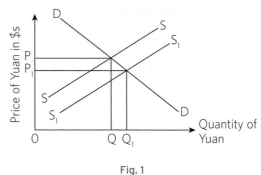

Fig. 1

Activity 2

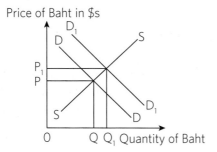

a. Japanese firms would buy Baht

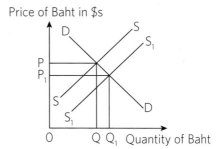

b. Tourists would sell Baht to buy rupee

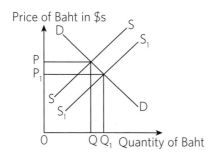

c. Thai banks would sell Baht to get the currency of Ghana

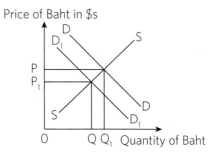

d. Fewer Bahts would be bought as fewer Thai products are being sold

Multiple Choice Questions

1. a

   A definition question.

2. d

   A definition question.

3. b

   A higher exchange rate makes exports more expensive and imports cheaper.

4. c

   The diagram shows that the value of the Naira has fallen due to an increase in its supply. Nigerians would sell the Naira to buy foreign currency in order to buy imports. a, c and d would all increase demand for the Naira.

Unit 51

Activity 1

a. A floating exchange rate is determined by market forces.

b. Certainty.

c. A high exchange rate may reduce inflationary pressure, as it means that import prices are low. This will keep down costs of production, reduce the price of finished imported goods and services and put pressure on domestic firms to keep their price rises under control. A disadvantage is that it may have a detrimental effect on the country's trade position, as it will mean that export prices are high and import prices are low.

Activity 2

a. expenditure reducing   b. expenditure switching   c. expenditure switching

d. expenditure switching   e. expenditure switching

Multiple Choice Questions

1. a

   If the value of the US $ is expected to increase in the future, people will buy it now. The higher demand will increase its price. b would reduce demand for the dollar. c and d would increase its supply.

2. d

   A straightforward question.

3. b

   The value of the £ has fallen. This will cause the price of UK exports to fall and the price of UK imports to rise. This is likely to mean that US will buy more of UK products.

4. a

Cutting government expenditure on benefits will reduce demand for all products including imports. b and c would raise demand and d would increase the price of exports whilst lowering the price of imports.

Unit 52

Activity 1

a. Free trade refers to the free movement of products across national boundaries. In such a case, there are no restrictions on the products bought and sold by firms and consumers to other countries.
b. A tariff and a quota. A tariff is a tax on imports and a quota is a limit on the quantity of goods that can be imported.

Activity 2

a. Dumping is the sale of products in a foreign market below cost price.
b. Anti-dumping duties are tariffs. Imposing them on Vietnamese shoes will raise their price. The impact of levying these duties will depend on the level they are set at. If they are set at a high level, they will make it difficult for Vietnamese firms to sell their shoes in the EU.
c. The EU shoe industry may collapse. The extract states that it contracted between 2000 and 2005. Other countries may enjoy a comparative advantage in shoe production.

Multiple Choice Questions

1. b

Increasing a quota limit would mean that more imports are being allowed into the country. a, c and d would all increase trade restrictions.

2. a

Imposing a tariff on manufactured goods will raise their price. Consumers will have to pay more for them, which will raise the cost of living. A tariff is also a source of government tax revenue.

3. d

A definition question. c is sometimes referred to as social dumping, as governments may feel compelled to lower or remove health and safety standards in order to attract foreign direct investment.

4. c

If infant industries have the potential to gain a comparative advantage, they may flourish and make an important contribution to the economy's output, employment and trade position. a and b are reasons for not supporting an industry. d is the declining industry argument.

Examination Practice

Multiple Choice Questions

1. When does free trade occur?
   a. When exports are directly exchanged for imports without the use of money
   b. When exports are subsidised by governments
   c. When goods are transported free of any direct charge
   d. When there are no import barriers placed on products

2. What is an advantage of international specialisation?
   a. Countries become more susceptible to external shocks.
   b. Countries can spread their risks over a range of products.
   c. There can be a more efficient use of resources.
   d. Those countries, with an absolute advantage, can gain at the expense of those with an absolute disadvantage.

3. What would increase a surplus on Namibia's balance of trade?
   a. European firms buying more food from Namibia
   b. European governments providing more foreign aid to Namibia
   c. Namibian firms selling more building materials in Namibia
   d. Namibian firms selling more insurance to other African countries

4. Which of the following is a credit item on Mexico's trade in services?
   a. Earnings from the sale of Mexican food in Peru
   b. Investment by Argentinean firms in Mexico
   c. Revenue received from Mexican insurance policies sold in Chile
   d. The money Mexican tourists spend in the US

5. What effect would the current account balance of a country, changing from a surplus to a deficit, is likely to have on its exchange rate and its unemployment rate?

	exchange rate	*unemployment rate*
a.	decreases	decreases
b.	decreases	increases
c.	increases	increases
d.	increases	decreases

6. Why might a fall in the exchange rate increase the rate of inflation?
   a. It will reduce employment.
   b. It will reduce a current account surplus.
   c. It will increase the cost of imported raw materials.
   d. It will increase the price of exports.
7. The table shows four economic indicators for four economies.
   Which country appears to exhibit the best economic performance?

	economic growth rate %	inflation rate %	unemployment rate %	current account balance ($m)
Country W	8	6	10	+50 000
Country X	5	4	8	-50 000
Country Y	3	2	3	-100
Country Z	1	-2	1	+100

   a. Country W
   b. Country X
   c. Country Y
   d. Country Z

8. A government increases tariffs on imports from its main trading partner. What is the likely consequence of this move?
   a. A fall in inflation
   b. A fall in trade barriers
   c. A rise in government revenue
   d. A rise in competitive pressures on domestic firms

9. Which of the following combinations of government measures would provide the maximum protection to the domestic car industry?

	Government subsidies to domestic producers	Tariffs on car imports
a.	decreases	increase
b.	decreases	decrease
c.	increase	decrease
d.	increase	increase

10. The table shows how a number of countries have altered tariffs and quotas on imports of TVs between 2000 and 2008. Which country had the greatest reduction in protection from TV imports in this period?

	Tariffs		Quotas	
	2000	2008	2000	2008
a.	20%	15%	200 000	180 000
b.	20%	25%	200 000	220 000
c.	20%	25%	200 000	160 000
d.	20%	15%	200 000	210 000

Structured Questions

1. Changes in the rate of exchange meant that exports of goods from Egypt decreased, as they became more expensive in other countries.
   a. What is meant by a rate of exchange? (3)
   b. Discuss the effect on production and employment, both in Egypt and in countries importing Egyptian goods, of an increase in price of Egyption exports. (7)
   c. Describe the structure of the balance of payments of a country. (4)
   d. Discuss what might lead to an improvement in the balance of payments of a country. (6)

   (Cambridge 0455 Paper 4 Q5 May/June 2005)

2. a. How does a specialisation in international trade benefit a country? (6)
   b. Some countries use protective measures in international trade. Decide two types of protection, a government can use in international trade. (4)
   c. Explain, with the use of one example, the meaning of natural resource of a country. (3)
   d. For many countries, international trade involves sale of their natural resources to other countries. Discuss whether it is wise for a country to exploit its natural resources rather than conserve them. (7)

   (Cambridge 0455 Paper 4 Q5 Oct/Nov 2005)

3. It was reported, in September 2002, that the Namibian dollar was gaining in strength and that its exchange rate against other currencies was fluctuating less.
    a. What does the report mean when it says that the 'exchange rate against other currencies was fluctuating less'? (5)
    b. Why do exchange rates fluctuate? (4)
    c. Discuss the consequences for an economy, if its currency 'was gaining strength'. (5)
    d. A country has a deficit on its balance of payments. Discuss two policies, other than changes in exchange rate, that a government might use to try and achieve a surplus rather than a deficit. (6)

    (Cambridge 0455 Paper Q6 Oct/Nov 2004)

Answers to Examination Practice Questions

Section 1

Answers to Multiple Choice Questions

1. d

   Wants are unlimited whereas resources are not. What we want is greater than what we are capable of producing. Over time, the quantity and quality of resources increases in most of the countries. This enables them to produce more. The growth in productive capacity, however, is exceeded by people's desire for goods and services.

2. d

   Both increase. A richer economy is likely to have more capital in particular. As the income of an economy increases, its citizens also tend to desire even more goods and services.

3. d

   Capital is goods used to produce other goods and services. c is an example of labour, b is saving and a is financial capital.

4. d

   In economics, the word 'land' covers all natural resources including sea water, forests and land itself.

5. b

   By rejecting the offer from her neighbour, the consumer is giving up the opportunity to have $200.

6. c

   From the man's point of view, the best alternative to being a builder is working as a gardener.

Suggested Answers to Structured Questions

1. a. If you decide to continue your studies and take further examinations, it means that you cannot use the time you will spend studying for other purposes. These may include resting, undertaking paid employment and pursuing leisure activities. If you consider undertaking paid employment as the best alternative to studying, the work is the opportunity cost. By studying, you are giving up the opportunity to work for the period of your educational course.

b. There are a range of factors, that would have to be taken into account, for deciding whether to study or to work. One is whether there is possibility of studying the desired subject at a higher level in an educational institution in your area. If not, you may have to consider studying in another area or country or you may have to think about another way of studying, such as undertaking a correspondence course.

Another factor concerns your self assessment of your performance in studies. If you think that you will struggle to pass the examinations or that you may not enjoy the course, studying may not be a good use of your time. In this case, you will be giving up the opportunity to earn money and gain work experience and possibly not gain much in return. If, however, you are prepared to work and think that you stand a good chance of passing the examinations, the decision to study may prove to be a good choice. Whilst you will be sacrificing some income now, your future career prospects and earning potential are likely to be significantly higher after pursuing higher studies. You may also gain a lifelong interest in some of the subjects you study and make some good friends. So, it is important that you examine the job opportunities open to you, given your qualifications and additional income earned with better qualifications relative to what can be earned without them.

If your courses and/or books and equipment have to be paid for, you and your family will also have to consider the financial sacrifices involved. To pay for your studies, you and your family may have to go without, for example, holidays or even some basic necessities. You may also have to undertake part-time employment, in order to finance your studies.

Whether your studies have to be paid for or not, your family may need your income now and to help support them, you may decide that you have to work now. This, however, is likely to reduce your life time earnings and consequently, the financial help received by your family from you in the future.

The key economic factors to be considered are your family's financial position, the cost of your studies and the difference made to your career choices and earnings by the qualifications gained by you.

2. a. Scarcity refers to a shortage or lack of something. Resources are scarce. There are not enough workers, machines, entrepreneurs and land to produce all the products people would like to have. As wants exceed resources, choices have to be made regarding the use of resources. To make the most efficient choices, it is important to consider the other possible uses of resources. Opportunity cost is the best alternative forgone. For instance, the opportunity cost of growing wheat on an area of land might be growing linseed.

Answers to Multiple Choice Questions

1. a

   In a market economy, consumers are sovereign. They decide what is produced. They signal their choices through the price mechanism.

2. c

   The equilibrium price is where demand and supply are equal. In this, it is $1.20 where demand and supply are 320 each.

3. d

   A fall in price will cause demand to extend and supply to contract, until they become equal and the market clears.

4. c

   A subsidy will cause supply to increase which, in turn, will lead to a lower price. a would cause a decrease in supply which would result in a rise in price. b and d would also lead to a rise in price. If beef becomes more expensive, some consumers may switch to lamb, causing the demand for lamb to increase. A successful advertising campaign would also result in an increase in demand for lamb.

5. d

   An advertising campaign will increase costs of production. However, it may also result in an increase in demand.

6. a

   Price elasticity of demand is a measure of the responsiveness of demand to a change in price. The formula is % $\triangle$QD/% $\triangle$P. In this case, demand rises by $5 from the original $10 (which is a 50% rise). Demand falls by 1 000 from its original 5 000 (i.e. a 20% fall). So PED = –20%/50% = –0.4.

7. d

   An increase in the number of substitutes is likely to make demand more sensitive to prices. Consumers will switch to a given product (from rival products) if its price falls and away from it (to rival products), if its price rises. a, b and c would all cause demand to become more inelastic. The lower the price of a product and the smaller the proportion of income spent on it, the less significant any price change is. The shorter the time period, the less is the chance for consumers being able to find alternatives.

8. b

    Inelastic supply is when a change in price causes a smaller percentage change in supply. a is elastic supply and d is perfectly inelastic supply. c can be rejected as price and supply are directly related.

9. b

    Recycling waste paper into newspapers will reduce the amount of waste buried in landfill sites and help preserve woods and forests. a, c and d will harm the environment.

10. b

    A subsidy given to bus companies should provide a number of advantages to people, other than the owners and workers of the bus companies and bus passengers. These include reduced congestion, reduced pollution and fewer accidents.

Suggested Answers to Structured Questions

1. a. The price of a good is determined by the interaction of demand and supply. Price will move to the equilibrium level. This where demand and supply are equal, as shown in Fig. 1.

    b. Worries about job security are likely to make people more pessimistic about the future and this is likely to decrease demand. High unemployment and a fall in income will reduce their ability to spend, again causing demand to fall. Fig. 2 shows the demand curve shifting to the left.

        Initially, the lower demand will result in the market being in disequilibrium with supply exceeding demand. There is a surplus of unsold products. Suppliers, seeing that they cannot sell all that they want at a price of P, will lower price. As Fig. 3 shows, market forces restore the market to equilibrium, with demand equaling supply at the new lower price of P_1.

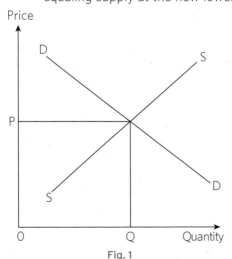

Fig. 1

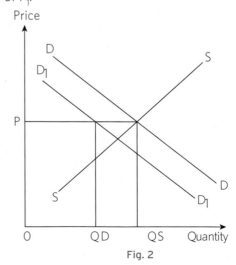

Fig. 2

2. a. An equilibrium price is a price at which demand and supply are equal. In such a situation, there is currently no reason for a price change. Fig. 4 shows that the equilibrium price is P since this is where the demand curve intersects the supply curve.

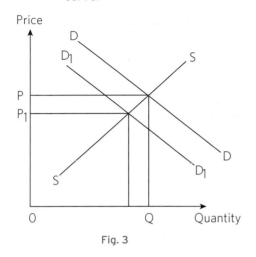

Fig. 3

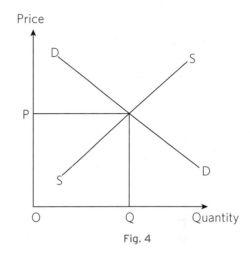

Fig. 4

In contrast, a disequilibrium price is a price at which demand and supply are equal. Fig. 5 shows a price set too high initially. Here supply exceeds demand and there is a surplus of the product in the market. Market forces will push the price down until demand equals supply.

It is also possible, at least for a period of time, to have a disequilibrium price set below the equilibrium. Fig. 6 shows that at a price of P, demand is greater than

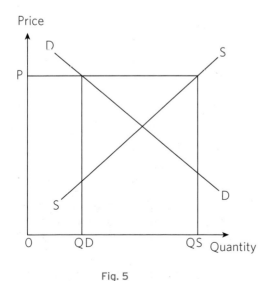

Fig. 5

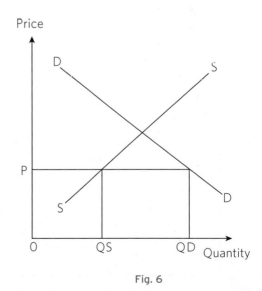

Fig. 6

supply and there is a shortage. The excess demand will drive the price up to the equilibrium level.

b. There are a number of reasons – some affecting demand and some affecting supply, to account for greater number of people travelling by aeroplane today than ten years ago. One is a rise in incomes. As people in most countries are becoming richer, they are choosing to take more holidays. They are also availing holidays in distant locations, which increases the chance of air travel. This rise in income has shifted the demand for air travel to the right as shown in Fig. 7.

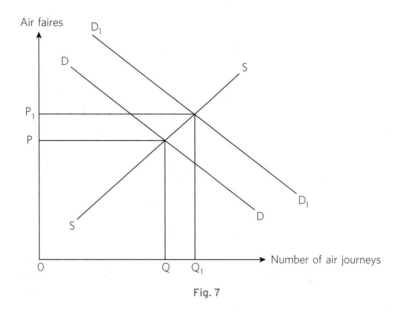

Fig. 7

Other reasons for more people travelling by air are the increased safety of aircrafts and globalisation. Over time, aeroplanes have become safer and the number of people killed in air crashes has fallen. After the attacks on the World Trade Centre in the US in September 2001, people did become worried about travelling by planes and demand for airtravel declined for sometime. However, since then demand has increased and continues to increase.

Globalisation means that more people are working and living for longer periods of time outside their home countries. As a result, people are travelling more by plane on business journeys and to meet their relatives.

Besides an increase in demand for air travel, supply of air travel is also increasing. There are more airlines flying within and between countries. For example, there has been a significant increase in the number of low costs airlines operating in India, the UK and the US.

Advances in technology, which have lowered the cost of carrying passengers, and the removal of restrictions on air traffic, have resulted in more airlines flying more planes both within and between countries.

Combined with the increase in demand, the increase in supply has resulted in a rise of passenger journeys undertaken by aeroplane. As air fares (on average) have fallen, it suggests that supply has increased by more than demand. Such a situation is illustrated in Fig. 8.

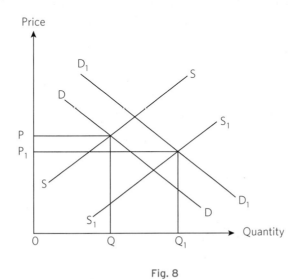

Fig. 8

c. Price elasticity of demand is a measure of the extent to which demand changes, as a result of a change in price. It is found by dividing the percentage in demand by the percentage change in price. The formula is:

$$PED = \% \, \Delta QD / \% \, \Delta P$$

There are a number of reasons for different goods having different price elasticities. The key reason is that some goods have close substitutes, whilst others do not. A good that has close substitutes of a similar price will have elastic demand. A rise in its price will cause a greater percentage fall in demand, as consumers can easily switch to rival goods. In contrast, a good that has no close substitutes will have inelastic demand. If it becomes more expensive, demand will fall by a smaller percentage as either there is no alternative or the alternative is not affordable.

The other reasons for differences in price elasticities are whether the goods are luxuries or necessities, the proportion of income spent on them, the flexibility to postpone their purchase and the extent to which the goods are habit forming.

- Luxury goods usually have elastic demand. If they become more expensive, people may decide to do without them. A fall in their price will make them affordable to more people. Necessities, however, such as soap are less sensitive to price changes.
- A product that takes up only a small proportion of income, for example a box of matches, is likely to have inelastic demand. A rise in price will not be very noticeable and will not alter the quantities bought by consumers significantly. On the other hand, if the price of a product takes up a large proportion of income then the price changes will probably cause the demand to alter by a greater percentage. People have to think carefully about whether they can afford to buy such goods.
- People will also be more sensitive to price changes, if their purchases do not have to made quickly. If some people are thinking about buying new cars to replace existing cars which are running quite well, not only is the purchase likely to take up a large part of their income but they also do not have to buy them immediately. If their prices rise, they may decide to delay their purchase. In contrast, demand for goods that have to be bought urgently usually have inelastic demand. If the roof on a house is damaged in a storm, it needs to be repaired immediately to prevent more damage. Even if the price charged by roof repairers rises, the occupants are likely to pay it.
- Demand for goods, such as cigarettes, that are habit forming is also inelastic. A rise in the price of cigarettes will cause a fall in demand but by a smaller percentage. This is because smokers find it difficult to stop smoking and even to reduce the number of cigarettes they smoke. Some will stop, some will cut back but many are likely to continue to smoke the same number.

d. Knowledge of price elasticity of demand is significant to a company selling holiday tours. It will help the company in its pricing strategy. If demand for its holiday tours is inelastic, it can raise revenue and profit by pushing up the price of its tours. Inelastic demand suggests that there are no close substitutes available.

If, on the other hand, demand is elastic, it is likely that the company faces some significant competition. In this case, the company has to think very carefully about raising the price of its tours. If rival companies do not increase their price, the company will lose market share. In fact, if demand is elastic, a rise in price will cause a fall in revenue and profit.

The company can, however, raise revenue by lowering price if demand is elastic. This is because demand will rise by a greater percentage than a fall in price.

There is no point, though, in reducing price and raising demand unless the company has the ability to sell more tours. If the company has the capacity, it will have to consider whether the additional revenue received from selling more holidays will be greater than the rise in costs experienced as a result of raising its output. If revenue does rise more than costs, the company will enjoy a rise in profit.

3. a. All four factors of production are involved in the RSPB's decision. The organisation has bought land, which is a natural resource. The decision to buy land and build visitor centres is making use of enterprise. This factor involves risk taking and organising the other factors of production. Labour, which is human effort, will be required to design and build the visitor centres. The visitor centres will be capital as they are man-made and provide a service.

   b. There are a number of advantages that the area may gain from the action of the RSPB. Having the visitor centres will be likely to attract tourists to the area. Tourism will create employment and income, both directly and indirectly. More tourists will increase the revenue of the tourist industry in the area and create more jobs in the industry. The tourist industry, in turn, will demand more products – some from other industries in the area. For instance, farmers may receive more orders for food and taxi firms may carry more passengers. Other industries in the area, that are not linked to tourism, may also benefit. This is because an expanding tourism industry, by raising income and employment, will increase demand for a range of products. Stopping construction on the area also protects the local environment. Air quality will improve and noise levels reduce. There are, however, some losses that the area may experience as a result of this decision. The area could have been used for housing. Building more homes would create income and employment for a period of time. It would have helped to reduce any housing shortages in the area. Factories and offices might also have been built there, which would have had a long term impact on income and employment.
   Determination of the most beneficial use of land depends on a number of factors. These include the size of the area of the land. For instance, if it is small it may not be possible to build many houses or offices or factories there. The land might also be very hilly and there may be a risk of erosion too. Other influencing factors include the need for housing, availability of appropriate infrastructure for housing and industry and relative amounts of income generated for the area by respective industries.

   c. (i) A private cost is a cost incurred by those directly involved in a production or consumption decision. In this case, it will be the RSPB's decision to build visitor centres.

One cost faced by it for building the visitor centres is the wages paid to masons. Other private costs include the cost of the land and the cost of building materials.

(ii) Social benefit is the total benefit arising from the consumption or production of a product. It consists of private and external benefits. The social benefit of the RSPB's action may include revenue, that the RSPB may receive from visitors to the site (a private benefit) and the conservation of birds and increased business for local shops and transport firms (external benefits).

d.   There are arguments both for the protection of rare birds being the responsibility of the government and for it being the responsibility of private charities.

It may be thought that the government may have to take responsibility to ensure an efficient allocation of resources towards the protection of rare birds. Private charities may not have sufficient finance to provide the necessary protection. They may not take into account the external benefits and costs, that their actions will cause. There is the possibility that the charities may underestimate or overestimate the extent to which rare birds have to be protected. If they underestimate it, some rare birds may become extinct. If they overestimate, too many resources will be devoted to protection of birds. For instance, land which could have been used for housing may unnecessarily be used for setting up bird reserves. Private charities may also charge high prices from visitors to the centres, which would make them inaccessible to the poor.

On the other hand, they may have special expertise (in this case in ornithology). Their need to attract donations from the general public provides both a carrot and a stick for them to achieve their objectives. They may also make decisions more quickly than a government and be less influenced by political factors.

Section 3

Answers to Multiple Choice Questions

1.   c

With money, people can make arrangements to borrow now and to pay bank loans in the future.

2.   c

One of the key functions of commercial banks is to lend. a, b and d are functions of a central bank.

3.   d

A rise in firms' profits will encourage people to buy their shares, as they will expect to receive higher dividends. A decrease in interest rates will also encourage people to buy shares. They will take some of their savings out of banks and other financial institutions, as they will now get a better return from buying shares.

4. b

A high demand for labour will mean that employers are willing and able to pay high wages. Also, a shortage of workers (low supply) will further necessitate a payment of higher wages to workers as employers, anxious to recruit workers, will be competing to attract skilled labour by offering better remuneration.

5. b

A rise in the qualifications needed to be a lawyer would reduce the supply of lawyers, causing the supply curve to shift to the left.

6. c

Demand for labour is based on demand for the products that workers produce. If more people visit the cinema, film production companies' profits will increase. This will encourage the companies to make more films and employ more actors. An increase in demand for actors will push up their wages.

7. d

An increase in labour productivity will raise the return received by firms from employing workers and hence is likely to push up wages. If unemployment decreases, it may become more difficult to recruit workers and so firms may have to raise wages.

8. c

If the strike involves most of the workers, a firm may experience a significant fall in output. a, b and d would all reduce the harmful impact of a strike. If the firm has large stocks, it can sell products despite none or fewer being manufactured during the strike. b would mean that consumers, disadvantaged by the strike, would not be able to switch to rival firms. d would be likely to mean that the effect of the strike would not be very damaging.

9. d

A relatively easy question. Tax free saving schemes will increase the amount earned by people from savings. a would discourage saving and b and c would reduce people's ability to save.

10. b

As households become richer, they are able to spend more on entertainment – both in absolute terms and as a percentage. They may spend more in absolute terms on food but in percentage terms it is likely to fall as, with more income, they spend more on non-essential items.

Suggested Answers to Structured Questions

1. a. There are a number of reasons for a worker to be prepared to work for low wages. One is **job satisfaction**. A worker may be able to earn more in another better paid job but prefer doing this job. Most very low paid jobs, however, are not very enjoyable. Many involve stringent physical labour and lack mental stimulation. One of the main reasons for people to be prepared to work for very low wages is because they **lack the skills**, experience and qualifications to gain better paid jobs. The work they do may be very low paid but it may still pay more than the benefits they might be able to receive if they were unemployed. Apart from being occupationally immobile, low paid workers may also be geographically immobile. Higher paid jobs may exist elsewhere in the country or in other countries but some workers may not be able to move due to, for instance, differences in the cost and availability of housing and family ties. A few workers may not be aware of availability of better paid jobs elsewhere and some may be prepared to accept very low pay for a period of time, in the hope of promotion and higher pay in the future.

   b. A worker may decide to move to another job, offering the same amount of pay, because of many reasons including proximity of residence to workplace, greater interest in job with more fringe benefits, better working conditions and better promotional prospects. Nearness of workplace to home will be likely to reduce the worker's transport costs and increase his or her leisure time. A more interesting job will keep the worker more motivated and may also help build up his or her skills. Jobs differ in the fringe benefits and working conditions they provide. A worker may be encouraged to move to gain, for example, a company car or free health insurance. Shorter working hours and longer breaks may also attract workers. A greater chance of gaining promotion (or quicker promotion) may also persuade a worker to switch jobs.

   c. Belonging to a trade union may bring a number of benefits to workers. The union can negotiate on their behalf for better pay and working conditions. **Collective bargaining** is likely to lend more strength to workers, than if they were to bargain individually. Unions may provide a number of other benefits for their members, such as strike pay, legal advice and financial support during a grievance dispute. In addition, they may give information about pensions and may also help to train workers.

   d. An older skilled worker's pattern of spending and saving may differ from that of a younger skilled worker in a number of ways. A skilled worker will be better paid than an unskilled worker. Having a higher income is likely to mean that the skilled worker will spend more in total than the unskilled worker, but a smaller proportion of total income. The skilled worker will be able to save some of his or her income. In contrast, the unskilled worker may have to spend all or most of his/her income to buy basic necessities, leaving little or no money to save.

The percentages that well paid workers and low paid workers spend on different items is also likely to vary. Low paid workers spend a higher proportion of their disposable income on food and a lower proportion on entertainment and leisure goods. A younger worker may spend more than an older worker (relatively) because he or she may be buying a home and furniture and supporting a young family. An older worker may have already bought most of the consumer durables he or she wants and is more likely to possess a home already. This older worker may be saving for his or her retirement or to help his or her children by either financing their education or supporting their purchase of a home.

2. a. In choosing an occupation, a person is likely to take into account the location, working conditions and promotional prospects. If a person can work close to home, he or she will spend less time and money in commuting. This will enable him or her to have more time for leisure. A person is likely to be attracted to an occupation which can be undertaken in a pleasant atmosphere and which has short working hours. Good career prospects may also encourage a person to take up an occupation. Other factors influencing the choice of profession include job security, status and fringe benefits.

    b. It is debatable which factor of production is most significant in the operation of a luxury hotel. They may all play a key role. A luxury hotel may be located in spacious grounds. Some may be close to beaches and areas of natural beauty. The hotel grounds, beaches and areas of natural beauty are natural resources which economists classify as land. A good location and attractive grounds are important in attracting customers.

    The role of the entrepreneur may be divided into two, in the case of a luxury hotel. The owner (or owners) will bear the uncertain risks. If it is a large hotel, a manager may be appointed to carry out the other functions – like organising the other factors of production. The success of the hotel will be heavily influenced by (i) the amount of finance the owner (or owners) has put into the hotel and (ii) the decisions taken by manager, such as the price to charge for the hotel's services. The workers, including chefs, cleaners and waiters will also play a key role. Friendly and efficient staff will create a good atmosphere in the hotel and encourage customers to return and avail the offered services. In addition to land, enterprise and labour, capital is also involved in the operation of a luxury hotel. Among the capital goods used to provide the service of the hotel are the hotel buildings, kitchen equipment and a computer.

c. There are two main categories of reasons which can account for the workers in the hotel being paid different wages. One is differences in characteristics of the workers and the other is differences in the work they perform. Older, more experienced and better trained workers are likely to be paid more than younger, less experienced and less well trained workers. So a gardener who has been employed by the hotel for some time will probably be on a higher wage than a young person who has just been taken on to work as a gardener as he may probably lack experience, need training and may be less productive.

The workers, carrying out skilled jobs in the hotel, such as the chef and accountant, are likely to be better paid than those performing unskilled jobs, such as cleaning and carrying bags. Jobs requiring high skills and qualifications tend to be well paid because there is a high demand for the workers who can undertake them and a low supply. Good chefs will have to undergo training and build up their skills and reputation over time. Attracting a good chef could increase a hotel's profits but there will be competition to attract his or her services. Both factors will mean the chef's wage is likely to be high. In contrast, the demand for low skilled workers tends to be less because they are less productive and their supply is higher, as the need for training and requisite qualifications is not the same as a chef. Low skilled hotel workers are often paid the national minimum wage in countries, which have such legislation.

Fig. 9 compares the wage rates of chefs and cleaners.

Not only is the demand and supply of chefs lower than cleaners, they are also more inelastic. This is because it is harder to replace chefs than cleaners if their wages rise and it takes longer for people to train and gain the qualifications needed to be a chef.

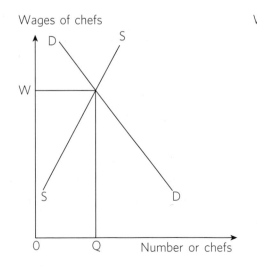

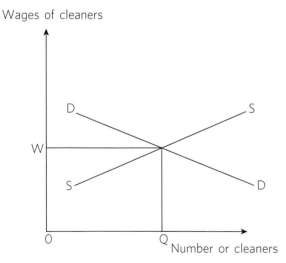

Fig. 9

Also, the cleaners are more likely to be casual workers than chefs. As a result, they are less likely to belong to a trade union or professional body and hence usually have less bargaining power. Working for shorter periods of time reduces their chances of promotion. Also, some of them work part time and accordingly receive less pay.

3. a. No, the figures do not indicate that the richest households spent less on food than the poorest households. The figures show the percentage amount spent and not the absolute amount.

    In absolute terms, the rich spend more on food, buying better quality produce. As they are richer, however, the amount they spend on all items is greater with their expenditure on food forming a smaller percentage of the total. For instance, a rich household may spend $500 a week whilst a poor household spends $50. This would mean that the rich household would be spending $65 (13%) while the poor household may be spending only $15 (30%).

    b. Faizal, being in a senior position, is likely to be earning more than Ali who has just started working. Being richer, Faizal is likely to spend a higher proportion of his disposable income on entertainment, leisure goods and services and other luxury products. Ali, in contrast, will not be able to devote much of his income to non-essentials. Ali will spend less in absolute terms, but a higher percentage of his income on food and other essentials goods. Ali may not save any of his income whilst Faizal is likely to save a proportion.

    c. People save some of their income, rather than spend it, for a number of reasons. One is to build up a fund of money that will provide them with income in the form of interest and which they can draw on during their retirement.

    Some people save to buy consumer durables such as televisions and some for foreign holidays. Others save for the future of their children, including financing their education.

    Many people save for precautionary reasons. They want to have some money that they can draw on to meet unexpected expenses, such as the need to pay for home repairs. These people often engage in contractual saving by investing in insurance policies.

    d. Higher consumer expenditure will increase the total demand in the economy. Higher total demand will encourage firms to increase their output. To produce more, they are likely to employ more workers. As a result, unemployment may fall. Greater competition for workers may push up wages too.

Higher output and higher incomes will raise government tax revenue. With this higher revenue, a government could spend more on, for instance, education, health care and transport infrastructure.

Higher output, lower unemployment and an increased ability of a government to spend on items that will raise the country's output in the future are clearly the advantages of consumer expenditure. There are, however, possible disadvantages of an increase in consumer expenditure. If the economy is producing as much or nearly as much as it is capable of, given existing resources and technological knowledge, there is a risk that more consumption would cause inflation or a trade deficit. Domestic firms would not be able to match higher demand with higher output. This would, consequently, push up prices and cause more imports to meet the domestic needs.

Section 4

Answers to Multiple Choice Questions

1. b

   The positive gap between total revenue and total cost is highest at 200 coats. Here, the profit is $600. At 100 coats it is $400, at 300 coats it is $500 and at 400 coats it is $400.

2. d

   It is only the public limited companies that can sell shares on the stock exchange. Private limited companies need to sell shares to known individuals. Partnerships and public corporations (state owned enterprises) do not have shares.

3. b

   Revenue is found by multiplying price by demand. Here the total revenue is:

Price per bar ($)	Total revenue ($)
4	40
3	45
2	40
1	25

   Revenue is maximised when price is $3.

4. c

   At Z, the total cost of production is WZ. Of this, YZ is the fixed cost and WY is the variable cost.

5. b

The firm's total revenue is $1 800 (200 x $9). Its average total cost is $6 (AFC + AVC) and so its total cost is $1 200 (200 x $6). Its profit is $600 ($1 800 – $1 200). This answer could also have been found by deducting average total cost from average revenue ($3) and multiplying the difference with output (200).

6. b

A perfectly competitive firm's output does not affect price. Its average revenue remains unchanged as its output changes.

7. c

The firm's total variable cost (TVC) initially rises slowly. This would be caused by reducing average variable costs (AVC). Then the TVC curve rises more slowly. This would be the result of AVC rising.

8. c

A definition question. AFC is TC/output.

9. c

A small firm is unlikely to have a complex management structure and hence can make decisions quickly. a, b and d are benefits of a large firm.

10. c

Vertical integration implies the merging of two firms at different stages of production. Vertical integration backwards occurs, when a firm merges with a firm closer to the source of supplies. b is vertical integration forward. There is no specific term for a or d.

Suggested Answers to Structured Questions

1. a. The factors of production are resources used to produce goods and services. They are in scarce supply. One factor of production is **land**. This refers to all the natural resources that are used in production. **Capital** is another factor of production and consists of man-made goods that make other products. The other two factors of production are human factors. One is **labour**, which consists of all human effort used in production and the other is **enterprise**, which involves risk taking and organising the other resources.

    b. There are a number of reasons for some firms to remain small. Some owners may choose to keep their firms small in order to retain control. Other owners may want their firms to expand, but may lack the requisite finance or the market. Banks may be reluctant to lend to small firms at low rates of interest and small firms are unlikely to be limited companies. Hence, they will not be able to sell shares. If the market for a product that a firm is producing is small, the firm will not be able to grow. A small firm may be making a specialised product with a limited demand or may be serving a small, local market.

c. In the first situation, it appears to be horizontal integration. In the second situation, it is vertical integration backwards

d. Horizontal integration may bring a number of benefits for the merged firms and consumers. The new larger firm may be able to take greater advantage of economies of scale including, for instance, technical, managerial and buying economies. With lower costs of production, the firm may be able to lower its prices and yet enjoy a rise in profits. Consumers may also benefit from an improvement in the quality of the firm's products brought about by operations on a larger scale and availability of more finance to spend more on research and development.

From the firm's point of view, horizontal integration has the benefit that it directly reduces its competitors by one and increases its market share. This greater market power, however, may disadvantage consumers if the firm uses it to raise price. There is also a risk that its costs and prices may rise, if the firm becomes too large and experiences diseconomies of scale.

Vertical integration backwards may also result in economies or diseconomies of scale. It may also have a number of other effects. It should guarantee supplies, which should mean that the firm and consumers will not suffer disruptions in supply and may raise the quality of supplies and final products. The supplies may be obtained at a lower price, which will reduce the firm's costs and possibly the price paid by the consumers. The firm may also use its ownership of a source of supplies to make it more difficult for its rivals to obtain the raw materials or to make them pay a higher price for them. This move could increase the firm's profit but may disadvantage consumers. There is also the risk that coordinating a firm, operating at two stages of production, may be difficult.

2. a. £5m is equal to 20% of Manchester United's profits. So, its profit is £5m x 100/20 = £25m.

b. Firms need to make profits to pay the entrepreneurs, to indicate the need for expansion and to provide the finance to support that expansion.

Profit is the reward for bearing risks and organising the other factors of production. People are unlikely to take the risk of losing their money, if the firm is not successful and probably not inclined to coordinate the other factors without the prospect of some financial reward.

If market forces are working efficiently, a rise in profit may indicate that demand for the product is increasing and more resources should be devoted for its production. Some of the higher profit made could be used to buy capital goods, which would enable the firm to produce more in the future. A profitable firm is also likely to find the borrowing and selling shares relatively easy.

c.   The price of shares in Manchester United Football Club had recently fallen because its profits had decreased. Also, it was expected that its profit in the next financial year would fall further. It had announced that there would be no special dividend paid out to shareholders. Such changes would have reduced demand for shares in the club. The changes would also have encouraged some shareholders to sell their shares in the club, as they would have expected the price to fall. Fig. 10 shows the decrease in demand and increase in supply, causing the price of shares to fall.

d.   There are a number of reasons why, as a director, I would be concerned by the fall in profits. One is that profits could fall further in the future. Revenue from televising of football matches was predicted to be reduced, the club would not be able to sell David Beckham again and the club was committed to large scale capital expenditure which would be incurred by adding 7 800 seats.
The fall in profits meant that no special dividend would be paid to shareholders. Such a decision, combined with the lower profits, would probably mean that the price of the club's shares would fall. This would make it more difficult for the club to raise finance for expansion.

There are, however, some reasons to be more optimistic. The club may make higher profits in the future. The extra seats should generate more revenue and the club may regain its top of the Premier League position. The club may also have more valuable players to sell and might not be paying out much to agents

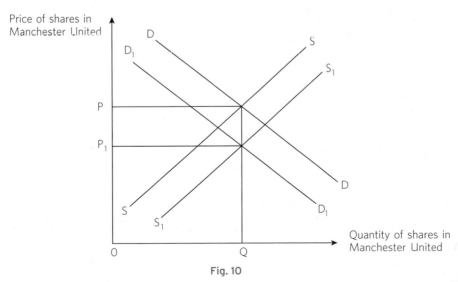

Fig. 10

of football players in the future. 2002/3 might have been an unusually bad year and even in that year, the club did manage to register a profit.

There are two general strategies to raise profits. One is to raise revenue and the other is to cut costs. I would suggest to the shareholders that revenue could be raised in a number of ways. If demand for the business's products is elastic, revenue could be raised by cutting price. In this case, demand would rise by a greater percentage than the fall in price. The business would, however, have to be confident that it could meet the higher demand at the same or lower average cost. In contrast, if demand is inelastic, revenue and profit could be raised by increasing price.

Revenue could also be raised by advertising, diversifying or merging. A successful advertising campaign would increase revenue by more than the cost of the campaign. Diversifying into new products may raise revenue, if demand for the products is increasing. The combined profit of a merged firm may be larger than the profit of the original business. Merging also reduces the competitors and may lower the average costs of a firm by enabling it to take advantage of economies of scale.

Average costs may also be lowered by spending some money on training of workers and capital investment. Better trained workers and new capital equipment are likely to be more productive and consequently, the average cost of products is likely to fall. The business should also ensure that any kind of wastages are avoided.

3. a. Profits would fall, if revenue decreases, costs increase or there is both a decrease in revenue and an increase in costs.

   There are a number of reasons for a decrease in revenue. People's incomes may fall, which would reduce their ability to buy products. Rival firms might have brought out better quality products or cut their prices. Tastes may change and the products produced by the firm might have become less popular. There might, for instance, have been a report stating that the products manufactured by the firm are harmful to health.

   The price of oil may have risen, which would have increased the firm's transport costs. The wages of its workers may have risen, not matched by a rise in productivity, or the costs of raw material could have increased.

   b. A firm can become larger as a result of internal or external growth. If a firm can gain more customers or can raise finance, it can open new or larger shops, offices or factories. More customers may be attracted by, for example, advertising and bringing out new products. Having more customers creates a need to expand and may provide the profit to finance the expansion. Finance may also be raised through borrowing or issuing shares. If a firm converts from being a private into a public limited company, it can sell its shares on the stock exchange. The more successful a firm is, the easier it should find to borrow or sell shares. Internal growth can enable owners to keep a better control and to achieve a desired size. External growth is quicker but there is a risk that owners will lose control and that the firm will become too large. External growth is achieved by merging with or taking over another firm.

c.   Three types of economies of scale, that a computer company may experience, are managerial, technical and financial. As it grows in size, a computer company can employ specialist workers. For example, it might employ specialist designers of computer hardware.
A computer company, producing on a large scale, can use expensive but very productive capital equipment. This is because it will have the volume to make full use of the machinery and will be able to spread its costs over a large number of computers.
The larger a computer company gets, the easier it may find to raise finance. It will become better known and have more collateral. This should encourage banks to give loans and people, to buy its shares.

d.   A company might change its use of different factors of production because demand for its products changes, the price of the factors or their productivity alters. If the company switches its production from mass-produced products to individually designed and produced products, it may employ less capital and more labour. A decision to move into a new line of production will draw on the skills of its entrepreneur (or entrepreneurs). If capital becomes more expensive, a company may switch from capital intensive to labour intensive methods (if it is possible to substitute the two). In contrast, advances in technology (which increase the productivity of machinery) will encourage it to use more capital.

Section 5

Answers to Multiple Choice Questions

1.   b
Economic growth occurs when the output (real GDP) of a country increases.

2.   c
The diagram shows that government expenditure rose whilst tax revenue fell over time. At first, tax revenue exceeded government expenditure and so there was a budget surplus. Then, government expenditure exceeded tax revenue and there was a budget deficit.

3. d

A decrease in VAT may encourage people to spend more. A rise in aggregate demand would reduce cyclical unemployment. a, b and c would all reduce aggregate demand, which would be likely to increase unemployment.

4. a

Increasing progressive taxes would reduce the disposable income of the rich whilst increasing welfare benefits would increase the income of the poor.

5. c

A rise in real GDP would be likely to encourage firms to hire more workers. Government tax revenue should rise and the standard of living should increase. The level of pollution may increase, but this would be a disadvantage rather than an advantage of economic growth.

6. d

People earning a high income would be paying income tax on a large proportion of their income and hence should benefit from a cut in income tax. Also, they are unlikely to receive housing benefit or unemployment benefit. Their children may be going to university and so a reduction in government expenditure on higher education would be a liability to them.

7. b

Competition policy is designed to encourage firms to act in a competitive way and to prevent uncompetitive practices. Predatory pricing reduces competition. c and d are fiscal policy measures.

8. a

A definition question.

9. d

As income rises, tax revenue from all types of tax is likely to increase in absolute terms. Revenue from a progressive tax will increase by a greater percentage, revenue from a proportional tax will rise proportionately and revenue from a regressive tax will increase by a smaller percentage.

10. d

By discontinuing the taxation of profits of firms, the sources of tax revenue (i.e. what can be taxed) will be reduced. Corporation tax is a direct tax. Its elimination is likely to encourage a rise in output and investment.

Suggested Answers to Structured Questions

1. a. A direct tax is a tax on the income of people and profits of firms. The burden of the tax is borne by the person or firm on which the tax is imposed. In the above statement, income tax is an example of a direct tax. An indirect tax is a tax on expenditure. The burden, or some of the burden of the tax, can be shifted on to another person. An example of an indirect tax is the tax on goods and services.

   b. Governments impose taxes for a number of reasons. These include – to raise revenue, to promote expenditure on merit goods, public goods and to help the poor. Taxes are also used to discourage the consumption of demerit goods and to turn external into internal costs.
   Besides correcting market failure, taxes are used to influence the distribution of income and to discourage imports. Progressive taxes help redistribute income more evenly amongst rich and poor. Tariffs placed on imports make them more expensive and are designed to encourage people to buy domestic goods rather than foreign products.
   In addition, taxes are used to influence aggregate demand. If a government wants to reduce aggregate demand (perhaps to reduce inflationary pressure) it will increase tax rates.

   c. (i) It would appear that the number of tourists in Singapore had increased. Government revenue from both indirect and direct taxes increased. Tourists spend money in a country and their demand generates income, not only in the tourist industry but also in other industries.
      (ii) Unemployment is likely to have decreased. Influx of tourists in Singapore would have created jobs, not just in the tourist industry but also in other industries. For instance, more people would have been employed in hotels, in transport and in unrelated industries as the higher incomes would increase aggregate demand.

2. a. Whilst a direct tax is a tax on the income of people and profits of firms, an indirect tax is a tax on expenditure. The burden of a direct tax cannot be shifted, unlike the burden of an indirect tax. Two examples of a direct tax from the information given are income tax and company (corporation) tax.

   b. There is a range of evidence that would be needed to investigate, to ascertain whether consumers were disadvantaged by the changes in the tax system. These include the impact on incentives, the distribution of income, productive and allocative efficiency. The shift from direct to indirect taxes might have increased the incentive for people to work and for entrepreneurs to start up new businesses and expand the existing ones. If this did occur, the quantity and quality of output may have risen and this would have benefitted the consumers. The rise in social security benefits, however, might have reduced the incentive to work.

Placing a tax on services would have widened the tax base but may have increased the price of a wide range of goods and services also. This rise might have caused inflation, if it had led the prices to increase over a period of time. This can be attributed to, for example, workers asking for pay rises to maintain the real value of their incomes. Inflation, however, might not have occurred since firms' overall costs may not have registered an increase due to the cut in corporation tax and even if prices had risen, it may not have caused workers to ask for higher pay as the cut in income tax would have increased their disposable income.

Indirect taxes tend to be regressive, whilst direct taxes tend to be progressive. So a shift towards indirect taxes would be likely to have benefitted the rich more than the poor. This would have caused a redistribution of income, although it would have been partially offset by the increase in social security benefits.

Consumers would benefit if the net effect of the changes in the tax system was to increase productive efficiency and allocative efficiency. Costs of production might fall and employment might rise due to the increased incentive to work and the cut in corporation tax.

Taxing certain products might have increased their price and lowered the quantity consumed. If services were originally over-consumed, imposing a tax on them might have increased allocative efficiency. If, on the other hand, some services were under-consumed, taxing them might have decreased allocative efficiency.

3. a. (i) See 2-a.
       (ii) A progressive tax takes a high proportion of the income of the rich. In contrast, a regressive tax takes a higher proportion of the income of the poor.

    b. (i) See 1-b.

    c. An increase in income tax rates can have a number of effects on an economy. Such a move will reduce disposable income. This, in turn, will be likely to reduce consumption. Lower consumption will discourage investment. A fall in consumption and investment will cause a reduction in aggregate demand. Fig. 11 shows that a fall in aggregate demand can reduce an economy's output.

Lower output may result in a rise in unemployment. The incentive to work will be reduced which will lead to cyclical unemployment. Besides this, there may be some voluntary unemployment also. The higher rates may discourage foreign direct investment and may encourage some workers to emigrate to countries with lower income tax rates.

A reduction in aggregate demand may, however, cause a fall in demand-pull inflation. Lower domestic expenditure may also result in an improvement in the current account position. This is because it is likely that fewer imports will be bought and so products, originally intended for the international market, may be diverted to the home market.

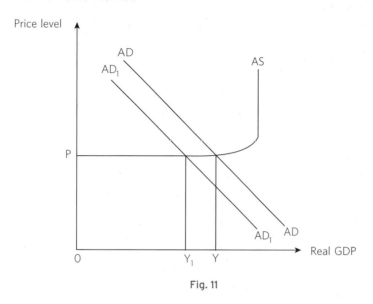

Fig. 11

In the short term, higher income tax rates will increase government tax revenue. If the government spends this tax revenue, aggregate demand may not fall. If the fall in consumption and investment is not offset by a rise in government expenditure, however, real GDP is likely to decrease. A lower GDP may mean that despite higher income tax rates, income tax revenue will decline as there will be less income available for taxing.

The effect of an increase in income tax rates will depend on the size of the rise, reaction of the people and the initial state of the economy. A small rise will obviously have less of an impact than a large rise. It is possible that a rise in income tax will reduce the expenditure by expected amounts. People may reduce their savings rather than their expenditure, if their disposable income falls. If an economy is operating at full capacity with inflation, a rise in income tax rates would be more beneficial than if it was operating with considerable spare capacity and high unemployment.

Section 6

Answers to Multiple Choice Questions

1. c

    Prices rose throughout the period. In 2009, the price level rose by 10%. In 2010, it still rose but by a smaller percentage. What occurred between 2009 and 2010 was actually a slowdown in the rate of growth of the price level.

2. c

    Inflation occurs when the price level, often measured by the consumer price index, rises. Inflation causes a rise in the cost of living and a fall in the value of money.

3. b

    If nominal incomes have risen, the money income level must have increased. This narrows the choice to b and d. If the money income level has risen and the price level has fallen, incomes will be able to buy more and so real incomes must have increased. If, however, the price level rises and rises by more than the increase in money incomes, real incomes must have fallen.

4. a

    Economic growth is an increase in real GDP. b, c and d may or may not have occurred.

5. d

    The unemployment arose because of a change in the structure of the call centre industry in the UK, with some work being transferred to other countries.

6. d

    A rise in the cost of transporting goods will increase firms' costs of production, leading them to raise price. a, b and c are all possible causes of demand-pull inflation.

7. a

    A country may increase its output by using up non-renewable resources. Unemployment is likely to fall and the government's ability to reduce poverty is likely to increase as tax revenue will rise. The productive capacity of the economy will also increase.

8. b

    If workers are more mobile, they will move more quickly between declining and expanding industries. This will reduce both frictional and structural unemployment. For cyclical unemployment to decline, aggregate demand would have to increase.

9. a

The HDI takes into account GDP, education and life expectancy. Both HDI and GDP include income. Neither HDI, nor GDP, take into account the gender equality or leisure.

10. b

A rise in pollution will reduce the quality of people's lives. d will increase living standards. a may be combined with a rise in the income of both the rich and the poor, but with a greater increase in the income of the poor. c means that the rise in real GDP per head would have understated the increase in products available for people to enjoy.

Suggested Answers to Structured Questions

1. a. A sustained increase in the general price level.

    b. Researchers calculate inflation by constructing a **weighted price index**. First they select a base year to ascertain the change in the general price level with respect to prices prevalent in base year. A number of households are asked to keep records of their expenditure. From the information gathered from this household survey, researchers decide the items to be measured and the weight attached to them. The higher the proportion spent on an item, the greater the weight ascribed to it. For example, if 10% of expenditure goes on food and 20% on transport, food would have a weight of 1/10 whilst transport would have a weight of 1/5. Changes in the prices of the items selected are found by visiting a number of trade outlets and obtaining information from, for instance, gas suppliers. The weights of the items in the basket of products are multiplied by their price changes to give a weighted price index. Then, the inflation rate is calculated. If, for instance, a consumer price index rises from 100 to 106, the inflation rate is 6%.

    c. The information may well be of concern to the Namibian economy. An inflation rate is relatively high and this could cause a number of problems. These include the menu and shoe leather costs. Firms would have to change prices in catalogues, for instance, on a regular basis and they would have to move money around in search of the highest interest rate. Lenders may lose out, whilst borrowers may gain if the rate of interest does not rise in line with inflation. The inflation, by creating uncertainty, may reduce investment and discourage foreign direct investment. This problem is more likely to occur, if the inflation rate is unstable. Namibia may experience balance of payments problems, if its inflation rate is higher than its competitors. If its price level is rising by more than that for rival countries, it is likely to export less and import more. It is interesting to note here that the price of imported products rose by the same percentage as Namibia's inflation rate.

In deciding whether a 10.6% inflation rate is a cause for concern, the Namibian government would also have to consider, whether it represents a rise or a fall from its inflation rate in previous years and the cause of the inflation. If the inflation is falling and is the result of demand-pull factors, it is likely to be less of a concern than a rising inflation rate caused by cost-push factors.

The Namibian government may also assess the impact of the rise in the price of particular items. For instance, the 20% increase in the price of medical and health services may be a cause of concern. This is a significant rise and calls for attention as health care is both an essential good and a merit good. On the other hand, the Namibian government may welcome the 9% rise in the price of tobacco as this is a demerit good.

2. a. Full-time jobs fell but part-time jobs rose. Total employment changed by – 42 600 + 1 500 = –41 100.

 b. The pattern of employment in Australia had changed in terms of the working hours and the type of industries attracting new workers.

 More people may be working part-time because there is a rise in demand for part-time workers and/or a rise in the supply of people wanting to work part-time. Employers may want to employ part-time workers because it gives them more flexibility and also because it is cheaper to employ part-time workers on an hourly basis. Part-time workers also often have fewer rights than full-time workers. Despite the lower pay and fewer rights, some people may want to work part-time. This may be because such work may allow them to look after children, undertake educational courses and pursue other interests.

 The decline in agriculture and rise in manufacturing is likely to reflect changes in demand and/or changes in costs. If domestic or overseas demand for manufactured products is rising, some of the economy's resources may switch from producing agricultural products towards manufactured products. As income rises, demand for services will also increase and again, this is likely to encourage a shift of resources.

 One of the factors that enables allocation of more resources for production of manufactured products and services is a rise in productivity. If the same agricultural output can be produced using fewer resources, this will exempt the resources to be used in the manufacturing and tertiary sectors. Over a period of time, a country may gain a comparative advantage in producing a particular product or products due to advancement in technology and better training. This should enable it to gain a larger market share and encourage an increase in output.

c. It is possible for the unemployment rate to fall whilst the numbers employed also decrease. This can occur, if the labour force fell. For instance, the labour force may initially be 30m, with 27m people being in employment and 3m being unemployed. In this case, the unemployment rate would be 3m/ 30m x 100 = 10%. If then the labour force fell to 25m, employment could fall to 23m whilst the unemployment rate would fall to 2m/25m x 100 = 8%.

d. Unemployment does provide some flexibility, making it easier for expanding firms to recruit more workers. It can also keep inflationary pressure down as rising aggregate demand can be matched by higher output. Also, the workers may become reluctant to press for wage rises for the fear of easy replacement by the unemployed labour. It is generally thought, however, that the costs of unemployment exceed any benefits. Unemployment imposes a number of costs on an economy. A key one is **lost output**. If the unemployed had been in work, more goods and services could have been produced and hence living standards could have been higher. Potential tax revenue is lost which may mean that taxes may be imposed at higher rates. The government may have to spend additional money on unemployment benefits, which could have been used for other purposes. The government may also have to spend more on health care and crime prevention, abetted by unemployment. This occurs as people tend to suffer from poor physical and mental health and also resort to crime, in some cases, when unemployed.

Magnitude of the cost of unemployment is influenced by its rate, duration and cause. A 10% unemployment rate will obviously have more serious consequences than a lower rate of 4%. In fact, a government may not be too concerned about a 4% rate, as it is close to full employment. Longer term unemployment is particularly serious as those affected may lose skills, miss out on training and lose the habit to work. Cyclical unemployment is more harmful than frictional unemployment, as it is likely to affect more people and last longer.

3. a. Economic growth is an increase in real GDP and, in the longer term, an increase in productive capacity.

b. Real means that the figure for gross domestic product has been adjusted for inflation. A rise in real GDP means that the economy has actually produced more goods and services.

c. No, whilst real GDP fell between 1999 and 2000, it grew between 1995 and 2000. The real GDP was higher in 2000 than in 1995. Of course, this does not mean that it increased each year – merely that it was higher at the end of the period than at the start.

d. (i) In percentage terms, the maximum economic growth was recorded by Equatorial Guinea. In absolute terms, South Africa had the largest increase in real GDP.

(ii) A wide range of information would be needed to decide whether one would be better off in Equatorial Guinea or South Africa, than in other countries. This includes information on employment prospects, working conditions and working hours. A person would enjoy a higher standard of living in a country with better employment prospects, as that would give him a good chance of finding a job, good working conditions and short working hours.

One would also require information on environmental and social conditions. The quality of life would be lower in a country with high levels of pollution and crime and poor housing conditions.

To decide whether one would be better off in the country, he would also need to examine information on tax rates, medical care, education and the country's relationship with other countries. Low tax rates lead to retention of greater income with people but it may mean that the provision of government services may be low and people have to pay for services like health care. People would like to live in a country with a high number of doctors per head, advanced medical care and good quality education. The quality of life could be adversely affected by living in a country at war with another country or which is susceptible to terrorist attacks.

Section 7

Answers to Multiple Choice Questions

1. d

   Some of the traditional characteristics of a developing country are *low rate of saving*, due to low average income and a *high rate of adult illiteracy*, due to a lack of educational provision. Other characteristics include a low life expectancy and a high rate of infant mortality. A high rate of adult literacy, a high school leaving age and a high level of labour skills are traditional features of a developed economy.

2. c

   A rise in the retirement age (meaning that people would retire later) would increase the number of people of working age. a and d would reduce the size of the working population. b does not change the size of the working population. People who are unemployed are still of working age and are already included in the labour force.

3. b

During childhood, people are dependent on others to provide goods and services for them. A rise in the birth rate will increase the number of dependants and will reduce the number of workers, for a period of time, as some parents will withdraw from the labour force to look after their children.

4. c

A fall in the average size of families would mean fewer children. a and b would increase the number of elderly dependants. d would be most likely to reduce the number of workers.

5. d

An increase in the birth rate and net immigration would increase the size of the population. As most immigrants tend to be aged between 20 and 40, it is likely to lower the average age of the population. a would reduce both the size and average age of the population. b and c may or may not increase the size of the population but they would increase the average age.

6. a

A cut in inheritance tax would mean that more money could be passed on to the rich. b and c would reduce the size of the holdings of the wealthiest. d would make it slightly more difficult for the wealthiest to accumulate wealth.

7. a

If non-renewable resources are used up quickly, country's ability to grow will be reduced. b, c and d would benefit a developing country.

8. d

A rise in living standards is likely to be accompanied by an improvement in health care and a fall in the infant mortality rate. a, b and c are all likely to rise.

9. b

Country b has the second highest percentage of population living in rural areas, the lowest percentage of children attending school and the lowest percentage of the population over 60.

10. a

If the birth rate is lower than the death rate, there will be a natural decrease in population. If there is net emigration also, the population must decline. The country's population may increase or decrease, in the case of b and c, depending on the relative size of the changes. d would result in an increase in the population.

Answers to Structured Questions

1. a. The rate of population growth tends to be higher in developing countries than that in developed countries, although there are exceptions to this. One major factor contributing to higher population growth is higher birth rates. The reasons include people relying on their children for support during their old age, high infant mortality rates and lack of awareness about contraception or reluctance to use it for religious reasons. Their death rates are below their birth rates and keep falling further, more rapidly.

   For developing countries, the natural change in population usually makes a positive contribution to population growth whilst migration makes a negative one. The reverse is the case with some developed countries. A number of developed countries are experiencing a natural decrease but net immigration, whilst in a number of developing countries there is a natural increase and net emigration.

   b. A government will try to limit the growth of its population, if it thinks that there is a risk of the country becoming overpopulated, insufficient resources to feed and house the population and risk of resources being overused and depleted. If the population size is above the optimum level, then more people in the country would reduce output per head. This would lead to a reduction in the material living standards of people. If there is already a food shortage, a rise in the birth rate may worsen the situation into a famine. Having more people may also put pressure on housing and result in a more rapid depletion of non-renewable resources.

   c. At a low level of development, most of a country's resources are likely to be employed in the primary sector. This sector is involved in the extraction of raw materials and agriculture. It also includes farming, fishing, forestry and mining. As a country develops, productivity in the primary sector rises, releasing resources. Incomes also rise, which leads to a demand for a greater range of products. The secondary sector becomes more important. At first, concentration is largely on low-skilled manufacturing. Then higher skilled and higher value added manufacturing grows in significance. As the economy becomes even more developed, the tertiary sector usually employs the highest percentage of resources. In developed countries, a high percentage of workers are employed in sectors such as education, health care and financial services and these areas account for a high percentage of the countries' GDP.

   d. There is a risk that having a higher proportion of older people in the population in developed countries will place an increased burden on the labour force. Older people may increase demand for health care, residential care and pensions.

The government might seek to finance these services by raising tax rates. This will reduce the disposable income of workers and might be politically unpopular. It could also switch some expenditure from, for instance, education but again this might not be popular.

There are a range of other policies, that a government can implement to deal with the situation. One is to raise the retirement age. This would directly reduce the cost of pensions and increase the tax revenue available, to spend on the health care and residential needs of the elderly. It can also encourage people to take out private pensions by giving them tax breaks on pensions. In addition, it can seek to increase the labour force by encouraging immigration or increase its quality by improving training and education. Having more or more productive workers may increase tax revenue and reduce the burden of dependency.

2. a. Among the indicators of the standard of living in a country are the real GDP per head, health care provision, the quality and quantity of education, housing, life expectancy and number of computers per head of the population.

    b. Poverty arises for a number of reasons. In some developing countries, some people are very poor whilst others are very rich. In other countries, a high proportion of the population live in absolute poverty. It is difficult to break out of this vicious circle of poverty. If a country has a low real GDP per head, its expenditure on education and health care is likely to be low. Savings and capital expenditure are also likely to be low. All of these factors will keep productivity and incomes low.

    Countries which rely on subsistence agriculture are likely to be poor. Even those developing countries, which rely on commercial agriculture, may struggle to raise incomes. Demand for agricultural products does not tend to rise in line with income. Also, their supply can be disrupted by weather and diseases and agricultural products of developing countries may face a number of trade restrictions posed by developed countries.

    Incomes can be kept down by high population growth. If there is a high birth rate, resources which could have been used to, for instance, improve transport infrastructure may have to be devoted for satisfying the needs of the rising population.

    A major cause of poverty is **unemployment**. Some developing countries experience high rates of unemployment. Poverty can also arise as a result of inappropriate government policies and government corruption. If, for instance, a government prints too much money, it can cause inflation which may lead to a loss of international competitiveness and a loss of jobs. If government officials pilfer some of the tax revenue raised – educational standards, health care provision and transport infrastructure will not be as high as possible.

c. While deciding upon the measures to raise the standard of living in a developing country, the factors restricting its growth have to be considered. If some people are experiencing a very low standard of living due to a very unequal distribution of income, the government could levy higher taxes on the rich and provide more assistance to the poor.

Improving education and health care would also improve living standards. It might be possible to switch some government expenditure away from other areas, such as defence, to areas which will raise living standards now and upgrade the future living standards too. If this is not possible, a government may have to borrow from an international organisation such as the World Bank or International Monetary Fund.

Diversion of resources into the secondary and tertiary sectors should raise incomes and living standards. This process might be assisted by the government encouraging the entry of multinational companies (MNCs) into the country, providing subsidies to infant industries and (for a period of time) protecting them from foreign competition.

Attracting MNCs into the country can improve living standards in a variety of ways. They may pay higher incomes than what are generally available in the country, increase employment, provide training, improve infrastructure and may introduce new technology. There is a risk, however, that some of their activities may reduce living standards and may deplete non-renewable resources. Helping infant industries grow may raise employment and income but they would have to be capable of reducing costs as they grow, so that they can be successful in the long term.

Measures to control population growth may help to improve living standards. Education, the provision of advice on family planning and financial incentives may reduce the birth rate. Having fewer children may improve the health of women, enable more women to work and reduce the pressure on health, housing and educational services.

Economists debate whether market forces or government intervention is more likely to increase income and living standards. Those who favour market forces would support measures such as privatisation and cuts in income tax. In contrast, those concerned with market failure are more likely to support measures such as the introduction of a national minimum wage and regulations on carbon dioxide emissions.

3. a A developing country is likely to have a higher proportion of its workers employed in the primary sector than a developed country. A higher proportion of the population in developing countries will probably work as farmers, miners and fishermen, for instance. The proportion of people in occupations linked to the

secondary sector changes, as development occurs. Some developing countries now have a bigger segment of people in the manufacturing sector. Some of these occupations are relatively unskilled, such as textile workers.

Most of the workers in developed countries are employed in tertiary occupations – working as doctors, lawyers and bankers. In fact, in a number of developed countries, more than 80% of workers are employed in this sector. Employment in the tertiary sector plays a less significant role in developing countries.

b. There are a range of other indicators, which are used to classify whether a country is a developing or developed one. Two key indicators are **real GDP per head and HDI**. A country may be classified as a developing one, if it has a low average income and a low level of development. Development measures not only income, but also the life expectancy and education. Other indicators include population growth, the number of consumer goods per household and the savings ratio.

Developing countries tend to have a higher population growth and a lower average age of population than developed countries. This difference arises largely because the birth rate of developing countries is higher than that of developed ones. Developing countries also have higher infant mortality rates.

People in developing countries tend to enjoy fewer consumer goods, such as computers and mobile phones. As income levels are lower, the savings ratio tends to be lower.

c. A multinational company (MNC) is one which produces in more than one country. It is usually a large, public limited company. A MNC can bring benefits to a developing country but it may also bring some disadvantages.

A MNC may create employment by hiring local workers. If the presence of a MNC does raise employment, it will be likely to reduce unemployment in the country. A MNC may pay higher wages than domestically-owned firms and provide high quality training for staff. MNCs can make a considerable contribution to a country's GDP and exports.

MNCs can also introduce new management ideas and new technology into a country. Domestic firms can pick up on these ideas and technology and may receive orders from the MNCs, for goods and services.

MNCs also contribute to tax revenue and may help to build infrastructure like roads, ports and improve energy supplies. Higher tax revenue will enable a government to spend more on health and education, which should boost economic growth and development. Improved infrastructure is likely to reduce costs of production and increase the country's international competitiveness.

MNCs' investment in developing countries, however, is not always beneficial. The top jobs in the MNCs may go to workers from the parent countries of MNCs. If MNCs are producing products made by domestic firms, they may cause some domestic firms to go out of business. If this is the case, the MNCs may not add to employment and, in fact, may reduce it. MNCs may pay higher wages than most of the other firms in the country, but the wages may still be lower than what they pay in their home countries.

The working conditions may not always be that good. One reason that a MNC may set up a factory or office abroad is to get round strict health and safety regulations at work and pollution limits at home. If a MNC accounts for a significant proportion of the host country's GDP and employment, it will be in a powerful position while making negotiations with the host government. It may use this bargaining power to block moves aimed at improving the working conditions and reducing pollution.

Another possible motive of a MNC may be to obtain raw materials. There is a risk that it will deplete the country's non-renewable resources quickly and then move to another country. It may also not contribute much to tax revenue and domestic income, if it sends most of its profits to its home country.

Section 8

Answers to Multiple Choice Questions

1. d

    Free trade occurs when there are no artificial restrictions placed on the export and import of goods and services. a is barter.

2. c

    International specialisation enables countries to concentrate on what they are best at producing. This should increase allocative efficiency. a is a disadvantage of international specialisation. b is the result of diversification rather than specialisation. International specialisation should enable countries, with both an absolute advantage and an absolute disadvantage, to gain.

3. a

    The balance of trade is the revenue earned from the sale of exported goods minus the expenditure on imported goods. a would increase export revenue. b would appear in current transfers and d in trade in services. c is an example of internal and not external trade.

4. c

   Credit items in the balance of payments are those which bring money into the country. c is a service sold abroad, which will bring income into the country. a is a credit item but it would appear in trade in goods. b is also a credit item but this would appear in the capital and financial sector as a transaction in liabilities. d is a debit item in trade in services.

5. b

   A deficit on the current account of the balance of payments of a country would probably mean that the country's exports have fallen whilst its imports have increased. As fewer exports are being sold, demand for the country's currency would fall. The rise in expenditure on imports would increase the supply of the currency. A fall in demand for and rise in supply of the currency would reduce its value. A reduction in exports and a rise in imports may suggest that output might be falling and unemployment rising.

6. c

   A fall in the exchange rate increases the price of imports. An increase in the cost of imported raw materials may result in cost-push inflation. A lower exchange rate reduces the price of exports, which would be likely to increase any current account surplus and increase employment.

7. c

   Country Y has a reasonable economic growth rate, an inflation rate which indicates price stability and an unemployment rate which may be equivalent to full employment. It does have a current account deficit but it is a small deficit.

8. c

   The government will receive tax revenue from tariffs. Such tariffs will increase the price of imported products and hence may cause cost-push inflation. An increase in tariffs will raise trade barriers and reduce competitive pressures on domestic firms by increasing the price products manufactured by rival firms.

9. d

   An increase in government subsidies to domestic producers and tariffs on car imports would reduce the price of domestically produced cars, relative to imported cars.

10. d

   Protection is reduced when tariffs are cut and quotas are increased. A reduction in tariffs would mean that the price, at which imports are sold, would be closer to the price charged by the producers. An increase in a quota means that more can be imported.

Suggested Answers to Structured Questions

1. a. In this context, a rate of exchange is the price of one currency in terms of another currency. For instance, £1 may be traded for $2.

    b. A rise in the price of Egyptian exports is likely to result in a fall in foreign demand for Egyptian products. Exports are a component of aggregate demand. Lower aggregate demand would be likely to reduce output, as shown in Fig. 12.

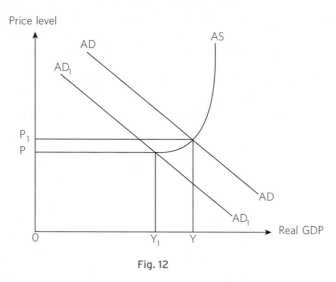

Fig. 12

The effect, however, will depend on the price elasticity of demand for exports. If demand is elastic, a rise in price will cause a greater percentage fall in demand for exports. This will lower export revenue and may have a significant impact on output and employment. If, however, demand is inelastic, a rise in price will cause a smaller percentage fall in demand and export revenue will rise. In this case, Egyptian firms may use the extra revenue to diversify into other areas and consequently, output and employment may not fall.

The effect on the countries importing Egyption goods will depend on the feasibility of purchasing products from other countries instead of Egypt (price considerations), the impact on their output, production and employment. If the rise in the price of Egyptian products makes their domestic products competitive, output and employment in the importing countries can rise. The third possibility is that the products can only be purchased from Egypt. In this case, the countries may continue to buy them at a higher price. This may push up inflation in the countries importing goods and higher inflation can reduce international competitiveness, output and employment.

c. There are three main sections of the balance of payments. The best known one is the **current account**. This includes trade in goods, trade in services, investment income and current transfers. Trade in goods is the export of goods, such as cars, minus the import of goods. Trade in services includes the exports and imports of services, for example, banking, insurance and tourism. Investment income is profit, interest and dividends earned abroad minus profit, interest and dividends earned by foreign nationals in the country. Current transfers includes items, such as wages sent home from abroad and wages sent out of the country by foreign nationals to their relatives abroad. The second section of the balance of payments is the **capital and financial account**. The main items in this section are portfolio and direct investment coming into and going out of the country. The third section is **net errors and omissions**. The balance of payments should balance but due to the complexity of the task of compiling it, some items are always left out and errors are introduced.

d. There are a number of factors that can lead to an improvement in the balance of payments of a country. One is a rise in incomes abroad. This may lead to a rise in demand for the country's exports.
Exports will also rise, if there is an increase in the country's international competitiveness. This can occur if the country's inflation rate falls and/or workers' productivity rises. Supply-side policies, such as education and training, may raise productivity. Producing better quality products or lower price products is likely to result in sale of greater quantities, both at home and abroad.
Exports can increase as a result of a fall in the exchange rate. A lower exchange rate makes exports cheaper and if there is an elastic demand export revenue increases.
Imports should fall as a result of a rise in the exchange rate. They, can also be reduced by subsidising domestic products or placing restrictions on imports. These restrictions include tariffs and quotas. In addition, a fall in domestic GDP may result in a fall in imports. Firms will buy fewer foreign raw materials and consumers will buy less of all products, including imports.
A strong domestic currency may attract foreign direct investment, which will bring money into the economy and will be recorded in the capital and financial account section.

2. a. Specialisation in international trade enables an economy to concentrate on what it is best at producing and importing other products. Specialisation should enable a country to use its resources efficiently and thereby, increase its output and the living standards of its inhabitants.

While deciding what products to specialise in, a country should focus on the area where its **comparative advantage** lies. A country is said to have a comparative advantage in a product, if it can produce it at a lower opportunity cost than other countries. If all countries specialise in products in which they have a comparative advantage, allocative efficiency should be achieved on a global scale.

b. The two most common methods of protection are **tariffs** and **quotas**. A tariff is a tax on imports. It is designed to discourage consumers from buying imports by making them more expensive, relative to domestic goods. A quota poses a limit on imports and reduces them directly. Firms wanting to import the product or products have to apply for or buy a licence.

c. A natural resource is one of the four types of resources, which are used in the production of other goods and services. This type of resource is found in/under the land or sea. Examples of natural resources include fishing grounds, forests and coal deposits.

d. There are a number of advantages in exploiting natural resources. For example, large fishing grounds may lend a comparative advantage to a country in the industry, enabling it to sell large quantities abroad and some at home. Exploiting rich fishing grounds, cutting down trees and mining coal can create income, employment and contribute to the balance of payments.

While making the decision on exploitation of its natural resources, a country has to take a number of factors into consideration. It may not currently have a comparative advantage in the products, which rely on these resources and may want to conserve them until it does. It may also want to conserve some resources for future use. This decision will, in turn, be influenced by the ease of replenishment of resources (renewable or non-renewable). If the resources in question are non-renewable, the country may want to conserve some of them to ensure future economic growth. If, however, there is a risk that the resources may not be in demand in the future, a country may want to exploit them now. For example, if it is thought that solar and wind power will replace coal as a source of energy in the future, it would make sense to mine and sell as much coal as possible now.

There is less worry about exploiting renewable resources, but in practice it can be difficult to decide whether a resource is renewable. In fact, the over-exploitation of a renewable resource can turn it into a non-renewable one. Excessive fishing, for instance, may eliminate a species if the number caught far exceeds that replenished through breeding.

3. a. Less fluctuation of the exchange rate against other currencies means that it was more stable. For example, earlier the value of the £ against the dollar might have changed from £1 = $2 to £1 = $1 to £1 = $3 within a week. Now, the value might have only fluctuated by $0.2 in a week.

    b. Exchange rates fluctuate because demand and supply conditions change. There are a variety of reasons for this. One is a change in exports and/or imports. If a country is, for instance, exporting more – demand for the currency will rise which will push up its price.

        A rise in the country's interest rate, relative to other countries, is likely to encourage foreigners to invest money into a country's financial institutions. This will again raise demand for the currency and its price.

        Changes in foreign direct investment also affect the exchange rate. If it is thought that the country's economic prospects are poor, foreign direct investment may fall and this would lower the exchange rate.

        The biggest cause of exchange rate fluctuations, however, is **speculation**. Some people and financial institutions buy currencies, when they expect their price to rise and sell, when they expect their price to fall.

    c. If a currency 'gains in strength', it means that it is rising in value. This means that the country's exports will rise in price whilst its import prices will fall. This may result in a deterioration of its current account position, especially if there is elastic demand for exports and imports. A fall in net exports would reduce aggregate demand which, in turn, would reduce employment.

        There can, however, be some beneficial effects of a rise in the exchange rate, especially if it is accompanied by greater stability. The country will be able to obtain essential imports at cheaper rates. A high exchange rate can benefit financial markets by attracting money into financial institutions and greater stability may attract foreign direct investment.

d. There his a range of policies, that a government may use, to turn a balance of payments deficit into a surplus. One is to impose **trade restrictions**. Tariffs are a tax on imports. The imposition of tariffs raises the price of imports and encourages domestic consumers to switch from imports to domestic products. There is a risk, however, that other countries will retaliate. If they do so, lower imports may be matched by lower exports and the balance of payments position will not improve. If a country is importing more goods than it is exporting due to high prices or low quality of domestic products, then imposing tariffs will not solve the problem.

The adoption of supply-side policies in the form of improved training and education, though taking longer time for implementation, may prove to be more effective. A more educated labour force should be more productive, capable of producing better quality products at a lower price. Such improvements should encourage both domestic and foreign consumers to buy more of the country's products and improve the balance of payments position.

Additional Structured Questions

Section 1

1. In Zimbabwe, a local community markets a tea which grows wild in their area. 'Communities should be able to manage their natural resources if they are to benefit, especially if they are to gain an economic benefit,' declared the project leader.
   a. Identify the factors of production. (4)
   b. Explain the benefits gained by the local community in Zimbabwe from the project. (6)

   (Cambridge 0455 Paper 2 Q2 May/June 2004)

2. All countries face the basic economic problem in relation to the factors of production. One country might allocate more resources to education and healthcare than another, but there will always be an opportunity cost involved in such decisions.
   a. Why do all countries face the basic economic problem? (4)
   b. State and explain the factors of production. (4)
   c. Define opportunity cost and explain why it is an important concept for economists. (4)
   d. Discuss whether a government should allocate more resources to education and healthcare than other forms at expenditure. (8)

   (Cambridge 0455 Paper 22 Q2 Oct/Nov 2011)

Section 2

1. a. Identify three causes of a change in the demand for a good. (3)
      'A combination of excess supply, weak consumer demand and competition from new channels, such as the internet, has pushed prices down in shops for goods, ranging from clothing to electrical products.'
   b. Using demand and supply analysis, explain whether the reasons given in the above extract would lead to the stated effect on prices. (7)
   c. Define price elasticity of demand and explain how is it calculated. (3)
   d. Discuss whether clothing and electrical products would be likely to have an elastic or an inelastic price elasticity of demand. (7)

   (Cambridge 0455 Paper 2 Q2 May/June 2004)

2. Recently, a number of governments have increased the subsidies granted to public transport. They have also increased taxes on the purchase of cars and on petrol used by private motorists.
   a. Explain the meaning of the word subsidy. (2)
   b. Use a demand and supply diagram to illustrate the effect of a subsidy. (4)
   c. Explain, using an example, what is meant by an external cost. (4)
   d. Discuss, using concepts of social costs and social benefits, the reasons for a government to subsidise public transport but tax private motorists. (10)

   (Cambridge 0455 Paper 4 Q7 May/June 2002)

Section 3

1. a. State four non-wage influences on an individual's choice of occupation. (4)
   b. Explain the primary, secondary and tertiary sectors of production and describe the change in importance of each sector with the development of a country. (6)
   c. Explain what is meant by a trade union. (3)
   d. Discuss the extent to which the relative strengths of trade unions influence the level of earnings in different occupations. (7)

   (Cambridge 0455 Paper 2 Q3 Oct/Nov 2006)

2. In Japan, persistent worries about job security, high unemployment and a steady fall in income have meant that consumers are buying less. This has caused the price of some products to fall. (*Far Eastern Economic Review* 25 May 2000)
   a. Explain how the price of a good is determined by market forces. (4)
   b. Use demand and supply analysis and diagrams to explain how the reasons given in the above extract can cause a fall in the price of a product. (6)
   c. How may a fall in prices affect consumer savings? (4)
   d. Discuss the factors that motivate consumers in deciding whether to spend or save. (6)

   (Cambridge 0455 Paper 4 Q2 May/June 2002)

Section 4

1. a. What is meant by fixed cost, variable cost and average total cost? (4)
    b. Discuss the effect on these costs, if a firm replaces labour with machines. (6)
    c. Some firms integrate with others. Explain the different forms of integration and suggest the reasons for integration to occur. (10)

    (Cambridge 0455 Paper 2 Q7 Oct/Nov 2006)

2. British Gas is a large profit-making public company in the UK. A publicity leaflet from the company stated that the number of customers it served had increased. It also said that the company was more willing to pay compensation to customers, for failure to meet required standards of service.
    a. Explain the principle of profit maximisation. (4)
    b. Discuss what might have happened to profits, as a result of each of the changes mentioned in the leaflet. (6)
    c. Describe briefly, the main types of business organisation and consider which of them is likely to be the most significant in a developed economy. (10)

    (Cambridge 0455 Paper 4 Q7 Oct/Nov 2003)

Section 5

1. a. Explain a market system. (5)
    b. Discuss when it might be desirable for a government to act as a producer of goods and services. (6)
    c. Sometimes the government does not act as a producer of goods and services, but still influences private producers. Explain how it might do this. (9)

    (Cambridge 0455 Paper 4 Q6 May/June 2005)

2. It was reported, in 2002, that people in Germany were expecting tax rises and an increase in unemployment.
    a. Distinguish between a direct tax and an indirect tax. Give an example of each. (4)
    b. Identify three types of unemployment and enumerate the causes of each. (6)
    c. Describe four main aims of government macroeconomic policy. (4)
    d. Discuss whether a rise in taxes can help to achieve any of these aims. (6)

    (Cambridge 0455 Paper 4 Q3 Oct/Nov 2004)

1. In 2004, economists were concerned about the inflationary impact of unusually high oil prices, which were caused by political uncertainty in the Middle East.
    a. Explain how inflation is measured. (6)
    b. Low inflation is one of the aims of government policy. Choose two other macroeconomic aims of the government and explain their meaning. (4)
    c. Explain how high oil prices may cause inflation. (4)
    d. Discuss the actions that a government might take, to control inflation. (6)

    (Cambridge 0455 Paper 2 Q4 Oct/Nov 2006)

2. 'Even after a decade of economic growth, with record trade and global investment, 24% of the world's population is still very poor and lives on an income of less than $1 a day per person.'
    a. Explain the concept of economic growth. (5)
    b. Discuss how trade and investment can boost economic growth. (5)
    c. Discuss whether economic growth should be the main aim of government policy. (10)

    (Cambridge 0455 Paper 4 Q7 Oct/Nov 2002)

Section 7

1. a. What determines the rate of growth of a population? (3)
    b. Contrast the expected age structure of the population of a developing country, with that of a developed country. (7)
    c. In some developing countries, life expectancy has been declining in recent years. This has been largely due to the spread of HIV/AIDS. Governments have allocated large amounts of expenditure for development of new hospitals and conduction of health and education programmes.

    Discuss the ways in which this policy might affect other major government economic policies. (10)

    (Cambridge 0455 Paper 4 Q6 Oct/Nov 2005)

2. 60% of the workforce in Java, which contains a large proportion of Indonesia's population, are rice farmers.
   a. Given this information, explain why Indonesia is likely to be a developing rather than a developed economy. (3)
   b. Describe the difference in living standards, that might be found in a developing economy compared with a developed economy. (7)
   c. Why do some countries have lower living standards of living than others? (6)
   d. Discuss two economic indicators, that can be used to measure the standard of living in a country. (4)

   (Cambridge 0455 Paper 4 Q5 Oct/Nov 2002)

Section 8

1. A recent journal article stated that poor nations should be allowed to protect their new industries from foreign competition.
   a. Explain what indicators might be used to determine that a nation is poor. (8)
   b. Describe the methods that might be used to protect domestic industries from foreign competition in international trade. (5)
   c. Discuss whether it is better for a country to engage in free trade or use some form of protection from foreign competition. (7)

   (Cambridge 0455 Paper 4 Q6 May/June 2006)

2. Demand for UK exports dropped considerably in November 2002, which pushed the UK further into a visible trade deficit – the largest since records began.
   a. Explain what is meant by a visible trade deficit and identify the part of the balance of payments under which it is be recorded. (3)
   b. Discuss whether it matters if a country has a visible trade deficit. (7)
   c. Describe the policies adopted by a government to bring a visible trade deficit into surplus. (4)
   d. Discuss the other consequences of pursuing two of the policies, mentioned by you in (c). (6)

   (Cambridge 0455 Paper 4 Q5 May/June 2004)

Useful Resources

Section 1

Newspapers and Magazines

Quality newspapers and economics magazines can help you to keep abreast of latest developments in your economy and the global economy. They can provide you with examples to illustrate your answers, statistical information and with articles that deepen and widen your knowledge and understanding.

Television and Radio Programmes.

A number of television and radio programmes focus on economic issues. Check listing schedules on a regular basis.

People

People can be a very useful source. Your teacher plays a key role in developing your understanding and skills. Your family and other members of your community may also be able to tell you about their experiences as workers, members of trade unions, savers and spenders. They may also share their view about economic events.

Books

I hope you will find this a useful book for your studies. You might also want to use the other book I have written for this level:- If you decide to go on to study AS or A level Economics, I have also written:

- AS Economics (Longman)
- Stanlake's Introductory Economics (Longman).
- A Level Economics Revision Guide (CUP)
- Economics Workbook (CUP)

The Internet

The internet can be a useful source of information but you must exercise caution while using it, as it offers an indiscriminate exposure to a plethora of information.

Two useful search engines are:
- www.google.com

- www.yahoo.com

There is also: **www.estima.com/weblinks.htm** – this links to economics resources sites.

Among the websites, that you might find useful, are:

- **www.bbc.co.uk** – This is the website of the British Broadcasting Corporation (BBC) of the UK. It is a good website for news and education.

- **www.bbc.co.uk/schools/gcsebitesize/business/** – A good revision site.

- **www.bized.ac.uk/virtual/economy/index.htm** – This site contains a range of economic information targeted at students, including a macroeconomic model.

- **www.commonwealth.org.uk** – A website that provides information about the economic performance of a large number of countries.

- **www.conference.board.org** – The website of the US Conference Board, which focusses on global economic issues.

- **www.econ.cam.ac.uk** – University of Cambridge's website, which contains some interesting articles.

- **www.federalreserve.gov** – The website of the US Central Bank. This provides information on monetary policy and the US economy.

- **www.gov.bw** – A good website on the economy of Botswana, produced by its government.

- **www.greenpeace.org** – Greenpeace's site provides information on environmental issues.

- **www.ictsd.org** – This is the website of the International Centre for Trade and Sustainable Development.

- **www.ifo.de** – German Institute for Economic Research. This provides (in English) information on economic growth and the performance of firms.

- **www.imf.org** – The website of the International Monetary Fund, that provides economic information on almost every country.

- **www.oecd.org** – Website of Organisation for Economic Cooperation and Development. This website provides information about the economic performance – including education and health care, of a number of countries.

- **www.twnside.org.sg** – Third World Network's website which includes a wide range of useful information on development.

- **www.un.org** – United Nations website with useful information about development.

- **www.worldbank.org** – The website of the World Bank. It is a useful source of information about development and economic performance.

- **www.wto.org** – World Trade Organization's website, that concentrates on international trade.

Index

under-production, 95
unemployment
  causal, 382
  causes of, 382–383
  changes in, 376
  consequences of, 383–385
  cyclical, 383
  demand deficient, 383
  effects of economy and, 384–385
  effects on unemployed, 384
  frictional, 382
  measures of, 381–382
  regional, 382
  search, 382
  seasonal, 382
  structural, 382
  technological, 382
unemployment and inflation, 328
unemployment rate, 310–311
unfairness, 102
United Nations, 417, 447
unit elasticity of demand, 74

V

variable costs, 250–252
VAT (value added tax), 335
velocity of circulation, 367
vertical integration, 275
vicious circle of poverty, 419, 421
voluntary export restraints (VERs), 494

W

wage, 162, 423
wage claims, basis of, 190
wage determination, 170–175
  effect of discrimination, 175
  government policies and, 172–173
  public opinion and, 174
  relative bargaining power of employers
    and workers, role of, 172

wage differential, 173
wage factors, 162–164
wage flexibility, 376
wealth inequality, 423
  measures of, 427
white collar unions, 188
windfall tax, 342
workforce or working population, 11
working conditions, 165
working hours, 165
World Bank, 417, 447–448

Y

yields, 157